*The Renaissance of Jewish Culture
in Weimar Germany*

MICHAEL BRENNER

The Renaissance of Jewish Culture in Weimar Germany

Yale University Press
New Haven & London

Published with assistance from the Lucius N. Littauer Foundation.

Set in Sabon type by The Marathon Group, Inc., Durham, North Carolina.
Printed in the United States of America by BookCrafters, Inc., Chelsea, Michigan.

Library of Congress Cataloging-in-Publication Data
Brenner, Michael.
   The renaissance of Jewish culture in Weimar Germany / Michael Brenner.
     p.   cm.
   Includes bibliographical references and index.
    ISBN 0-300-06262-1 (hc : alk. paper)
        0-300-07720-3 (pbk. : alk. paper)
   1. Jews—Germany—Intellectual life.
2. Germany—Intellectual life—20th century. I. Title.
DS135.G33B74   1996
943'.004924—dc20   95-30449
                               CIP

A catalogue record for this book is available from the British Library.

The paper in this book meets the guidelines for permanence and durability of the Committee on Production Guidelines for Book Longevity of the Council on Library Resources.

10 9 8 7 6 5 4 3 2

Portions of Chapter 4 appeared in an earlier form as "An Unknown Project of a World Jewish History in Weimar Germany: Reflections on Jewish Historiography in the 1920s," *Modern Judaism* 13 (1993): 249–267. Reprinted by permission of the Johns Hopkins University Press.

For my parents

Contents

Acknowledgments

This book would not have been possible without the instruction and assistance that teachers, colleagues, and friends provided me throughout my years of studying, researching, and writing. Growing up in Germany's postwar Jewish community, I was constantly confronted with the complexities of German-Jewish existence. My mother's childhood memories of the Weimar days in Dresden and my father's recollections of the rich Jewish culture in interwar Krakow provided my first links to a Jewish past irretrievably lost. I am profoundly grateful for my parents' constant efforts to make me aware of the varieties of Jewish life. Without their continuous inspiration and encouragement, I would have never embarked on the journey that led to my studies in Jewish history in Heidelberg, Jerusalem, and New York.

Among the many teachers I have had the privilege to study with, I must single out Professor Yosef Hayim Yerushalmi, who not only provided me with countless answers to the complex problems of Jewish history but—more important—taught me the art of formulating questions. His unique combination of vast erudition and methodological sophistication nourished my curiosity to explore new paths of Jewish history. My own search for a fresh perspective on German-Jewish history was deeply inspired by the stimulating advice I received from him. He has been a *Doktorvater* in the best tradition of this German term.

Special thanks to Professor Michael A. Meyer of the Hebrew Union College in Cincinnati, who critically examined almost every detail of the manuscript. While working on this book, I have had the opportunity to get to know him as a meticulous editor and a warm human being who provided support and assistance wherever possible. I have profited from the intellectual rigor and scholarly advice of Professor Fritz Stern, whose insightful comments on earlier drafts of this book were a constant reminder to view Jewish culture in the context of German society as a whole. Professors Michael Stanislawski and Atina Grossmann enriched my studies at Columbia University and provided assistance during this book's many stages of development. I am grateful to Irene Heskes, Paul Mendes-Flohr, Alan Mintz, Benjamin Ravid, Alexander Ringer, Ismar Schorsch, Jack Wertheimer, and Harry Zohn, whose expertise benefited various chapters of this book.

During the two years I spent researching in Berlin, I received numerous comments on my work from the participants of the doctoral colloquia on German-Jewish history and their organizers, Professors Reinhard Rürup, Stefi Jersch-Wenzel, and Monika Richarz. I am particularly grateful for the stimulating suggestions provided by Professors Shulamit Volkov and Jacob Toury of Tel Aviv University. My students, in courses I taught on various aspects of modern Jewish culture at the Freie Universität Berlin, Indiana University, and Brandeis University, contributed many fresh ideas.

I benefited immensely from the comments made by my friends and colleagues on various drafts of this book. Stefan Rohrbacher, himself a product and a historian of German Jewry, engaged me in fruitful discussion from the first days I showed interest in the study of Jewish history. Michael Berkowitz, Arthur Brenner, and David Myers reviewed large parts of the manuscript. Because this work deals with a variety of cultural expressions, I consulted a number of specialists. I learned much about Yiddish literature from Delphine Bechtel, about Jewish art from Inka Bertz, about Jewish social welfare from Sharon Gillerman, about German-Jewish literature from Katharina Ochse, about Jewish education from Claudia Prestel, about a sociological approach to Jewish history from Nusi Sznaider, and about the experience of East European Jews in Germany from Yfaat Weiss.

I am grateful for their academic advice and their friendship. To have met them during my years of study and research is reward enough for the many lonely hours spent in libraries and archives. Otto Bohlmann and Jenya Weinreb of Yale University Press gave me the benefit of their expertise and insightful comments.

I have left until last one friend whose help was invaluable. John Efron not only assisted me with style and language but also provided substantial comments concerning the content of my work. Despite his busy schedule, he always had time for my many inquiries.

If teachers, colleagues, and friends provided comments and insights to this dissertation, my wife, Ilana, contributed something even more important: intellectual inspiration, the constant reminder of the existence of another world beyond my own research, and the shared love for our daughter, Simone.

It is my pleasure to thank the institutions that enabled my study and research. The Studienstiftung des deutschen Volkes, the Deutscher Akademischer Austauschdienst, Columbia University, the Center for Israel and Jewish Studies, the Memorial Foundation of Jewish Culture, and the Franz Rosenzweig Center for the Study of German-Jewish Culture and Literature in Jerusalem provided generous grants and fellowships.

Many archives and archivists extended their hospitality and assistance. Fred Grubel, Frank Mecklenburg, and Diane Spielmann at the Leo Baeck Institute in New York provided personal advice and professional assistance, as did Aryeh Segall and Hadassah Assouline at the Central Archives for the History of the Jewish People in Jerusalem. My thanks to the other archives who furnished material: the Central Zionist Archives in Jerusalem, the Manuscript Division of the Jewish National and University Library in Jerusalem, the Schocken Institute in Jerusalem, the Brandeis University Archives in Waltham, the Vanderbilt Divinity Library in Nashville, the YIVO Institute in New York, the Bundesarchiv Potsdam, the Geheimes Staatsarchiv Preußischer Kulturbesitz in Merseburg, and the Leipzig Stadtarchiv. Finally, I wish to thank Professor Benjamin Ravid of Brandeis University for his permission to work with the archival material in the estate of his late father, Professor Simon Rawidowicz.

Introduction

I discovered that one does not easily cease to be Jewish, and that self-rejection never solves anything. . . . I decided that henceforth I would tell others and myself: "Yes, I am Jewish—what of it? Yes, to some extent and on several points I am *different* from my fellow citizens, from other men."

—Albert Memmi, "Does the Jew Exist?" in *Commentary* (1966)

The image of Weimar Jewry, overshadowed by its tragic end, is that of "Jews beyond Judaism"—Jews who failed to create a particular culture and only contributed to German culture before they were reminded in 1933 of their Jewishness. In the tradition of what is generally known as Fall and Decline History, historians often conceived of the development of German Jews between their emancipation and their ultimate destruction as a linear retreat from Jewish traditions and a gradual absorption within German culture. "It has become a common view," as Fritz Stern critically remarks, "to hold that German Jewry somehow represents the epitome of craven assimilation and submission."[1]

Although a number of important studies have helped to unveil the finer points in the complex picture of German-Jewish history during the nineteenth and early twentieth centuries, Gerson Cohen's assessment that German Jewry's "internal Jewish life . . . has not yet won the place it deserves in contemporary historiography" remains valid for the Weimar period (1918–1933).[2] Countless studies focus on individual Jews and their contributions to Weimar culture, but not a single work is devoted to Weimar's indigenous Jewish culture. Similarly, none of the standard works on Weimar culture mentions Jewish culture, although Jews often figure prominently in their analyses.[3]

The complexities of Weimar Germany's Jews are revealed in their attempt to negotiate the narrow path that allowed for the persistence of a distinct Jewish identity within a non-Jewish society. The basis for such a path was the systematic construction of what Franz Rosenzweig referred to as a particular Jewish sphere—intended not as a spiritual ghetto but as a cultural realm compatible with participation in the larger non-Jewish society and culture.[4] Those who were part of such a Jewish sphere had multiple identities and lived in a variety of worlds: the same writers drew inspiration from German myths and Hasidic tales, the same educators were active in the adult education movements of the German *Volkshochschule* and the Jewish *Lehrhaus,* the same painters depicted German soldiers and East European Jews, and the same architects built department stores and synagogues.

Although a growing number of German Jews actively participated in a Jewish cultural sphere during the Weimar period, I do not argue that they constituted the vast majority of German Jews. Their activities represented merely one of the ambiguous tendencies of Weimar Jewry, as described by Ismar Schorsch: "If one sector of the community is indeed best accounted for in terms of spiritual bankruptcy, the behaviour of another sector constituted a dramatic polar opposite, whose singular achievement was to deepen and culminate the development of a distinct Jewish subculture in a relatively open and voluntaristic setting."[5]

Those varieties of cultural and political identification were often present within one family. In the memoirs of his youth, Gershom Scholem portrays a family that epitomizes in microcosm the diversity of German Jewry at the beginning of the twentieth century. Young Gerhard (Gershom) was the only one of four brothers who possessed a drive to learn more about Judaism and to identify with Zionism. Although he was later to become a world-renowned professor of Jewish mysticism, he was not the most famous of his brothers while still in Germany. This honor went to his brother Werner, who represented the Communist Party in the Reichstag from 1924 until 1928. Another brother, Erich, was a member of the liberal Deutsche Demokratische Partei and adhered to the ideology of the mainstream organization of German Jews, the Central Association of German Citizens of the Jewish Faith. The oldest brother, Reinhold, was a German nationalist and supported the conservative Deutsche Volkspartei.

Although Gershom Scholem's search for a lost Judaism was unique within his family, it was emblematic for numerous Jewish intellectuals of his generation and represented a particular version of a common phenomenon of Weimar society—the revolt of the son against the father.[6] About the same time that Scholem studied Jewish history and mysticism, Franz Kafka became an enthusiastic consumer of Yiddish theater and Hebrew literature, and Franz Rosenzweig—on the verge of converting to Christianity, as several of his cousins had done before him—embarked on his journey to Jewish culture. They all had grown up without much or any Jewish knowledge. The remnants of Jewish culture left to their parents were, as Franz Kafka recalled in the *Letter to His Father,* "too little to be handed on to the child; it all dribbled away while you were passing it on."[7]

Kafka never sent this letter to his father, who would not have understood it, anyway. To him, as to the fathers of Gershom Scholem and Franz Rosenzweig, Jewishness had become a rather curious hereditary relic to be preserved in some way, but not imbued with any concrete content. Kafka's and Scholem's great-grandfathers had grown up in modest conditions in a closed Jewish society; their grandfathers had smoothed the way for economic success and integration into German culture; their fathers continued this path and assumed that their children would one day do the same. That Kafka's generation did not do so has reasons that are rooted in the general development of German society in the early twentieth century, as well as in specific developments concerning German Jews.

In the nineteenth century, to most Germans—Jews and non-Jews alike—Judaism and modern culture seemed separated by an unbridgeable gulf. It was an unwritten law that in order to become Germans, Jews would leave behind the world of the Talmud and Hebrew liturgy and would instead adopt the culture of Goethe and Beethoven. When German Jews were granted legal equality in the constitution of the Second German Reich in 1871, they had, in their own minds, by and large fulfilled this condition. The study of traditional Jewish sources and the knowledge of Yiddish and Hebrew had been largely restricted to a small and ever diminishing Orthodox minority, while European literature, music, and art had found their way into all German-Jewish homes.

Hannah Arendt summed up this development among German Jews of the nineteenth century in her own pointed and perhaps exaggerated way: "Jews who wanted 'culture' left Judaism at once, and completely, even though most of them remained conscious of their Jewish origin. Secularization and even secular learning became identified exclusively with secular culture, so that it never occurred to these Jews that they could have started a process of secularization with regard to their own heritage."[8] Even such a sympathetic observer as Thomas Mann made a clear-cut division when speaking about Judaism and modern culture. In a description of a visit to his future father-in-law, he felt the need to state to his brother Heinrich that "one is not at all reminded of Judaism among those people; one feels nothing but culture."[9]

When Thomas Mann uttered this statement, a new interest in Judaism was visible among German Jews, for which Martin Buber coined the term "Jewish renaissance."[10] Three generations after German Jews had begun to move "out of the ghetto," the question of what formed the nature of their Jewishness had become ever more acute. To be sure, some Jews in Weimar Germany remained Orthodox, and others preserved traditional Jewish customs in their homes.[11] And some continued to adhere to at least a Liberal definition of religious Jewishness. Religion alone, however, proved a fragile basis for self-definition among a highly secularized Jewish population, one that came to disavow most ritual practices of Judaism. Those Jews who rejected both the view that Judaism could be defined in purely religious terms and the view that Jews should assimilate completely into German society were thus confronted with the central problem of Jewish existence in modern secular society: How to create a new form of Judaism, and what content to give it?

"Post-assimilated" Jews could neither restore the Jewish traditions of the past under changed historical conditions nor reverse the profound socioeconomic and intellectual transformation that the previous generations had experienced. As Eric Hobsbawm has argued, modern societies constantly redefine the framework of traditions that constitute the very basis of their existence. They resurrect certain elements of an allegedly golden tradition and adapt them to the new conditions of a changing society, or use them for different purposes than originally intended. What seems to be a retrieval of authentic traditions becomes, rather, a modern construction or invention of a tradition.[12]

The Jews of modern Germany serve as an example par excellence of a minority population inventing or reinterpreting its tradition.[13] In a new context and used for different purposes, traditional texts, artifacts, and even songs attained a new meaning and thus became new traditions themselves. Multivolume encyclopedias redefined Jewish knowledge, modern translations represented classical Jewish texts in new garb, Jewish museums displayed ceremonial artifacts in a secular framework, arrangements of Jewish music transformed traditional folk songs and synagogue liturgy for a concert audience, and popular novels recalled selected aspects of the Jewish past. As historian Pierre Nora has observed with respect to other societies, *lieux de mémoire*—places of memory, such as archives and monuments, festive anniversaries and encyclopedias—had replaced *milieux de mémoire,* spontaneous collective memory, among German Jews, as well.[14]

Jewish culture in Weimar Germany was characterized neither by a radical break with the past nor by a return to it. Indeed, it used distinct forms of Jewish traditions, marking them as authentic, and presented them according to the demands of contemporary taste and modern cultural forms of expression. What might have appeared as authenticity was in fact a modern innovation. Much of Jewish culture in Weimar Germany was, to rephrase Goethe's Mephistopheles, *ein Teil von jener Kraft, die stets das Alte will und stets das Neue schafft* (a part of that power which ever wants the old, yet forever creates the new).

Jewish culture, in the context of this book, comprises all literary, artistic, and scholarly expressions promoted by such institutions as schools and theaters, publishing houses, cultural associations, and clubs that consciously advanced a collective identity among German Jews, which differed from that of their non-Jewish surroundings.[15] This does not mean that all those educational projects, publications, and artifacts aimed at an exclusively Jewish audience; most of them, however, contained a specific message to their Jewish addressees.

It follows that German-Jewish culture must not be misunderstood to mean *any* literary, scholarly, or artistic production created by German-speaking Jews. A story written by Stefan Zweig, a book published by S. Fischer, a painting by Max Liebermann, or a lecture by Sigmund Freud were not necessarily relevant for Jewish culture. The Weimar constitution was not a Jewish document just because its author, Hugo Preuss, was Jewish. Similarly, the *Berliner Tageblatt*—published by Rudolf Mosse—was not a Jewish newspaper (even if antisemites referred to it as *Judenblatt*), nor was the theory of relativity a Jewish theory because Albert Einstein was a proud Jew. Weimar's Jewish culture was not necessarily high culture. Some of its products may indeed be classified as first-rate cultural creations, but others are second- or third-rate works. Because the impact of cultural products is not necessarily related to their quality, they may still be relevant in this context.

In analyzing the Jewish culture of Weimar Germany, one must choose between two methodological approaches. The first is to select one institution, journal, or personality as an example of a larger process; the second is to draw a picture of the variety and richness of the phenomenon as a whole. I have opted for the second alternative because only such a view can grasp the principal characteristic of the cultural sphere created by German Jews: the simultaneous establishment of diverse cultural forms of expression. Even using such an approach, I cannot include *all* aspects of the Jewish cultural sphere in Weimar Germany but must focus on its most important and representative phenomena.

The process of establishing a distinct Jewish sphere in various cultural branches was expressed by a discourse whose basic patterns were taken over from the larger German society and transformed into a distinctly Jewish context. Those patterns were the quest for community, the synthesis of knowledge, and the search for authenticity. Based on the contemporary German pursuit of a genuine *Gemeinschaft* (community) as opposed to *Gesellschaft* (society), German Jews believed that they needed to strengthen their sense of community in order to revitalize Jewish culture. True culture, they asserted, could be created only by men and women who were deeply anchored in the common ground of a Gemeinschaft. When creating their own sense of Gemeinschaft, German Jews were drawn to many of the same ideas that attracted non-Jewish Germans, such as the power of irrationalism, the hunger for wholeness, and the obsession with statistics and hygiene.

Once such a community was established, its members had to acquire basic knowledge about its traditions and values. This realization proved especially important for German Jews alienated from Judaism. Reflecting the calls of the time for a coherent presentation of knowledge, they created institutions of learning and publications that would transmit a comprehensive and all-inclusive knowledge of Jewish matters. The Jewish cultural renaissance was not content to spread theoretical knowledge but promoted an allegedly authentic Judaism, just as German society propagated genuine forms of culture, as opposed to what was conceived as the decadent and superficial civilization of the modern Western world.

In Part I, therefore, I examine the quest for community among German Jews on two levels. First, an analysis of the changing self-definition within the Liberal majority of German Jews reveals a gradual shift from a community of faith to a community of fate and common descent. This shift was achieved mainly by a reconsideration of the spiritual Jewish heritage.

Whereas rationalist thought and individual faith had been the principal characteristics of nineteenth-century Liberal Jewish ideology, in the Weimar period mysticism, Romanticism, and the collective experience became increasingly significant. On a second level, the changing definition of Jewish community (*Gemeinschaft*) was expressed within the local institutions of the Jewish community (*Gemeinde*). Transcending its nineteenth-century identity as a purely religious community, the Jewish Gemeinde in Weimar Germany was increasingly dedicated to secular tasks in the areas of social welfare, culture, and education. It recalled the premodern Jewish community, the *Kehillah*, but resembled more closely the structure of contemporary German municipal administrations.

A similar leaning on ancient Jewish traditions can be observed in the analysis of the transmission of Jewish knowledge in Part II of this study. Franz Rosenzweig's Jewish Lehrhaus—the most important Jewish institution for adult education in Weimar Germany—borrowed its name from the traditional Jewish house of learning, the beth midrash, but had little in common with it. Instead, the Lehrhaus was an offspring of contemporary German debates on education reform that resulted in a broad network of institutions for adult education. Like these Jewish educational institutions, the two multivolume Jewish encyclopedias conceived in Weimar Germany aimed at restoring Jewish knowledge, but in fact re-created Jewish knowledge. The fact that the *Jüdisches Lexikon* granted more space to the "godless Jew" Sigmund Freud than to the famed medieval scholar Nahmanides points to a significant shift in the understanding of Judaism as a secular culture.

The final part of this book is concerned with the use of allegedly authentic models, or topoi, for new purposes in the realms of literature, music, and art. By juxtaposing the "non-Jewish" assimilated German Jew with the imagined authenticity of East European and oriental Jews, Jewish writers, artists, and musicians hoped to regain authenticity themselves. In search of Jewish authenticity, German Jews were confronted with the presence of the East European Jewish intelligentsia that had settled in Germany during the years after the First World War. The encounter of those two groups is the subject of the final chapter.

Recognizing the significance of the creation of modern Jewish culture in Germany does not mean that it has to be viewed as a success story. Although one must admit its achievements, one should beware of idealizing them.[16] It is the historian's task to consider the potentials and limits, achievements and failures of the changing face of modern German-Jewish existence. The fifteen years of Weimar Germany were too brief a period to permit any definitive evaluation of the Jewish culture that developed during that time. This culture was brought to an end not by its own weaknesses but by those of the larger society. The forced revival of Jewish culture that followed after 1933 was only a macabre epilogue to a story that had not yet fully unfolded when the heavens over Germany darkened.

Part I

The Quest for Community

1

Pre-Weimar Origins

From Mendelssohn on . . . the Jewishness of every individual has
squirmed on the needle point of a "why."

—Franz Rosenzweig, *The Builders* (1923)

The first half of the nineteenth century marked, as Eric Hobsbawm
wrote, "the greatest transformation in human history since the remote
times when men invented agriculture and metallurgy, writing, the city and
the state."[1] Dynasties fell, new states emerged, political ideologies from
socialism to liberalism and nationalism were born, the working class rose,
and industrial mass production began. Although no one in Europe
remained unaffected by the political, social, economic, and cultural innovations of this period, some groups experienced the change more dramatically than others. The lives of Jews in Germany were radically altered by
those developments. At the beginning of the nineteenth century they occupied a clearly defined place in society. With few exceptions, they spoke their
own language, used Hebrew script, lived in separate quarters, dressed differently from other Germans, married among themselves, sent their children to Jewish schools, and shared particular values and beliefs. But by the
middle of the nineteenth century, a rapidly increasing number of German
Jews had moved to towns and parts of towns that hitherto had been closed

to them, sent their children to nondenominational schools, and knew their Goethe and Schiller better than any Jewish Bible commentator. In short, German Jews had moved "out of the ghetto," to borrow the title of Jacob Katz's pioneering study on this subject.

This period brought about a decisive transformation not only for Jews, but for Judaism as well. After the erosion of premodern Jewish society, with its clear-cut boundaries, the need to achieve new self-definitions by creating invisible borderlines arose. Officially, Judaism was reduced to a religious denomination, divided into various streams, such as the Reform movement and Neo-Orthodoxy. The irony of such a definition of Judaism in purely religious terms was that it occurred at a time of increasing secularization. Just when the affiliation with Judaism was officially reduced to synagogue attendance, fewer and fewer Jews observed the commandments of Jewish law.

Along with this process of confessionalization, German Jews created secular forms of culture to express their Jewish distinctiveness. Those forms meant a departure from pre-modern Jewish life and a construction of a new Jewish self-definition. German Jews selected certain aspects of the rich Jewish heritage and integrated them into modern European culture, as expressed in the realms of scholarship, art, and literary fiction. The result was the formation of a new tradition that had enduring influence on Jewish existence in the modern world.[2]

There were three steps in the development of a secular Jewish culture in Germany prior to the days of Weimar. The initial phase encompassed most of the nineteenth century, beginning with the foundation of the Verein für Cultur und Wissenschaft der Juden (Society for Culture and Science among Jews) in 1819 and concluding with the rise of Zionism in the 1890s. The first products of modern secular Jewish culture often served the apologetic purpose of promoting a view of Judaism that would further the cause of emancipation. During the second phase, starting in the 1890s, secular Jewish culture began to attain a more autonomous role. Art, literature, music, and scholarship were no longer instruments in the fight for freedom but the main ingredients of a new conception of Judaism that was decisively shaped by the ideological reorientation among the major currents of German Jewry. World War I, finally, constituted a decisive period of transition for modern Jewish culture.

BETWEEN ACCULTURATION AND DISTINCTIVENESS: NINETEENTH-CENTURY ROOTS

The Verein für Cultur und Wissenschaft der Juden, founded in Berlin in 1819, was the first institution to define its purpose explicitly as the promotion of Jewish culture. The title of the Verein left no doubt that it considered culture in close relation to *Wissenschaft,* which in German means both science and scholarship. In early-nineteenth-century Germany the connection between culture and Wissenschaft did not pertain specifically to Jews. Wissenschaft had become the intellectual ideal of the time. At the newly founded University of Berlin, new critical and scientific methods were introduced in the study of history by Barthold Niebuhr, in law by Karl Friedrich von Savigny, and in philosophy with Johann Gottlieb Fichte's *Wissenschaftslehre.* Overshadowing them all, in 1818 Hegel's philosophy began to emanate from the university.

The Verein grew out of a *Wissenschaftszirkel* (scientific circle), in which Jewish students of the University of Berlin delivered lectures in 1816 and 1817 on a broad variety of (non-Jewish) topics. The circle's transformation into a study group dedicated to distinct *Jewish* topics in November 1819 can be explained only partly by the anti-Jewish riots that affected many German-Jewish communities a few months earlier. Those events may have triggered the formation of the Verein, but the deeper causes of its existence are to be found within the general intellectual trends of the time.[3]

By the end of the eighteenth century, the cosmopolitan ideals of the Enlightenment had been superseded by the particularist ideals of the nation. In the subsequent period of Idealism and Romanticism Herder's assertion that every nation possessed its particular *Volksgeist* (national spirit) became for philosophers and poets the basis of a distinct German patriotism. Under the impact of the Wars of Liberation against Napoleon, the philosophical and poetic search for a German Volksgeist attained a political tone, as expressed in Fichte's *Speeches to the German Nation* (1807–1808) and Ernst Moritz Arndt's anti-French poems. The concept of a Volksgeist did not leave Jewish students unaffected. As modern students of philosophy, they no longer identified with the universalist ideals of Lessing and Mendelssohn, but as Jews they were not accepted as part of the German Volksgeist by its most important proponents, such as Fichte and Arndt. To solve this dilemma, the founders of the Verein came together in search of a distinct Jewish Volksgeist, one that could be identified only by means of Wissenschaft.

The Verein existed for only five years and published no more than one volume of its periodical, the *Zeitschrift für die Wissenschaft des Judentums*. When it dissolved in 1824, some of its members had converted or were on the verge of converting to Christianity to gain their "entrée billet into European culture," as the Verein's most famous member, Heinrich Heine, formulated. Although the practical accomplishments of the Verein can hardly be called a success, its founders planted the seeds for one of the most important developments of modern Jewish culture. Their achievement was the foundation of the scientific study of Judaism, *Wissenschaft des Judentums*. Leopold Zunz, Isaak Markus Jost, Immanuel Wolf, and other founders of the Verein approached traditional Jewish sources quite differently from the many generations that had studied the same sources before. They no longer interpreted them as the divine laws governing their daily lives but regarded them as historical documents that deserved to be studied scientifically.

With the old Jewish community and its institutions in the midst of upheaval, the Verein constituted an attempt to form a new kind of elite community centering around the scientific study of Judaism. In a letter expressing his disillusion after the failure of the Verein in 1824, Zunz reminded Wolf that the "five to ten enthusiastic men" who founded it in 1819 hoped "like Moses" to propagate a new spirit among their Jewish contemporaries. History itself became, as Yosef Hayim Yerushalmi remarked, "what it had never been before—the faith of fallen Jews."[4] In other words, the preoccupation with the Jewish past was transformed into a new tradition that would preserve Jewish distinctiveness in the future. The fathers of the Verein did not consciously create such a new tradition but had several other motives.

One such motive was pragmatic and concerned the status of German Jews. By proving to the non-Jewish world that Jews had a rich cultural heritage worthy of scholarly study, the Verein hoped to further the cause of legal equality. As Michael Meyer has written, the founders of the Verein intended to "gain respect in an intellectual milieu where science was the reigning value."[5] Immanuel Wolf, one of the founders of the Verein, declared in his outline of Wissenschaft des Judentums that "scientific knowledge of Judaism must decide on the merits or demerits of the Jews, their fitness or unfitness to be given the same status and respect as other citizens."[6]

The scholarly studies of Leopold Zunz aimed in a more direct way to achieve emancipation for German Jews. Like Wolf, Zunz believed that the "equality of the Jews in customs and life will follow from the equality of Wissenschaft des Judentums."[7] In *Gottesdienstliche Vorträge der Juden, historisch entwickelt* (1832), he documented the long tradition of Jewish sermon literature and thus rebutted the Prussian government's dismissal of German synagogue sermons as innovations in Jewish liturgy. Five years later, in his study on Jewish surnames, *Die Namen der Juden,* Zunz proved the ancient origin of many "non-Jewish" names among Jews, in reaction to a decree that forbade the use of Christian surnames among Jews.

A second motive, the construction of an "essence of Judaism," was as important as the Verein's fight for emancipation. Immanuel Wolf identified the "fundamental idea of Judaism" in the "idea of unlimited unity in the all" and argued that "all that has come forth from Judaism everywhere bears the imprint of this basic idea and reveals it in every form."[8] If Judaism could be reduced to a religious idea, then Jewish history was the history of this idea and its interpretation by various religious sects. When another member of the Verein, Isaak Markus Jost, wrote a modern history of Judaism, its title, *Geschichte des Judentums und seiner Sekten* (History of Judaism and of its sects, 3 vols., 1857–1859), revealed it to be the history not of a people but of a religious denomination. In his earlier work, the nine-volume *Geschichte der Israeliten* (History of the Israelites, 1820–1828), Jost had recalled Wolf's principal understanding of Judaism by setting out to investigate Judaism "in order to apprehend its essence."[9]

Although the Verein had limited success in promoting a new secular faith, the scientific preoccupation with Judaism became one of the most popular means of expressing Jewish self-definition among nineteenth-century Jewry. When Liberal Jews opened a rabbinical seminary in Berlin in 1872, they called it Hochschule für die Wissenschaft des Judentums, and the conservative rabbinical seminary in Breslau named its periodical the *Monatsschrift für Geschichte und Wissenschaft des Judentums.* Its long-time editor, Heinrich Graetz, became the most prominent representative of the second generation of Wissenschaft des Judentums, and his *Geschichte der Juden von den ältesten Zeiten bis auf die Gegenwart* (History of the Jews from antiquity to the present) became the classic of modern Jewish historiography.

Wissenschaft was but one pillar in the secularization of Jewish culture. When the Verein dissolved, parallel developments integrating Jewish thought into European culture were well under way in the realm of literature. Heinrich Heine, a member of the Verein, was the most prominent of the German-Jewish writers in the nineteenth century who included Jewish topics in their literary oeuvres. By using the German language to express Jewish themes, these authors differed from most contemporary East European *Maskilim* (Enlighteners), who advocated the introduction of modern secular Jewish literature in Hebrew.

As Leopold Zunz made clear in his programmatic essay *Etwas über die rabbinische Litteratur* (On rabbinic literature, 1818), Jewish literature had never been restricted to Hebrew or other Jewish languages. Some of the most important Jewish sources were the Aramaic Talmud, the Greek works of Philo of Alexandria, and the Arabic writings of Maimonides and Yehuda Halevi. Yet a fundamental difference separated those works from German-Jewish literature of the nineteenth century. Most of the literary products written by Jews in non-Jewish languages before the eighteenth century came out of a Jewish system of belief and a more or less autonomous Jewish cultural framework. Their authors knew Hebrew and produced other writings in Hebrew, and their non-Hebrew writings remained known within the Jewish world largely because of Hebrew translations and commentaries.

Thus in 1818 Zunz was able to include any work of a Jewish author within his definition of Jewish literature. Only a few years later, when the oeuvres of many authors could be divided into Jewish and non-Jewish works, Zunz's original definition was no longer valid. Although Heine's *Rabbi von Bacherach* was one of the most impressive achievements of modern Jewish literature, his *Deutschland, ein Wintermärchen* certainly could not be construed as a Jewish book. The same distinction can be made in the work of Berthold Auerbach and other German-Jewish writers of the nineteenth century. By the end of the nineteenth century, definitions of Jewish literature included only those works by Jewish authors that dealt with Jewish topics and aimed at least partly at a Jewish audience.[10]

Beginning in the mid-nineteenth century, this sort of literature was promoted by German Jews who established Jewish book clubs, publishing houses, and literary societies. Liberals, the Orthodox, and later Zionists created German-Jewish literary spheres in which they depicted their particular milieux and glorified their heroes. The pioneering figure in the advancement of a distinct German-Jewish literature throughout the nineteenth century was the Liberal rabbi and journalist Ludwig Philippson. He published five volumes of novels and novellas on various aspects of Jewish history, and, more important, in 1837 he founded the *Allgemeine Zeitung des Judentums,* which was to be the leading German-Jewish journal for the next seventy-five years. Its purpose was not only to inform about daily events and to advance religious reform but also actively to promote German-Jewish literature. For Philippson, German-Jewish fiction had a clearly defined pedagogical purpose. In an age characterized by the steady decline of familiarity with traditional Jewish sources, a historical novel helped to popularize positive themes of Jewish history and ingredients of Jewish tradition that would otherwise vanish.

In the nineteenth century German Jews produced hundreds of novels, novellas, dramas, and poems on Jewish topics. This dissemination of German-Jewish literature was in part the result of Philippson's organizational talents. In addition to his journal he established, in 1851, the first Jewish book club. His Institut zur Förderung der israelitischen Literatur (Institute for the Promotion of Jewish Literature) had about thirty-six hundred subscribers and published about eighty Jewish novels and short stories, as well as scholarly works. Seven volumes of Heinrich Graetz's *History of the Jews* appeared under the auspices of the institute, as did a German translation of the novel *Alroy,* written by the most prominent European author of historical Jewish novels, Benjamin Disraeli.[11]

When the institute closed in 1874, novels, tales, poems, and dramas on Jewish topics had replaced, for many German-Jewish readers, traditional Jewish homiletics, legal discussions, and even Jewish source books. The two favorite topics of German-Jewish literature throughout the nineteenth century were the Sephardic Jewish heritage, which provided the material for a glorious Jewish past, and East European and rural German-Jewish life, which was both romantically idealized and dismissed as barbarian "half-Asia," to use the title of a novel by Karl Emil Franzos.[12]

Most of those literary products did not aim consciously at constructing a modern secular Jewish culture but used secular means to further the cause of emancipation on the grounds that Judaism was a religion. German-Jewish authors turned to the Jewish community of medieval Spain as a paradigmatic model of Jewish integration and acculturation. They constructed a myth of harmonious Spanish-Jewish coexistence and at least partly rejected their own Ashkenazic heritage. In Philippson's words, "The Jew was not only the decayed inhabitant of the German and Slavic ghetto; he was also the noble Andalusian, the rich merchant, the studying rabbi; he lived free and productively at Euphrat and Tigris, he took active part in the course of world history."[13] Philippson's message was clear: if the Andalusian Jew was a respected member of Spanish society and the Babylonian Jew lived with equal rights in a non-Jewish society, why couldn't the

German Jew in a modern and enlightened world attain the same status? For Philippson, German-Jewish literature was not to be restricted to the "dirty *Judengasse* or the modern *Salon*"—the two extremes of the German-Jewish experience—but had to promote the integration of German Jews as German citizens of Jewish faith.

Moritz Oppenheim, the first professional Jewish painter in Germany, had a similar vision. Born near Frankfurt in 1800, he grew up in a religious Jewish family but discarded Jewish traditions when he studied art in Munich, Paris, and Rome and became friendly with the leading German painters of his time. Under the protection of Baron Carl Mayer von Rothschild, he earned fame as a portraitist in the first half of the nineteenth century. Only late in his life, between 1865 and 1880, did Oppenheim turn systematically to Jewish themes. His *Bilder aus dem altjüdischen Familienleben,* created during those years, were the most popular nineteenth-century depictions of Jewish life and adorned many a Jewish home in imperial Germany.

Oppenheim advocated both the identification of German Jews as German patriots and the perseverance of Jewish religious traditions, thus anticipating the formula of "German citizens of the Jewish faith." One of his earlier paintings depicted a German-Jewish soldier returning from the War of Liberation against Napoleon. In the original version of 1833–1834, the soldier displayed the Iron Cross as a reward for his bravery on the battleground. The home of the soldier's Orthodox father contained a portrait of Frederick the Great next to a Hebrew passage of the Bible, and the *Vossische Zeitung* under an open Talmud volume, thus idealizing German-Jewish symbiosis.

In his collection on Jewish family life, Oppenheim illustrated clean and orderly synagogues adorned with flowers and paintings, bourgeois living rooms with servants removing the precious china plates, and well-educated and even better dressed Jewish children listening to the benedictions of their fathers. As Ismar Schorsch noted, those "genre and historical paintings were entirely in tune with the prevailing Biedermeier appetite for depiction of the past." The spirit behind those paintings was the optimistic vision of a harmonious German-Jewish coexistence. Like the Verein in the realm of Wissenschaft and the Institut in the field of literature, Moritz Oppenheim "translated . . . emancipation ideology into the medium of art."[14]

These three aspects of Jewish culture—Wissenschaft, literature, and art—shared the conflicting goals of creating a broad spectrum of Jewish culture while serving an ideology that reduced Judaism to the narrow sphere of the synagogue. As long as this ideology remained prevalent, it prevented a conscious redefinition of Judaism outside the religious realm. But developments within the Jewish community of fin-de-siècle Germany brought a twofold change. The majority of Liberal Jews for the first time created mass organizations that were not dedicated to a religious purpose, and a small minority of Zionists officially redefined Judaism in terms of a nation.

FROM RELIGIOUS DENOMINATION TO SECULAR CULTURE

When German Jews entered the twentieth century, they did not know what to expect from the future. The immediate past had resonated with ambiguous messages. They had become equal citizens according to the 1871 constitution of the Second German Reich but remained excluded from the ranks of officers of the Prussian army, from government posts, and from most of academia. They had achieved considerable wealth but were not invited to certain social occasions. They had won their long battle for legal emancipation but were confronted with a new kind of antisemitism that recognized no religions, only races.

The decade between 1893 and 1904 marked an era of consolidation in the development of modern German-Jewish culture between its formative period during the nineteenth century and its culmination in Weimar Germany. Secular forms of Jewish literature, Wissenschaft, and art that had existed earlier were now autonomous. Artists, rather than promoting the cause of emancipation, were establishing secular forms of Jewish culture that would be a new basis for future generations of German Jews to identify with Judaism.

With the foundation of the Centralverein deutscher Staatsbürger jüdischen Glaubens (CV, Central Association of German Citizens of the Jewish Faith) in 1893, the defense of emancipation became the privilege of lawyers and politicians instead of scholars, writers, and artists. The CV, founded at the peak of political antisemitism in imperial Germany, was officially defined as an organization representing a religious group, but it acted in an almost exclusively secular fashion. Its aim was the acceptance not of religious beliefs but of civic rights, its arena not the synagogue but the courtroom and the parliament, its chief representatives not rabbis but lawyers and politicians. The establishment of the CV marked the first time that German Jews organized to defend their rights, and their first employment of the modern mass organizations. Together with other Jewish mass organizations of quite different character, such as the Alliance Israélite Universelle in France and the Bund in Russia, the CV decisively transformed the religiously dominated Jewish organizational framework.

The CV's original aim of defense against antisemitism was soon supplemented by a second major task, when its representatives recognized that "one has to know the object one is defending."[15] Liberal Jews thus began the systematic promotion of Jewish culture. The seeds planted by such men as Zunz, Wolf, Philippson, and Oppenheim now began to bloom.

The causes for this development must be seen in the context of cultural transformation in fin-de-siècle Germany. German culture during this period was characterized not only by the awakening of nationalist thought and neo-Romantic ideas but also by the rise of various subcultures. Most important were the Catholics, the workers, and the Polish immigrants in the Ruhr region.[16] The rise of nationwide Jewish cultural associations established around the beginning of the twentieth century was part of this fragmentation of German culture. Between 1893 and 1904, those newly founded institutions included the Union of Associations for Jewish History and Literature, various Jewish libraries, the Society for the Promotion of Wissenschaft des Judentums, a central archives for Jewish community records, the *Germania Judaica* dedicated to publishing detailed accounts of local German-Jewish history, Jewish sporting clubs and student fraternities, B'nai Brith lodges, associations promoting statistics and folkloristics among German Jews, and the Jewish Women's League.

Jewish contemporaries were well aware of the revitalization of a distinct Jewish culture. Rabbis and Jewish community officials had complained for decades about the decline of Jewish knowledge and culture, but around the turn of the century a new tone was discernible in their public statements. Typical of this view was a lecture delivered in 1904 by Rosalie Perles, the widow of the rabbi of Königsberg:

> Let us imagine that our grandfathers—especially those who had . . . feared a gradual assimilation within the non-Jewish surroundings—would return to life and step in front of us. How they would be amazed by the thorough changes that their descendants underwent! How they would be astonished that the assimilation, which they had feared so much, did not occur, that instead exactly the opposite happened! . . . What would our grandfathers see today? The [Jews of] today proudly display their Judaism, no matter to which class or occupation they

belong. Jewish artists, painters, and sculptors tend to depict Jewish topics, which are known to them from the Jewish *Volksseele* or their history, or are of the present time. The Jewish element can be felt even more in the realm of music. There are long concert evenings with Jewish melodies, Jewish folk songs and liturgical music, which are performed by our best singers. There are recitals of Jewish poems and legends, and dramatic poets often go back into biblical times. Some revive our old prophets on the stage, while others describe the life of the *Ostjuden* or of the Palestinian settlements. . . . Our grandfathers would not have had to worry so much, had they seen this future while they were still alive.[17]

The grandfathers might have been impressed had they seen their descendants' renewed interest in Judaism. More probably, however, they would have been bemused and troubled by the emergence of a Jewish culture that had little to do with the Judaism they knew. Instead of attending synagogue services, their grandchildren listened to liturgical music in concert halls; instead of living according to religious laws, they read novels on traditional Jewish life in Eastern Europe; instead of performing a Yiddish *Purimshpil,* they attended a modernist German drama on a biblical theme. The Jewish renaissance in literature, art, music, and scholarship was no return to traditional Judaism but an attempt to integrate selected aspects of this tradition into the framework of a modern secular culture. And it was the task of the modern organizations to promote such a renaissance.

Rosalie Perles's speech appeared in the yearbook of the Union of Associations for Jewish History and Literature, a driving force behind the transformation of Jewish culture. Its activities constituted one of the major forces promoting modern Jewish culture in imperial Germany. The forty-eight local Vereine für jüdische Geschichte und Literatur (VJGLs) existing during the early 1890s formed a Germany-wide union (Verband) in December 1893, only a few months after the founding of the CV. Gustav Karpeles, Philippson's successor as editor of the *Allgemeine Zeitung des Judentums,* became its first president.[18]

The VJGLs helped to spread Jewish literature systematically among assimilated Jews and to provide a central agency for the coordination of the scattered local initiatives. One of their most important tasks was the publication of their yearbook. First issued in 1898, the yearbook contained a review of events concerning Jews and Judaism during the past year, reports of the activities in the various branches, and a number of literary and historical articles. The low price of the yearbook (seventy-five pfennigs per volume) enabled its high circulation, which reached seventy-five hundred in 1909.[19]

The yearbook actively promoted the production of German-Jewish literature by printing short stories and plays with Jewish themes. In addition, the VJGLs opened libraries that housed traditional and modern Jewish literature. In most small and medium-size towns they were the only Jewish libraries. In large cities they offered a broader spectrum of contemporary Jewish literature than other libraries. The library of the VJGL in Berlin, for example, contained more than sixty Jewish journals and newspapers, and a rich selection of books.[20]

Among the VJGLs' activities was the popularization of Jewish scholarship through lectures on a variety of topics related to Jews and Judaism. The yearbook published a list of lectures and helped to organize visits of lecturers to the smaller VJGL branches. For several years, a few branches offered adult education courses on Jewish history, Jewish religion, and Hebrew.[21] During one semester, approximately one thousand lectures were delivered in about 150 local chapters.[22]

Although the VJGLs and other cultural Jewish organizations of imperial Germany did not challenge the basis of emancipation, according to which Judaism was purely a religious denomination, they constituted a first step in the process characterized by Ismar Schorsch as a development "from confession to culture."[23] The main task of Jewish culture became the reeducation, or to use a contemporary term, the re-Judaization of acculturated German Jews.

BIRTH PANGS OF A RENAISSANCE

If 1893 saw the first stirrings of a reorientation among German Jews, 1897 marked the beginning of a revolution for Jewry as a whole. In August, Theodor Herzl convened the first Zionist Congress in Basel, an event that caused tempestuous discussions among the Jewish communities of the world. For some he was the Messiah leading Jews back to their Holy Land, for others he was a secular savior from misery and persecution, and a third group regarded his plans as an essential threat to their well-being in the diaspora. Most German Jews belonged to the third category. When Herzl chose Munich as the meeting place for the first Zionist Congress, the German Rabbinical Assembly, fearful that the convention would arouse accusations of Jewish disloyalty to Germany, opposed his decision and thus prevented a meeting on German soil.

But the Zionist cause had its German supporters, represented by the Zionist Federation for Germany. Although the Zionists were a minority within German Jewry, they had a prominent part in the development of the World Zionist Movement before World War I. Herzl's two successors were German Jews, German was the official language of the Zionist Congresses, and the German city of Hamburg was chosen as the site of the 1909 Zionist Congress.

The Zionist movement emerged as a reaction to two developments: the increasing antisemitism in Eastern and Central Europe and the rapid process of alienation from Judaism among European Jews. Zionism offered a remedy for both: the establishment of a Jewish state would result in the disappearance of antisemitism and would revitalize Jewish identity. Although most Zionists believed in both goals, some had different priorities from others. For such political Zionists as Theodor Herzl, physical danger constituted the heart of the Jewish problem in Europe. Their most important task was therefore the establishment of a Jewish homeland. To relieve the Jews from such immediate threats as the pogroms in Russia and the riots after the Dreyfus affair in France, Herzl even considered accepting Jewish settlement in a territory outside Palestine. Be it in the Land of Israel or in East Africa, Jews had to form a state of their own and become a people with a territory.

Cultural Zionists, in contrast, emphasized the spiritual needs of the Jewish people. They did not overlook the immediate physical threat but considered it a lesser evil than the alienation of Jews from Judaism. They argued that Jews would survive as people but, because of their rapid assimilation, might not survive as Jews. Zion was to be a spiritual center for the worldwide revitalization of Judaism. Ahad Ha'am (the pen name of Asher Ginzberg), the leading spirit of cultural Zionism and editor of the Odessa Hebrew journal *Ha-shiloah,* believed that not all Jews would and could settle in Palestine but that all Jews would profit from the establishment of a spiritual center.

Zionists were divided not only by ideological differences but also by geographical barriers. While to Ahad Ha'am and other East European Zionists the revival of Hebrew was essential, in Germany, with its highly acculturated Jewish population, such a demand would have been illusionary.[24] German Zionists thus had the difficult task of promoting a national Jewish culture that was not expressed in a language of its own. How did German Zionists define this culture using the same language as that of the non-Jewish surroundings?

An exceptional spirit and a well-organized framework was needed to create the basis for a national Jewish culture under those conditions. A leading figure of German Zionism emerged in the person of Martin Buber, whose own roots were outside Germany. Born in Vienna in 1878, he grew up in Galicia with his grandfather, Salomon Buber, a renowned scholar of Midrash. As a student, Martin Buber came to Leipzig before the turn of the century and stayed in Germany until the Nazi period. Buber's dominant role in the development of modern German-Jewish culture may have been widely accepted because he belonged to many different worlds. He was at home in Galicia's *Haskalah* (Jewish Enlightenment) and in Germany's intellectual circles; he was a Zionist, but his marriage to a Bavarian-born woman (who converted to Judaism) connected him with his German surroundings; his rediscovery of Jewish mysticism was embedded in a general preoccupation with Eastern spirituality and German mystics. When promoting a modern Jewish culture, Buber consciously borrowed his concepts from the larger society.

In an essay of 1900 Buber first introduced the term *Jewish renaissance,* defining it as the "resurrection of the Jewish people from partial life to full life." This resurrection, Buber emphasized, was possible only by combining Jewish traditions with a modern sense of aesthetics. Just as the Italian Renaissance in the fifteenth century was not a return to ancient culture, so the Jewish renaissance of the twentieth century was to be not a return to premodern times but rather the birth of a modern Jewish culture.[25] Buber's call for renewal reflected the fin-de-siècle Zeitgeist, which regarded the beginning of the new century as the awakening of a modern age, the *Moderne.* The designation of the new style emerging in art as *Jugendstil,* or art nouveau, represented such a self-conception. Using the same terminology, Jewish student circles called themselves *Jung-Juda,* and the modern literary and artistic creativity among cultural Zionists soon became known as the Young Jewish Movement.[26]

At the Fifth Zionist Congress in Basel in December 1901, Buber appeared as a spokesman for the small Demokratische Fraktion, the faction within the Zionist movement that most vehemently promoted the renewal of Jewish culture. His presentation of the immediate agenda for a Jewish renaissance included four principal tasks: the promotion of Jewish art, the establishment of a publishing house as the center for a specific Jewish literature, the spread of modern Jewish culture in newspapers and journals, and the modernization of Jewish scholarship.[27]

The creation of a modern Jewish art seemed most urgent. As Buber emphasized in his Congress speech, "The specific characteristics of a nation find their purest expression in artistic creativity. . . . Thus, our art is the best way for our people to [find] itself."[28] If Jews were to be a nation and establish their own state, they were to have not only their own politics and politicians but also their national art and their own artists. Buber's speech fits in the context of German society. The existence of a genuine German national art was a prominent topic in the contemporary intellectual discourse among artists, art historians, museum directors, and novelists. Of course, they did not agree about the nature of such a particularly German art. To some, the Gothic style was genuinely German; for others, Albrecht Dürer was the personification of German art. In his best-selling novel *Rembrandt als Erzieher* (1890), Julius Langbehn declared that Rembrandt van Rijn was the embodiment of German art. For most art historians, it was easier to state what German art was not than what it was. When the progressive director of the Berlin Nationalgalerie—dedicated to the motto *Der deutschen Kunst*—began to acquire the works of French Impressionists, a storm of indignation among nationalists shattered his plans and ultimately caused his resignation.[29]

Adherents of a national German art could refer to Gothic architecture, to Dürer's masterpieces, and even to the greatest Dutch painter, but their Jewish counterparts were in a more difficult situation. In Judaism, art had traditionally been restricted to the religious sphere and included synagogue decorations, ritual objects for the Jewish home, book illustrations, and tombstone engravings. In the absence of appropriate models, a national Jewish art had to be invented or, rather, constructed out of traditional Jewish motifs and contemporary styles of art.

The artist who personified such an approach was Ephraim Mose Lilien. Like Buber, Lilien grew up in Galicia and came to Germany shortly before the turn of the century.[30] Together with Buber, he participated as a member of the Demokratische Fraktion in the Fifth Zionist Congress, where he organized the first Jewish art exhibit. During the first years of the twentieth century, Lilien established a new Zionist iconography by integrating Jewish motifs into contemporary trends of European art. Depicting old Jews with long white or black beards, heroic images of the Jewish Scriptures, and idealized portraits of the Holy Land, Lilien chose themes that could be immediately identified as Jewish. At the same time, his style reflected art nouveau. Milly Heyd has analyzed in detail Lilien's adaptation of the British artist Aubrey Beardsley.[31] Lilien also embraced prominent motifs from the socialist movement, for which he had worked prior to his involvement in Zionism. Socialists and Zionists shared the utopian vision of a new and better society, a recurring motif in Lilien's book illustrations. The rising sun, prominent in socialist iconography, symbolized for Lilien the renaissance of the Jewish people. His sun rose behind the pyramids of Egypt and contained the Hebrew inscription *Zion,* thus marking a modern exodus from slavery to freedom.[32]

Lilien was heavily influenced by a third source of contemporary culture: German neo-Romanticism and its emphasis on the national character of art. This influence became visible in the publication usually considered the first product of the Young Jewish Movement, the book *Juda* (1900), a collection of poems and illustrations glorifying ancient Israel. Lilien was the illustrator, and the poems came from the pen of a rather unlikely figure: the non-Jewish conservative aristocrat Börries von Münchhausen, who later rose to prominence as a protagonist of Nazi Germany's culture and committed suicide in the wake of Germany's defeat in March 1945. Even at the time of his collaboration with Lilien, Münchhausen was known as a proponent of *volkisch* (German nationalist) literature, who declared that Jews could not contribute to German literature but should be assisted in their attempt to create their own national culture.[33] This odd couple, Münchhausen and Lilien, worked on *Juda* in an atmosphere that evoked the oaks and firs of German *Heimatliteratur* rather than the palm trees of the biblical Orient: "A bright room below the gable next to the tower was prepared for the artist. Beside his drafting table stood my desk. The windows were wide open, the smoke of the potato fires wafted through Thuringian land, and its smell pervaded our room."[34]

For the young Zionist movement, the poems of a German aristocrat glorifying Israel appeared a confirmation of its own ideas. Zionist Theodor Zlocisti exclaimed, "It came like a natural law" that the first ones to recognize Jewish aristocracy were aristocrats themselves.[35] And Theodor Herzl addressed a moving letter to Münchhausen just after *Juda* appeared: "When I entered the Zionist Movement some years ago, and tried to open the eyes of those who did not want or attempt to understand our cause, I already annunciated your coming, my dear Lord. I did not know your name, but I knew you would come. I promised that our movement would enthuse a Byron, just as once the cause of the Greeks was spread by another tribe."[36]

Not just Zionists enthusiastically welcomed *Juda.* The Austrian writer Stefan Zweig was so impressed that he wrote a long introduction to a volume of Lilien's works in 1903. *Juda* was, in Zweig's words, "the first page in the history of the nationally conscious [Jewish] art." Zweig went on to predict that "*Juda* is the first link in a chain, the end and the greatness of which are still incalculable."[37]

Ephraim Mose Lilien, scene from *Juda,* 1900: the Jew in exile is contrasted with the rising sun, labeled Zion.

Indeed, *Juda* marked only the modest beginning of the Young Jewish Movement. Three years after the creation of *Juda,* Lilien continued to contribute to the artistic creations of the Young Jewish Movement with his *Lieder des Ghetto* (Songs of the ghetto). This time his illustrations accompanied poems of an East European Jew of proletarian background, like Lilien himself. In the poems Morris Rosenfeld, a Polish Jewish socialist who had immigrated to the United States, described the harsh working conditions of the Jewish masses of the old ghettos in Eastern Europe and the immigrants' lives in America. Whereas in *Juda* Lilien had depicted the young Zionists' dreams of Palestine, *Lieder des Ghetto* reflected their parents' world. Not surprisingly, Münchhausen rejected the socialist tendencies of this book. In a review he admitted, "Poet and artist are totally strange to me, where they express the democratization of social thoughts. I have known Judaism only as a proud and aristocratic Judaism. Here, I find a plebeian Judaism and Social Democratic ideas."[38]

Ideas that seemed un-Jewish to the German aristocrat soon became the embodiment of Jewish art for many of his contemporaries. Just as *Juda*

was, in the words of Zionist Sammy Gronemann, a "favorite book of the
Jewish house and was not missing on any bar-mitzvah table or under any
Jewish Christmas tree," Lilien's other works enjoyed enormous popularity
among German Zionists.[39] Within a few years his version of modern
Jewish art was popularized and commercialized in the form of souvenir
postcards showing scenes from Palestine, Congress delegate cards depicting
Jewish symbols, stamps for the Jewish National Foundation, and cigarette
boxes featuring portraits of Zionist leaders. Those artifacts, together with
Lilien's illustrations—among them a portrait of his father as an exploited
East European Jewish proletarian and a depiction of the nude Theodor
Herzl—began a new tradition in Jewish art.[40]

A single artist, however, does not a movement make. To establish itself
as an independent force in German-Jewish culture, the Young Jewish
Movement needed a center from which to coordinate its efforts. The creation of publishing houses and journals thus received priority in the
Zionist circle of Buber and Lilien. Only a few months after Buber had
demanded the establishment of a publishing house in his speech at the
Fifth Zionist Congress, he founded the Jüdischer Verlag in Berlin in 1902
as a "central agency for the promotion of Jewish literature, art and scholarship."[41] During more than three decades of existence, the Jüdischer
Verlag achieved most of its goals by publishing a broad variety of translations from Hebrew and Yiddish literature, scholarly works on Jewish
issues, and a wide spectrum of German-Jewish literature and Zionist ideology. The preeminent role of art in the creation of a modern Jewish culture was underlined by a collection of seven essays on Jewish artists edited
by Martin Buber, published in 1903. Ernst Simon, Buber's student and
friend, recalled the publications of the Jüdischer Verlag as a "new type of
German Jewish book lacking that petty bourgeois flavour of tract literature which had hitherto nearly always clung to Jewish books. The aim was
to bring it up to the highest standards of the best contemporary output
and thus to open up a new approach to the cultured public of the higher,
emancipated classes."[42]

Buber's initial plan to place an intellectual journal, *Der Jude*, at the heart
of the Jüdischer Verlag failed because of financial quarrels with the World
Zionist Organization.[43] Another Zionist, Leo Winz, established the journal
Ost und West in 1901. Until Buber finally began publication of his journal
in 1916, *Ost und West* was the principal journal of the Jewish cultural
renaissance, containing numerous illustrations, short stories, and poems
expressing a "Jewish art and literature that was not produced accidentally

by Jews . . . but that strives to shape—in content and form—the characteristics and the destiny of our people [*Stamm*]."[44]

After his failure to launch *Der Jude* in April 1903, Buber temporarily
retreated from his manifold organizational activities. When he returned to
the Jewish public with his edition of the Hasidic tales of Rabbi Nahman in
1906, he did so as a spiritual leader. His Hasidic tales had an enormous res-
onance and were the basis for a renewed interest in Judaism among many
assimilated German Jews. One of the reasons for their success was the general revival and popularization of myth and mysticism. The poet Stefan
George and his circle used Germanic myths and Eastern spirituality as
sources for modern literary creativity, the publisher Eugen Diederichs made
a variety of classic mystical texts available in modern translations, and in
the same year in which Buber's *Rabbi Nahman* appeared the socialist
Gustav Landauer published the first modern translation of the great
German mystic Meister Eckhart.

Buber himself was a central figure of this trend. He had written his dissertation on the German mystics Nicholas of Cusa and Jakob Boehme, and
his *Ecstatic Confessions* (1909) contained descriptions of mystical ecstasy
in various cultures. By turning to Hasidism, Buber not only reflected the
contemporary revival of mystical traditions but also revolted against nineteenth-century Wissenschaft des Judentums, which tried to present Judaism
as a "clean," rational religion, free of mysticism and superstition. In the
nineteenth century even the most passionate chronicler of Jewish history,
Heinrich Graetz, had been anxious to depict the Jewish religion as rational.
Singling out Maimonides and Mendelssohn as the heroes of Jewish history,
he dismissed Hasidism as the "daughter of darkness."[45]

By the turn of the century, a renewed interest in the fields previously
neglected by Wissenschaft des Judentums became apparent. A decade
before Martin Buber published his first Hasidic tales and a generation
before Gershom Scholem established Jewish mysticism as a modern scholarly discipline, a small circle of German-Jewish intellectuals led by the
young Hamburg rabbi Max Grunwald founded the Gesellschaft für
jüdische Volkskunde (Association for Jewish Folkloristics) in 1898,
reflecting the spread of folkloristic societies in Germany during the
1890s.[46] One of the Gesellschaft's major tasks was the study of popular
Jewish mystical traditions. Its journal, the *Mitteilungen für jüdische Volkskunde* (1898–1929), contained articles about Polish Hasidim and Caucasian mountain Jews, itinerant singers and *Wunderrebbes,* and such
uncanny creatures as demons of the night, evil spirits, and all kinds of

ghosts. Like the fathers of the Verein für Cultur und Wissenschaft der Juden, the founders of Jewish folkloristics were eager to present a certain version of Judaism to the non-Jewish world. Their version, however, differed substantially from that of the Verein. During the eight decades between the foundations of the two associations, Jewish society and antisemitic stereotypes had been transformed significantly. To most Germans, Jews now represented the antithesis of the neo-Romanticist ideals of the time: they were mainly urbanized, not tied to the soil, and they lacked genuine folk traditions. Judaism, once attacked for its superstition, was now criticized for being a *Verstandesreligion* (religion of reason).

This transformation of antisemitism is expressed in one of the most popular books of the time, Julius Langbehn's *Rembrandt als Erzieher*, in a passage juxtaposing premodern Jews with assimilated modern Jews: "Rembrandt's Jews were real Jews, who wanted to be nothing but Jews, and they also had character. This is the exact opposite of today's Jews: they want to be Germans, Englishmen, Frenchmen, etc., and through this have become characterless." Such respected intellectuals as historian Jakob Burckhardt criticized the "wealthy Israelite" of Berlin rather than the poor superstitious village Jew.[47] Grunwald and his circle understood that one could no longer refute antisemitic stereotypes by portraying Judaism as rational. The ideal Jew presented in their publications was the mystic or the Jewish counterpart to the neo-Romanticist ideal of the peasant, be it in the form of Caucasian mountain Jews, Ethiopian Falashas, or rural Jews of Germany.

Grunwald and his colleagues took the refutation of antisemitic stereotypes seriously, but their main addressees were acculturated German Jews, who had no Grimm brothers to record their folk tales and customs. Grunwald attempted to "help to create a solid basis for the future of our people" by reviving forgotten traditions. As if in response to Moritz Steinschneider's alleged statement that Wissenschaft des Judentums wanted only to give the remnants of Judaism a decent burial, Grunwald emphasized his opposition to any attempt of "preserving mummies."[48] His ideal was the practical application of scholarship. A Purim play discovered in Poland could be used in Hamburg, for example, and a decoration of a Hungarian synagogue could be reproduced in Vienna.

The rise of Jewish folkloristics as a subdiscipline of Wissenschaft des Judentums was only one aspect of the large-scale transformation that led to an emphasis on the present and future of Jewish existence, instead of on a pure examination of the Jewish past. The Office for the Statistics among the Jews established "sociology of the Jews" as a subdiscipline of Wissenschaft des Judentums, and the Society for the Promotion of Wissenschaft des Judentums aimed at a popular presentation of the scholarly results of the first century of Wissenschaft des Judentums.[49] All those organizations were influenced by Martin Buber's demand to replace Wissenschaft des Judentums with Jewish Wissenschaft, which would fulfill two major aims: "First, to understand what one loves. Second, to investigate what our people needs and what it will expect."[50]

When Martin Buber delivered this programmatic statement in 1901, the revitalization of Jewish culture in Germany seemed far off. But only a few years later the organizational framework for a systematic cultural renaissance had been built. The first German-language Jewish publishing house, the Jüdischer Verlag, promoted both Jewish art and literature, as did the journal *Ost und West*. In the realm of scholarship, a significant shift signaled the practical application of the research into the past for establishing a modern and mostly secular Jewish culture. The foundation for the realization of Buber's vision was laid in the two decades before World War I. During those years, however, only a small, mostly Zionist minority of German Jews became actively involved in this newly emerging Jewish cultural framework. It took the war to change this situation.

HOPE AND DISILLUSION: THE WAR

Not all German Jews were happy about the outbreak of the war, but they had reason to maintain high hopes. The Kaiser's famous promise that from then on there would be no differences between classes, parties, and religions was greeted enthusiastically by the Jewish population. What peace had not achieved—the full integration of Jews into German society—war would establish. The bonds of solidarity among Christian and Jewish soldiers, fighting together and dying in the same trenches, would eliminate the remaining barriers and stereotypes.

Like Max Weber, who initially believed that "this war is really great and wonderful beyond expectation," philosopher Hermann Cohen, the most prominent German-Jewish thinker, expressed his pride in living to see Germany's heroic hour. In his essay "Deutschtum und Judentum" (Germanness and Jewishness), he argued that it was the special task of the Jews to spread the supremacy of German culture among their coreligionists of other European countries.[51] Just as Social Democrats submitted themselves to the emperor's call for weapons, German Zionists left no doubt that they would do their duty as German soldiers, and a group of Zionists even returned from Palestine to fight for their German fatherland.[52]

Indeed, the First World War brought forth a decisive change in the development of German-Jewish relations, but it was not the change that German Jews had envisioned. Instead of resulting in the social acceptance of the Jews, the war led to their brutal disillusionment. Many had lasting memories of the antisemitism in the trenches. For some, this experience led directly to Zionism.[53] Those who were already Zionists and had initially welcomed the war, such as writer Arnold Zweig, expressed increasing doubts about their commitment to a German state that had made its Jewish soldiers subject to a specific census, the so-called Jew count, in 1916.[54] Most significant, such Liberal Jews as writer Georg Hermann abandoned their belief in successful assimilation. In a moving essay Hermann, the author of *Jettchen Gebert*—the enormously popular novel of 1906 about an assimilated Jewish family in Berlin—confessed that his lifelong identification with Germanness had been an illusion: "Whether we wanted it or not," he wrote a year after the war, "we had to rediscover our Judaism. . . . We experienced a great disappointment with the Germans and we continue to do so."[55] With similar frustration, Ernst Toller adapted his wartime experience for his drama *Die Wandlung,* in which Friedrich, an assimilated Jew, remains an alien to his non-Jewish comrades, even after winning the Iron Cross.

Even the twelve thousand Jewish lives lost on the battlefield were not sufficient to create the "community of the trenches" envisioned by Isidor Landau. Instead, the war strengthened the ties of many acculturated German Jews with the Jewish community. Ernst Simon, who became aware of his Jewishness during World War I, recalled the feelings after the war: "We became mature and thereby able to experience Judaism as something positive. . . . Here was the Gemeinschaft that we had sought our whole lives."[56]

German Jews found their solidarity strengthened by their encounter with East European Jewry during the war. In 1925 Alfred Döblin wrote that in his visit to Poland he met Jews for the first time, reiterating what many German-Jewish soldiers had experienced a decade earlier: the conviction that genuine Judaism was to be found only in the East. German Jews were directly confronted in the East with a world they previously knew, at best, from Martin Buber's *Hasidic Tales*. And those who did not go East as German soldiers had the opportunity to meet *Ostjuden* in Germany. Between 1916 and 1920, seventy thousand East European Jews moved to Germany as industrial workers or merchants and artisans, bringing with them their own culture.[57]

The immigration of East European Jews radically transformed Germany's Jewish community. Non-German citizens constituted about a quarter of Berlin's Jewish community and were even the majority in such communities as Leipzig, Dresden, and Hamborn. In many communities the Ostjuden, who were deeply rooted in Jewish traditions, contributed decisively to the renaissance of Jewish culture. At the same time the encounter with East European Jews encouraged German Jews to overcome their internal divisions. All major streams of German Jewry considered the encounter significant. For Liberal Jews, the Yiddish-speaking Ostjuden represented a cultural outpost of Germanness, for Zionists they embodied authentic Judaism, and for the small segment of Orthodox German Jews, East European Jewry was a religious inspiration. Although the *Burgfrieden* (civic truce) declared by the emperor proved short-lived for Jews, as for other segments of German society, a more lasting Burgfrieden was achieved in the German-Jewish community, with East European Jews functioning as a bridge between the various German groups.

The first phases of such a development had been visible before the war. The title of the journal *Ost und West* is evidence for the new importance of East European culture to German Jews after the turn of the century. On the eve of World War I, the writer Fritz Mordechai Kaufmann founded a pan-Jewish review (*Alljüdische Revue*), called *Die Freistatt,* whose main purpose was the promotion of East European culture. Transcriptions of Yiddish texts and translations of Hebrew sources occupied an important place in the journal. In his programmatic outline, Kaufmann defined his journal as a vehicle for overcoming the divisions among the various factions separating German Jewry. To reach this goal, he solicited contributions from representatives of all religious and political sects, but especially "outsiders and heretics."[58]

The *Freistatt* never became a significant pan-Jewish review and was dissolved in 1915 after only two years of existence, but two journals established in 1916 proved more successful. Twelve years after his initial plan, Martin Buber finally succeeded in launching his monthly, *Der Jude.* During its eight years of existence, *Der Jude* became the most important intellectual forum of modern German Jewry. In the second volume, appearing in 1917, Franz Kafka published for the first time two of his animal stories ("Jackals and Arabs" and "A Report for an Academy"), Arnold Zweig contributed "from the battlefield" on Jew and European, the anarchist

Gustav Landauer reflected on Strindberg and Shakespeare, and the leader of socialist revisionism, Eduard Bernstein, described how he grew up as a Jew in the diaspora. Buber, who a decade earlier had introduced the Ostjude as a literary figure, endeavored to present the real lives of East European Jews in his journal by publishing statistics and accounts of contemporary political developments in Eastern Europe.

Der Jude was clearly Zionist in orientation but was open to all Jewish intellectuals. Buber's main concern, like Kaufmann's, was to overcome the deep divisions that separated German Jewry. In the preface of the first issue of *Der Jude,* Buber expressed his conviction that "our time . . . is the beginning of a genuine concentration and unification" for German Jewry.[59] By providing German Jewry with a first-rate intellectual platform, *Der Jude* was to further this process.

The bi-weekly *Neue Jüdische Monatshefte* began to appear in October 1916, almost synchronously with *Der Jude.* More than any other Jewish journal, it was dedicated to the creation of a united German-Jewish Gemeinschaft.[60] The *Neue Jüdische Monatshefte* was the only German-Jewish journal edited jointly by leading Liberal Jews and Zionists. Its five editors were the Liberal philosopher Hermann Cohen; the chairman of the CV, Eugen Fuchs; moderate Zionists Adolf Friedemann and Franz Oppenheimer; and Alexander Eliasberg, a translator of Hebrew and Yiddish literature.

Such an unprecedented collaboration was possible only because of the war. In 1916 the major German-Jewish organizations formed a common framework for the first time by creating the Komitee für den Osten (KfdO). This organization (enlarged to the Vereinigung jüdischer Organisationen Deutschlands, VIOD, in 1918), which aimed both at assisting East European Jews suffering the miseries of war and at furthering specific German war interests in the East, published the *Neue Jüdische Monatshefte.* It was only natural, then, that East European Jews were the dominant topic during the five years of the journal's existence. More than a third of its articles (122 out of a total of 347) were devoted to cultural, historical, or political issues of East European Jewry. But the journal also became a central agency for the promotion of German-Jewish culture. For example, Franz Rosenzweig's open letter to Hermann Cohen that would later lead to the establishment of the Akademie für die Wissenschaft des Judentums was published by the *Neue Jüdische Monatshefte* in 1917.

Afer the war ended, the old divisions began to reappear. The KfdO and the VIOD dissolved, and the *Neue Jüdische Monatshefte* had to suspend publication in 1920 because of inflation. The personal losses were no less significant. Hermann Cohen died in 1918, and Gustav Landauer, who had contributed to *Der Jude* and opened the Jüdisches Volksheim in Berlin, was killed for being one of the leaders of the short-lived Bavarian Soviet Republic.

The ambiguous path of German Jewry became conspicuously manifest at the turning points of German history. As in 1871, in 1918 Jews became both further integrated into German society and more conscious of their distinctiveness. As Jews rose to the ranks of ministers and officers, antisemitic agitators experienced unprecedented success. But unlike events of 1871, the forces separating German Jews from the larger German society in 1918 proved stronger than the tendencies integrating them. Thus by the early days of Weimar Martin Buber's prophecy of 1916 had come to pass: "From all the letters I received from the front, from all talks with those who returned home, I got the same impression—one of a general strengthening of ties with Judaism. . . . Some will defect from Judaism. . . . But those who remain true to Judaism will be attached to it more strongly than before: more seriously, more actively, more responsibly."[61]

2

Gemeinschaft and Gemeinde: The Ideological and Institutional Transformation of the Jewish Community

Das Idol dieses Zeitalters ist die Gemeinschaft. Wie zum Ausgleich für die Härte und Schalheit unseres Lebens hat die Idee alles Süße bis zur Süßlichkeit, alle Zartheit bis zur Kraftlosigkeit, alle Nachgiebigkeit bis zur Würdelosigkeit in sich verdichtet.

—Helmuth Plessner, *Grenzen der Gemeinschaft* (1924)

The trauma of World War I dashed the hopes that German Jews had, to be finally included in a German *Volksgemeinschaft*. Still, they shared with their non-Jewish neighbors the need to establish new forms of community. Some satisfied this need by emphasizing their Germanness, others became socialists or communists, and many found refuge in the rediscovery of a Jewish Gemeinschaft. Only a few weeks after the outbreak of World War I Martin Buber anticipated this strengthening of Gemeinschaft in a speech later reprinted as the opening essay in *Der Jude*:

> In the tempest of events the Jew has had the powerful experience of what Gemeinschaft means. . . . The most essential weakness of the Western Jew was not that he was "assimilated" but that he was atomized; that he was without connection [to the Jewish community]; that his heart no longer beat as one with a living Gemeinschaft. . . ; that he was excluded from the life of the people and their holy Gemeinschaft. Judaism was no longer rooted, and the uprooted roots [*Luftwurzeln*] of his assimilation were without nourishing force. Now, however, in the catastrophic events that he experienced with his neighbors, the Jew discovered with shock and joy the great life of Gemeinschaft. And [this discovery] captured him.[1]

Buber and his fellow Zionists believed that the nineteenth-century confessionalization of Judaism had led to an atomization among German Jews,
whose Judaism was now defined not as a framework for communal life but
as a private religious faith of individual German citizens. Indeed, by the end
of the nineteenth century religion had become a divisive force among a populace split into Orthodox, Liberals, and nonbelievers. Unlike in Eastern
Europe, the Jewish population of Germany was not distinguished from its
non-Jewish surroundings by such visible factors as languages or neighborhoods. What then was the source of this image of communion that was in
the minds of the members of this fragmented community?[2]

Buber's reference to a "community of blood" was familiar to many
Zionists, who employed ethnic terms to define their ties to other Jews.[3] Liberal Jews, though rejecting the concept of a Jewish nation, also employed
such ethnic terms as *Abstammungsgemeinschaft* (community of common
descent) to express their belonging to a Jewish Gemeinschaft.[4] This definition of Gemeinschaft included all children of Jewish parents, regardless of
what they believed or how they acted. When such acculturated German
Jews as Walther Rathenau spoke of a Jewish *Stamm* (and compared it to
the Bavarians or the Saxons) to emphasize their Germanness, they clearly
departed from the nineteenth-century conception of Jewish identity as
purely religious.[5] This Gemeinschaft of common descent remained, however, an invisible community, whose members could not be identified by
dress, language, or religious practice.

Weimar Germany's organized Jewry aimed to change this rather vague
sense of Gemeinschaft into a concrete culture, thus transforming an invisible community into a visible one.[6] The sections of this chapter explore
three aspects of the changing conception of community among German
Jews: the influence of the debate about Gemeinschaft on the self-conception of Liberal German Jews; the transformation of the Gemeinde, the local
Jewish community, from an essentially religious congregation into a mainly
secular institution; and the central role of cultural institutions within such
a transformed Gemeinde.

THE IMPACT OF INTELLECTUAL TRENDS ON
LIBERAL JUDAISM

German Jews probably had stronger ties to nineteenth-century
German liberalism than most other segments of the German population,
because their legal equality and acceptance in German society depended to

a large extent on the success of liberal politics. The liberals promised to emancipate German Jews not because of love for Judaism but because of their firm principle that the inhabitants of a country should not be divided into first- and second-class citizens.

German Jews adopted many of liberalism's principles. Most Jews voted for the liberal parties and supported constitutional government;[7] they adhered to the principle of free trade, which suited their economic interests; and most German Jews replaced their traditional synagogue service with modern liturgy and introduced such aesthetic innovations as choir and organ. They firmly defended such liberal principles as personal freedom, individualism, rationalization of religion, and the belief in progress. They welcomed their transformation from the ethnically distinct German-Jewish society of the ghetto into a denomination of German citizens of Mosaic (or Israelite) faith.

Jews adhered to liberal doctrines as long as they were convinced that liberalism would pave the way for them to be accepted into German society. When the influence of liberal parties in German politics decreased, however, the social integration of Jews was blocked, and new antisemitism became more visible in the Bismarck era. When even the liberal parties hesitated to attack antisemitism openly and refused to admit Jewish candidates in the leading positions in national elections at the end of the *Kaiserreich*, many German Jews lost their faith in liberalism.

An increasing number of Jews thus shifted their vote to the Social Democratic Party (SPD). Although the economic interests of most German Jews conflicted with those of the Social Democrats, twelve out of fourteen (unbaptized) Jewish members of the Reichstag of 1912 belonged to the SPD. In Weimar Germany, when the SPD gained respectability and the liberals lost further political ground, Jewish votes went equally to the SPD and the liberal parties, and to a smaller extent to the conservatives and the Catholic Center Party.[8]

In comparison to German society as a whole, in which the ideals of nineteenth-century liberalism were rapidly waning and liberal parties gradually disappeared from the political scene, Weimar Jewry appeared to be one of the last strongholds of liberal traditions. Contrary to the consensus among historians, however, the "symbiosis between Liberalism and the Jews" did not persist from emancipation until the years after 1933.[9] Most Jews in Weimar Germany would not have objected to being characterized as liberals, and the major Jewish organizations still referred to themselves as liberal, but their understanding of liberalism had undergone a profound transformation. During the two decades preceding the Nazi rise to power, Liberal Jews abandoned such traditions as a purely religious definition of Judaism, dominance of rationalist thought, and cultural optimism.

Three facets of the quest for community characterized the transformation of Liberal Judaism in Weimar Germany: the construction of a community based on common ethnicity rather than individual faith, as expressed by Germany's most important Jewish organization, the CV; the emphasis on nonrational elements within the Jewish religion by a new generation of Liberal rabbis; and the Romanticist antimodernism of the Jewish youth movement. All three elements signified a gradual departure from the nineteenth-century ideology aimed toward the acquisition of political equality. This departure signaled a shift in the traditional affinity between liberals and Jews and the construction of a new collective Jewish identity.

When the CV was founded in 1893, it defined itself as an *Abwehrverein,* an association whose purpose was to defend the legal equality of German Jews and fight antisemitism. By the First World War, however, significant changes in the CV's ideology had taken place. The CV had assumed the role of a *Gesinnungsverein,* which regarded the strengthening of the Jewish identity of its members as one of its most important tasks. Ironically, increasing antisemitism led to the political organization of German Jews and ultimately to a rediscovery of positive values in Judaism.[10]

This change was first expressed clearly in a speech that Eugen Fuchs, the CV's chief thinker who would later become its president, made in 1913. Fuchs admitted that the original purpose of the CV was no longer sufficient: "We started as an Abwehrverein, and the more we practiced Abwehr the more we realized that Abwehr could not be done without knowledge, and without pride. . . . We became more contemplative, more positive, and more Jewish."[11] Fuchs introduced a new element into the self-definition of Liberal German Jews when he emphasized that they were bound not only by a common religion but also by the consciousness of common descent (*Stammesbewußtsein*).[12] Fuchs concluded that the term *Centralverein deutscher Staatsbürger jüdischen Glaubens* was outdated: "If I could create a new formula today, I would say, 'We are a Centralverein of Jewish Germans.'"[13]

The new emphasis on Jewish Stammesbewußtsein and on positive values of Judaism brought a renewed sense of Gemeinschaft to German Jews. One ought not to forget that Fuchs's speech was directed mainly against Zionism and its notion of a Jewish nation. Because Liberal Jews vehemently rejected the existence of a Jewish nation (at least in Germany), they had to find an alternative to the Zionist sense of Gemeinschaft. In a relatively secularized society, religion was no longer a sufficient basis for community, and defense against antisemitism could hardly be regarded as an ideal common ground. Therefore, such terms as *Stammesgemeinschaft* and *Schicksalsgemeinschaft* (community of common fate) were gradually integrated into the ideology of the CV during World War I and in the Weimar period. Both terms indicated the search for a new sense of *Gemeinschaft,* a word much used and often misused in Germany, especially with reference to Ferdinand Tönnies' sociological study *Gemeinschaft und Gesellschaft* (Community and society).

Originally published in 1887, *Gemeinschaft und Gesellschaft* attracted little attention beyond the academic realm. When a second edition appeared in 1912, however, the book was widely discussed, and during the Weimar years it was republished in several editions and popularized in many different versions.[14] The sudden interest in Tönnies' study was part of a passion for the term *Gemeinschaft* in Weimar Germany. Nationalist ideologues and politicians propagated a *Volksgemeinschaft,* Protestant theologians and Catholic social reformers spoke of a new religious community, philosophers discussed a *Philosophie der Gemeinschaft* and an artificial Gesellschaft, and the youth movement aimed for the ideal of a genuine Gemeinschaft.[15] Opponents of an idealized sense of Gemeinschaft, such as the philosopher Helmuth Plessner, seemed like lonely prophets who had to admit that the quest for community had become the "idol of our time."[16]

Tönnies did not explicitly evaluate the terms *Gemeinschaft* and *Gesellschaft.* For him Gemeinschaft represented "organic" relations, such as families, neighborly relations, and village communities, whereas he saw Gesellschaft reflected in "mechanical" relations like business associations and urban administration. Tönnies envisioned the integration of certain forms of Gemeinschaft within a modern Gesellschaft, but the popularizers of his theories condemned modern Gesellschaft for representing a society of uprooted individuals and longed for a renewal of a genuine Gemeinschaft.[17]

Eugen Fuchs's comments must be seen in the context of the public discussion of Tönnies' book. Fuchs made it clear that Jews formed an organic Gemeinschaft rather than a mechanical Gesellschaft. What Fuchs only cautiously mentioned in 1913 was openly adopted by a younger generation of CV leaders in the 1920s. In February 1928 the CV's syndic, Ludwig Holländer, rejected the definition of German Jewry in terms of religious denomination. He was not reluctant to express bluntly that German Jewry was partly an *Unglaubensgemeinschaft* (community of lack of faith) rather than a *Glaubensgemeinschaft* (community of faith) and left no doubt that common descent united German Jews.[18]

In a much discussed article in the *Europäische Revue* of October 1930, Erich von Kahler, a Jewish historian and philosopher, tried to integrate the theory of Jewish descent into a systematic philosophical framework based on the difference between the character (*Wesensart*) of Jews and that of other Germans. Kahler was well known in German intellectual life primarily because of his critique of Max Weber's "Wissenschaft als Beruf" (Wissenschaft as vocation), which he published under the title "Der Beruf der Wissenschaft" (The profession of Wissenschaft).[19] Influenced by the neo-Romantic ideas of the George circle, Kahler rejected Weber's liberal rationalism as well as that of the principal philosopher of Liberal Judaism, Hermann Cohen, and the founders of the CV. Kahler believed that Jews should admit that they were a distinct Stamm, different from the German *Stämme*. Unlike the antisemites, however, Kahler denied that this difference should lead to the exclusion of Jews from German society. Quite the contrary: *because* of their difference, Kahler argued, German Jews could contribute much to German society. This was exactly the reverse of the original ideology of the CV. Instead of claiming that individual Jews should be integrated into society on the basis of their equality with non-Jewish Germans, Kahler maintained that the German-Jewish Stamm should be tolerated in German society because of its differences.[20]

Kahler did not represent the CV, but one of the younger CV leaders explicitly endorsed Kahler's view. The CV's Bavarian syndic, Werner Cahnmann, assured Kahler that "there are no basic differences whatsoever between our views and yours." In a second letter, Cahnmann went further: "I am of the opinion that our friends in the camp of liberalism and Enlightenment . . . are dangerous friends for us. Because rationalism dissolves all kind of distinctive existence [*Sonderart*]. . . , it also dissolves distinctive Jewish existence. . . . The maintenance [of a distinctive Jewish existence] is only possible in alliance with the Romantic forces in German Bildung."[21] Cahnmann explicitly referred to Kahler when he published an article in *Der Morgen* in which he demanded the integration of German Jews, as a group with distinctive characteristics, into German society. As Cahnmann recalled, a "small-scale internal revolution" took place in the CV during the late 1920s, and his ideas, reversing nineteenth-century emancipation ideology, were shared by an increasing number of leading CV members.[22]

The changing position of the CV represented only one facet of Jewish liberalism in Weimar Germany. Its emphasis on the Stammesgemeinschaft should not be confused with the abandonment of religion. In his memoirs Caesar Seligmann, a Frankfurt rabbi and longtime president of the Union of Liberal Rabbis in Germany, juxtaposed the passivity of Liberal Judaism at the end of the nineteenth century with its fresh spirit in the first decades of the twentieth century.[23] Seligmann may have exaggerated the extent of revitalization of Liberal Judaism, in which he played a leading part, but a variety of documents and personal recollections leave no doubt that a changing spirit was perceived among Liberal German Jews around the turn of the century. In many respects this change was a reaction to contemporary Jewish and non-Jewish movements: the rise of Zionism, the popularity of East European Jewish spirituality as Buber presented it, and a parallel renewal of religiosity in Protestant and Catholic circles.[24] More deeply, it had the same causes as those movements: the search for spiritual support in an age increasingly dominated by materialism, and the longing for religious and ethnic roots in a rapidly urbanizing, anonymous society.

One of the main features of the transformation of Liberal Judaism in Weimar Germany was its gradual detachment from the optimistic belief in human reason and progress. This development must be seen in relation to the general intellectual framework, and especially to contemporary Protestantism. Belief in human reason, scientific progress, and the settlement of theological questions by historical analysis had characterized Protestant liberalism from Friedrich Schleiermacher to Adolf von Harnack, but these beliefs were shattered in the early twentieth century. In 1906 Albert Schweitzer pointed to the self-deception of historical analysis in *The Quest for the Historical Jesus,* and a decade later Rudolf Otto rediscovered the "numinous element" in the Old Testament and stressed the nonrational elements in Luther in *The Idea of the Holy* (1917), the most widely read theological work in Weimar Germany. Between 1922 and 1933 "postliberal" thinking was published in the journal *Zwischen den Zeiten* (Between the times), a forum in which a younger generation of theologians rejected their teachers' rational belief in progress.

A similar development occurred in the field of philosophy. The official summary of the tenth convention of the German Philosophical Society in Leipzig in 1928 emphasized, "The discussions in Leipzig and their aftereffects revolved in large part around the problem of the irrational."[25] It was certainly no coincidence that the rising star among German philosophers in the last days of Weimar was Martin Heidegger, whose Philosophy of Being repudiated both rationalism and scientific progress.

In Jewish thought this trend was best characterized in Franz Rosenzweig's *Star of Redemption,* the three parts of which reflected different aspects of the "new thinking" as expressed by a Liberal German Jew. The first section stresses the subjectivity of truth; in the second section Rosenzweig analyzes the continuous relationship between humans and God on the basis of revelation; the final portion argues for the existence of Jewish history outside the course of general history.[26]

The Star of Redemption was a reaction to the elimination of the concept of revelation in Judaism by many nineteenth-century German-Jewish thinkers. This development was related to the more general cleansing of nonrational elements from Judaism, which found a last expression in *The Religion of Reason out of the Sources of Judaism* (1919), the posthumously published work of Rosenzweig's own teacher, Hermann Cohen. Cohen, the neo-Kantian philosopher of Marburg who in his last years taught at the Liberal rabbinical seminary in Berlin, represented a nineteenth-century view shared by the bulk of contemporary Liberal rabbis and the first generations of scholars of Wissenschaft des Judentums. In their view, the emphasis on revelation and other concepts originating beyond human reason constituted an aberration from the rational course of Jewish history and the rational essence of Judaism. They had a special disdain for Jewish mysticism, as illustrated by the words of the Posen rabbi Philipp Bloch, told in anecdotal form by Gershom Scholem. Impressed by Bloch's immense collection of Kabbalistic works, a young scholar inquired of him why he read so much mystical literature. The old rabbi looked at his library and replied, "What, am I supposed to *read* this rubbish, too?"[27]

The premier figure of Liberal Judaism in Weimar Germany, Rabbi Leo Baeck, signaled the changing spirit of Liberal German Judaism in his second edition (1922) of *The Essence of Judaism,* originally published in 1905 as a reply to Adolf Harnack's *Essence of Christianity.* In the first edition Baeck basically had adopted the rational framework of Hermann Cohen, but the second edition included significant modifications. Baeck never refuted his rationalist outlook, but as historian Michael Meyer summarizes, in the revised version of *Essence of Judaism* the "moral and rational elements in Judaism, as well as its universal goals, are increasingly balanced by their polar counterparts, which achieve equivalent importance. However strong the moral bond between God and humans, Baeck came to believe that religion encompassed more. It was forced to acknowledge the unfathomability of the Divine, to appreciate what reason could not fully grasp."[28]

As Albert Friedlander noted, Baeck's prototype in Jewish philosophy was not the rational Maimonides, who was celebrated by Baeck's predecessors, but the nonrational Yehudah Halevi.[29] Unlike Philipp Bloch and many of his older colleagues, Leo Baeck considered Kabbalistic literature a source of inspiration for modern Liberal Judaism. Baeck's publications after World War I concentrated increasingly on topics of Jewish mysticism.[30] In his obituary for Nehemias Anton Nobel, an Orthodox rabbi of Frankfurt, Baeck appreciated first and foremost Nobel's reintegration of mystical elements into Judaism.[31]

Leo Baeck succeeded Nobel as president of the General Rabbinical Association of Germany in 1922 and became the leading representative of the German rabbinate throughout the remainder of the Weimar period. His colleagues also integrated nonrational elements into Liberal Judaism. When asked to define Liberal Judaism in a short essay, Leipzig Liberal rabbi Felix Goldmann stressed the relations between Hasidism and Liberal Judaism. Goldmann saw Hasidism no longer as a "daughter of darkness which is born in the dark and continues to walk on dark paths" (Graetz) but as "born in the spirit of liberalism." On the other hand, the Enlightenment philosopher Moses Mendelssohn, the undisputed hero of nineteenth-century Liberal Jews, was now seen as "having contributed little to the religious development" of Judaism; his friends and successors—much celebrated a generation before—were called by Goldmann in 1919 the representatives of "Protestantism in Jewish garb" [ein jüdisch frisierter Protestantismus].[32]

The changing mood among Liberal German rabbis was clearly reflected in their annual conventions. During the first postwar meeting, in 1921, Rabbi Max Dienemann of Offenbach delivered a speech called "On the Importance of the Irrational for Liberal Judaism." In this lecture, which amounted to a systematic criticism of nineteenth-century religious Jewish Liberalism, Dienemann voiced his deep shame over "our superficiality and our lack of depth." Dienemann confessed that the rationalization of Judaism by Liberal Jews had torn the roots from the tree of Judaism and gradually dried it out. He complained that the partial replacement of Hebrew by German as the language of prayer and the abolition of several Jewish rituals and laws had negative repercussions. "One thought purely rationally; one imagined that the better one understands his prayers, the more one would pray. But one did not think of the nonrational element of the emotion, which is tied to the Hebrew language." The time of rationalism had passed: "It is a characteristic of our time that the irrational is dominant, that one cannot answer questions—as has been done in the previous era—out of contemplation, cool examination, rational thought, explanation, and scientific orientation, not at all out of clarity, but out of the dark, the instinctive, the inexplicable, the mystical forces."[33]

Dienemann, who later became the editor of the most prestigious Liberal German-Jewish journal, *Der Morgen,* and the last president of the Union of Liberal Rabbis in Germany, welcomed this development. He believed that it brought new life to Judaism and that therefore the task of Liberal Judaism was to integrate nonrational elements into its ideology: "Today, thank God, one again knows that reason is not the ultimate force. One feels mysteries and is willing to immerse oneself in them. One hungers for positive emotions, for steadfastness and support, one is tired of the individual way of life and recognizes community and feelings of togetherness. . . . It is our task to create a synthesis of the rational and the irrational forces."[34]

An even stronger push away from rationalism was visible among the younger generation of Liberal German rabbis, as represented by Max Wiener. Wiener, born in 1882, grew up in the Silesian town of Oppeln while Leo Baeck, then a young rabbi, was serving there. Wiener's and Baeck's paths were to cross several times. On completion of his rabbinical studies, Wiener became an assistant rabbi to Baeck in Düsseldorf, and after Wiener went to Stettin for a short stay, they became colleagues as *Gemeinderabbiner* of Berlin. While Baeck was still wavering between rationalism and nonrational elements, Wiener's break with nineteenth-century Liberal traditions was complete. In his programmatic speech at the convention of Liberal German rabbis in Berlin in January 1922, Wiener held Judiaism's nineteenth-century rational weltanschauung responsible for the poor condition of modern Jewish religiosity.[35] He demanded a religious renewal based on the integration of nonrational elements—the feeling of belonging to the Jewish people and the self-consciousness of the particularity of the Jews as a chosen people—into modern Judaism. As Wiener's biographer, Robert S. Schine, has observed, Wiener's "historical-metaphysical irrationalism" constituted an assimilation of Romantic nationalism into Liberal Judaism.[36]

For Wiener, religious acts based on revealed law, not rational doctrines, were the basis of Judaism. His critical position toward the development of German Judaism in the nineteenth century was also reflected in his book

Jüdische Religion im Zeitalter der Emanzipation (Judaism in the time of emancipation). This work was one of the most important studies written by a Liberal rabbi in the Weimar period and served as an epitaph for Liberal Judaism in Germany. When it was published in 1933, both Liberalism and Judaism had become invectives.

Leo Baeck, Max Dienemann, and Max Wiener represented the new leadership of the Liberal German rabbinate.[37] While such scholars as Gershom Scholem started to grasp the importance of the mythical element in the Jewish religion, such rabbis as Baeck, Wiener, and Dienemann tried to reintegrate nonrational elements into theological interpretations of contemporary Judaism. This process constituted a reversal of the rational Enlightenment traditions that had emphasized the common elements of all monotheistic religions and culminated in the propagation of one deistic faith. The renewal of nonrational traditions paved the way for marking once again the borderlines that separated religions. After a century of increasing acculturation, Liberal German rabbis felt the need to stress the distinct character of Judaism and thus strengthen the collective identity among German Jews.

In an increasingly nonliberal environment, many German Jews were hesitant to continue liberal traditions. Franz Rosenzweig most eloquently summarized the crisis of Liberal Judaism in his poignant words, "The Liberal German-Jewish standpoint on which almost all of German Judaism had enough room for nearly a century has become so tiny that apparently only one person—I myself—can live there. Poor Hermann Cohen."[38]

The transformation of Liberal Judaism was most dramatically expressed by the younger generation. In his pioneering study on the German youth movement, Walter Laqueur distinguishes the prewar *Wandervogel* era from the Weimar period, dominated by the *Bünde*. Emerging out of the hiking traditions of the Wandervogel, the Bünde clung to a blend of Romanticism, teetotalism, nationalist thought, and a strong belief in the principle of leadership. When antisemitism in the youth movement became palpable shortly before World War I, Jews founded their own movements. The first was Blau-Weiss (established in 1907 in Breslau and in 1912 nationwide), a Zionist organization that transformed elements of German nationalism into Jewish nationalism. The influence of the German Wandervogel youth movement on the Blau-Weiss was obvious. Its hiking tours and songs expressed a Romantic love for nature and the collective experience. Zionist ideals were prominent in the Blau-Weiss program, but often, as the seventeen-year-old Gerhard (Gershom) Scholem criticized, these ideals remained theoretical.[39]

The Liberal Jewish youth also adopted the essential elements of the German youth movement, giving first priority to ties with nature and organizing countless hiking tours. The bulletins of the Liberal youth movement were full of letters in which idealistic Jewish youngsters explained to their worried bourgeois parents or to "effeminate" brothers why they went for one-week hikes, slept in tents, and ate from tin plates. The Jewish youth movement shared with its non-Jewish counterpart a general rejection of the bourgeois home, with the added incentive that the Jewish homes may have been even more bourgeois than those of many of their non-Jewish comrades.

The Jewish and non-Jewish youth movements shared an immense admiration for spiritual leaders. What Gustav Wyneken and Hans Blüher had been for the Wandervogel and the Bünde, Martin Buber was for many young Jews.[40] Without taking Buber's philosophy too seriously, the youth movement adopted his Romanticism and his call for originality and saw in the East European Hasidim an equivalent to the German peasant ideal. The terminology of the Jewish youth movement imitated that of the German youth movement. There were Jewish *Knubbels* and *Pimpfe, Führer* and *Schwarze Haufen.* In letters of 1925 among members of the Kameraden youth group, the greeting *Heil* was still commonly used. It was partially replaced by the Hebrew *Shalom* in later years.[41]

In the 1920s about one-third of young German Jews belonged to one of the Jewish youth organizations. The mainstream Verband der jüdischen Jugendvereine had forty-one thousand members. Although most of them were children of CV adherents, this organization differed from its parent organization in its idealization of healthy rural life and small-town Jewish communities. Like Zionist youth groups, it "rejected liberalism, rationalism, materialism, and solutions that revolved around the individual."[42] For all the youth groups, Jewish issues were important. Most German Jewish families practiced shallow forms of Judaism, and Jewish children rejected this shallowness as part of the bourgeois spirit of their parents. The *Kameraden* began to study Hebrew and organize reading sessions of the new Buber-Rosenzweig edition of the Bible. As one of them recalled, they "somehow sought a Jewish way of life. All this search was based more on Romanticism than on a deep religious urge. . . . One section of the Kameraden came to the conclusion that they were Germans by language, way of life, and homeland, but Jews by 'blood.' "[43]

Another section of the Kameraden stressed its ties to the German home-land. But both groups expressed their affiliations in similar terms; while the German Jews gathered around their campfires and recited Martin Buber's *Hasidic Tales,* the Jewish Germans met at medieval castles to read Stefan George. Although they rejected the Zionist idea of a Jewish nation, the Liberal Jewish youth organizations adopted much of the Zionist agenda of a revival of Jewish solidarity. If they read Buber or George (and most read both), they did it as Jews who were in search of a new sense of Gemeinschaft, one that was no longer phrased in the language of rationalism.

Hiking tours, though important to all German youth groups, were more significant for young Jews. No other group had undergone as rapid an urbanization as German Jews. At the beginning of the nineteenth century they lived almost exclusively in villages and small towns, and a hundred years later they were highly concentrated in big cities. In 1933, one-third of Germany's half-million Jews lived in Berlin. Jews were often stereotyped as urban dwellers, and both youths and adults were eager to prove that Jews actually had strong ties to nature.

In his article "Community in the Big City," Leo Baeck summarized the dangers of urban life, its anonymity, and its numerous temptations, which had not existed in the traditional rural Jewish community, but Baeck also mentioned the social and cultural advantages of the urban Jewish community.[44] Criticism of modern urban life and idealization of rural Jewish life and East European Jewry were sometimes voiced in the language of neo-Romanticism and cultural pessimism. As members of Zionist youth organizations recalled, Hermann Hesse's *Demian* and Oswald Spengler's *Demise of the West* were just as popular as Theodor Herzl's *Old-New Land* and Martin Buber's *Hasidic Tales.*[45]

Spengler's cultural pessimism was not restricted to the youth movement or Zionist circles. When the B'nai Brith lodge of Germany published a special journal for its 1921 meeting, it stressed the difference between culture and civilization. Lodge member Fritz Kahn—author of *Die Juden als Rasse und Kulturvolk* (The Jews as a race and a people of culture, 1920)—expressed in specifically Jewish terms the ideas of Spengler, Thomas Mann, and others who juxtaposed German culture and Western civilization. Civilization, Kahn maintained, was modern urban life adopted by Jews only after they had been absorbed into European society in the nineteenth century, whereas culture was truly representative of Judaism: "*Zivilisation* surrounds us when we ride on the electric streetcar through the bustle of the streets, when we hear the evening telegrams on illuminated squares. . . , and when a Mercedes whizzes by with sixty horsepower. . . . But when we have entered our house, and see from inside the splendor of the Sabbath candles. . . , when we enter the room from which the millennia-old *Schir hamalaus* sounds . . . in this hour we are surrounded outwardly and inwardly by culture."[46]

By the end of the 1920s, when the youth movement had become a substantial part of the cultural life of German Jews, its activities were increasingly integrated into the institutional framework of the Jewish community. The demand of Brunswick rabbi Paul Rieger that Jewish communities grant generous financial subsidies for youth activities and establish permanent homes for Jewish youth (*Jugendheime*) was realized in most large communities.[47] The Jewish community of Breslau, for example, established a Jugendheim that became the center of a rich cultural program with a library and a number of special events in music, literature, and sports. The Jewish community of Hamburg opened a *Jugendamt* (youth welfare office) in 1921, which was followed by a *Landjugendheim* (countryside youth center) ten years later. Some communities employed special youth rabbis, who would concentrate all local youth activities under the auspices of a distinct *Jugendgemeinde* (youth community).[48]

The Jewish youth movement arose on the eve of World War I in opposition to the established Jewish organizations and institutions.[49] During the fifteen years of the Weimar period it contributed significantly to the transformation of the Jewish establishment and its most important pillar, the local Jewish community. In the youth movement the new sense of Gemeinschaft among German Jews first found its institutional expression.

THE TRANSFORMATION OF THE LOCAL JEWISH COMMUNITY

English makes no distinction between *Gemeinschaft* and *Gemeinde,* and both words are usually rendered as community. In German, the two terms have different meanings: *Gemeinschaft* refers to a general communal solidarity, and *Gemeinde* usually stands for an institution representing a certain form of Gemeinschaft, such as a municipal administration or a religious congregation. The traditional Jewish Gemeinde, the *Kehillah,* was a semiautonomous institution representing the local Jewish population. When Jews began to gain political equality, the Kehillah lost its legal and cultural autonomy in Central European and Western European countries. In contrast to the Jewish congregations of most other countries, which were voluntary unions fulfilling mainly religious purposes, the Jewish Gemeinde in Germany retained some of the characteristics of the pre-modern Kehillah.[50]

The German-Jewish Gemeinde remained a publicly constituted corporation, based on the principle of compulsory membership and empowered by the state to levy taxes on its members. It included all the Jews in any one place of residence, and anybody who left it left Judaism at the same time. In 1876 this rule changed slightly, when the Prussian *Austrittsgesetz* enabled Jews to be members of separatist communities without leaving Judaism. Neither this nor later legal reforms, however, significantly altered the character of Jewish communities. Most German Jews remained within the structure of the Gemeinden, to which they paid their taxes.

The modern German-Jewish Gemeinde had lost much of the traditional Kehillah's autonomy, but it was more comprehensive than a religious congregation. The representatives of the Gemeinden could emphasize different aspects of the communities' activities at different times. In the early nineteenth century, most communities adopted as their official designation the term *Israelitische Religionsgemeinde* or *Kultusgemeinde,* thus underlining their religious character. In the nineteenth century, the Religionsgemeinde contained such secular institutions as schools, hospitals, and old-age homes, but the synagogues were its undisputed center. Consequently, internal debates between Liberals and Orthodox focused mostly on issues of synagogue decorum, such as the introduction of organ music and the status of the rabbi.

With the emergence of Zionism at the turn of the twentieth century, this situation began to change. Following Theodor Herzl's appeal for the "conquest of the *Gemeindestube,*" the Zionists soon emerged as a third party in the elections for the assemblies of representatives of the Gemeinden.[51] By reopening the debate on the self-definition of Judaism, they also questioned the self-definition of the Jewish Gemeinde. According to the Zionists, Jews were united not by religion but by nationality, so they intended to transform the Gemeinde from a Religionsgemeinde or Kultusgemeinde into a broad local framework representing a national minority (*Volksgemeinde*).

Before World War I, major changes could not be made in the Gemeinden because of the undemocratic voting system and the small size of the Zionist electorate. After 1918, however, the Jewish communities underwent a process of democratization that ultimately led to their profound transformation. The most visible change occurred on the supralocal level. The Liberal establishment successfully resisted Zionist attempts to establish a democratically elected Jewish Congress in Germany, but such elections took place in the supracommunal organizations that had been established shortly after World War I in the two largest German states. Jewish parliaments were elected for the first time in Bavaria in 1921 and in Prussia in 1925.[52]

Members of the old establishment in the local Jewish communities initially resisted such a development, without being able to prevent it. Most Jewish communities, reflecting other political developments in Germany, introduced universal suffrage on the basis of proportional representation in the Weimar period. With a few exceptions, they granted voting rights to women, immigrant citizens, and non-tax-payers.[53]

The democratization of the Jewish community was intimately connected with its politicization. The *Jüdisches Jahrbuch für Gross-Berlin* described this change: "The question of 'liberal or conservative' was not enough to describe all the problems. The profound question, what Judaism and Jewishness meant, broadened the hitherto existing questions and led, by its divergent answers, necessarily to the creation of new parties."[54] The new parties emerging within the Jewish community were built around political platforms, not religious concepts. In Berlin, parties ranged from the socialist Poalei Zion, led by Oskar Cohn, former Social Democratic member of the Reichstag, to the Deutsche Liste of Max Naumann's extremely conservative Verband nationaldeutscher Juden. A manifesto of the Poalei Zion from 1920 illustrates the degree to which the Jewish community's election campaigns had become politicized and secularized: "The legend that the Jewish people is only a religious community must be brought to an end. All concerns of worship [*Kultusangelegenheiten*] must be eliminated from the tasks of the community and shall be given to a voluntary organization. The community must contain all affairs of culture and learning, education and instruction, immigration and migration, legal and political protection, economic need and housing problems, gymnastics, sport, and statistics." The Nationaldeutsche Juden also advocated the secularization of the Jewish community, though its members had different motives. In the same election campaign they distributed leaflets saying, "The election campaign must not be a struggle of religious conceptions, it must be a decisive struggle about our Germanness [*Deutschtum*]!"[55]

The most important party to emerge after World War I was the Jüdische Volkspartei (JVP), an alliance of Zionists, Ostjuden, Orthodox, and lower-middle-class Jews. The principal goal of the JVP was to transform the Jewish community into a Volksgemeinde. Although it sought to care for the

"The contestants line up": Berlin Jewish community elections, 1919. Cartoon from *Der Schlemiel,* drawn by Ludwig Wronkow. Photograph by Jim Strong. Courtesy of the Leo Baeck Institute, New York.

religious needs of its members, the JVP considered social welfare and cultural activities most important. In a pamphlet of 1919, a leading JVP activist envisioned the Volksgemeinde as the "representation of the Jews as a national minority that autonomously determines its cultural activities based on its particular *Volkseigenart.*"[56]

The main rivals of the JVP were the long-established Liberals, who fought officially for the continuation of the Kultusgemeinden, in which religious institutions would remain central. By the end of the 1920s many elections had been reduced to a duel between the Liberals and the JVP. Those two parties received 87 percent of the vote in the 1930 Berlin Gemeinde elections, although ten parties had nominated candidates. The third major faction, the Orthodox, received less than 5 percent of the vote.[57]

The biggest success for the JVP was the overthrow of the Liberals in Berlin, where they had been the majority party for more than half a century. In the elections of 1926 the Liberals lost their absolute majority, and a coalition of JVP and Orthodox determined the community's fate during the next four years. For the first time a Zionist, Georg Kareski, became the head of Germany's largest Jewish community.[58]

In most other communities the Liberals suffered perceptible losses but held sway. In Hamburg and Cologne they lost their absolute majorities and were dependent on coalitions with their longtime opponents, the Orthodox.[59] In Dresden, Leipzig, and Chemnitz the Liberals maintained their majorities only because of an undemocratic voting system, according to which the minority of German Jews was reserved a majority of seats in the assemblies. In Breslau, the shifting of power was arranged by peaceful agreement: the assembly of representatives was enlarged in 1930 from twenty-one members to twenty-three, and the number of Liberal members was reduced from thirteen to eleven.[60] In some smaller communities with large numbers of East European Jews, the JVP succeeded in gaining the absolute majority; for example, in Duisburg in 1928 the JVP won more than 60 percent of the vote.[61]

Even where the Liberals retained the majority, the concept of a Religionsgemeinde was sacrificed for the concrete needs of German Jewry. No matter which party dominated, by the late 1920s the large Gemeinden had in fact become "cities within cities," administering hospitals, old-age homes, orphanages, banks, unemployment assistance, schools, adult education institutions, art collections, libraries, statistics offices, and more. The annual budget of the Berlin Jewish community, with 170,000 members and 1,500 paid officials, was more than 10 million marks. The segment of the communities' annual expenses distributed in the religious sector decreased steadily. By the late 1920s synagogue attendance on the High Holidays slipped below 50 percent in Berlin, Frankfurt am Main, and other large cities. At the same time, participation in the secular community elections increased. Even in Berlin, 60 percent of the community (more than seventy-seven thousand people) went to the polls in 1930, and in many smaller places election turnout was about 90 percent.[62]

Although the Weimar period clearly witnessed a progressive secularization—in the Catholic and Protestant communities as well as in the Jewish one—there were also tendencies of religious revival. Not only did such figures as Leo Baeck, Martin Buber, and Franz Rosenzweig engage in creative religious thought, but everyday religious practice also made a comeback. Among the Liberals, a growing number of young rabbis hoped to attract younger people to Judaism with educational programs, and the opening in 1929 of the first Berlin community synagogue with mixed seating appealed to women, who demanded a more equal role in prayer. The Orthodox segment of the community changed, too. A new type of rabbi, like Nehemias Anton Nobel of Frankfurt and Joseph Carlebach of Hamburg, reached out to non-Orthodox Jewish students and intellectuals. By their new approaches toward Jewish mysticism or by their modern pedagogical techniques, those leaders of Weimar's Orthodox Jewry were indeed able to awaken new interest in Judaism—though not necessarily in Orthodoxy—on the fringes of Jewish society.

FROM KULTUSGEMEINDE TO KULTURGEMEINDE

The development of three cultural institutions—local Jewish newspapers, modern Jewish libraries, and Jewish schools in urban areas— reflected the transformation of the Jewish community. The Gemeinde attempted to halt the spread of private Jewish cultural institutions and associations and instead advocated that they be included under its auspices. Before World War I less than a handful of Jewish communities issued their own news bulletins, but in 1932 more than forty local Jewish newspapers had a combined circulation of about 310,000.[63] The Gemeinden integrated formerly private Jewish libraries into their framework, took over or subsidized Jewish schools, and replaced such private associations as the Associations for Jewish History and Literature and the B'nai Brith lodges as the centers of Jewish adult education.

In the premodern Kehillah the transmission of essential information about the principles and activities of the Gemeinde, from the administration to its members, was arranged on the daily basis of informal contact. The members of a Jewish community lived close to each other, met for regular prayer, and were subject to the authority of the local Jewish community. With the loss of communal ties in the age of political equality and the rapid population increase of urban Jewish communities, many Jews were no longer informed about the activities of their community. The Frankfurt community, for example, had grown from 3,000 to almost 30,000 during the nineteenth century, and the Berlin Gemeinde, with more than 170,000 members, had become an entirely anonymous apparatus for most of them.

The increasing atomization of a rapidly urbanizing Jewish population forced the Gemeinden to create institutional frameworks that would renew the contact between the communities' administration and their membership. The Gemeinden thus established their own publication organs, usually called *Gemeindeblatt* or *Gemeindezeitung*. In the late nineteenth century, such local newspapers existed only in a few communal or supracommunal organizations, such as those in Baden (founded in 1884) and Cologne (founded in 1888). Berlin launched its Gemeindeblatt in 1909, when the community already had more than a hundred thousand members.

During the Weimar years every large community and many small ones created a Gemeindeblatt. By 1933, forty-two such communal newspapers had appeared, constituting almost half the Jewish journals circulating in Germany.[64] They reported news from the Jewish world, announced regular activities of the community and its institutions, and published lists of those who joined and defected from the communities. The officials of the Jewish communities realized that the Gemeindeblatt provided a unique opportunity to promote Jewish knowledge among a highly assimilated urban Jewish population. In contrast to such older Jewish journals as the Liberal *Allgemeine Zeitung des Judentums* (founded in 1837) and the Orthodox *Der Israelit* (founded in 1860) or the later-established mouthpieces of the CV (*Im deutschen Reich,* 1895) and the Zionist movement (*Jüdische Rundschau,* 1896), the local Gemeindeblatt was distributed freely to every household registered in the Jewish community and was the only means the community had of reaching all its members.

The publications had two tasks, as formulated in the programmatic statement of the first issue of the Berlin Jewish Gemeindeblatt. First, they filled the gap between the community administration and its members and encouraged everyone to participate in Jewish life: "The knowledge of the individual member about the community events has dwindled, and as a consequence interest in community activities has declined as well. In this respect, the Gemeindeblatt wants to create a change." Second, the Gemeindeblatt had a more general aim: "It should publish articles about the essence of Judaism, its tasks, and its particular character, its teachings and its writings."[65]

Many communal newspapers went far beyond the role of local news bulletins and developed into attractive journals concerning all matters of interest to Jews. During the late 1920s the communal newspapers increased their efforts to attract the attention of members whose contact with the Jewish community was tenuous. In 1928 the Berlin Jewish community hired the former editor of *Ost und West,* Leo Winz, to professionalize the management of the local Gemeindeblatt. He significantly changed the appearance of the paper and its advertising strategies.[66] The Gothic script was modernized into Latin letters, and the title page became an aesthetically refined frontispiece. Winz transformed the Gemeindeblatt into a voluminous journal of forty-eight, sometimes even sixty-eight, pages with numerous illustrations. Some issues included competitions for prizes, and some were special editions on topics chosen to attract readers. Winz's advertising strategies were so successful that the Berlin Gemeindeblatt no longer depended on community subsidies. Its circulation rose from an average of fifty-eight thousand in 1928 to seventy-seven thousand in 1931, with individual issues reaching eighty-seven thousand. Winz left no doubt about the purpose of those measures: "The Gemeindeblatt has to become a publicity tool of the first rank, in order to promote the Jewish interests of the members of the Jewish community. As a result of such an aroused interest there will naturally be an increasing participation in community activities."[67]

The Gemeindeblatt of the Berlin Jewish community was the Jewish newspaper with the highest circulation in Germany. All other communal newspapers had a circulation of less than ten thousand. Nevertheless, many of them were of high literary quality and were significant in their promotion of Jewish culture in Weimar Germany.[68] Among the smaller community newspapers, the *Bayerische Israelitische Gemeindezeitung (BIGZ)*, published by the Bavarian Union of Jewish Communities, must be singled out. Edited (from 1930) by Ludwig Feuchtwanger, a brother of the writer Lion Feuchtwanger, the *BIGZ* followed the first cautious steps in the Christian-Jewish dialogue, analyzed the contemporary development of Zionism, reviewed the most recent Jewish literature, discussed modern Jewish philosophy, and reported on matters of communal life. Like most community newspapers, the *BIGZ* recorded the views of the factions within the community, without taking sides in internal struggles. (The neutrality of the communal bulletins was generally respected.) The *BIGZ* succeeded in recruiting many young, first-rate Jewish intellectuals as contributors, among them Gershom Scholem, Hannah Arendt, and Leo Löwenthal.[69]

Newspapers and journals were a relatively new way to express Jewish culture, but the classical medium of the book was also used to promote a modern Jewish cultural identity. Traditionally, every Jewish community had its beth midrash (house of study), with a library consisting of the classic religious texts and their interpretations. During the nineteenth century those texts became irrelevant for most German Jews, and the libraries were used almost exclusively by rabbis, scholars, and the small minority of Orthodox Jews. When at the end of the nineteenth century Jewish libraries became popular again, their shelves were filled with a different kind of literature: novels, dramas, poems, and critical essays written in German about Jewish history and contemporary issues. Most of the users of these libraries were unable to read Hebrew or follow the traditional talmudic interpretations. The first director of the World Zionist Archives, Georg Herlitz, wrote in 1928: "It is a long way from those [traditional] synagogue libraries to the community libraries of our time. . . . Those synagogue libraries contained Jewish books for experts of Jewish knowledge, whereas the community libraries of today contain mainly instructional books about Judaism for general readers. . . . Today, the main purpose is not the deepening of already existent knowledge about Judaism but the initial spread of such a knowledge."[70] The first Jewish reading halls to hold modern and mostly secular Jewish literature were opened in Germany's larger cities at the end of the nineteenth century by private associations. In Berlin the first such organization to establish a Jewish library was the Verein Jüdische Lesehalle und Bibliothek in 1895, and similar foundations in other cities followed suit. Within ten years the Berlin Jewish library was significantly enlarged. With an annual average of twenty-four thousand readers, the library moved several times to larger locations, increased its stock of books, and established additional reading hours.[71]

In 1920 the Lesehalle, shattered by the postwar economic crisis, was integrated into the Jewish community as a branch of its library, which had been founded in 1902.[72] This measure initiated a broad extension of the Berlin Jewish community's library network. By 1932 the Gemeinde had set up nine branches, with about seventy thousand volumes, in various sections of the city.[73] The main reading room of the library had become a meeting point for the local Jewish population. There Gershom Scholem met the Hebrew writer Shmu'el Yosef Agnon, "where he tirelessly leafed through the Hebrew card catalogue." Asked by Scholem what he looked for, Agnon supposedly replied, "Books that I have not read yet."[74] Although the Gemeinde library had acquired some remarkably rare books and Hebrew manuscripts, they were not its most important holdings. In contrast to other large Jewish libraries in Berlin, such as the rabbinical seminary libraries or the Staatsbibliothek and the Universitätsbibliothek, the main objective of the Jewish community library was not to become a place of scholarly research but to provide popular books and a large selection of newspapers for a highly acculturated Jewish audience.

Franz Rosenzweig compared the potential readers of Jewish libraries with the four types of children discussed in the Passover Haggadah. Whereas professional libraries were for the "clever child," the natural audience of the Gemeinde library was the "child who does not know how to ask"—those assimilated Jews who had to be taught how to approach their lost cultural heritage. The main task of the Gemeinde library was, according to Rosenzweig, to make such an audience curious to learn more about Judaism. The Berlin library was Rosenzweig's model for such an approach:

Next to the main lending library there is a reading room, whose open stacks hold not only the volumes that serve the expert as indispensable tools but also modern works that provide the nonexpert with the ability to take the first steps into the world [of Judaica]: books of history, philosophical representations of Judaism, modern Bible commentaries, finally—and especially important—the classics in modern translation. This is a collection of books for the curious. And this curiosity is today the natural situation of three-quarters of the members of an urban Jewish community.[75]

On Rosenzweig's initiative, the Frankfurt Jewish community enlarged its library in the 1920s and established a reading room according to the Berlin prototype. Similarly, in 1920 the Jewish community of Munich revived its "completely neglected" Jewish library.[76] Other communities followed, and by 1932 libraries existed in more than thirty Jewish communities. Among these towns were such small places as Neuwied and Speyer, where every community member was asked to donate one book.[77]

As in Berlin, the local Jewish reading hall in Hamburg had been founded as a private initiative around the turn of the century. It was closed during the economic crisis of 1921, when the Jewish girls' school claimed its rooms. The private association that had established the library urged the Jewish community to finance its reopening, arguing that "several Jewish students had to leave Hamburg in order to write their dissertations on Jewish topics in other cities."[78] After protracted negotiations the Gemeinde agreed in 1923 to finance and extend the library "with regard to the middle and lower classes of the Jewish population who are no longer able to keep Jewish newspapers and buy Jewish books."[79]

The Gemeinde took over the formerly private library, united it with smaller local Jewish libraries, and reopened it in 1928 as the *Gemeinde-bibliothek,* the official community library. Professor Isaak Markon, a leading Hebraist who had taught at the universities of Petersburg and Moscow and at the Orthodox rabbinical seminary in Berlin, was hired to be its director. He intellectually enriched the library and the entire Jewish community of Hamburg.

During the remaining years of the Weimar era the number of readers at the reopened Hamburg library grew steadily from an average of five hundred per month in 1929 to six hundred per month a year later to one thousand readers per month in 1931.[80] The most popular books were novels by German-Jewish authors, such as Jakob Wassermann, Max Brod, Stefan Zweig, Arnold Zweig, and Jacob Loewenberg, a local author. Translations from Yiddish literature and Hasidic tales were also well liked. Only three years after its reopening the library was called the "intellectual center of the Jewish community."[81]

Other institutions also claimed to be the community's intellectual center. First among them was the Jewish school. When acculturation progressed and the number of Jewish pupils at non-Jewish schools increased in the second half of the nineteenth century, the Jewish school lost its predominance in the education of Jewish children. At first glance, the further decline in the number of Jewish schools until the rise of Nazi Germany appears a continuation of this trend. Although 492 Jewish elementary schools existed in 1898, only 247 remained in 1913, and 141 were left in 1932.[82] This dramatic development was caused by the rapid urbanization of German Jewry, which forced the closure of many Jewish schools in rural areas, and by the belief of most Liberal Jews that the abolition of separate Jewish schools would constitute an important step toward their complete integration into German society.

As a more detailed analysis reveals, however, the closure of Jewish schools in rural areas was one of two major currents in the development of Jewish educational institutions during the Weimar period. In big cities, new Jewish schools were reestablished and already existing schools were enlarged and increasingly supported by the Jewish communities. The rural schools threatened by closure usually had fewer than ten pupils, but most of the new schools in large cities soon counted a few hundred students. In some Jewish communities with established Jewish school systems—Hamburg, Frankfurt, and Cologne—about every second Jewish child attended a Jewish school in 1932. Berlin never reached such a ratio, but the opening of five Jewish elementary schools in the German capital between 1919 and 1927 marked a clear revival of separate Jewish education. In other cities, such as Munich, Nuremberg, and Duisburg, no Jewish schools had existed for decades, but such institutions were reestablished during the 1920s, either by the Jewish community or by Orthodox associations.

Children of Orthodox Jews, Zionists, and East European Jews constituted most pupils in Weimar Germany's Jewish schools. Despite the vehement opposition of Liberal leaders to education that separated students along religious lines, a minority of Liberal Jews also began to send their children to Jewish schools. They were motivated partly by the realization that most interfaith schools (*Simultanschulen*) remained dominated by the guiding principles of the Christian religion, celebrated Christian holidays, and required attendance on the Sabbath. Of the few schools that distanced themselves from Christian doctrine, most were situated in workers' neighborhoods and were unattractive to middle-class Jewish parents.[83] An additional reason for the increased attendance at Jewish schools in big cities was the spiraling rate of antisemitic incidents in non-Jewish schools. Two years before the Nazi rise to power a former student of both Jewish and non-Jewish schools recommended that Jewish children attend the Jewish school in Breslau, and his main argument was the absence of antisemitism in a Jewish milieu: "How happy is the child who spends his time free of the hatred of Gentile companions."[84]

Most of the new Jewish schools of the Weimar years were established by the Orthodox separatist communities. Those schools, however, often recruited pupils who were not Orthodox. When the Orthodox congregation Ohel Jakob in Munich opened a Jewish elementary school in 1924, its sixty-four pupils hailed mainly from the Orthodox and East European Jewish communities. By 1932 its student body had doubled, with 42 percent of the pupils coming from Liberal Jewish homes. During the same period the attendance of Jewish pupils at non-Jewish public elementary schools dropped from 586 to 278.[85]

In Bavaria's second largest community, Nuremberg, the situation was similar. Jewish schools were nonexistent until the Orthodox association Adas Israel established an elementary school in 1921, which five years later became an institution of the local Gemeinde. This school grew from 80 pupils in 1921 to 180 pupils in 1928. Thus, before 1933, 30 percent to 40 percent of Jewish children in Bavaria's two largest cities attended a Jewish elementary school. Those numbers are especially significant given that for decades there had been no Jewish school in those communities.[86] Outside Bavaria, new Jewish elementary schools were established in Breslau (in 1920 and 1921), Duisburg (in 1925), and several other cities.[87]

The development of Jewish education in Weimar Germany was best reflected in its center, Berlin. Before World War I Germany's largest Jewish community had two lower-grade secondary schools but no elementary school. During the Weimar years, five Jewish elementary schools were founded. One of them belonged to the Orthodox separatists and another one remained a private school, but three schools were integrated into the framework of the Jewish community. The Rykestraße school was founded in 1924 as a private school but was taken over by the Jewish community in 1929. The two other schools were opened as *Gemeindeschulen* during the rule of the alliance between the JVP and the Orthodox. When the Liberals regained power in 1930, they cut the schools' subsidies but let them remain institutions of the community. The number of students attending Jewish schools in Berlin rose from 1,170 in 1913 to 2,713 in 1930 and reached a peak of almost 3,000 in 1932. The proportion of Jewish pupils in Berlin who attended Jewish schools thus had increased to about 20 percent by 1932.[88] In many smaller cities of Prussia almost every second Jewish child attended a Jewish school. In 1930, when the Orthodox high school of the separatist Adass Jisroel congregation in Berlin held its first *Abitur* exams (which qualified students to attend a university), the Berlin Jewish community made public its plan to establish its own high school and a yeshivah, but neither of those institutions was created before 1933.[89]

In other cities, however, the Jewish high school system started to expand before 1933. Four of Germany's ten Jewish high schools existing in the 1920s had been established during the previous decade, and many of the others were significantly enlarged during this period. All the new schools—Leipzig (1913), Cologne (1919), Berlin (1919), and Breslau (1921)—were founded by the Orthodox but included students who were children of non-Orthodox parents. In Breslau the initial resistance of the Liberals and some Orthodox to the school had diminished by the time of its tenth anniversary in 1931.[90] At other places too, Jewish schools were initially rejected by the Liberal establishment as an attempt at renewed ghettoization but were gradually accepted as necessary institutions in times of virulent antisemitism.

Because of the economic crisis, most Jewish schools—founded as private institutions—could no longer exist with exclusively private funding and therefore turned to the Gemeinde for financial support. At the same time Jewish high schools received official state recognition and enabled their students for the first time in the history of Jewish education in Germany to graduate with the Abitur. Both developments occurred in the three cities with the best developed Jewish educational systems in Weimar Germany: Hamburg, Cologne, and Frankfurt.

Although the mostly Liberal establishment of the communities did not favor the creation of religious schools, they avoided the closure of already existing Jewish schools and granted increasing financial support. The Cologne Jewish community, for example, concluded a contract in 1928 with Jawne, its Orthodox high school, that guaranteed annual subsidies for a period of five years in exchange for community control over the school.[91] In Hamburg, the girls' high school of the Jewish community grew from 350 to 600 pupils in the Weimar years because it absorbed the students of a private Jewish girls' school that had to be closed.[92]

For the first time in its 125-year history, the Frankfurt Philanthropin (the only non-Orthodox Jewish high school in Weimar Germany) enabled its students to graduate with an Abitur degree after the school was recognized as a *Realreformgymnasium* in 1928. Jawne followed a year later, and the Hamburg Talmud Tora high school for boys was accredited the equivalent status as an *Oberrealschule* in 1932, after the school underwent pedadogical reforms under the direction of Joseph Carlebach in the early 1920s.[93]

The development of the Frankfurt Philanthropin reflects the increase in numbers of students attending Jewish schools and their new self-perception. During the 1920s, the Philanthropin established an elementary school and a kindergarten. This expansion enabled Frankfurt Jewish children to attend a Jewish school from kindergarten until high school graduation. As a result, in 1930 the number of students at the various Philanthropin schools reached an unprecedented high of 900. About the same time, the Orthodox schools of Frankfurt had 1,160 pupils.[94] As in Hamburg and Cologne, every second Jewish pupil in Frankfurt attended a Jewish school during the Weimar years.

Founded in 1804, the Frankfurt Philanthropin, offering courses in secular subjects and the German language to as yet unemancipated German Jews, furthered equality and acculturation throughout the nineteenth century. In the Weimar years, however, the Philanthropin began to promote Jewish knowledge and Jewish consciousness. Religious education was expanded from three to five hours per week. Boys were required to cover their heads during Hebrew lessons in obedience to religious ritual, and for the first time strictly Orthodox teachers were employed. Books with Jewish content became more widely read, and in the late 1920s a permanent study group was established to discuss "problems of Judaism."[95]

Most Jewish schools similarly strengthened their Jewish education. The study of modern Hebrew, as introduced by Joseph Carlebach in Hamburg, soon became obligatory in other Jewish high schools.[96] Non-Jewish subjects were taught regularly, but curricula allowed Jewish matters to be emphasized even in courses on nonreligious subjects. The director of the Breslau Jewish high school encouraged teachers to assign essays on "Jewish experiences" in German lessons, discuss Jewish heritage in history lessons, sing Jewish melodies in music classes, and introduce female students to the customs of a Jewish home in home economics classes.[97]

In spite of those efforts, Jewish subjects remained restricted to three to five hours per week. The study of Hebrew was mostly rudimentary, and basic religious education was still the major objective of those lessons.

More important was the creation—partly voluntary and partly forced—of a Jewish milieu, caused by the return of the Jewish denominational school. Together with the extension of the Jewish community's social welfare network and the establishment of the Jewish youth movement, the exclusively Jewish social environment in these schools nourished the ideals of a Jewish Gemeinschaft within Weimar Germany.

Although the Jewish high schools promoted the study of a modern curriculum within a Jewish milieu, a small but visible movement advocated a return to a premodern framework of Jewish education. About the middle of the nineteenth century, the last yeshivot—academies for the study of Talmud—in Germany had disappeared, though they were still flourishing in Eastern Europe.[98] With the influx of East European Jews in the late nineteenth century, the yeshivah returned to Germany. In 1890 Salomon Breuer, the Hungarian-born rabbi of the local separatist community, opened a yeshivah in Frankfurt am Main. Although it drew a few students from local Orthodox families, most of its pupils came from Eastern Europe, especially from Hungary. With the establishment of the Breuer Yeshivah, Germany won a place on the map of religious Jewish education in Europe. For the first time in more than a century, Jewish parents sent their sons from distant places to Germany in order to study Talmud.[99] After World War I Joseph Breuer succeeded his father as director of the yeshivah, and he significantly expanded and reorganized it. To cope with the increasing number of students of both German and East European background, four additional teachers had to be employed in the early 1920s.[100] Immigration from the East helped to establish yeshivot in other German cities as well, such as Berlin, Cologne, Leipzig, and Nuremberg.[101] What to East European Jews was a continuation of traditional learning appeared to German Jews to be innovation. When Rabbi Joseph Carlebach established a yeshivah in Hamburg in 1921, a contemporary observer stressed the extraordinary importance of this development for German Jewry: "We felt that what was taught to this youth was something *totally new,* something never heard of in Hamburg during the last hundred years."[102]

Germany's three rabbinical seminaries, founded in the last third of the nineteenth century, flourished in the Weimar period. The Orthodox Hildesheimer Rabbinerseminar in Berlin's Artilleriestraße increased its student body to accommodate the influx of East European Jews. The number of students soon exceeded the number of vacancies in the rabbinate. The Rabbinerseminar began to offer Bible and Talmud courses for a broader Orthodox audience, ranging from schoolchildren to businessmen. According to its annual report of 1924, the institution had "come much closer to what was undoubtedly the intention of the founder of this Seminary, that is, to make it a centre for all those who wish to train in the spirit of Orthodox Judaism."[103]

The Liberal Hochschule für die Wissenschaft des Judentums—located in the same street—also recruited a new type of student, but one of a different kind:

> The 'new student' had neither shared the traditionalist climate of the small Jewish community, nor did he possess any sizable fund of Jewish learning. In all probability, one of the Jewish youth-movements which had sprung up in recent years had made him aware of the Jewish problem. He had read, though not necessarily understood, Buber and later Rosenzweig, and he was bursting with questions and eager to acquire a Jewish philosophy. He was deeply emotive, penitently aware of his insufficiency of Jewish learning, and sincerely anxious to acquire it together with a firmly founded Jewish *Weltanschauung*. The difference between learning and *Weltanschauung* was not settled in his mind either. He looked forward to a university education, but felt strongly that getting only a university education, as perhaps his family expected, was wrong from the Jewish point of view. Some of those post-war students were considering professional careers in the Jewish field, possibly the rabbinate, but all that would depend on the clarification of their Jewish problems and the answer of the *Lebensfragen* which they expected to get in the classrooms of the *Hochschule*.[104]

One of the regular guests at the Hochschule in the winter of 1923 was a rather unusual figure, who had just come to Berlin from Prague. Franz Kafka found a second home in the Artilleriestraße, as he wrote to a friend. The Hochschule was for him a "refuge of peace in wild and woolly Berlin and in the wild and woolly regions of my mind. . . . A whole building of handsome lecture rooms, large library, peace, well heated, few students, and everything free of charge."[105]

The Jewish Theological Seminary in Breslau, the center of Positive-Historical Judaism (the German counterpart to Conservative Judaism), enrolled its largest student body in 1930, just a year after its seventy-fifth anniversary. Like the Berlin Rabbinerseminar and the Hochschule, the Breslau Seminary extended its reach by offering evening courses for adults and members of Jewish youth groups.[106]

The range of educational possibilities illustrates the ambiguity that characterized Weimar Germany's Jews: one segment of Jewish students received very little Jewish education (or none at all) in school—mostly reduced to a weekly lesson in religion—while another growing segment attended

Jewish elementary schools and high schools or even yeshivot and rabbinical seminaries, grew up in a Jewish milieu, and obtained at least a basic knowledge of Judaism.[107]

Although the end of separate Jewish schools in Germany seemed close at hand at the beginning of the twentieth century, most observers agreed that a revival of Jewish education was well under way during the Weimar years: "The Jewish elementary school is no longer the problem child of responsibility-conscious Jewish circles. It has forcefully proved itself. . . . All levels of the Jewish population in its social, religious, and political varieties today send their children to the Jewish elementary school. . . . The present growth of Jewish elementary schools in big cities clearly reflects the living spirit of certain streams within German Jewry."[108] Indeed, the increasing attendance at urban Jewish schools reflected a more general trend among adults. Many German Jews who had not attended Jewish schools and had grown up in assimilated Jewish families began to participate in the newly established Jewish adult education system, which will be discussed in the next chapter.

Part II

The Transmission of Knowledge

3

A New Learning: The Lehrhaus Movement

I learned much Torah from my teachers. More than from them I learned from my colleagues and the most I learned from my students.

—Babylonian Talmud, Makkot 10a

The renewed sense of community among German Jews was only the first step toward a Jewish cultural renaissance. Those who revitalized their solidarity—in terms either of a Jewish nation or of a community of common fate and descent—wished to know more about the group they belonged to. Richard Koch, one of the leading teachers at the Frankfurt Jewish Lehrhaus (house of study) articulated this desire in his almost prophetic words of 1923: "If our historical suffering should recur one day, then we want to know why we suffer; we do not want to die like animals, but like humans who know what is good and what is best. . . . Often enough others and we ourselves have told us that we are Jews, that we have faults and virtues. We have heard it too often. The Lehrhaus shall tell us why and for what purpose we are Jews."[1]

Many German Jews, who were constantly reminded of their Jewishness, increasingly wondered why, and for what purpose, they were and remained Jews. The Lehrhaus and other Jewish adult education institutions of Weimar Germany tried to provide an answer by offering a systematic reappropriation of Jewish knowledge. As the founders of a Jewish Lehrhaus stated in 1925, Jewish adult education aimed at "digging out the lost treasure and reopening the blocked source."[2] The notion that Jewish knowledge had been gradually lost during the nineteenth century, or, to use Franz Kafka's words, had "dribbled away" while it was passed from one generation to another, is as problematic as the demand for its systematic reappropriation.[3] The transmission of Jewish knowledge in Weimar Germany was a process that contained both restorative and innovative elements. Restorative, because its declared aim was to make classical Jewish texts and traditions available to Weimar Germany's Jews; innovative, because both the means of transmission and the conditions of reception were far removed from the world of premodern Jewry.

Three aspects of the Lehrhaus movement—its place in the German adult education movement, its vision of a New Learning, and its impact on German Jewry—provide some insight into the dialectics of the appropriation of Jewish knowledge in Weimar Germany. Adopting basic elements of both the traditional Jewish beth midrash and the recently developed German Volkshochschule (institution for adult education), the teachers of the Lehrhaus did not simply "dig out" traditional Jewish knowledge but laid the foundation for a new type of Jewish Bildung, which would respond to the needs of a population at home in both European and Jewish cultures. The Lehrhaus teachers were not rabbis or activists in the Jewish community but physicians, chemists, and lawyers who had received little Jewish education as children and who only recently had moved from the periphery to the center of Jewish society.[4]

FRANZ ROSENZWEIG AND THE FRANKFURT JEWISH LEHRHAUS: BETWEEN BETH MIDRASH AND VOLKSHOCHSCHULE

When Franz Rosenzweig opened the Frankfurt Free Jewish Lehrhaus in August 1920, he broke new ground. In imperial Germany, Jewish adult education had been restricted to sporadic lectures organized by such institutions as the Association for Jewish History and Literature and the B'nai Brith lodge. Although those lecture programs had a spirit similar to that of the Lehrhaus and shared its aim, only the Lehrhaus achieved a systematic transmission and reconceptualization of Jewish knowledge that appeared attractive to a large number of acculturated German Jews.

The roots of the Lehrhaus reveal little of its later form. The Lehrhaus grew out of the Frankfurt Gesellschaft für jüdische Volksbildung, founded in 1919 by Georg Salzberger, a Liberal rabbi who, as an army chaplain in World War I, had lamented the lack of Jewish knowledge among Jewish soldiers.[5] The Gesellschaft, which provided Jewish adult education in the form of popular lectures (*Volksvorlesungen*) and excursions to historic Jewish sites, would have hardly differed from similar institutions in imperial Germany had Franz Rosenzweig not become its director. Rosenzweig not only introduced the name *Lehrhaus* but initiated a profound change in its approach to Jewish adult education.

What distinguished the Lehrhaus from its precursors was first and foremost its theoretical framework. For Rosenzweig, Jewish learning constituted the only means of reorganizing and revitalizing Jewish life. In this respect, the Lehrhaus represented a tendency that could be observed among various groups of Jewish intellectuals in Weimar Germany who shared the aim of re-creating "genuine" Jewish life through learning. Like groups of non-Jewish intellectuals (the most famous being that of Stefan George), the Jewish groups were organized around one dominant figure. They included the study group of the charismatic Rabbi Nehemias Anton Nobel in Frankfurt,[6] the Talmud study circle of Salman Baruch Rabinkow in Heidelberg,[7] the private kosher psychoanalytic clinic in Heidelberg where Frieda Reichmann cultivated both Torah and Freudian analysis,[8] the wartime Berlin Volksheim of Siegfried Lehmann, and the Berlin group centered around an obscure scholar of Jewish mysticism, Oskar Goldberg.[9]

The Frankfurt Free Jewish Lehrhaus cast a much wider net than these small and exclusive groups. During the six years of its existence, 64 teachers offered 90 lecture courses and 180 study groups and seminars for up to 1,100 students per semester. The Lehrhaus was a financially independent adult education institution, frequented by all social strata and age groups of the Frankfurt Jewish population. It was conceived, directed, and always dominated by Franz Rosenzweig.

More than any other German Jew, Franz Rosenzweig helped to build a distinct, modern Jewish culture, while remaining deeply rooted in his German surroundings. He identified with Liberal German Judaism but shared the Zionists' radical critique of assimilation.[10] For Rosenzweig "Zionism, a diagnostician of genius but most mediocre healer, has recognized the disease but prescribed the wrong treatment."[11] The diagnosed disease was the progressing ignorance of Judaism among German Jews. Rosenzweig knew as well as the Zionists that a radical treatment was necessary to save the patient, as "Jewish study and teaching, Jewish learning and education—they are dying out among us."[12] In contrast to the Zionists' treatment of emigration and the establishment of a Jewish state, Rosenzweig prescribed a reclaiming of Jewish knowledge within the diaspora.

The first patient to be treated by Rosenzweig was himself. Born into a respected and acculturated Jewish family of Kassel in 1887, he was intellectually close to his baptized cousins and was almost ready to embrace Christianity when he discovered his own Judaism on the eve of World War I. The young scholar, who wrote his doctoral dissertation on Hegel with the preeminent historian Friedrich Meinecke, was deeply immersed in European Bildung. Rosenzweig showed immense knowledge of the foundations of Christianity but lacked basic information on Judaism. He decided that he at least had to become familiar with the religion he intended to abandon. Thus began his remarkable return to his Jewish origins. By autodidactic study during the war, he acquired a solid knowledge of Jewish sources, and within a few years he emerged as one of the most profound thinkers of Judaism in Germany.[13]

In the trenches of World War I Rosenzweig produced the major philosophical work of modern German Judaism, *The Star of Redemption;* also during the war he called for a renewal of Jewish education and scholarship. While already suffering from a progressive paralysis that would lead to his premature death in 1929, he co-translated the Hebrew Bible with Martin Buber. At the core of his endeavor to retrieve the lost ties to Judaism for himself and for German Jews was his concept of Jewish adult education, as propagated in his essay "Bildung and No End" (1920).[14]

The New Learning, as presented in that essay and subsequent ones, had two major elements. Rosenzweig's first principle was that only by learning could German Jews regain the basis for Jewish life that had gradually disappeared during the nineteenth century. An institute for Jewish learning should therefore not merely transmit knowledge but should provide German Jews with the necessary tools to rebuild a distinctive cultural identity and strengthen their sense of Gemeinschaft. His second principle concerned the methods of teaching. In contrast to Old Learning, which started from the Torah and led into life, the New Learning had to lead from the world of alienated Jews back to the Torah.[15]

Rosenzweig immediately aimed at transforming his theoretical outline of New Learning into practice. Shortly before writing "Bildung and No End," he was invited, in 1919, to join the Jewish school in Hamburg as its assistant director.[16] Rosenzweig was inclined to accept this offer, but then influential members of the Frankfurt Jewish community expressed their interest in bringing him to Frankfurt. In the fall of 1919 he visited the Orthodox Frankfurt rabbi Nehemias Anton Nobel, who initially intended to arrange a match for the still unmarried scholar. Rosenzweig left Nobel without a bride but with the promise of a job in Frankfurt as the director of the new Jewish adult education institution.[17]

After preparing for his new post by organizing a Jewish adult education program in Kassel in the spring of 1920,[18] Rosenzweig introduced his own concept of Jewish adult education and replaced the term *Volksvorlesungen* with *Freies Jüdisches Lehrhaus*. Although *frei* (free) had several possible connotations—open to anybody, open in spirit, and without the requirement of exams (not, however, free of tuition)—Lehrhaus clearly referred to the Hebrew beth midrash. As an institution for Jewish learning and interpreting Jewish law, the beth midrash dated from talmudic times. Rosenzweig not only translated the term into German but also adopted the institution to the needs of a modern and highly secularized Jewish community.

As early as 1893, Gustav Karpeles, the first president of the Association for Jewish History and Literature (Verein für jüdische Geschichte und Literatur), was confronted with the problem of using the traditional institution to meet new needs. He demanded a revival of the beth midrash "under the different conditions which have been created by modern culture." For Karpeles, the "beth ha-midrash of the future [was] the Jewish Literaturverein."[19] The activities of the Association for Jewish History and Literature over the following four decades did not meet the high expectations of its founder. Although thousands of lectures helped to promote Jewish knowledge, the communal spirit of the beth midrash, fostered by conversations and discussions among its participants, was entirely absent in the Literaturverein.

The Frankfurt Lehrhaus, however, did to some extent recapture the communal spirit of the beth midrash. It became a place where members of different classes of the Jewish population met in an atmosphere of free interchange of opinions between teachers and students. Rosenzweig preferred study groups in which a small number of students worked intensively to lectures that attracted a large audience but did not require active participation. He was willing to integrate a wide range of topics into the Lehrhaus program, provided that the teacher was inspiring enough. Non-Jewish topics were as welcome as Jewish ones, but the program focused on a center: the acquaintance with the Hebrew language and such essential

Jewish sources as the Bible and the Talmud.[20] As Rosenzweig wrote shortly before beginning his work at the Lehrhaus, the only law of the Lehrhaus must be "Nulle dies sine linea hebraica" (No day without a Hebrew line).[21] Rosenzweig himself who taught Hebrew in the Lehrhaus, and his wife took over his classes after his illness prevented him from teaching.

In spite of the intended resemblance between the beth midrash and the Lehrhaus, their differences were more apparent than their similarities. Two profound assumptions of learning in the beth midrash—that students knew the basic Jewish sources and that students and teachers observed religious Jewish laws—were absent from the Lehrhaus. Because students at the Lehrhaus lacked the most basic knowledge of Judaism, the Lehrhaus had to function as a Jewish primary school (*heder*), as well. In contrast to newly founded Orthodox educational institutions in some major German Jewish communities, the Lehrhaus did not constitute the institutional center of a strictly observant Jewish community.

Rosenzweig and his colleagues at the Lehrhaus have often been portrayed as *ba'alei teshuvah,* secularized Jews who returned to an Orthodox mode of life, just as the Lehrhaus was simply considered a revived beth midrash. Such a view is misleading, because it overlooks the innovation of the enterprise. The men and the few women of the Lehrhaus did not wish to return to a premodern Jewish society; rather, they selected certain aspects of Jewish traditions and learning that they wanted to appropriate for contemporary life and thought. Rosenzweig never abandoned his predilection for the European style of life and Bildung. Although the Lehrhaus might have been a window to the traditional Jewish world embodied by the beth midrash, it never became a door through which accultured German Jews left European culture behind.

To find the major influence on Rosenzweig's concept of a New Learning, one must look to contemporary German discussions on education reform rather than to traditional Jewish forms of learning. In his study of the German academic community, Fritz Ringer noted three major tendencies in discussions of education during the Weimar period: attempts to attain a "wholeness" of knowledge, the search for rootedness, and the demand for a *Lebensphilosophie* (philosophy of life). These tendencies were shared by philosophers and historians, conservatives and modernists, representatives of the universities and the secondary school system. A few examples may help to illustrate the new trends in educational reform in Weimar Germany.

Reform-minded thinkers insisted that the principal task of the teacher was to create new values and to get involved in contemporary questions of politics and philosophy, in short, to transmit knowledge that was immediately usable. When Max Weber attacked the prevailing intellectual trends that identified the academic teacher with the healer of contemporary problems in his famous speech "Wissenschaft as a Vocation" (1919), he had little practical impact. In contrast to Weber, most of his contemporaries disagreed with Tolstoy's statement that Wissenschaft "gives no answer to our question, the only question important for us: What shall we do and how shall we live?"[22]

The search for truth and for a Lebensphilosophie within public education and the academy remained prominent during the Weimar period, as did the demand for a wholeness or synthesis of learning. In German high schools the new approach of *Deutschkunde* (German culture) aimed to convey a total view of the students' historical roots.[23] On a different level, philosopher Max Scheler criticized the increasing specialization of the universities and demanded the combining of compartmentalized results of research into one wholeness. This synthesis would be achieved by people's universities, which were to exist side by side with the traditional universities.[24]

There are many parallels between Rosenzweig's call for a New Learning and the attempts to reform the educational system at German schools and universities. The longing for rootedness was implicit in the New Learning, which aimed at rediscovering the principal sources of Judaism unknown to most German Jews. Like Max Scheler, Rosenzweig demanded a wholeness of Jewish learning in the curriculum he proposed in "It Is Time" (1917) and in his later programs for the Frankfurt Lehrhaus, which would have to offer "a curriculum as encyclopedic as possible—in other words, an education [*Bildung*]."[25] Most important, however, was the influence of Lebensphilosophie. Like non-Jewish educational reformers, Rosenzweig despised the "old university," with its purely academic program. When offered an academic position as historian by his teacher Friedrich Meinecke, Rosenzweig declined and made clear how little an academic career that was detached from "life" meant for him.[26]

Rosenzweig's concept of New Learning did not favor the pure accumulation of knowledge or practical information but outlined a learning that was meant to instigate a complete change in mode of life. As expressed in the two last words of his *Star of Redemption,* education should lead "into life." Jewish adult education was to fill the vacuum that the dissolution of the traditional Jewish community had left. The Lehrhaus was to become the "very center of a Jewish life."[27] The Jewish home had lost its Jewish atmosphere, Jewish law had lost its authority, and the synagogue had lost its religious depth, Rosenzweig argued, and he continued to ask the question, "What, then, holds or has held us together since the dawn of emancipation? . . . The answer is frightening. Since the beginning of emancipation only one thing has unified the German Jews in a so-called 'Jewish life'; emancipation itself, the Jewish struggle for equal rights."[28]

The Lehrhaus was to produce a new type of Jew, who would proudly identify with a positive content of Judaism instead of reducing his or her Jewish identity to the struggle for equality and against antisemitism. In his essay on Jewish education, Rosenzweig emphasized that the task of the Lehrhaus was to produce not books or theoretical knowledge but a new human being: "Books are not now the prime need of the day. But what we need more than ever, or at least as much as ever, are human beings—Jewish human beings."[29] Rosenzweig believed that the Lehrhaus would create a stratum of lay Jews who would be equipped with broad and deep Jewish knowledge.

Like Rosenzweig's philosophy of life, his concept of the Lehrhaus was influenced by contemporary intellectual discussions. In imperial Germany, adult education had been mainly restricted to the well-organized Catholic and Social Democratic frameworks, and until 1918 there existed only five independent Volkshochschulen. With the new government of Weimar, adult education attained a new prominence. The Weimar constitution of 1919, in article 148, explicitly declared the support of the Volkshochschule a purpose of the Reich and the German states, and the Prussian office of cultural affairs received an independent section (*Referat*) for matters of adult education. In 1919 alone, 135 new independent Volkshochschulen were established, and by the end of the 1920s 215 had been created.[30]

The German Volkshochschule grew out of earlier European attempts to create systems for adult education. Around the turn of the century several German universities adopted the British idea of university extension and established popular courses and lectures for nonacademics. At the same time, the Danish Grundtvig schools, which aimed not at imitating university courses at a less-advanced level but at creating a new kind of nonacademic learning among a predominantly peasant population, were introduced to northern Germany. Unlike the "extensive" courses, whose main task was the transmission of knowledge, the "intensive" Grundtvig schools envisioned a type of learning that would directly influence its students' conditions of life. The German Volkshochschulen were intensive because they provided new forms of Bildung for the individual as well as the transmission of knowledge in the traditional sense; at the same time they resembled the extensive courses in the composition of their students, who were mainly from the lower-middle-class urban populace.[31]

The Lehrhaus was not a pure imitation of the German Volkshochschule and its educational concepts. It developed genuine theories of adult education. Still, Rosenzweig's distancing of the Lehrhaus from the Volkshochschule cannot conceal the strong influence that the German Volkshochschule had on the Lehrhaus.[32] Rosenzweig himself referred to one of the most important theoretical outlines of the Volkshochschule movement when he introduced himself to the representatives from the Jewish associations in Frankfurt.[33]

The critique of contemporary German society by leaders of the German adult education movement was strongly reminiscent of Franz Rosenzweig's analysis of German Jewry; both complained about the lack of rootedness, community, and spiritual orientation. A closer look at the most important outlines and programs of German adult education in the early years of Weimar reveals striking parallels to those of the Lehrhaus. Almost all those programmatic statements emphasized the need of the Volkshochschule to build a new sense of community among the German people, a role the Lehrhaus was to play among the Jewish population. The most important association of independent adult education institutions, the Hohenrodter Bund, emphasized in its guidelines of 1923 that the "ultimate aim of adult education activities is the creation of a genuine Volksgemeinschaft."[34] Like Franz Rosenzweig, the fathers of the German Volkshochschule reflected the Lebensphilosophie of the time. Bildung was not a goal in itself but a means to create a happier individual and a better society.[35]

Anonymous lectures could not live up to those ideals. Instead the Volkshochschule developed the concept of the small and intensive study group (*Arbeitsgemeinschaft*). Like the larger Volksgemeinschaft, the Arbeitsgemeinschaft emphasized the sense of community by uniting teachers and students as participants in a dynamic exchange of ideas. The intensive study group soon became a symbol for the Volkshochschule itself, and a journal on German adult education founded in 1919 was called *Die Arbeitsgemeinschaft*.[36]

The personal connection between the Volkshochschule movement and the Lehrhaus teachers can be observed most clearly among Rosenzweig's most important colleagues, Eduard Strauss and Martin Buber. Before teaching at the Lehrhaus, chemist Eduard Strauss had already been an experienced instructor in Frankfurt adult education programs. He also contributed to the theoretical debate concerning the reform of adult education after the First World War. In an essay of 1920, Strauss identified three urgent tasks for modern adult education: to answer the contemporary search for a *Sinngebung* (ultimate meaning) of life, to provide a wholeness of knowledge and thus to counteract the growing drive for specialization, and finally to work as a group, in Gemeinschaft. Strauss tried later to materialize his aims in a Jewish framework, the Lehrhaus, but the 1920 essay is general in tone and reflects the overall discussion in the adult education movement after the war.[37]

Martin Buber—the most prominent teacher of the Frankfurt Lehrhaus— participated in German adult education and helped to reshape it. A conference for the renewal of education took place in his Heppenheim home in June 1919. Buber was also an active participant at the conferences of the Hohenrodter Bund.[38] Like Strauss, Buber saw the Volkshochschule as an instrument to overcome what he regarded as the present crisis of culture by leading the alienated masses back to a cultural Gemeinschaft. Outside Frankfurt, teachers at non-Jewish institutions for adult education, such as Paul Eppstein in Mannheim and Karl Adler in Stuttgart, were active in the establishment and development of local Jewish Lehrhäuser. They guided the development of the German adult education movement and helped to transmit the principles of the Volkshochschule to the Lehrhaus movement.[39]

Although evidence points to the strong influence of German educational debates and the model of the Volkshochschule on the development of the Jewish adult education movement, this interconnection was limited because of the situation of the Jewish minority in Germany. In contrast to the mainly proletarian background of the general Volkshochschulen students, most attendants of Jewish adult education institutions came from the middle classes, and often the upper middle classes.[40] The more fundamental difference that distinguished the Lehrhaus movement from other German educational reforms was the desire to preserve a cultural distinctiveness. The Lebensphilosophie represented by the Lehrhaus was not that of a society in search of new values but that of a minority struggling for its cultural survival, while its distinctiveness was increasingly stressed by external forces.

What held true for the general educational debate can also be maintained for the specific case of the Volkshochschule: the Jewish adult education movement adopted many ideas of the Volkshochschule, but their conditions and aims were quite different. The Lehrhaus thus imitated neither the beth midrash nor the Volkshochschule but constituted a distinctive path of adult education.

LEARNING IN REVERSE ORDER: THE STUDENT AS TEACHER

Conventional methods of learning would not suffice to attract German Jews who were alienated from existing Jewish institutions. Jewish knowledge in Germany had become increasingly professionalized and concentrated in the hands of rabbis, teachers, and a few Orthodox Jews. Rosenzweig had this dilemma in mind when he demanded a "learning in reverse order" to inspire the practical engagement of those Jews who lacked knowledge of their Jewish heritage. Unlike the founders of the Frankfurt Volksvorlesungen, Rosenzweig preferred teachers in his Lehrhaus to be men and women with little or no knowledge of Judaism.

> For the teacher . . . cannot be a teacher according to a plan; he must be much more and much less, a master and at the same time a pupil. It will not be enough that he himself knows or that he himself can teach. He must be capable of something quite different—he himself must be able to "desire." He who can desire must be the teacher here. The teachers will be discovered in the same discussion room and the same discussion period as the students. And in the same discussion hour the same person may be heard as both master and student.[41]

In his opening address at the Frankfurt Lehrhaus, Rosenzweig further specified the meaning of the New Learning in its Jewish context:

> A new "learning" is about to be born—rather, it has been born. It is a learning in reverse order. A learning that no longer starts from the Torah and leads into life, but the other way round: from life, from a world that knows nothing of the Law, or pretends to know nothing, back to the Torah. That is the sign of the time. . . . There is no one today who is not alienated, or who does not contain within himself some small fraction of alienation. All of us to whom Judaism, to whom being a Jew, has again become the pivot of our lives—and I know that in saying that I am not speaking for myself alone—we all know that in being Jews we must not give up anything, not renounce anything, but lead everything back to Judaism. From the periphery back to the center; from the outside, in. This is a new sort of learning. A learning for which—in these days—he is the most apt who brings with him the maximum of what is alien.[42]

Based on Rosenzweig's principle of learning in reverse order, the composition of the faculty became the most striking characteristic of the Frankfurt Lehrhaus. As Ernst Simon remarked, it was the "first time in the history of Judaism that the Rav was sitting on the same bench as the *am-ha'arets* [a person without adequate knowledge in Jewish sources and traditions], not only in order to hear, in order to learn, but also as instructor."[43] More than that, Rosenzweig made it clear that the am-ha'arets and not the rabbi occupied the central role in the teaching body of the Lehrhaus. Only two rabbis were among the most important teachers: Nehemias Anton Nobel, whose charisma influenced a variety of Frankfurt Jewish intellectuals, and Georg Salzberger, a Liberal Jew who had initiated the Gesellschaft. Rosenzweig did not consider either of them a pillar of the Lehrhaus. He had great esteem for Nobel as a rabbi and a preacher but felt that "he had no idea what the Lehrhaus was about. For him it remained the Volkshochschule."[44] Rosenzweig tolerated Salzberger because he was the founder of the Gesellschaft and because Rosenzweig needed an official rabbi (*Konzessionsrabbiner*). Rosenzweig thought that Salzberger did not really fit into the program, "but because he is a nice person . . . he belongs to us, just as a solid editor of the local news belongs to an international newspaper."[45]

The typical Lehrhaus teachers were *à la recherche du Judaïsme perdu* (in search of a lost Judaism). Having grown up in assimilated homes without much knowledge of Jewish sources and traditions, the teachers had to acquire this knowledge outside home and school—usually against the wishes of their families. This renewed interest in Judaism was at least in part a reaction to an older generation still practicing some Jewish traditions that were devoid of spiritual content. The classic literary depiction of this situation is Franz Kafka's *Letter to His Father*:

> I could not understand how, with the insignificant scrap of Judaism you yourself possessed, you could reproach me for not making an effort . . . to cling to a similar, insignificant scrap. It was indeed, so far as I could see, a mere nothing, a joke—not even a joke. Four days a year you went to the synagogue, where you were, to say the least, closer to the indifferent than to those who took it seriously. . . . That's how it was in the synagogue; at home it was, if possible, even poorer, being confined to the first Seder, which more and more developed into a farce, with fits of hysterical laughter. . . . I have received a certain retrospective confirmation of this view of Judaism from your attitude in recent years, when it seemed to you that I was taking more interest in Jewish matters. As you have in advance an aversion to every one of my activities and especially to the nature of my interest, so you have had it here too. But in spite of this, one could have expected that in this case you would make a little exception. It was, after all, Judaism of your Judaism that was here stirring, and with it also the possibility to enter into a new relationship between us. . . . But it never came to test. Through my intervention Judaism became abhorrent to you, Jewish writings unreadable; they "nauseated" you.[46]

The natural route of modern Jewry, as it appeared to the father of Franz Kafka and many of his contemporaries, was a path that led away from Judaism (without officially renouncing it) and straight into German or Czech or French society. Their children, however, no longer deemed the path of their fathers and grandfathers worthy of imitation. Instead, they pointed out that full integration into German society existed only in their fathers' fantasies. Gershom Scholem remarked in his memoirs that despite his father's attachment to the German national identity, all his parents' friends were Jews, and neither he nor his parents were ever invited to the homes of non-Jewish colleagues or schoolmates. In view of the social limitations of legal equality, both Gershom Scholem and Franz Rosenzweig accused their fathers and grandfathers of having given up centuries-old Jewish traditions without having obtained a secure place in German society in exchange.[47]

Rosenzweig's, Scholem's, and Kafka's lives were only the most famous examples of the "internal journey of 'dissimilation'" typical for many young Jews in Weimar Germany, including teachers and students of the institutions of Jewish learning.[48] At the Frankfurt Jewish Lehrhaus, Jewish intellectuals who had experienced a similar journey were the teachers of those still to embark on one. The inner circle of the Lehrhaus included biochemist Eduard Strauss, physician Richard Koch, archaeologist Rudolf Hallo, and educator Ernst Simon, and lawyer Rudolf Stahl as the Lehrhaus secretary. They were not "professional Jews" but pursued their various careers while working in the Lehrhaus. They perfectly fit Rosenzweig's conviction that "he is the most apt who brings with him the maximum of what is alien."

The generational conflict was clearly portrayed when young Ernst Simon returned home from his first Kol Nidre service on the eve of Yom Kippur, the Day of Atonement. When he entered the house, his parents had just come in—not from the synagogue but from the movies. Simon, who became an observant Jew, soon chose to leave his parents' home. Similarly, Richard Koch's parents celebrated Christmas and Easter, and only his grandmother observed the most important Jewish holiday, Yom Kippur. Rudolf Stahl reported that his "Jewish education at home was nil." Like Simon, Stahl became conscious of his Judaism only after he became the target of antisemitism in school.[49]

Rudolf Hallo had been most estranged from Judaism. Hallo, a childhood friend of Rosenzweig, grew up in an assimilated Jewish upper-middle-class family in Kassel and later sought to find in Protestantism the spirituality he had never encountered in Judaism. Unlike Rosenzweig, however, Hallo went so far as to accept baptism; he converted to the Protestant faith at the age of seventeen. It was only then that he began to reflect about his Jewishness and systematically taught himself Jewish knowledge. After he became engaged to a Jewish woman, Gertrude Rubensohn, in 1920, he officially returned to Judaism.[50]

Rosenzweig was Hallo's guide back to Judaism and into the Frankfurt Lehrhaus. Rosenzweig chose his childhood friend to replace him as the main administrator of the Lehrhaus after he became ill. In the same way Rosenzweig personally recruited most of his other colleagues at the Lehrhaus. After the resignation of Rudolf Hallo, Rosenzweig was determined to engage the young lawyer Rudolf Stahl as the Lehrhaus secretary. When Stahl was not prepared to accept this position because of career considerations and because he lived outside Frankfurt, Rosenzweig remained unconvinced: "Nothing helped. He said, 'You are the one I want,' and I had to give in. Rosenzweig was what one might call a dictator." He also convinced Koch and Simon to join the Lehrhaus, although they initially resisted. Koch was taken by surprise when Rosenzweig approached him through their common friend Eduard Strauss. Koch argued that he lacked qualifications to teach in a Jewish institution, whereupon Rosenzweig insisted on his cooperation and emphasized, as Koch said, "that he needed my collaboration exactly because of this fact. He needs somebody who does not understand anything of the matter."[51] Ernst Simon recalled his recruitment in almost the same words: "Franz Rosenzweig urged me to teach there. I told him that I did not know anything and that I had just started to make myself acquainted [with Judaism]. 'Well, [Rosenzweig replied,] that's exactly what [our new methods] are about.'"[52]

Rosenzweig's closest collaborator was biochemist Eduard Strauss, whom Gershom Scholem called the "true star of the Lehrhaus."[53] He was an original Jewish thinker who decisively shaped the Lehrhaus and who was the only person to teach there from its opening until its closing.[54] Born in 1870, he grew up without much knowledge of Judaism. His active engagement in Judaism was inspired in the years preceding World War I by Martin Buber's writings on Hasidism. In 1919 he started a Bible-reading class at a Liberal Jewish youth organization in Frankfurt, and in the same year he became the president of the newly established Hermann-Cohen-Loge, a social and intellectual center for many young Jews from assimilated families who were interested in their Jewish roots.

As president of the lodge, Eduard Strauss created the motto "Judaization of Judaism" (Verjudung des Judentums). The task of the lodge was for him to "make a *conscious* Jew out of every member and to assure that he remains such."[55] Like Hermann Cohen, Strauss left no doubt that he felt both German and Jewish. Strauss recognized more lucidly than Cohen, however, that there was not much content left in the Judaism of most German Jews, and he considered it his most urgent task to help re-create a spiritual basis for Jewish life in Germany. In an address to a Liberal Jewish youth group, Strauss demanded, "Nobody can deprive you of your *Deutschtum*—let the others say whatever they want! You have to make your *Judesein* so strong (and if you believe it is lost, you will easily regain it) that you feel there is no stronger constructive force than this one!"[56]

In his essay "Judentum und Zionismus" (1919), Strauss gave credit to the Zionists' recognition of the spiritual crisis of modern Judaism but disagreed with the Zionist solution; he stressed that it was possible to be an opponent of assimilation without becoming a Zionist. This third path between Zionists' reducing Judaism to a nation and Liberals' reducing Judaism to a religious denomination attracted Rosenzweig's attention. Here was another German Jew who recognized the necessity of reconstructing a spiritual basis for German Judaism without opting for Zionism. Rosenzweig visited Strauss in Frankfurt in September 1919; a close friendship developed between the two men that was to last until Rosenzweig's death ten years later. In Strauss Rosenzweig had found what he never believed he would find: not a spiritual father like Hermann Cohen, not a younger disciple, but a colleague who would think and feel like him.[57] Rosenzweig addressed his program of adult education, "Bildung and No End," to Eduard Strauss. Strauss—together with Nobel—convinced Rosenzweig to come to Frankfurt and direct Jewish adult education. In turn, Rosenzweig persuaded Strauss to transfer his Bible class from the Liberal Jewish youth organization to the Lehrhaus.[58]

It is characteristic of the teaching methods of the Lehrhaus that Strauss, the principal Bible instructor, knew no Hebrew. In the first years he read with his students from the Luther translation, and in later years he used the first volumes of the Buber-Rosenzweig translation as they were being published. As one of the participants in this Bible lecture class recalled, it was as if a "lost treasure of one's own possessions was refound."[59] The special aura of Strauss's class was described by Gershom Scholem, for a short time Strauss's colleague at the Lehrhaus:

His equal was hardly to be found in Jewish circles but only among Christian revival movements. His crowded Bible lessons were speeches of an 'awakened one' who spoke out of the spirit. If one may be permitted to use the language of Christian sects, they were pneumatic exegeses. . . . His listeners were spellbound, as though they were held by a magic circle; anyone who was not susceptible to this kind of talk stopped coming, and this is what happened to me. Strauss had no prior Jewish background, and without being tied to Jewish tradition he nevertheless constituted the pure case of a Jewish pietist.[60]

There were two major exceptions to the generalization that the Lehrhaus teachers did not have much experience with Judaism. Nahum Glatzer, a young East European Jew with a solid background in Judaism, and Martin Buber, the best-known German-Jewish thinker in Weimar Germany, came from the heart of Jewish society.[61] Buber was not connected with the Lehrhaus until Rosenzweig visited him in his Heppenheim domicile—fifty miles from Frankfurt—in December 1921. Abandoning his principle that *amei-ha'arets* (the plural form of *am-ha'arets*) should constitute the pillar of the Lehrhaus, Rosenzweig invited Buber as a permanent lecturer: "Only on the trip home did it occur to me that it was cheaper to transport the prophet than twenty of his disciples," Rosenzweig recalled.[62]

Buber's involvement in the Lehrhaus not only brought a famous name to the institution but also meant a decisive boost for Buber's own career. The teaching of a series of lectures or seminars was a new experience for Buber, who was used to giving single lectures. In the Lehrhaus he began a teaching career that he later pursued at such institutions of higher learning as the University of Frankfurt and the Hebrew University in Jerusalem. Moreover, the Lehrhaus became a testing ground for the practical application of teaching methods about which he had long theorized, and a place where he first explored his future writings. Buber's courses were among the best attended in the Lehrhaus, second only to those of Nobel, who counted about three hundred students in his lectures.[63]

Together with Strauss's Bible readings and Simon's classes on Jewish history, Buber's lectures and study groups on a variety of topics became the core of the Lehrhaus program in the years after Rosenzweig stopped teaching. Buber's lectures contributed much to the Lehrhaus' reputation among Frankfurt Jewish intellectuals as a fashionable place. This reputation even extended to the local high schools. Once a worried father told Buber, "with some disapproval, that his eleven-year-old daughter had said to him that she wanted to visit Buber's lecture because in her school 'propaganda' was made for it."[64]

Martin Buber helped to realize an important goal set by Rosenzweig: to attract not only schoolgirls but also the "crepe-de-chine" audience, the upper-middle class of the Frankfurt Westend.[65] As Nahum Glatzer recalled, Rosenzweig wanted the educated Jew to become ashamed of knowing so little of Judaism: "Rosenzweig, half jokingly, half seriously, spoke of 'smuggling' Judaism into the general education so dear to the Jew."[66] According to Ernst Simon, "Rosenzweig provided Jewish Bildung with an aristocratic, saucy, frolic, easy, and secure atmosphere; here blows metropolitan air, a breeze of modernity, instead of this poor people's atmosphere that in former times made everything Jewish so unattractive."[67]

Rosenzweig remained the leading spirit of the Lehrhaus as long as it existed. His dominating role, which Gershom Scholem called his "dictatorial inclinations,"[68] was best expressed in his relationship with Rudolf Hallo during the latter's administration of the Lehrhaus. Hallo, who gave courses on a variety of topics, including the Hebrew language, Bible, Jewish history, and rituals, retired from his administrative post after only one year. His decision was caused by a personal conflict with Rosenzweig, which revealed Rosenzweig's strong conviction that the personal and academic spheres were not separable. Rosenzweig not only suggested that Hallo study Talmud daily—which Hallo gladly did—but also demanded that he adopt an Orthodox way of life. This Hallo was unprepared to do.[69]

The popularity and success of the Lehrhaus could never have been achieved without Rosenzweig's predilection for symbols and minute details. There was, for example, a long argument over the date to be printed on the Lehrhaus programs. Rosenzweig was not willing to use the Christian date and insisted on listing the date according to the Jewish calendar. This plan, however, was rejected by the Frankfurt Jewish community leaders, who regarded the Jewish calendar as antiquated. As a result no date appeared on the programs, only the number of years since the Lehrhaus was opened. Rosenzweig remarked jokingly, "And thus we count our own era since the creation of the Lehrhaus."[70]

Part of Rosenzweig's pragmatism was his detailed financial plan to keep the Lehrhaus "free" and independent. Tickets for the courses were sold on the basis of self-estimation into various income groups. When urged to lower the relatively high upper price of six marks for one class (in 1921), Rosenzweig strongly opposed the idea.[71] He stressed that the main purpose of the high price was to make the institution respectable. He intuited that well-to-do bourgeois would rather attend expensive courses than cheap ones. The same motive led him to change the name of the institution from the proletarian Volksvorlesungen to Freies Jüdisches Lehrhaus, which sounded more attractive to an upper-middle-class audience.[72]

Rosenzweig rejected the plans of the main sponsor of the Lehrhaus—businessman Henry Rothschild, in whose house Rosenzweig lived—to make its financial survival dependent on the contributions of passive members of a Lehrhaus Association. In response to Rothschild's plan, Rosenzweig came up with a new idea that would exclude passive membership: the sale of subscription tickets for two hundred marks (this price rose to six thousand marks in times of inflation). Rosenzweig figured out that this would both increase the number of students and make a significant financial contribution to the Lehrhaus budget. Rothschild was skeptical about the new plan and bet Rosenzweig that fewer than ten people would be willing to pay such a high price. Rosenzweig won the bet, and within one year there were sixty-four subscriptions.[73]

Rosenzweig's concept of new Jewish learning centered around intimate and active study groups. But he needed some form of bait to attract larger numbers of students. Disappointed that only five hundred participants had registered for the twelve classes during the first year of his activities, he thought to increase this number by inviting illustrious names who would draw various groups of people into the Lehrhaus. Journalist and writer Siegfried Kracauer was to tempt the intellectual circle around the *Frankfurter Zeitung,* and feminist Dora Edinger was to lead the "ladies for peace and freedom" (*Tanten für Frieden und Freiheit*) into the Lehrhaus.

The list of instructors of the Lehrhaus reads like a Who's Who of German Jewry: it included Leo Baeck, the leader of Liberal German Judaism, and Nathan Birnbaum, a representative of the Orthodox group Agudat Israel (and former Zionist). Zionist Gershom Scholem taught a seminar on the Zohar (a classical text of Jewish mysticism), and German nationalist Alfred Peyser spoke on the Verband nationaldeutscher Juden. Psychologist Erich Fromm instructed his students on the Jewish sect of the Karaites, and future sociologist Leo Löwenthal taught a course on figures at the margins of Jewish history. Galician-born Hebrew writer and later Nobel prize winner Shmu'el Yosef Agnon recited from his writings, and non-Jewish German writer Alfons Paquet told of his impressions of Palestine. The famous leader of the German Jewish women's movement, Bertha Pappenheim (the president of the Jewish Women's League in Germany and Freud's Anna O.), read from the memoirs of Glückel von Hameln (a Westphalian Jewish widow of the seventeenth century), and philosopher Leo Strauss taught a seminar on Spinoza. Father Hermann Schafft led a lecture group on attitudes of Christians to the Old Testament, and journalist Siegfried Kracauer spoke on modern religious trends.

The fresh faces among the teachers could not conceal for long the crisis that began only three years after the Lehrhaus opened. This predicament was tied to the fatal illness of the school's founder. In the early years of his progressive paralysis Rosenzweig was still able to lead most of the affairs, but his condition deteriorated rapidly. Rosenzweig's last class, relocated to a large room of his private apartment, was held in the summer of 1922. In 1924 he could no longer use the typewriter specially designed for him. Although he could dictate letters to his wife or his secretary using a special system, he restricted his daily work to essential issues, which in his last years meant mostly the Bible translation that he had started with Buber.

Nevertheless, Rosenzweig remained the official head of the Lehrhaus. Although his illness also paralyzed, to a certain extent, the organization of the Lehrhaus, it seemed inappropriate to replace him. Rudolf Hallo's short interlude as the Lehrhaus' de facto administrator only accentuated the difficulties of directing the Lehrhaus. After Hallo's resignation in 1923, the leadership of the Lehrhaus was to be shared between Rosenzweig, Buber, Koch, Simon, and Strauss. As often happens in jointly led enterprises, however, quarrels began to occur. Hallo's forced retirement started a whole series of dissensions among the institution's leaders, which culminated in Simon's refusal to participate in the collective leadership. Strauss's charismatic role aroused the opposition of several Lehrhaus activists, among them Hallo and Simon.[74]

Martin Buber was another target of pointed criticism from some of his Lehrhaus colleagues, especially Ernst Simon. Simon accused Buber of tolerating "partly hysterical, partly shameless questions" of mostly female participants in Buber's courses, which led to a "dabbling of souls, a most repulsive game" (*Gemansche der Seelen, das über alles widerwärtige Spiel*). For Simon, Buber's uncritical response to the most personal and most vulgar questions constituted the greatest danger to the future existence of the Lehrhaus. In fact, it was noted that the Lehrhaus was in danger of becoming a consulting institution for the students' personal problems.[75]

The Lehrhaus continued its regular program until 1926, but the leadership crisis left its imprint. Of course, other factors contributed to the gradual fading of the initial Lehrhaus spirit. The flair of novelty had disappeared, and with it many students who had attended only a few classes because of their curiosity. A further reason for the suspension of the regular Lehrhaus program was the high demand on its students. Rosenzweig's goal was for the students ultimately to change not only their theoretical knowledge but also their way of life. By emphasizing this aim in the Lehrhaus program, Rosenzweig alienated a large number of hesitant students who were not ready to go that far.

Not all Lehrhaus teachers were amei-ha'arets, who were eager to acquire Jewish knowledge. Some were young Jews of Orthodox background, for whom the Lehrhaus was a stop on their way to estrangement from Judaism. Erich Fromm, who later became a famous psychologist, was the most prominent example. Fromm, having produced a dissertation on the sociology of diaspora Judaism, was proposed several times as director of the Frankfurt Lehrhaus but taught there only briefly. Having grown up in a prominent Orthodox family in Frankfurt, he belonged to almost all intellectual Jewish circles in the Frankfurt area, including the study group of Rabbi Nobel and the Talmud group of Rabinkow in Heidelberg.[76] After teaching at the Lehrhaus, Fromm joined the Heidelberg "Torah-Peuticum" of Frieda Reichmann, whom he later married. In the words of Gershom Scholem, his Judaism was "analyzed away" in Heidelberg. Finally, Fromm was associated with another Frankfurt school of mostly Jewish intellectuals, the emerging Institute for Social Research.

Another former Lehrhaus teacher who soon dissociated from the Lehrhaus and found his home in the Institute for Social Research was sociologist Leo Löwenthal. He too participated in Rabbi Nobel's study group and, like many other Lehrhaus teachers, came from an assimilated family. As he later recalled, his temporary involvement in the Zionist movement, his activities at the Lehrhaus, and his decision to keep a kosher home for a short while were reactions to his upbringing. He did all this, he said, "probably largely out of a rebellion against my parents. My parents symbolized, so to speak, everything I didn't want—bad liberalism, bad enlightenment, and two-sided morality."[77]

There was of course a certain degree of irony involved in a rebellion that was a return to religious traditions. Still, Löwenthal, Scholem, Kafka, and Rosenzweig vehemently opposed the paths their fathers had chosen. As a consequence, they paid for their rebellion with a more or less vehement rejection by their fathers (not, in most cases, by their mothers). For some of them—Rosenzweig and Scholem—this rebellion led to a lasting identification with Judaism. For others, such as Löwenthal, it was only a stop on their journey away from the supposedly hollow forms of their parents' bourgeois lives.

After 1926 the Lehrhaus program was reduced to Strauss's Bible-reading course (which had already existed before the Lehrhaus was established), a class in biblical exegesis, and the annual Nobel lectures. Despite this de facto suspension, the Lehrhaus cannot be characterized as a failure. With the concept of learning in reverse order, Rosenzweig made an innovative contribution to Jewish education and to adult education in general. The quantitative achievements of the Lehrhaus also should not be forgotten. At its peak it enrolled about 1,100 students of various ages, professional backgrounds, and affiliations with Judaism.[78] Although they constituted only about 4 percent of a Jewish community of 27,000, participation was extremely high compared to that of non-Jewish adult education institutions, which usually were attended by less than 1 percent of the population.[79]

Rosenzweig's great achievement was to make acculturated German Jews ashamed that they knew so little about Judaism. To use his own words, he smuggled Jewish knowledge into the general Bildung so dear to German Jews. His colleague Richard Koch pointed out that a hundred years earlier a Lehrhaus would have been an institution for the promotion of European Bildung among German Jews, whereas it actually served to integrate Judaism into their general Bildung.[80]

Did the strengthening of Jewish identity, as intended by the teachers of the Lehrhaus, mean a weakening of their German identity? Was it a flight from the heights of German Protestant culture into the world of their blood, as historian Friedrich Meinecke thought about Rosenzweig? According to Franz Rosenzweig, just the opposite was the case. He maintained that "Judaization made me not a worse but a better German."[81] Still, for many German Jews of assimilated background, to get acquainted with Judaism meant to recognize the limits of their integration into German society. For Richard Koch, for example, the relation between Deutschtum and Judentum could never mean "to unite, only to get along with each other" (*Es handelt sich bei 'Deutschtum und Judentum' immer um vertragen, nie um vereinigen*). Koch believed that Jewish characteristics were visible even among the most assimilated German Jews; they would be never fully accepted as Germans and would do better not to be too involved in German politics or academics. As proof of the Jews' will to retain their distinctiveness, Koch mentioned the unwillingness of even assimilated Jews for their children to marry non-Jewish Germans.[82]

This was the opinion of a Liberal German Jew only a few years after Hermann Cohen's enthusiastic wartime idealization of a German-Jewish symbiosis. As an immediate reaction to Cohen's essay "Deutschtum und

Judentum," the young German soldier Franz Rosenzweig had written to his parents during the war about what he regarded as a basic misunderstanding of the "German-Jewish symbiosis":

> To be a German means to feel responsibility for the German people as a whole; to harmonize not only with Goethe and Schiller and Kant but also with the others, and especially with the inferior and average, with the assessor, the little public servant, the fat-headed peasant, the stiff *Oberlehrer* [senior teacher]. The real German must love them all or suffer for them all . . . just as we blush when the average Jew compromises us. . . . Cohen confounds what he finds as a European in Deutschtum with what the German finds in it. . . . In Cohen there is only *Europäertum;* he lacks genuine Deutschtum.[83]

Most teachers of the Frankfurt Jewish Lehrhaus regarded themselves as Liberal German Jews, not Zionists. They taught in German, felt German, and intended to remain in Germany. They reacted sensitively, however, to the increasing antisemitic attacks. If they were to be robbed of their Germanness one day, then they would possess a second cultural heritage, as Richard Koch stated (his words are quoted at the beginning of this chapter). The retrieval and renewal of this heritage was no local Frankfurt story. Even though the Frankfurt Lehrhaus dissolved in 1926, its impact on German Jewry was enduring. Similar institutions of Jewish adult education, following Rosenzweig's model, were established all over Germany during the Weimar period.

THE LEHRHAUS AS A GERMANY-WIDE MOVEMENT

The Frankfurt Lehrhaus was undoubtedly the most innovative and important institution of its kind. But this does not explain why scholars have studied only this Lehrhaus and have ignored the widespread network of Jewish adult education institutions in Weimar Germany.

The Frankfurt Lehrhaus was preceded by the Jewish Volkshochschulen in Berlin and Breslau and by a less intensive program of adult education in Munich, all founded in 1919. During the Weimar years, Jewish institutions for adult education existed in seven of the ten largest Jewish communities in Germany, and in several smaller communities. All such institutions founded after Franz Rosenzweig transformed the Frankfurt Volksvorlesungen into the Lehrhaus adopted the name and parts of the program of the Lehrhaus. Instruction in the Hebrew language was essential to all Lehrhaus and Volkshochschule programs, as was the study of the basic

Jewish sources, the Bible and the Talmud; intensive study groups were organized to recruit a core of serious students, and illustrious lecturers were invited, to attract outsiders.

However strong the connections between the Frankfurt Lehrhaus and other similar institutions were, they did not exclude regional and local particularities; every institution had its leading personalities, its specific thematic emphasis, and its own methods. German Jews were divided into different political and religious groups and were also separated into rural and urban, rich and poor, and German-born and foreign-born Jews. Further, regional and local differences existed among most urban middle-class Liberal Jews. Like the non-Jewish population, Jews from Munich felt like Bavarians, and Jews from Berlin identified themselves as Prussians. Liberal Bavarian Jews successfully opposed the establishment of a Jewish umbrella organization representing all Jews of the Reich because they feared Prussian domination, and Prussian Zionists accused their Bavarian colleagues of "having breathed too much Bavarian air for years."[84]

Institutions for adult education reflected local needs and circumstances. In Berlin, which had a large population of East European Jews and many lower-middle-class German Jews, programs emphasized issues of social welfare and economy, whereas in Mannheim—a city with strong musical traditions—the Lehrhaus considered Jewish music an important element of its program. More often, however, the interests of the leader determined the character of the institution. Because it is impossible in this framework to provide detailed histories of each institution for Jewish adult education, I shall focus on two models of Jewish adult education outside Frankfurt, each of which constituted a new approach to Jewish learning: the Berlin Jewish Volkshochschule, which emphasized contemporary Jewish issues, and the Stuttgart Lehrhaus, which made a pioneering attempt to establish a Christian-Jewish dialogue.

Systematic Jewish adult education in Berlin originated in World War I, when Ismar Freund, legal adviser to the Berlin Jewish community, urged the community's board to consider the establishment of a system of adult education. Freund stated, "In recent decades, interest in Jewish issues has increased among those circles that earlier had been indifferent." In order to address this development, Freund recommended the foundation of a Jewish version of the Volkshochschule that had just been established in major German cities.[85]

Freund's initiative was supported by various Jewish organizations, ranging from the Berlin Zionist Association to the B'nai Brith lodge. After the end of the war, their united efforts were successful: in February 1919 the Freie Jüdische Volkshochschule opened its doors. The new institution had high expectations, as the opening address of Rabbi Julius Bergmann illustrated. He compared the Volkshochschule to the University of Berlin. The university had contributed to the renewal of German culture in the early nineteenth century, and its Jewish counterpart was to become the pillar in the revival of Jewish knowledge in the twentieth century.[86]

Teaching methods at the Volkshochschule were rather conventional, focusing on instructors who may be called professional Jews. Learning in reverse order never caught on in Berlin. During a stay in Berlin in 1920, Rosenzweig collected information on the Berlin Jewish Volkshochschule and expressed his profound doubts about the methods of Jewish adult education practiced there: "What I was told about its decline has strengthened my opinion that things cannot be worked out by relying solely on the system in Berlin. . . . The Berlin Volkshochschule did not attain the goal it set itself: to reach those people who were totally indifferent; only those who had already been interested before came."[87]

Rosenzweig's negative evaluation of the Berlin Volkshochschule did not do the institution justice. The number of registrants rose from 1,560 in 1921 to 2,000 in 1924, reaching almost the number of students of the general Berlin Volkshochschule.[88] Some classes attracted as many as 250 attendants. Taking into account the enormous range of cultural programs offered in Berlin and the competing lecture series of other Jewish institutions, this was a respectable figure. This success was partly due to a well-organized advertising campaign and the convenient system of purchasing tickets, which were available in the secretariat of the Jewish community, in Jewish bookstores, and in the largest department stores of Berlin, Hermann Tietz and Kaufhaus des Westens, both owned by Jews.

The Berlin Jewish Volkshochschule had its own element of New Learning, related neither to new teaching methods nor to a new type of teacher but to a new curriculum. Although there were classes on the Bible, the Talmud, Jewish history, and the Hebrew language, the increasing politicization within the Berlin Jewish community as well as the economic crisis led to a growing concentration on contemporary political, social, and economic issues. Such new sciences as sociology, ethnology, and psychology became most popular at the Volkshochschule, where they were taught for the first time within a distinctly Jewish framework.

Universities offered no academic study of modern Judaism, and rabbinical seminaries concentrated on medieval and ancient topics, so the

Berlin Jewish Volkshochschule was the first institution to offer a systematic study of contemporary Judaism, including courses in Jewish sociology, economic history, and modern Jewish literature. The Volkshochschule also organized debates on contemporary Jewish issues, including a series of Contradictory Evenings (*Kontradiktorische Abende*), in which opposing views were directly interchanged. In the framework of these discussions, leading Liberals defended their position against Zionist representatives on the issues of Jewish schools, the tasks of the urban community, and the relation between Judaism and communism.

Many teachers at the Volkshochschule were young scholars who later established their respective careers in Israeli or American universities. Gershom Scholem, then twenty-five years old, gave the first class of his long teaching career in the Berlin Jewish Volkshochschule on the history of Jewish mysticism. He recalled that his course was "astonishingly well attended," and among his students were "some unusual seekers, like one of Berlin's best-known violin makers and the later abbot of a Buddhist monastery and propaganda center in Ceylon."[89] Three of Scholem's later colleagues at the Hebrew University in Jerusalem also taught at the Volkshochschule. Historian Fritz Baer began his teaching career with a course there on Jewish life in Christian Spain. Martin Buber spoke in a lecture series on modern humanity and religion in the fall of 1930. Harry Torczyner, who later taught Bible in Jerusalem under his Hebrew name Tur-Sinai, was a regular teacher at the Volkshochschule.

In contrast to the Frankfurt Freies Jüdisches Lehrhaus, the Berlin Freie Jüdische Volkshochschule had neither a dominant leader nor a particular theory of teaching. This worked both to its advantage and to its disadvantage. On one hand, the institution lacked the genius of Franz Rosenzweig and his New Learning; on the other hand, its success was not dependent on one person. The Frankfurt Lehrhaus closed because its leader was no longer able to manage the institution and because his program proved to be too ambitious in the long run. The Berlin Volkshochschule, in contrast, was run by an executive committee with rather uncharismatic but effective members that guaranteed a continuous program.[90]

Having observed the Jewish adult education institutions in Germany's two largest Jewish communities, we shall turn our attention to a Lehrhaus in a smaller community. The Stuttgart Lehrhaus was a child of the Frankfurt institution of the same name, which it resembled closely, though it was much smaller. It grew out of the personal friendship that developed between Stuttgart textile merchant Leopold Marx and Martin Buber. When

Buber first came to Stuttgart to deliver a series of lectures in February 1925, he stayed with Marx, and the two men discussed the impact of the Frankfurt Lehrhaus on the Jewish population. Buber encouraged the still-skeptical Marx: "It is possible everywhere. There have to be only people who want it." Marx remembered, "I could not forget Buber's answer. . . . I perceived it as a mission I had to fulfill." In less than a year Marx was able to open the Stuttgart Lehrhaus.[91]

Stuttgart had a Jewish population of five thousand in the 1920s. Marx described the community's knowledge of Judaism as follows: "There were only two or three Zionists in addition to the East European Jews and the academicians who came from northern Germany. For the others, Jewish consciousness was restricted to occasional prayer — if they went to synagogue — and the fight against antisemitism and for equal rights. . . . Jewish knowledge existed only among the Orthodox and those who had to teach it professionally. On the other hand, there were a considerable number of academics and people with a high degree of general Bildung."[92]

Marx's bleak picture is somewhat exaggerated, as there existed in Stuttgart an active B'nai Brith lodge and other cultural Jewish associations, which organized a variety of activities. But Marx was right that Stuttgart lacked a modern institution that was able to attract Jews from the margins of the community. In September 1925 he sent to all community members a letter that called for a reappropriation of Jewish knowledge.[93]

In accordance with Rosenzweig's principle of learning in reverse order, professional Jews were initially relegated to second rank. The Liberal chief rabbi of Stuttgart was not even consulted in the preparations for the foundation of the Lehrhaus.[94]

In his opening address in February 1926, Leopold Marx emphasized the novelty of the idea of the Lehrhaus. He and his colleagues did not intend to found another yeshivah, a "breeding-place for Talmud disciples detached from the world [*eine Pflanzstätte weltabgewandten Talmudjüngertums*], a place which is as foreign to us progressive Europeans as a museum piece of an ethnological collection. No! We do not want to turn back the wheel of history. . . , we do not want to sacrifice a dot of our Germanness and Europeanness and cosmopolitanism, and nevertheless we want to found the Jewish Lehrhaus."[95]

Introductions to basic Jewish sources and to the Hebrew language were at the core of the Lehrhaus curriculum, as in most other Jewish institutions for adult education, but the Stuttgart Lehrhaus was the first such institution to promote Christian-Jewish dialogue. In Weimar Germany a small number of Christian scholars and theologians were interested in serious discussion with their Jewish colleagues, thereby breaking with the traditional missionary approach that characterized mainstream Christian interest in Judaism. One of them was Lambert Schneider, a young Christian publisher, who initiated a new Jewish translation of the Bible.[96]

When Schneider conceived of this translation, the only person he could imagine as translator was Martin Buber, who was known not only as the author of Hasidic writings and philosophical works but also as the principal Jewish representative of Christian-Jewish dialogue. Buber earned this reputation chiefly because of his establishment of the interfaith religious journal *Die Kreatur*. Together with his coeditors, Protestant psychiatrist Viktor von Weizsäcker and Catholic theologian Joseph Wittig, Buber made *Die Kreatur* the major platform of religious socialism and Christian-Jewish exchange during the four years of its existence (1926–1929).[97]

The Lehrhaus movement constituted the forum for another kind of Christian-Jewish dialogue. Several Jewish adult education institutions integrated lectures and debates with notable Christian scholars into their programs. The small Jewish Lehrhaus of Wiesbaden, near Frankfurt, organized a series of lectures titled "The Position of the Religions Toward the Social and Political Problems of Today," including an evening with Paul Tillich on religious socialism and the Protestant Church, attended by several hundred auditors.[98] After an unsuccessful attempt to arrange a series of interfaith debates in the Frankfurt Lehrhaus, Martin Buber turned the Stuttgart Lehrhaus into the center of Christian-Jewish dialogue. In 1928 and 1929 he participated in four discussions on Judaism and contemporary religious questions, concentrating on such topics as religion and nationhood, or religion and revolution.

Buber's partners in the debates—Theodor Bäuerle, director of the local Volkshochschule; historian Hermann Hefele; writer Wilhelm Michel; and Jakob Wilhelm Hauer, a scholar of religion—offered a diverse spectrum of Christian views on contemporary issues.[99] Their discussions centered on the relation of the two religions to authority, nation, politics, and Jesus. Most of the talks emphasized the differences between Judaism and Christianity rather than their similarities. A "Public Dialogue on Church, State, Nation, and Jewry," which took place in January 1933 between Buber and liberal theologian Karl Ludwig Schmidt of Bonn, was—like most of the earlier dialogues—unsatisfying. Buber's demand that interfaith dialogue should in future avoid assertions of irreconcilable truths was dismissed by Schmidt, who showed little inclination for compromise and concluded his rebuttal to Buber with the following words: "Were the Church more Christian than it is, the conflict with Judaism would be sharper than it can now be. . . . We Christians must never tire of keeping this conflict alive."[100]

Instead of pointing to a common ground for Jews and Christians, the debates accentuated the line dividing the two groups—a dividing line that became concrete a few days after Schmidt's visit at the Stuttgart Lehrhaus, when Adolf Hitler was installed as Germany's chancellor. By then Jakob Wilhelm Hauer, one of the participants in the earlier Lehrhaus debates, had become a leading figure in the racist Deutsche Glaubensbewegung, which aimed at "liberating" Christianity from its Jewish roots.

A short summary of the remaining major institutions of Jewish adult education in Weimar Germany will illustrate the general outline they shared and the specific local characteristics separating them from each other. The model of the Berlin Jewish Volkshochschule was adopted by the only other Jewish institution of that name, founded in Breslau in the fall of 1919.[101] As in Berlin, professionals taught most classes. The instructors included the professors of the local rabbinical seminary (the conservative Jüdisch-Theologisches Seminar), local rabbi Hermann Vogelstein, and Jewish teachers. The Jüdisch-Theologisches Seminar had a decisive influence on the establishment of the Jewish Volkshochschule, and its programs often read like popular versions of the rabbinical seminary's catalogues, thus representing the British model of university extension rather than Rosenzweig's vision of learning in reverse order.

The highlight of the Breslau Jewish Volkshochschule was the semester opening addresses, usually delivered by prominent Jewish writers. The Volkshochschule succeeded in having the most famous Jewish writers of the German literary scene—among them Max Brod, Georg Hermann, Lion Feuchtwanger, Arthur Hollitscher, Else Lasker-Schüler, Martin Buber, and Franz Werfel—speak about Jewish topics.[102]

The Breslau Volkshochschule functioned without interruption during the Weimar period and was the center of popular Jewish learning in eastern Germany. Although the instruction may have been more superficial than in Frankfurt because of the lack of intensive seminars and study groups, it had a broader impact on the local community. The twenty classes of the school's first year were attended by twelve hundred students "from all social classes and religious streams." The local Jewish newspaper concluded that the "Volkshochschule had filled a genuine need for the widening and deepening of Jewish knowledge" among Breslau Jews.[103]

Most smaller Jewish adult education institutions represented a combination of the Frankfurt and Berlin models. As in Berlin, their teachers were usually professional Jews, and the local rabbi was usually instrumental in founding the Lehrhaus. This was true of Paul Lazarus in Wiesbaden (1921), Emil Schorsch in Hannover (1928), Hugo Schiff in Karlsruhe (1928), and Max Grünewald in Mannheim (1929). In Munich the situation was more complicated. The first courses of adult education (*Lehrkurse*) were organized there by the Association for Jewish History and Literature in November 1919. Until the mid-1920s the Munich Lehrkurse were kept at a modest scale, an average of three or four courses per semester, and the courses usually met only four or five times. When the young rabbi Max Elk came to Munich in 1925 to fill the new post of a youth rabbi, he reorganized the Lehrkurse into a Lehrhaus that was modeled on the Frankfurt institution. A year later Elk left Munich, and the Lehrhaus was subsequently run by journalist Ludwig Feuchtwanger, brother of writer Lion Feuchtwanger.[104]

Although the principle of learning in reverse order was not much used in the smaller institutions, most of them were careful to integrate another of Rosenzweig's principles: the reappropriation of Jewish sources. Rabbi Emil Schorsch of the Hanover Lehrhaus calculated that because assimilated German Jews were unfamiliar with the Talmud, its exotic feel would have a stronger attraction for them than would any topic about which they had some superficial knowledge. "Just as a child is first more interested in the lions of Africa than in the moles living in his parents' garden, so many Jews prefer to begin with the Talmud, which is totally unknown to them, than with the study and understanding of the prayer book."[105]

The Mannheim Lehrhaus proved especially creative when confronted with the question of how to attract previously indifferent members of their community. Addressing this issue, Rabbi Max Grünewald wrote a *Lehrkantate,* a didactic musical play after the model of Bertolt Brecht. Performed by 250 members of the local Jewish community during Hanukkah of 1930 in Mannheim's largest recital hall, it was attended by a significant number of Mannheim Jews (see Chapter 6). The Lehrkantate illustrated how cooperation among the various adult education institutes was possible. One year after its Mannheim performance, it was adopted by the Cologne Lehrhaus and was successfully performed there.[106]

The position of the Frankfurt Lehrhaus as the center of Jewish adult education in Germany was underlined by the export of its teachers. Many of them gave lectures and courses at a variety of already extant Jewish institutions for adult education and were instrumental in establishing new ones.

For example, Martin Buber, Ernst Simon, and Erich Fromm were frequent lecturers at the Munich Lehrhaus. Simon was a particularly prominent speaker in many cities and, at one point, was suggested as a possible director of the Stuttgart Lehrhaus.[107] Buber, in addition to being the guiding spirit of the Stuttgart Lehrhaus, gave the opening address at the Cologne Lehrhaus in 1929 with a reading of his Bible translation. Two years later, this institution had about five hundred attendants.[108] Rudolf Hallo—Rosenzweig's successor in Frankfurt—continued adult education classes in his home town of Kassel, after his retreat from Frankfurt.[109] The secretary of the Frankfurt Lehrhaus, Rudolf Stahl, opened a small Lehrhaus when he returned as a lawyer to his home town of Nauheim. Soon afterward he was able to report to Rosenzweig that "much life and inspiration came to the quiet little community of N."[110]

Even more enthusiastic was Rabbi Lazarus of Wiesbaden, who called the local Lehrhaus the "center of all the Jewish intellectual life of the community."[111] Indeed, in many smaller communities the Lehrhaus gave new meaning to Judaism for those Jews who had been unattracted by the pre-existing network of synagogues and the few social and cultural associations. Leopold Marx summarized the achievements of the Lehrhaus as follows: "The Lehrhaus has succeeded in creating the beginning of a *movement*. . . . Either by the new contact with the Bible, by the original force [*Urgewalt*] of the original language [*Ursprache*], or by a moving word from Martin Buber—here many of us found a totally new, previously unknown meaning for our Judaism."[112]

Although designed for adults, the Lehrhaus often became a meeting point for certain groups among the local Jewish youth. Like the eleven-year-old girl who rushed into the Frankfurt Lehrhaus because it was fashionable, other Jewish adult education institutions were frequented not only by adults but by youngsters. In Berlin, Frankfurt, and Cologne young Jews even founded their own educational institution, the Schule der Jüdischen Jugend. No longer content with the teaching methods of the Berlin Jewish Volkshochschule, this School of Jewish Youth closely copied the Frankfurt model. During the fall trimester of 1930, the Schule der Jüdischen Jugend in Berlin was frequented by four hundred students who participated in twenty-four courses.[113]

Franz Rosenzweig, when viewing the overall development of Jewish adult education in Weimar Germany, might have been more satisfied than he was ready to admit. In every community with a Lehrhaus or Volkshochschule, a new kind of lay intellectual Jewish leadership was educated.

Stemming mostly from assimilated families, those young professionals, academics, and merchants went the opposite way from their grandfathers: deeply embedded in general Bildung, they acquired a basic, sometimes solid knowledge in Judaism. Although their number was limited, they represented a tendency that was also perceptible in the areas of scholarship, literature, and art.

Rosenzweig and his colleagues were certainly successful in making alienated Jews curious about Judaism. Thousands frequented lectures, seminars, and working groups at the various Jewish adult education institutions all over Germany. Rosenzweig's larger and much more ambitious aim, however, to construct a new Jewish lifestyle from the theoretical basis acquired in those courses, was not as well achieved. His demand that the community members lead what he defined as a Jewish life caused tensions even in the inner circle of his own Lehrhaus and ultimately contributed to its premature dissolution. At the institutions outside Frankfurt, the task of building a new Jewish life through acquired Jewish Bildung was not usually considered a high priority.

In this sense, the Lehrhaus movement was like the German Volkshochschule, which also attracted considerable numbers of students but did not achieve its goal of transforming German society through education. When the German Volkshochschule's ideals of a new Volksgemeinschaft took shape in 1933, they did so in a form quite unintended by most of the Volkshochschule's liberal-minded founders. In the same year, the Lehrhaus movement entered a new chapter of its existence. Under the leadership of Martin Buber, for the first time a nationwide organization emerged, providing a framework for the increasing number of German-Jewish adult education institutions. The conditions and aims of the organization were entirely different from those of Weimar days, but the base provided by Franz Rosenzweig and his Lehrhaus movement were a consolation to German Jews in their most desperate hour.

4

Toward a Synthetic Scholarship: The Popularization of Wissenschaft des Judentums

[It is our task] to build up a continuously developing inventory of Judaism, to see what we are, what we have, and what we are able to do.

—Martin Buber, "Jüdische Wissenschaft," *Die Welt* (1901)

In the face of Germany's political revolution after World War I, German academia readdressed some of its most existential issues. A central question concerned the integration of learning and life. Challenged by Max Weber's celebrated lecture of 1919, "Wissenschaft as a Vocation," the proponents of a Lebensphilosophie vehemently argued for the reintegration of learning and weltanschauung, and demanded as the primary tasks for future scholarship a synthesis and a wholeness, instead of specialization and diversification.[1]

This hunger for wholeness was also reflected in the development of Wissenschaft des Judentums. Many of its representatives demanded a return to the classical religious texts and a synthesis of Jewish culture. As we have seen, the period between the turn of the century and World War I constituted a phase of transformation for Wissenschaft des Judentums. After the emergence of Zionism, such new subdisciplines as ethnography and sociology inspired the study of contemporary Judaism and its ethnic distinctiveness. Together with such associations as the Society for the Promotion of Wissenschaft des Judentums and the Associations for Jewish History and Literature, those subdisciplines marked a growing fragmentation and secularization of Wissenschaft des Judentums, whose institutional framework previously had been restricted to rabbinical seminaries. Those tendencies were still visible during the Weimar years, but the most significant change in Wissenschaft des Judentums after World War I was its popularization (this term is meant not to be derogatory but to express the attempt to spread knowledge of Judaism among broad sections of the Jewish population). Most proponents of Wissenschaft des Judentums in Weimar Germany were thus in basic agreement with the principles of Jewish adult education institutions: both groups attempted to raise the standard of Jewish knowledge among Jews. Their approaches, however, differed. Wissenschaft des Judentums had three goals: renewed access to basic Jewish sources through modern translations, promotion of the wholeness of Judaism by the compilation of encyclopedias, and the establishment of a synthesis of Jewish history through plans for a multivolume, multiauthored work.

In the Weimar period, the further secularization of Wissenschaft des Judentums resulted in the establishment of the Akademie für die Wissenschaft des Judentums—a secular research institute that sought to integrate the various subfields of research—and in German universities' partial recognition of Jewish studies as a discipline.[2] The Akademie für die Wissenschaft des Judentums was originally conceived as a means of popularization of Wissenschaft des Judentums. In 1917 Franz Rosenzweig had suggested, in an open letter to Hermann Cohen, the establishment of an academy of Judaism as a place of instruction for teachers of Jewish religion and as a future center of a revitalized Jewish scholarship. The academy was supposed to produce a new type of scholar-teacher and thus become an instrument for a systematic reappropriation of Jewish knowledge among German-Jewish youths.[3]

When the Akademie was founded under the leadership of historian Eugen Täubler, in 1919, Rosenzweig's plans were virtually ignored. Täubler, a disciple of Theodor Mommsen and himself a preeminent scholar of ancient history, saw his main task to be raising the standard of Jewish scholarship to the level of European academic research. He aimed to prove to the academic world that Wissenschaft des Judentums deserved to be considered as seriously as other scholarly disciplines. To attain this goal, Täubler drew up the first plan for systematic research on Judaism, to be undertaken outside the traditional rabbinical seminaries. Even though the academy never lived up to the ambitious plans of Eugen Täubler and his successor, philosopher

Julius Guttmann, it was the first institution in Germany to push for the study of Judaism on a professional basis in a highly specialized secular framework.[4]

Täubler's wish to attain recognition for Jewish studies outside Jewish circles harked back to the beginnings of Wissenschaft des Judentums. Virtually all its leading representatives, including Leopold Zunz, Abraham Geiger, Moritz Steinschneider, and Heinrich Graetz, had fought for the establishment of a chair of Hebrew literature, Jewish theology, or Jewish history at a German university. When renowned non-Jewish theologians and philologists supported an initiative instigated by the Berlin Jewish community on the eve of World War I, the creation of such a chair seemed imminent.[5] No chair dedicated specifically to Jewish studies, however, was established during the war or the Weimar period.

A look at the status of Jewish studies in other countries may be useful in evaluating the situation in Germany. Although at the beginning of the 1920s the field of Jewish studies existed mainly in rabbinical seminaries, at the end of the decade it had become an established discipline on three continents. In 1925 Harvard University had initiated a professorship in Hebrew literature and philosophy that was to be occupied by Harry A. Wolfson. Four years later Salo W. Baron was chosen as incumbent of the first chair of "Jewish history, literature, and institutions," which had been established with the proceeds of a private endowment fund at Columbia University.[6] In 1925 two other institutions for Jewish scholarship were established: the Hebrew University opened its gates in Jerusalem and provided Jewish studies with a new center, and the Vilna-based Yidisher Visnshaftlekher Institut (YIVO, Institute of Jewish Research) was organized to explore the history and culture of the Jews in Eastern Europe.[7]

No comparable chair or institution was founded in Weimar Germany, but a lectureship for religion and Jewish ethics was established at the University of Frankfurt am Main. The lectureship was significant largely because its longtime incumbent was Martin Buber. Along with a few similar lectureships at other universities, such as Giessen and Leipzig, the Frankfurt position marked a first, albeit cautious, step to free Jewish studies from its isolation at the rabbinical seminaries and to make it accessible to Jewish and non-Jewish students in a secular setting.[8]

The growing specialization of Wissenschaft des Judentums was further underlined by the spread of professional journals in various subdisciplines. This process had been introduced before World War I by the foundation of the *Zeitschrift für Demographie und Statistik der Juden* and the *Mit-*

teilungen für jüdische Volkskunde, in the subfields of Jewish sociology and ethnography. In the Weimar period they were joined by new journals in the realms of Jewish genealogy (*Jüdische Familien-Forschung*), social welfare (*Jüdische Arbeits- und Wanderfürsorge*), bibliophilia (*Soncino-Blätter*), and German-Jewish history (*Zeitschrift für die Geschichte der Juden in Deutschland*). An attempt to establish a modern Jewish theological periodical was brought to a premature end by the rise of the Nazis.[9]

It is impossible to separate the process of specialization and increasing secularization of Wissenschaft des Judentums from its simultaneous popularization. In fact, the same scholars were connected to the major projects representing both tendencies. Ismar Elbogen, the coeditor of the *Zeitschrift für die Geschichte der Juden in Deutschland,* was to edit a multivolume universal Jewish history, and Franz Rosenzweig, the original initiator of a plan for the academy, and Martin Buber, the lecturer of Jewish religion at Frankfurt University, collaborated in producing the most remarkable Bible translation in Weimar Germany.

HEBREW IN GERMAN GUISE: TRANSLATIONS OF JEWISH SOURCES

Five generations passed between the first cautious attempts by German Jews to become part of German-language culture and their exclusion by the guardians of an Aryan race. Nothing illustrates better the intellectual development of German Jews during this period than a comparison of the two Bible translations that introduced and concluded the time span. In 1783, precisely 150 years before the writings of Jewish authors were burned by Nazi students, Moses Mendelssohn laid the foundations for a rapidly emerging German-Jewish culture. Mendelssohn's German Pentateuch was not just a translation and interpretation of the Holy Scripture but also a gateway to German culture for many a German Jew. The first Jew to undertake a German Bible translation, Mendelssohn used Hebrew characters, because the average German Jew was not able to write and read German in Latin or Gothic letters.

Martin Buber and Franz Rosenzweig, who began their joint translation a few years before the extinction of German-Jewish culture, had a starting point diametrically opposite to that of Mendelssohn. Five generations after Mendelssohn, German Jews felt at home with the German language and literature but were no longer able to read their most important text in the Hebrew original. Whereas Mendelssohn aimed at teaching German to his fellow Jews, the two modern translators hoped to lead German Jews back to the Hebrew language.

By creating what appeared to many readers to be a Hebraized German, the two translators provided even those who were unable to understand Hebrew with a certain sensibility for the sound of the language. More important, many German Jews—especially the young people—were convinced that the Buber-Rosenzweig Bible constituted a document that was particularly theirs. They could understand it because it was written in German, and they could claim that it was essentially Jewish because its German language differed substantially from accepted norms. The translation thus had two effects in the renaissance of Jewish culture: first, it enabled German Jews to reencounter their most important text in an attractive and modern way; and second, its "non-German German" fostered the growing sense of cultural distinctiveness among German Jews.

German Jews had produced numerous Bible translations in the period between that of Mendelssohn and that of Buber and Rosenzweig, but no others were as significant. Neither the popular Zunz translation (1837) nor the Liberal and Orthodox versions of Ludwig Philippson (1841–1854) and Wohlgemuth-Bleichrode (1899) followed Goethe's famous dictum, according to which the translator should create a third element between the original and the target language.[10] The success of Buber and Rosenzweig in presenting such a third element—a Hebraized German—indeed constituted a pioneering enterprise. Before analyzing the effect of this Hebraized German and its reception among various segments of German Jews, I shall briefly recount the history of the Buber-Rosenzweig translation.[11]

On the eve of World War I, Buber planned a Bible translation together with two prominent representatives of the German literary scene, Moritz Heimann and Efraim Frisch. When they abandoned their plan, Buber waited a decade before returning to the idea. In 1925 Lambert Schneider asked Buber to translate the Old Testament as the first and central work of Schneider's publishing firm, and Buber reacted positively. He accepted on condition that he collaborate with Franz Rosenzweig, who had rendered Hebrew prayer texts and poems from Yehuda Halevi into German during the postwar years.

In spite of his progressing paralysis, Rosenzweig took an active part in the translation until his death in 1929. Thereafter, Buber continued the work alone; more than thirty-five years after beginning, he concluded the project by translating the two books of Chronicles in his new home in Jerusalem. As Gershom Scholem emphasized in his speech at the completion of Buber's translation in 1961, the primary intention of the project was to lead the German-Jewish reader back to the original source. For Scholem the most visible message of the Hebraized German text was, "Go and learn Hebrew!"[12] In the introduction to his celebrated German translation of the medieval Hebrew poetry of Yehuda Halevi, Rosenzweig had made clear that this was indeed his most important goal. He opened his text with the motto of the translator Friedrich Leopold von Stolberg: "O dear reader, learn Greek and throw my translation into the fire."[13]

Rosenzweig was not the first to take this motto seriously. It was the guiding principle behind such German translations as Klopstock's Horace, Schlegel's Shakespeare, and—first and foremost—Hölderlin's Sophocles and Pindar. Buber and Rosenzweig had Hebraized the German language just as those poet-translators had Hellenized, Latinized, or Anglicized it. The principle common to the Romantic German translations of ancient literature and the neo-Romantic Buber-Rosenzweig Bible was called by George Steiner an "anti-Enlightenment tactic of linguistic nationalism."[14]

For Buber and Rosenzweig, linguistic nationalism meant the creation of an essentially Jewish Bible translation, just as Martin Luther had produced the first piece of modern German literature with his sixteenth-century Bible translation. In one respect, Buber and Rosenzweig's task seemed even more difficult than Luther's: they had to express Jewish distinctiveness in a non-Jewish language. One sign of this approach was that they translated the Hebrew names for the biblical books into German rather than use the common Latin form, so *Bereshit* became *Im Anfang* instead of Genesis.

To express cultural distinctiveness through translation was a goal that was by no means generally accepted by contemporary translators, and another Jewish intellectual suggested quite a different purpose for translation only a few years before Buber and Rosenzweig embarked on their enterprise. In his essay "The Task of the Translator" (1923), Walter Benjamin argued that all existing languages derived from and returned to a common universal root. It was the task of the translator to restore, at least partially, this "pure language." This aim was in blatant contrast to both the German Romantics and the Jewish neo-Romantics, who were in search of the linguistic characteristics representing specific national cultures.[15]

Their shared search, however, could not conceal the difference between Hölderlin and Schlegel on one hand and Buber and Rosenzweig on the other. For the first two, the national element was associated with the target language, whereas for the second pair it was associated with the original language. The German Romantics used foreign sources to reveal the historical development of German; Buber and Rosenzweig, in contrast, used translation into German as a medium to re-create a renewed linguistic affinity between German-Jewish readers and the ancient Jewish culture behind the Hebrew sources.[16] They sought to introduce acculturated German-Jewish readers to Israel's *Ursprache* (original language) and primal religious sensibility.

Buber and Rosenzweig had to contend with a number of difficult problems of translation, which they hoped to solve by developing their own principles. Because they understood all biblical books as part of one coherent text, they had to use the same German expression for a particular Hebrew term throughout the Scripture, even if biblical criticism had attributed the verses in question to different sources. A second principle was based on Buber's assumption that the biblical text had originally been spoken. The essentially oral character of the Bible was to be retained by rendering the German translation aurally as closely as possible to the original Hebrew. A famous example appears in the first sentences of Genesis. Most German editions of the Bible translated the term *tohu va'vohu* (without form and void) as *wüst und leer* or *öd und wüst*. Neither German translation conveyed the aural affinity of the two Hebrew words. To rectify the problem, Buber and Rosenzweig created the phrase *Irrsal und Wirrsal.*[17]

Another important principle of translation was the preservation of the multitude of associations connected with certain terms in the original language. The Hebrew *ruah,* for example, means both "wind" and "spirit." Usually, German Bible translators had used the definition that best suited the immediate context, thus losing the term's crucial ambiguity. In the Buber-Rosenzweig translation *ruah* is translated as *Braus,* a term coming close to the twofold meaning of the original. Finally, Buber and Rosenzweig render the tetragrammaton with the pronominal form as *Ich, Du,* or *Er.*[18] Thus, the whole biblical text reads as a dialogue between God and His People. Buber and Rosenzweig may have done this not only because of Buber's general philosophy of dialogue but also as an invitation to German Jews to renew this dialogue.

Most German Jews reacted positively to the first volumes of the Buber-Rosenzweig translation, but a few voices raised considerable protest. Just as the two translators identified with different streams of German Judaism, the translation's reception cannot be neatly separated along factional lines.

Liberal rabbi Benno Jacob, himself a renowned translator of Hebrew texts, praised the intention of Buber and Rosenzweig to restore the original

Hebrew behind the German. As Gershom Scholem later believed, Jacob regarded the premier aim of the translation to be an appeal for the reader to study Hebrew: "I know no other translation which so very much replaces the original and yet so very much presses one to learn the original itself."[19] For other Liberal Jewish critics, the reading of the Buber-Rosenzweig translation *was* already a kind of study of Hebrew. The poet Margarete Susman wrote, "In this work, we possess at the same time the ancient Hebrew Bible and the modern German Bible." She went on to say that the "landscape is really that of the biblical land of ancient times; the altar has again become the wild, blood-spattered sacrificial table; the people are figures of the ancient Middle East."[20] Susman found in the translation what many German Jews had identified in Buber's early writings on Hasidism: a Jewish authenticity that had been lost in the Bible translations of the nineteenth century. The changes within Liberal Judaism, noted in Chapter 2, were also reflected in Liberal responses to the Buber-Rosenzweig Bible. Recognizing the Romanticist tradition behind the translation, Liberal Berlin rabbi Arthur Loewenstamm appreciated the work as a necessary replacement for what he considered rationalistic Bible translations of the nineteenth century. Rationalism was no longer sufficient, Loewenstamm argued, to express the full depth of the human soul. The new translation was full of a "new healthy Romanticism that leads into the . . . depths of our souls."[21]

Jewish actors recited parts of the Buber-Rosenzweig translation together with readings from Heinrich Heine and Peter Altenberg, Jewish schools used the translation in their religious education, and Jewish newspapers recommended the work as the most appropriate Hanukkah present.[22] It is no surprise that among the German-Jewish youth movement, the Romanticism of the Buber-Rosenzweig translation was received enthusiastically. Reading circles were dedicated to the recitation of the new translation, and the 1927 convention of the former members of Kameraden had discussions focusing on it.[23] One activist of the youth movement recalled that "there was hardly a meeting, a seminar, a conference, or a camp of Jewish youth organizations where Bible study was not part of it. . . . Had the generation of young Jews that went through the Buber-Rosenzweig school of Bible reading and Bible interpreting been permitted to grow up and to remain together, they would have become the most Bible-conscious Jews since the days before the ghetto walls had fallen in Europe."[24]

What attracted the youth movement repelled parts of the German-Jewish intelligentsia. The Buber-Rosenzweig Bible aimed at restoring religious immediacy and thus was part of the Lebensphilosophie behind the Lehrhaus and certain trends of Wissenschaft des Judentums. For the Frankfurt cultural critic Siegfried Kracauer, the translation was archaic, reactionary, and dangerously close to German nationalism; it sounded like "Bayreuth and Valhalla"—a criticism shared in principle by Walter Benjamin. From a different angle, literary critic Emanuel Bin Gorion (the son of Hebrew writer Micha Josef Berdyczewski) added his voice to the choir of negative criticism by calling "Buber's Bible" artificial, antiquated—in short, "totally superfluous."[25]

Buber and Rosenzweig neither identified with the principles of Protestant Bible scholarship nor entirely rejected them, as Orthodox Jewish scholars did. It is therefore unsurprising that Orthodox Jews reacted ambivalently to the translation. Although they could not agree with the unorthodox methods of translation, they repeatedly pointed to their positive side effects. Joseph Wohlgemuth, editor of the journal *Jeschurun* and himself a translator of the Bible, expressed the ambiguous feelings of Orthodox Jews: "Only a decade ago, I would have taken a translation of *our* Bible by Buber only hesitatingly into my hands. Whoever has gone so far astray [*abgeirrt ist*] from *our* original source of life according to the Torah . . . cannot be the interpreter of the word of our living God." Similarly Rosenzweig, a student of Hermann Cohen, could not be "spirit of our spirit" (*Geist von unserem Geiste*). In spite of his reservations, Wohlgemuth recognized that unusual means may have been necessary to make acculturated German Jews familiar with the classic Jewish texts and ultimately to lead them back to an Orthodox way of life.[26]

The more extreme representatives of the Orthodox camp did not let such pedagogical excuses for the use of Bible criticism pass. The editors of the mouthpiece of separatist neo-Orthodoxy, *Der Israelit,* were especially infuriated because the work's implicit criticism of Orthodox Bible interpretation might not be recognized immediately by its readers: "The sword wrapped in cotton can hit more severely than the openly presented sword."[27]

The Zionist view was best expressed by Ernst Simon, who hailed the translation of his Lehrhaus colleagues as the "first genuine encounter of the Jewish-Hebrew Bible and the spirit of the German language." He stated that because the Luther Bible, with its Christian interpretation, remained unacceptable to most German Jews, the Buber translation was their introduction to the holy character of the Scripture.[28] The comparison with the Luther Bible was a common theme of the Zionist reviews of the Buber-

Rosenzweig translation. One reviewer maintained that just as Luther had grasped the German Volkseigenart in his translation, so too had Buber and Rosenzweig created a new linguistic expression for the Jewish Volkseigenart by capturing the Hebrew melody (*nigun*) in German guise.[29]

Although contemporary readers and critics, as well as the translators themselves, usually emphasized the Jewish character of the translation, it was actually more influenced by German culture than Jewish tradition, just as the Lehrhaus—in spite of its name—developed more from the Volkshochschule than from the beth midrash. Neither traditional Jewish sources nor contemporary Orthodox and Liberal Jewish Bible commentaries had as much influence on Buber and Rosenzweig's final work as had the writings of German Romanticism, particularly Herder's interpretation of the language of the Hebrew Bible and Grimm's magisterial German dictionary of the early nineteenth century. Many critics read such terms as *Braus* and *Irrsal und Wirrsal* as new creations, but the translators used them in close accordance with Grimm's dictionary. To avoid the non-Jewish connotation of their references, Buber and Rosenzweig jokingly referred to the author of the dictionary as "Reb Grimm" and rendered the common abbreviation "R" (which Protestant Bible scholarship had introduced for the anonymous *Redaktor* [editor]) as *Rabbenu* (Hebrew for "our teacher").[30]

Compared with the novelty and idiosyncrasy of the translation techniques involved in creating the Buber-Rosenzweig Bible, the other Jewish Bible translations undertaken in Weimar Germany were conventional. In 1924 the Berlin Jewish community adopted the suggestion that Liberal rabbi Siegmund Maybaum had made three decades earlier to publish a scholarly Bible translation for Liberal German Jews. Several Liberal German rabbis, among them Emil Bernhard-Cohn, Max Dienemann, Benno Jacob, and Caesar Seligmann, cooperated in the translation, and the leading Bible scholar at the Hochschule für die Wissenschaft des Judentums, Harry Torczyner, was commissioned for the editorial work. Most of the text was completed before 1933, but Torczyner's thorough revisions took several years. The first volume appeared only in 1937, under conditions quite different from those of the Weimar period.

Whereas the Torczyner Bible constituted a scientific counterpart to the Buber-Rosenzweig Bible, Lazarus Goldschmidt's "unique splendorous edition" (thus the subtitle) was its bibliophilic counterpart. Published in a limited edition of three hundred copies, it interested a small group of bibliophiles. Goldschmidt, a Lithuanian-born orientalist who also translated the

Quran into German, was much better known for a project that he had begun around the turn of the century and concluded in the Weimar period: the first complete German translation of the Babylonian Talmud.

The Talmud translation was based on his critical Talmud edition, which questioned numerous traditional interpretations. This was reason enough for the Orthodox to vehemently oppose the translation. The non-Orthodox Jewish press, in contrast, praised Goldschmidt's initiative, mentioning that the translation made a vast fund of knowledge available to German Jews who could not read the Aramaic original. Still, it remains unclear who actually bought the twelve volumes containing approximately ten thousand pages of the Talmud translation. For Orthodox Jews, study of the original was irreplaceable, and for most of Weimar Germany's Jews, who no longer followed religious Jewish laws, the Talmud had lost its relevance to daily life. Unlike many sacred books, the Talmud is not the kind of edifying literature that average German Jews would bother to read on their own in their spare time. Selling almost ten thousand complete sets was thus a remarkable success for the Jüdischer Verlag, which published the work.[31] If the Goldschmidt translation was neither studied nor read systematically, it may have been bought in order to be displayed next to other examples of "classical" literature in a German-Jewish living room.[32]

The Weimar period was the first time in which a substantial number of young Jewish women entered the field of Wissenschaft des Judentums and became Jewish scholars. Representative of their work were the studies on the Prussian state and the Jews by Selma Stern (later known as Stern-Täubler), the studies on Jewish art by Rachel Wischnitzer, and the studies on the Salon women by Hannah Arendt. More important, a few classics written by or for Jewish women became accessible to German-Jewish women in modern translations. These translations aimed to create a new Jewish consciousness among their readers.

Bertha Pappenheim created the most important of these translations, a modern German version of the seventeenth-century Yiddish memoirs of Glückel von Hameln, a remarkable Westphalian Jewish woman. Her memoirs described the fate of a merchant's widow at the time of the Shabbatean movement. Pappenheim (a direct descendent of von Hameln) also translated into German the best-known Jewish classic for women. This work was the so-called women's Bible, the *Tse'enah u-re'enah*. A digest of parts of the Hebrew Bible and popular legends, this Yiddish-language book composed by Jacob ben Isaac Ashkenazi in the sixteenth century constituted almost the entire literary diet of Jewish women before the Enlightenment (although it had not originally been intended for a female audience). Well aware of the original spirit of this women's Bible, which was part of the tradition excluding women from traditional Hebrew studies, Pappenheim tried to turn the initially degrading character of the book into its opposite in her translation of 1930. As she made clear in her preface, her translation was meant to make emancipated Jewish women conscious of their cultural heritage as women and as Jews.

Pappenheim's translation of the *Tse'enah u-re'enah,* like the Buber-Rosenzweig Bible and the Goldschmidt Talmud, was read in a context totally different from that of the original versions. Whether German Jews read those texts because of deep religiosity or literary curiosity, in a secular society the books no longer functioned as the bases for the religious laws that governed premodern Jewish life. For most readers, moreover, those works had lost their centuries-old associative frameworks. If a passage of the Buber-Rosenzweig Bible were read in a Jewish youth group, few if any members would complement it with Rashi's traditional commentary. Many of them, however, would connect it with the better-known Christian interpretations, including Luther's translation, Rembrandt's biblical paintings, and Bach's spiritual music.

By translating the Bible and the Talmud, the scholars of the Jewish renaissance intended to restore to German Jews the basis of Jewish knowledge in the traditional Jewish society. Isolated from the traditional cultural framework, however, their translations became new sources, read differently and used with new intention. In this respect, the translators of Jewish sources were confronted with the same contradictions as the contemporary editors of Jewish encyclopedias. They, too, seemed to restore traditional Jewish knowledge while they actually combined restorative elements with innovative ones.

JEWISH KNOWLEDGE FROM A TO Z: THE *JÜDISCHES LEXIKON* AND THE *ENCYCLOPAEDIA JUDAICA*

The collating of knowledge has been only one of the functions of modern encyclopedias. Often, encyclopedias have been regarded as a means for the promotion of a particular worldview or philosophical system. The best-known example, Diderot's *Encyclopédie,* broke with established tradition and intellectual authorities in order to pursue its editors' ideological principles. The German *Brockhaus* of the mid-nineteenth century symbolized the unity of German language and culture despite Germany's political fragmentation. The German-Jewish encyclopedias of the twentieth century—the *Jüdisches Lexikon* and the *Encyclopaedia Judaica*—were not such audacious enterprises, and yet they, too, clearly exceeded the limits of a reference work. On one hand, they constituted systematic attempts to reconstruct as much as possible of the lost cultural memory of German Jews, and, on the other hand, they actively created a new associative framework, in which modern secular elements joined traditional elements. The encyclopedias included entries on a wide variety of topics, discussing both German-Jewish novels and the Talmud, both socialist Jewish movements and Hasidism, and the *Jüdisches Lexikon* allotted more space to the entry on Sigmund Freud than to the one on the medieval rabbinic authority Nahmanides.

The aim of the editors of German-Jewish encyclopedias was threefold: first, to restore the treasure of Jewish culture to the Jewish community (and to illustrate it to the non-Jewish world); second, to consolidate the leading role of German Wissenschaft des Judentums among international Jewish scholarship; and third, to create a modern Jewish consciousness among German-speaking Jews by redefining the contents of Judaism.

As early as the eighteenth century, the Swiss philosopher Johann Georg Sulzer had recognized the importance of encyclopedias in the process of modern nation building: "Such a work is a treasure of highest importance for a nation."[33] Indeed, many of the small nations that came into existence after World War I used encyclopedias to convey to their respective populations a cultural memory.[34] Although a German-Jewish encyclopedia certainly was no replacement for a national Jewish encyclopedia in Hebrew, its Zionist editors considered the project a preparatory stage—to enhance the collective consciousness of German-speaking Jews as a distinct group with its own history and culture—for a Hebrew version.

The idea of a Jewish encyclopedia was neither new nor restricted to the German context. A few years before the close of the nineteenth century, the Hebrew writer Ahad Ha'am explained in a letter to his Maecenas, Kalonymos Ze'ev Wissotzky, the urgent need for the creation of a Jewish encyclopedia:

> I always see in front of me this "cursed" question: How are we going to transmit to our children a thorough and intelligent understanding of Judaism, to the extent that they would love it, honor it, and be willing to sacrifice themselves for it? . . . After examining this problem, again and again, I came to realize that, if there is going to be an answer, it will have to be the same one that was given by Rabbi Juda the Nasi, Maimonides, and Rabbi Joseph Caro as a solution to the

problem of Torah-studying in their days: We need again a new book, written in easy Hebrew, that would include information on every aspect of Judaism.[35]

Ahad Ha'am was referring to his own project of a Jewish encyclopedia, the *Otsar Ha'Yahadut,* which never materialized. Several other encyclopedias, begun by such East European Jewish scholars as Joseph Klausner and Nahum Sokolow, also failed.

The situation in Germany during the nineteenth century was not much different. When Heinrich Graetz was asked, in 1887, to suggest a project to commemorate his seventieth birthday, he singled out as the most urgent desideratum the creation of a (German-language) Jewish encyclopedia. The project was begun, but like earlier attempts by David Cassel, Moritz Steinschneider, and Ludwig Philippson, it was laid aside after the first promising steps.[36]

The center of Jewish encyclopedic activities thus shifted to North America, where the sense of ethnic definition among the Jews was stronger than in imperial Germany and where the economic situation of the Jewish population was more favorable than in tsarist Russia. The first modern multivolume Jewish reference work, the *Jewish Encyclopedia,* was initiated and edited by the Austrian journalist Isidore Singer in New York, after a futile search for patrons in the Old World. Its twelve volumes, appearing between 1901 and 1905, bore witness to a gradual shift of the center of Jewish studies from Europe to the United States. Although many European scholars initially expressed staunch doubts about a project of this scale organized in the United States, even the most severe critics had to admit its success. Singer created a solid scholarly reference work that is still frequently used.[37]

The *Jewish Encyclopedia* served as the prototype for a sixteen-volume Russian Jewish encyclopedia, the *Evreiskaia Entsiklopediia* (1908–1913), and was followed suit by the ten volumes of the Hebrew *Otsar Yisrael* (1907–1913). In Germany, plans for a Jewish encyclopedia were laid to rest for three decades, following the failure of Graetz's proposal of 1887. When the plan to compile a *Jüdisches Lexikon* finally materialized in Weimar Germany, it was initiated not by one of the luminaries of Wissenschaft des Judentums but by a young archivist who had grown up without much Jewish knowledge and who had just completed his university studies. Georg Herlitz, born in Upper Silesia to an acculturated German-Jewish family, had acquired his Jewish knowledge as a student at the Hochschule für die Wissenschaft des Judentums. Herlitz thought of his studies at the Hochschule not as a preparation for his rabbinical career but as an opportunity to conduct a personal search of Judaism.

When Herlitz launched his plan for a compendium of Jewish knowledge, he found a collaborator in his former fellow student Bruno Kirschner. Both Herlitz and Kirschner had come to the Hochschule searching for a Lebensphilosophie; neither of them found it in Liberal Judaism, but instead the two became active in the Zionist student association. Rejecting rabbinical careers, both chose professions unusual for graduates of the Hochschule. Herlitz became the director of the newly established Zionist Organization's archives in Berlin, and Kirschner was employed by a large insurance company.

They both felt the need not only to acquire Jewish knowledge but also to transmit it to those who did not have the opportunity or the willingness to study at a Jewish institute of higher learning. Herlitz's initial plan was to create a small compendium for the internal use of Jewish student associations. When Kirschner became involved through the mediation of the director of the Jüdischer Verlag—Ahron Eliasberg—he insisted on creating a scholarly work on a larger scale.[38]

The early concepts of Herlitz and Kirschner were rather vague. The title of their project constantly changed, as did its scope. The date of publication announced in the *Jüdischer Verlag* was 1922.[39] At the end of 1922, material for more than a thousand pages had been prepared, but the completion of the project was not yet in sight. In a new outline the encyclopedia grew to four volumes, and publication was postponed.

Monetary inflation, which reached its peak in the fall of 1923, certainly contributed to the delay. The change of directors at the Jüdischer Verlag was another factor. Ahron Eliasberg, who had cooperated with Herlitz and Kirschner from the beginning, was replaced by Prague Zionist Siegmund Kaznelson in 1921. Although Kirschner was careful to adhere to scholarly standards and thus intended to further expand the projected four volumes, Kaznelson urged the two editors to accelerate their work and to reduce its bulk. In addition, he was instrumental in recruiting six "expert editors."[40]

The diverging views of Kaznelson and Kirschner overshadowed the last period of editorial work. After the appearance of the first volume in 1927, Kirschner resigned from his post as editor. In an angry letter to all participants, he accused Kaznelson of adorning the project with the celebrated names of the expert editors, while neglecting the plans of the two initiators. In addition, he criticized the unharmonious working atmosphere of "daily conflicts, resistance, intrigues, sabotages, and the ignoring of our editing activities." The prevalent tendency under Kaznelson's guidance was, according to Kirschner, "to finish quickly, no matter how."[41]

Indeed, Kaznelson succeeded in publishing the *Jüdisches Lexikon* within a short time (publication began in 1927 and was completed in 1930) and received for this work—despite Kirschner's complaints—mostly positive reviews. The four-volume limit was observed by the artificial division of the fourth volume into two parts. The four volumes, bound in five, consisted of 7,834 columns, or almost 4,000 pages. They contained about 15,000 entries and approximately 2,000 illustrations, compiled by more than 300 participants.[42]

Kaznelson's rush was caused not just by general financial considerations but also by the concrete pressure of a competitive enterprise. Only a few months after the appearance of the first volume of the *Jüdisches Lexikon,* the publication of another German-language Jewish encyclopedia, the *Encyclopaedia Judaica,* commenced. Like the *Lexikon,* the *Encyclopaedia* was the product of the cooperation of two initiators. Otherwise, the two projects had little in common during their initial phase. The backgrounds of the two pairs of editors were different, as were their original purposes, the scopes of the projects, and their places of publication.

In contrast to the German background of both Herlitz and Kirschner, the two initiators of the *Encyclopaedia,* Nahum Goldmann and Jakob Klatzkin, were both of East European origin and well versed in traditional Judaism. Herlitz and Kirschner remained virtually unknown, but Goldmann and Klatzkin became illustrious figures in Jewish history: the first as longtime president of the World Jewish Congress, the second as a Jewish philosopher and Zionist thinker. Lithuanian-born Goldmann moved with his family to Frankfurt am Main at the age of six, when his father got a job there as a Hebrew teacher. Jakob Klatzkin, son of a famous rabbi in Belorussia, studied in Switzerland and Germany, where he got to know the young Nahum Goldmann and his father. As an already renowned Hebrew writer and philosopher, Klatzkin renewed his friendship with Nahum Goldmann after World War I. In the postwar years both edited a short-lived Zionist periodical (*Freie Zionistische Blätter*) and retreated for a few months to the Bavarian artists' resort of Murnau.[43]

When the two moved to Berlin in 1923, they took with them the plan to establish a Hebrew publishing house, the Eschkol-Verlag.[44] All the intended publications of Eschkol—"classical Hebrew literature in modern scholarly editions"—would center around a projected ten-volume Hebrew encyclopedia. In their preliminary program of the encyclopedia in 1924,

Goldmann and Klatzkin referred to a committee of scholars and writers, consisting of Ahad Ha'am, Leo Baeck, Simon Dubnow, Ismar Elbogen, and Gotthold Weil, among others.[45]

In this early phase, Goldmann and Klatzkin clearly had in mind a Hebrew publication, though they thought that a possible German edition "might be published . . . in an abridged version."[46] At a later stage, Goldmann and Klatzkin envisioned the simultaneous publication of the *Encyclopaedia* in Hebrew, German, and English. Goldmann recalled this project as his first experience in international Jewish affairs: "Since it was to be a trilingual reference work, it was to be internationally financed. Committees would have to be set up in various countries, including America, to secure the scholarly and financial cooperation of the Jewish communities. What the scheme in fact amounted to was a kind of world Jewish organization, which was to represent the major achievement of modern Jewish scholarship."[47]

Because of financial problems, however, the *Encyclopaedia* was not published in all three languages. Goldmann returned home empty-handed from a tour to America that had aimed at enlisting support for the English edition. Similarly, Anthony de Rothschild of London, to whom Albert Einstein had introduced Goldmann, did not grant financial support. The Hebrew edition suffered a serious setback after Hayim Nahman Bialik's Devir publishing house refused to cooperate in the project. Goldmann almost abandoned the entire enterprise, but he then received unexpected support from Jakob Goldschmidt, the managing director of the Darmstadt und National Bank and a leading German-Jewish philanthropist.[48]

With Goldschmidt's support, Goldmann and Klatzkin could proceed with the publication of the German edition. Between 1928 and 1934, ten volumes of the German *Encyclopaedia* appeared, and two Hebrew volumes of the *Encyclopedia Yisra'elit: Eshkol* were published in 1929 and 1932. The English edition was to be postponed until the completion of the German one.[49]

Thus the *Encyclopaedia Judaica,* planned as an international publication, became an essentially German-Jewish piece of work. It was initiated by two Jewish intellectuals living in Berlin, compiled mostly by German-Jewish scholars, addressed to a German-Jewish audience, and—apart from the two Hebrew volumes—composed exclusively in German. Ismar Elbogen, the assistant editor, was the leading Jewish historian in Weimar Germany and taught at the Hochschule für die Wissenschaft des Judentums. Most of the eighteen departmental editors lived in Germany as well. As was the case with the *Lexikon,* the intended scope of the *Encyclopaedia* was exceeded. The projected limit of ten volumes was reached in 1934, with the tenth volume containing entries through the letter *L.* The remaining volumes never appeared, as a result of the political developments in Germany.[50]

The *Lexikon* and the *Encyclopaedia,* originally conceived from different perspectives, shared some characteristics: both became means to raise the level of Jewish knowledge among the German-speaking Jewish population; both were based on solid scholarly endeavors; and some participants and a few editors, such as Ismar Elbogen and Max Soloweitschik, worked on both projects.[51] Still, a major difference between the two projects remained visible: the *Lexikon* was addressed chiefly to the lay Jewish population, whereas the *Encyclopaedia* aimed at both lay readers and professionals.[52] It thus consisted of lengthy central articles and concise peripheral entries. Some of the central articles in the *Encyclopaedia,* such as the three-hun-dred-column entry on Bible, were of book length. The most intellectually significant contribution of the *Encyclopaedia* was its emphasis on aspects of Jewish history and culture that had been widely neglected by traditional Wissenschaft des Judentums. The social and economic history of the Jews was explored more thoroughly than the traditional history of suffering and scholarship (*Leidens- und Gelehrtengeschichte*), as reflected in Graetz's *History of the Jews.* Lengthy entries on taxes, the Jewish workers' move-ment, the Jewish community, and trades underlined this tendency. Not one of the sixteen articles covering more than fifty columns was dedicated exclusively to intellectual history. Instead, the articles included an entry on Jewish community studies, a largely sociological treatment of talmudic issues, and a thorough discussion of Yiddish culture and literature.

By adopting the Anglo-Saxon system of identifying the authors of indi-vidual articles rather than publishing articles anonymously, as is common in German encyclopedias, the editors hoped to produce a few original con-tributions by authors whose fame exceeded the narrow realm of Jewish studies. The two Jewish encyclopedias did not attract Jewish authors as famous as the contributors to the *Encyclopedia Britannica,* whose thir-teenth edition of 1926 contained entries by Albert Einstein, Sigmund Freud, and Leon Trotsky. But a few authors whose specialties lay outside Jewish issues were recruited. Albert Einstein was not among the contribu-tors, but his cousin, the famous musicologist Alfred Einstein, was. Walter Benjamin, too, wrote an article for the *Encyclopaedia.* He was assigned the topic "Jews in German Culture" in the article on Germany and produced his first major piece on a specifically Jewish topic for this purpose.[53]

The work of Benjamin's friend Gershom Scholem occupied an important place in the main corpus of the *Encyclopaedia*. His hundred columns on Kabbalah were Scholem's first book-length general discussion of this topic. This largely forgotten piece of work is an important source on early Kabbalah scholarship and on Scholem's scholarly development. Moreover, it represented the will of the editors to allot to the new discipline of Kabbalah a prominent place in the project. Scholem's entry on Kabbalah was the third-longest article in the entire ten volumes.[54]

The editors' intention to emphasize the new subdisciplines of Wissenschaft des Judentums, such as statistics and folkloristics, was even more evident in the compact *Jüdisches Lexikon*. One of the most fascinating entries is the almost seventy-column article on statistics. In more than one hundred tables and two maps, leading Jewish sociologists summarized the most recent results of Jewish populational and occupational statistics. Numerous articles on folkloristic aspects of Judaism made the scholarly results of this young discipline available to the public for the first time. The Zionist orientation of the *Lexikon* was underlined by the inclusion of such entries as "Workers' Question in Palestine" and by the reprint of the Balfour Declaration on an entire page. In the *Encyclopaedia,* where those contemporary issues were less emphasized, lengthy articles on the Hebrew language and the city of Jerusalem indirectly supported the Zionist cause.

It would, however, be a distortion of the two reference works to depict them as exclusively Zionist enterprises. Although the publishers and chief editors of the encyclopedias were Zionists, their main financial backers were not.[55] Both works aimed at a much larger audience than the Zionist minority among German Jews. In order to reach more people, both the *Lexikon* and the *Encyclopaedia* included numerous articles by non-Zionist authors. Especially in the sensitive area of contemporary Judaism, the editors tried hard to create a balanced depiction of the various factions within the Jewish community. Nahum Goldmann, who was responsible for articles covering contemporary Judaism in the *Encyclopaedia,* chose as coeditor the Liberal rabbi Benno Jacob. The contributions on Liberal and Orthodox German Jews and their organizations were left to their own representatives. Following this principle, Ludwig Holländer, the director of the CV, was assigned the article on his organization, and Orthodox leader Jacob Rosenheim wrote a long entry on the organization he represented, Agudas Israel. These articles unavoidably propagated non-Zionist positions.

The struggle for a balanced depiction led sometimes to contradictions. The term *assimilation,* for instance, was defined in a quite different way in the contributions of the young Zionist historian Hans Kohn and of Ludwig Holländer. Not denying that assimilation made Jews more aware of the problems of modern Jewish society, Kohn emphasized that it created the type of uprooted Jew who does not feel deep bonds to any specific place. Often, he maintained, assimilation led to undignified and hypocritical behavior. Holländer, in contrast, claimed that assimilation meant "unprincipled adjustment of the Jews to their non-Jewish surroundings."[56]

To gain popularity among a great number of German Jews, the encyclopedias had to be more than informative, objective, and scholarly compendia; they also had to be attractive. Indeed, both reference works were not just practical sources of reference but also belles lettres in the literal sense: beautiful books printed on high-luster paper and adorned with numerous black-and-white and colored illustrations. Moreover, each volume of the *Lexikon* contained several pages of traditional Jewish sheet music. Sales figures reveal that both encyclopedias were successful, and the *Jüdisches Lexikon* became an especially popular work and one of the bestsellers of the Jüdischer Verlag.[57]

As a means of popularization of the knowledge of Judaism, the two projects—especially the *Lexikon*—could be compared to the *Konversationslexikon,* the term used for a general encyclopedia in nineteenth-century German. Although the Jewish encyclopedias were not conceived as general encyclopedias, they too were to enable German Jews to engage in substantive—albeit not too specialized—conversation on Jewish topics, just as they would converse on German literature, French fashion, and American jazz dance. The editors of the two encyclopedias might have had Frau Oberamtmann Rollmaus, a figure from Gustav Freytag's popular novel *Verlorene Handschrift,* in mind when speculating about the possible effect of their products. Frau Rollmaus could tell everybody a bit about Englishmen and Tartars, comets and poets, and they may have envisioned German Jews conversing on Khazars and Karaites, Kabbalists and Kalonymides. But they might also have thought of the limits of their projects by remembering Frau Rollmaus' children, who revealed that all her knowledge was based only on her readings of the Konversationslexikon.

Most critics enthusiastically welcomed the publication of both reference works as the best means to complement the Jewish bourgeoisie with a good portion of Jewish Bildung. The *Jüdische Rundschau* stated an opinion shared by non-Zionists: "In recent years, there has been a sharp increase in the demand for Jewish knowledge. After a generation that became ever more remote from Judaism, we see now a generation that wants to regain access to the knowledge which had been lost by the development of the last century. . . . We believe therefore that the *Jüdische Lexikon* has come at a right moment, and fulfills an important function in the process of re-Judaization of the present Jewish generation."[58]

Franz Rosenzweig also expressed this view in his comment on the *Encyclopaedia* in the Liberal periodical *Der Morgen*. Like Ahad Ha'am, he considered a modern Jewish encyclopedia similar in importance to the monumental traditional Jewish reference works from the Talmud to Maimonides' Mishne Torah to the Shulhan Arukh. For Rosenzweig, the modern encyclopedias were significant because they "did not presuppose anything, not even the knowledge of Hebrew letters." He expressed his hope that the *Encyclopaedia Judaica* would find its place among "the necessary interior of any Jewish home," between the Konversationslexikon and the piano.[59]

Compared to the praise that both works received, negative criticism was negligible. Orthodox circles rejected the encyclopedias' view concerning traditional Jewish sources, thus echoing their position toward the Buber-Rosenzweig Bible translation.[60] The most vehement attack against the *Jüdisches Lexikon* was written by Talmud translator Lazarus Goldschmidt, who listed scores of errors and inaccuracies and concluded that the *Lexikon* lacked any significance as a reference work and should not be used.[61] The only Zionist equivalent of Goldschmidt's critique came from the one-time editor of the *Lexikon,* Bruno Kirschner.[62] There is reason to suppose that the harsh criticisms of both Goldschmidt and Kirschner had personal rather than professional motives; Goldschmidt may have been disappointed because he was not asked to participate, and Kirschner's opinion may have been influenced by his quarrel with the publisher and his resignation from the editorial board.

In no other place and time were two such important Jewish reference works produced. The *Jüdisches Lexikon* and the *Encyclopaedia Judaica* were among the outstanding creations of the Jewish cultural renaissance during the Weimar period. With their monumental projects, the creators of the encyclopedias hoped to launch a new phase of German-Jewish scholarship. Instead, however, their work became the grandiose eulogy of German-Jewish history during its twilight hour.

IN SEARCH OF SYNTHESIS: THE TOTAL VIEW OF JEWISH HISTORY

In his magisterial study of the German academic community between 1890 and 1933, Fritz Ringer viewed the search for synthesis as one of the most characteristic traits of the "German mandarins" in the Weimar period: "Synthesis, the whole, understanding, viewing: the slogans were always the same. Biologists and physicians meant to study the whole organism; pedagogues and psychologists, the whole man. In sociology and in economics, it was the whole community."[63] One is tempted to add Jewish studies to Ringer's listing of disciplines. Like biologists, sociologists, and economists, scholars of Judaism in the Weimar period were eager to present a synthesis of their previous research. This drive for wholeness was in large part a reaction to the increasing specialization of the discipline. Not willing to close themselves off in an ivory tower of highly specialized subdisciplines, the leading representatives of Wissenschaft des Judentums searched for ways to expose the Jewish public to popular, and at the same time scholarly, summaries of the first century of research in the field.

The most ambitious attempt to present an all-inclusive "Outline of Wissenschaft des Judentums" was initiated by the Society for the Promotion of Wissenschaft des Judentums in the early twentieth century. As early as 1903, the newly founded society published its plan to collect the results of one hundred years of research in thirty-one monographs on various areas of Jewish scholarship. In the three following decades, some of those monographs were completed. Many of them still serve as important summaries of their specific fields of research or as original contributions to Jewish studies.[64]

While the society was instrumental in initiating several other "grand projects," such as the *Corpus Tannaiticum* and the *Germania Judaica*,[65] the Zionist Jüdischer Verlag contributed most to the construction of a total view of Jewish history and culture. Both the *Jüdisches Lexikon* and the Goldschmidt Talmud translation were published by the Jüdischer Verlag. In the field of Jewish history, the Jüdischer Verlag issued the pioneering ten-volume *World History of the Jewish People* by Russian-Jewish historian Simon Dubnow. Dubnow, who lived in Berlin between 1922 and 1933, had originally written his oeuvre in Russian, but it appeared first in German translation (1925–1929).

Dubnow was much praised by scholars and the public for having provided a Jewish history that included aspects of social and economic history ignored by Graetz. At the same time, however, questions arose concerning Dubnow's assumption that one scholar could single-handedly write a critical history of the Jews. Among the critics was Ismar Elbogen, the chief Jewish historian of Weimar Germany. Elbogen was convinced that because of the rapid expansion of Jewish scholarship in the first third of the twen-

Ismar Elbogen lecturing at the Hochschule für die Wissenschaft des Judentums. Courtesy Bildarchiv Abraham Pisarek, Berlin.

tieth century, only a collaborative effort was appropriate for such a monumental project of Jewish history.[66]

Elbogen himself was involved in two attempts to write a collaborative Jewish history, both which had to be abandoned prematurely. In 1924, Elbogen had initiated a newly revised edition of Graetz's standard Jewish history. In a memorandum in which Elbogen laid out the concept for this new edition, he stressed that a new Jewish history could no longer be written from the perspective of the nineteenth century; in this memorandum he sought to moderate Graetz's harsh judgments on the Catholic Church and medieval knighthood, and to integrate more Jewish history of Eastern Europe, Palestine, and North America.[67] It is not entirely clear why the revised edition of Graetz's Jewish history never materialized, but apparently the objection of Graetz's descendants played a part in the failure of the project.[68]

When Elbogen embarked for the second time on a voluminous historical project, it was not a revision of any former project but an entirely new enterprise. Its initiator and supposed publisher was Peter Reinhold, a former (non-Jewish) minister of finance in the government of the German Reich. The project constituted the first plan for a multiauthored, multivolume Jewish history, to be written by a dozen or so of the most prominent Jewish historians in various countries.[69] Furthermore, this *History of the Jews from the Earliest Times until the Present Age* would have been of special interest for the Anglophone Jewish world, as it was intended to be published simultaneously in German and English. The participation of scholars of several countries and the bilingual edition pointed to the international spread of Wissenschaft des Judentums. At the same time, the leaders of the project tried to stress the preeminent position of German scholars in the discipline by choosing a German editor and a German publisher.

Elbogen asked for contributions in early 1929 and set a deadline of March 1931. Each of the twelve volumes was to be limited to 550 pages; an initial edition of five thousand copies would be printed in each language. According to Elbogen, the work was to be based on the research by the contributors in their areas of specialization, "but the material shall be composed in such a fashion that it is easily readable for educated amateurs. Notes shall be restricted as much as possible; indispensable discussions on the clarification of scholarly problems shall be put to the end."[70]

One of the proposed contributors, Cecil Roth, emphasized in his initial response to Elbogen's invitation—which he accepted with the "utmost gladness"—that the project was "something for which there is a crying need in the Jewish world today from every point of view, and which should earn you the gratitude of every person, whether Jew or Gentile, who is interested in our glorious past."[71] Of the seventeen persons whom Elbogen approached in 1929, only three declined to participate and one postponed his decision. Most started their work in the following year. With a few exceptions, the fourteen participants represented the elite of Jewish scholarship in six countries: from Germany, Ismar Elbogen, Leo Baeck, Eugen Täubler, Selma Stern-Täubler, Bernhard Kahn, and the two Russian emigrés, Simon Dubnow and Mark Wischnitzer; from England, Cecil Roth; from Italy, Umberto Cassuto; from France, Maurice Liber; from Palestine, Yitshak Fritz Baer and Elias Auerbach; and from the United States, Jacob Mann and Solomon Zeitlin.

In January 1930 Elbogen informed his publisher that the contributors for five volumes had already begun their work. The first chapters of the project were thus under way when later in the same month Peter Reinhold sent an alarming letter to Elbogen, informing him to "suspend the work for our common project for the time being" for financial reasons, obviously caused by the worldwide economic crisis.[72]

Reinhold continued to assure Elbogen that the delay was only temporary.[73] By 1932, Elias Auerbach had finished his first volume on the early history of the Jewish people. Because the future of the project as a whole was unclear, he had it published separately by Reinhold's K. Wolff publishing house. Auerbach's study, *Wüste und gelobtes Land* (Desert and promised land) is characterized more by its popular style than by its scholarly innovations. In a letter to Sigmund Freud, Arnold Zweig recommended Auerbach's book, saying that "it makes extremely stimulating exciting reading and is written with exemplary objectivity." Freud indeed read the book as preparation for his work on Moses but found it disappointing.[74] When *Wüste und gelobtes Land* appeared, Elbogen still believed that his project would be realized. As late as 16 January 1933, he informed Cecil Roth that "now the publishing house is hopeful again and wants to start the subscription for the whole series this fall." As this same letter shows, Roth had already completed his contribution on England.[75] He later recalled that the "section of the Jews in England which I prepared in connexion with this project served as the nucleus of my History of the Jews in England."[76]

Elbogen's confidence proved to be unwarranted, however. This time the stumbling block was not an economic crisis but a political catastrophe. Only two weeks after Elbogen's letter to Roth, Adolf Hitler was appointed chancellor of the German Reich. The political change had immediate implications for Peter Reinhold's publishing house. Instead of a Jewish history, he published Arthur Gobineau's *Essay on the Inequality of the Human Races,* "in order to give the publishing house [which had been owned by Kurt Wolff] an Aryan face."[77]

Economic and political developments deprived the Jewish world of a project that would have become a unique contribution to the popularization of Jewish studies. Moreover, such a synthesis of Jewish historiography from scholars of many countries would have indicated to later generations the status of Jewish studies in the 1920s. For us, it remains to list this project as the ambitious, perhaps too ambitious, culmination of various attempts to present the results of the first century of Wissenschaft des Judentums to the Jewish community at large, and thus to contribute to the process of reappropriation of Jewish knowledge.

In his penetrating analysis of Wissenschaft des Judentums, Gershom Scholem repeatedly pointed to what he identified as a dialectical process immanent in the development of this discipline throughout its existence in Germany. Quoting Moritz Steinschneider's statement (mentioned in Chapter 1) on granting the remains of Judaism a decent burial by means of scholarship, Scholem went on to say,

> A breath of the funereal did in fact cling to the atmosphere of this discipline for a century; occasionally there is something ghostlike about this literature. Yet at the same time the positive element quite unintentionally asserts itself. In many of these scholars, romantic enthusiasm overcomes their original intention of liquidating, spiritualizing, and de-actualizing Judaism. It drives them to positive insight far removed from what they originally envisioned.[78]

Although the essence of Scholem's analysis is certainly correct, his tendency to designate the positive elements of Wissenschaft des Judentums as an unintended side effect of its overall achievements requires correction. Such a view—already doubtful concerning many of the nineteenth-century scholars of Judaism—easily leads to a distorted image when dealing with their successors in the early twentieth century.

Scholem was not only a critic but also a product of Wissenschaft des Judentums. In his emphasis on stronger connections between Jewish scholarship and Jewish life, he was part of a trend that dominated this discipline in Weimar Germany. The translation of essential sources, the transmission of the wholeness of Judaism, and the projected compilation of a synthesis of Jewish history were several expressions of this trend. And one might add other examples, such as the establishment of new subdisciplines within Wissenschaft des Judentums.

Jewish genealogy and social welfare research attempted to address concrete needs of German Jews by means of scholarship; the first aimed at facilitating individuals' search for their roots in the faceless modern society, and the second sought to alleviate the worsening socioeconomic crisis affecting the Jewish population of Weimar Germany. By the late 1920s all three rabbinical seminaries had introduced courses on contemporary Jewish developments, covering both welfare issues and demography.

Ismar Elbogen maintained in a 1922 summary of the first century of Wissenschaft des Judentums that living Judaism "must constitute the focus . . . and the leading idea" of Jewish scholarship.[79] When clarifying this demand a decade later, Elbogen went so far as to state that "Wissenschaft des Judentums loses its right to existence if it is not attached to living

Judaism."[80] He thus encouraged the study of such new subfields as Jewish art, music, and sociology. The numerous projects initiated to convey the substance of Judaism to the Jewish population formed the most significant attempt to guarantee the further right to existence of Wissenschaft des Judentums. In a pugnacious attack on the Jewish Hegelianism of the founders of the discipline, Zalman Rubaschoff (Shazar), a historian who later became president of Israel, called their products the "first fruits of de-Judaization." Yet when Rubaschoff wrote these words in 1918, the first fruits of what contemporaries called the "process of re-Judaization" had begun to grow.[81]

Part III

In Search of Authenticity

The Invention of the Authentic Jew: German-Jewish Literature

> In spite of the barbarous fur cap which covers his head, and the still
> more barbarous notions which fill it, I esteem the Polish Jew more
> highly than his German counterpart, even though the latter wears a
> beaver on his head and carries Jean Paul in it. . . . The Polish Jew with
> his dirty fur cap, vermin-infested beard, smell of garlic, and his jabber is
> certainly preferable to many other Jews I know who shine with the mag-
> nificence of gilt-edged government bonds.
>
> —Heinrich Heine to Christian August Keller (1 September 1822)

On the eve of World War I, a debate in one of the most prestigious
German cultural journals attracted the attention of a great part of the
German literary world. Moritz Goldstein, a young Zionist, published an
article in the conservative *Kunstwart* in which he criticized the control that
Jews wielded over German literature. According to Goldstein, this situation reflected the extremely unhealthy state of German and Jewish culture.
He suggested, therefore, that German Jews should retreat from their conspicuous position in German literature and instead concentrate on Jewish
culture. More specifically, he called for the creation of a distinct German-
Jewish literature, written by Jewish authors on Jewish topics for a Jewish
audience.[1]

A major criterion of such a German-Jewish literature was, according to
Goldstein, the creation of a new type of fictional Jew:

The Jewish drama, *the* Jewish novel has not yet been written. The creation of a
new type of Jew—not in real life, but in literature—is of utmost importance in
this respect. We all see life, people, and nature as our artists present them to us.

But what kind of Jew did they show us? . . . The demonic-wicked Shylock and
the good-natured comical Jewish peddler; until now there exist almost only those
two extremes. The Jew of our likeness, our Jewish ideal of the Jew, is still
lacking. Jewish writers, to work [*heran*]![2]

In Weimar Germany, Jewish writers, no matter what their background
and style, were strikingly uniform in their depictions of Jewish characters.
While most portrayed the assimilated "non-Jewish" German Jew negatively,
they constructed fictitious counterimages of what appeared to them to be
authentic Jews, such as East European Jews, oriental Jews, or heretical-mes-
sianic figures. What made those characters look authentic in the eyes of
acculturated German Jews was that they appeared to be unaffected by
Western civilization. By speaking a Jewish language, being well-versed in
religious traditions, and proudly displaying their Jewishness, the characters
symbolized a direct link with their ancestors. Their interpretation of their
ancestors' tradition could lead to internal conflict and even revolt—as was
the case with Jewish heretics—but never to the shallowness that many
German-Jewish writers identified with modern Judaism in the West.

The Jewish cultural renaissance, represented by the search for community and the transmission of knowledge, also took place on a third level.
This level was the longing for Jewish authenticity, as expressed in the
realms of literature, music, and art. While scholars, rabbis, communal
leaders, and teachers aimed at the reconstruction of Jewish Gemeinschaft
and the promotion of Jewish knowledge, the writers and artists discussed
in the following two chapters envisioned the ultimate fulfillment of this
renaissance by creating ideal types of Jews.[3]

This idealization of authentic Jewish characters and its implicit critique
of Western civilization reflected a tendency in contemporary German literature. Many popular writers in Weimar Germany evoked positive images
from distant realms in time or space to offer remedies for what they perceived to be the malaise of modern European civilization. This technique
became a prominent literary motif, known as Exoticism.[4] The construction of the authentic Jewish ideal, however, went beyond general Exoticist
tendencies.

Non-Jewish German writers turned to Eastern spiritualism, Native
American mythology, or, for that matter, Jewish mysticism (as in Gustav
Meyrink's best-seller of 1915, *Der Golem*) for images, but the German-
Jewish writers discussed here described a culture related to them histori-
cally and emotionally. By selecting what appeared to them as genuine and,
at the same time, exotic Jewish traits, they were able to construct alterna-

tive Jewish identities for themselves, at least in the realm of literature. Referring to Martin Buber's depiction of Hasidism and his reception among many groups of German Jews, Paul Mendes-Flohr termed this search for alternative identities an "aesthetic affirmation of Judaism."[5] In their daily lives, those writers continued to be an integral part of German culture and Western civilization, but in their literary dreams many of them admired the apparently authentic Jewish world of Eastern Europe and the Orient.

THE GERMAN JEW BETWEEN ANTISEMITISM AND SELF-DENIAL

Zionists like Moritz Goldstein were not the only Jews to demand the creation of a literary Jewish ideal. Ludwig Geiger, a Liberal Jew and editor of the *Allgemeine Zeitung des Judentums,* had, a few months before the appearance of Goldstein's essay, envisioned the "German Jew, as we would like him to be: assiduous, solid, diligent, always aiming at the highest, working only for others, never pushing himself forward, faithful, abstinent, but still able to enjoy the happiness that he always longed for, without having fought for it recklessly."[6] Geiger's vision of the upright German-Jewish patriot, accepted as an equal by German society, never became the basis for the literary depiction of German Jews in Weimar Germany. Instead, most Jewish writers characterized their German-Jewish protagonists as uprooted individuals, torn between antisemitism and denial of their Jewishness.

Intensified antisemitism was important in the works of German-Jewish authors. In some cases, the contemporary context was veiled behind the mask of a historical novel, as in Lion Feuchtwanger's best-seller *Jud Süß* (1925), about the rise and sudden fall of the seventeenth-century Württemberg court Jew Joseph Süß Oppenheimer, who was publicly executed once his patron had died. The parallels to the tragic fate of Weimar Germany's Jewish foreign minister, Walther Rathenau, were obvious to most readers. As Feuchtwanger recalled, he initially intended to write a novel about Rathenau and his murder by rightist extremists in 1922, but he ultimately pondered the "same problematics, only two centuries earlier."[7]

In other cases, contemporary antisemitism was depicted with almost prophetic literary skills. The Austrian-Jewish writer Hugo Bettauer described the expulsion of Viennese Jews as early as 1922, in his "utopian novel" *Die Stadt ohne Juden* (The city without Jews). His plot became the basis for a

widely discussed movie and for a literary remake set in Berlin, Artur Landsberger's "tragic satire" *Berlin ohne Juden* (Berlin without Jews, 1925). As
both authors were to experience, their novels were neither utopian nor
satiric. Bettauer was killed in his office in Vienna in 1925 by a German
nationalist, and Landsberger committed suicide in 1933, when his literary
scenario became reality.

Like Feuchtwanger's character Jud Süß, Bettauer's and Landsberger's
German (and Austrian) Jews were incarnations of what Isaac Deutscher
has called the "non-Jewish Jew."[8] They were reminded of their Jewishness
mainly because the outside world viewed them as Jews, not because they
found any particular value in Jewishness. It is the Jewish hero of Bettauer's
novel who states, "The leaven, which is added to the bread dough, tastes
quite awful, but still one cannot make bread without it. In the same way,
one has to regard the Jews: leaven, in itself unpleasant and even damaging
in too-large quantities, but in the right mixture indispensable for the daily
bread."[9]

A brief analysis of two of the best-known Jewish characters in the writings of Weimar Germany's Jews—Kurt Tucholsky's Herr Wendriner and
Jakob Wassermann's Gregor Waremme—will further illustrate the ambivalent attitude of German-Jewish writers toward Judaism. Between 1922 and
1930 Tucholsky, the most pungent political satirist of Weimar Germany,
published sixteen essays about the fictional Wendriner in Germany's
leading leftist magazine, *Die Weltbühne*, under the pseudonym Kaspar
Hauser. In his long monologues in Berlin dialect mixed with a few Yiddish
expressions, Herr Wendriner advocated an authoritarian education for his
children, talked about betraying his wife, and favored a nationalist German
policy. Among contemporaries, Herr Wendriner was seen as the typical
restless, self-centered, materialistic, "non-Jewish" German Jew. In the last
and most biting essay, Tucholsky told of Herr Wendriner's compromising
with a—then still fictitious—Nazi dictatorship. Wendriner, in possession
of a "yellow card," was certain of his immunity as a "protected citizen"
and welcomed the discipline created by the new regime ("Na, jedenfalls
herrscht Ordnung. Also, Ordnung herrscht mal"), while justifying antisemitism toward the Ostjuden.[10]

Like Herr Wendriner, Gregor Waremme, alias Georg Warschauer, was the
opposite of the ideal German Jew envisioned by Ludwig Geiger. Waremme-
Warschauer was the Jewish protagonist in Jakob Wassermann's *Der Fall
Maurizius* (The Maurizius case, 1928), one of the most popular novels by a
Jewish author in Weimar Germany.[11] As his two names suggest, Waremme-

Warschauer, born in Germany to parents of East European Jewish background at the end of the nineteenth century, was a split personality. In his rejection of his Jewishness and his failure to be accepted as a German, he seemed like a caricature of the radically assimilated German Jew. He converted to Christianity, invented for himself a new Christian childhood, and strove, unsuccessfully, to be recognized as a German ultra-nationalist.

Other German-Jewish characters in contemporary novels of Jewish authors, such as Alfred Engländer in Franz Werfel's *Barbara oder die Frömmigkeit* (1929) and Dr. Trebitsch in Joseph Roth's *Das Spinnennetz* (1923), also denied their Jewishness. The fictional Dr. Trebitsch, depicted as a leader of a secret right-wing antisemitic organization, was modeled after Arthur Trebitsch, an Austrian Jew who considered himself a follower of Otto Weininger and who figured prominently in the development of the Austrian Nazi movement. It was certainly no coincidence that a few years later philosopher Theodor Lessing published the first systematic study on Jewish self-hatred, including the case of Arthur Trebitsch.[12]

Such fictional German Jews as Herr Wendriner and Warschauer-Waremme were depicted as outsiders in German society, which to a certain degree reflected the experiences of their creators. Tucholsky abandoned the Jewish religion and converted to Protestantism during World War I.[13] Like Heine's conversion a century earlier, Tucholsky's dissociation from the Jewish religion did not make him more respectable in the eyes of his numerous enemies. He shared Heine's ambivalent feelings toward Germany and left the country before 1933. Tucholsky's ruthless critique of assimilated German Jews was often mistaken for Jewish self-hatred, as Heine's remarks about his fellow German Jews had been.

Unlike Tucholsky, Jakob Wassermann never dissociated himself from the Jewish community; however, his repeated efforts to be recognized as both German and Jew ended in utter failure. His moving confession *Mein Leben als Deutscher und Jude* (My life as German and Jew, 1921) depicts the dilemma of his split identity. Although he tried hard to become a German writer, in the end he had to realize that he was never recognized as such:

> I had imagined that I had given the Germans an essentially German book, a book grown out of the soul of the people, so to speak. I imagined that because a Jew had written it, I had proved that a Jew could establish his oneness with the nation, could overcome the prejudgment of his alien character not only by resolve and by seizing opportunities, but by the inner nature of his being. But these expectations were disappointed. . . . The German public could not be permitted to see that a Jew had written so peculiarly German a book.[14]

A decade before the Nazis rose to power, Wassermann admitted the "hopelessness of all efforts. . . . Vain to live for them [the Germans] and die for them. They say: he is a Jew."[15]

Critics during the Weimar period and later have accused Wassermann and Tucholsky of Jewish self-hatred or self-denial. In his study *Der jüdische Selbsthaß* (Jewish self-hatred, 1930), Theodor Lessing included Wassermann as one of his examples.[16] A few decades later, Gershom Scholem awarded Tucholsky the dubious honor of being "one of the most gifted, most convinced, and most offensive Jewish anti-Semites [who accomplished] on a definitive level what the anti-Semites themselves were unable to bring about."[17] The implicit identification of the author with his literary characters is, however, in both cases based on a misperception and overlooks the critical distance of Tucholsky and Wassermann from their German-Jewish protagonists. The characters are portrayed negatively not because they are Jewish but, on the contrary, precisely because they are "non-Jewish Jews" denying their Jewishness.

Tucholsky's private statements leave no doubt about his disgust for the extremely assimilated Jew, whom he called the German Jew. His biting critique culminated in a letter to his brother Fritz two weeks before his suicide in Sweden in 1935: "Undoubtedly the German Jews were the worst of all—because they have adapted all the bad characteristics of the krauts [*boches*]. The Germans are not Judaized—but the Jews are *verbocht*."[18] As soon as the fictional German Jews leave Germany, however, they become less detestable and sometimes even return to traditional Judaism. Waremme-Warschauer, for example, discovered the traditional sources of his Jewishness when, after long wanderings, he visited Hasidic Jews in the United States.[19]

Like many other German-Jewish writers, Tucholsky and Wassermann rejected the image of an assimilationist Jewish community while praising what they regarded as authentic Jews outside Germany. The Wendriners and Waremmes thus represented only one side of a more complex literary scenario. For Tucholsky, whose first article in *Die Schaubühne* (later to become *Die Weltbühne*) was a tribute to Yiddish theater, the Ostjude embodied many of the positive qualities he yearned for among German Jews.[20] Wassermann, to whom the Ostjude was not a positive counterpart to the German Jew, constructed another authentic Jewish ideal in the form of the oriental Jew.

THE JEW AS ORIENTAL

Wassermann, unlike Tucholsky, considered the European or Western Jew a most pitiable creature, representing "shame, misery, humbleness, darkness." For him, however, the Asian Jew meant "power, honor, glory, and great deeds." Referring to these two types of Jews, Wassermann left no doubt that the "task of the modern Jew is mainly to forget the first and to adopt the latter."[21] In one of his speeches on Judaism, titled "The Spirit of the Orient and Judaism," Martin Buber made a similar distinction: he classified Judaism together with Chinese, Indian, and Middle Eastern cultures as part of the Asian spirit, opposed to occidental civilization.[22] Asked by Buber to elaborate on this contrast, Wassermann contributed an essay to the almanac of the Prague Zionist student organization, *Bar Kochba*. Under the title "The Jew as Oriental," Wassermann characterized Western Jews as Jews without foundations, members of a community destined to fade away gradually. In contrast, the oriental Jew is "certain of himself, of the world, of humankind. . . . He is free, while they are slaves. He speaks the truth, while they are lying. He knows his sources, he lives with his mothers, he rests and creates, while they are the eternally wandering unchangeables [*Unwandelbaren*]."[23]

Wassermann never specified whom he identified as oriental Jews. For him, as for many other German-Jewish writers, the oriental Jew was a symbolic contrast to the stereotype of assimilated German Jews, rather than a specific type in Jewish history. This counterimage could be a biblical warrior or a talmudic sage but was always immediately identifiable as an authentic Jew, both externally (by dress and language) and by distinct intellectual values.

The glorification of the Orient as a source of profound spirituality and wisdom was not reserved for Jewish authors. What contemporary authors meant by "the Orient" was not the geographical region but an idea that emerged in the minds of Western intellectuals. In Germany the connection between spirituality and the Orient had deep roots, reaching from Goethe's *Westöstlicher Diwan* and Friedrich Schlegel's *Über die Sprache und Weisheit der Inder* to Schopenhauer's fascination with esoteric Hindu traditions and Nietzsche's tribute to Persian wisdom in *Also sprach Zarathustra*. This stereotype was further promulgated in Weimar Germany by such different writers as Hermann Hesse and Oswald Spengler.

The Jewish expression of the oriental motif cannot be reduced to a mere by-product of this general trend. Wassermann, who felt little affection for

East European Jews, chose as the incarnation of Eastern spirituality not just *any* oriental characters but oriental *Jews*. Although Gershon Shaked explains Wassermann's idealization of oriental Jews by saying that they appeared to him "almost 'non-Jewish,'" the opposite argument seems more plausible.[24] One should take seriously Wassermann's search for a literary ideal within the world of Judaism and may therefore suggest that fictional oriental Jews were positive characters because they embodied everything Wassermann regarded as genuinely Jewish, whereas Wassermann rejected the "Waremmes" because they appeared non-Jewish to him. Wassermann, though not a Zionist, prided himself on having helped to initiate the Zionist movement. In a usually overlooked letter to the *Jüdische Rundschau,* he claimed that the prologue of his first novel, *The Jews of Zirndorf,* which focused on the Shabbatean movement, may be considered "one of the most important causes of the emergence of the entire Zionist movement."[25]

Such a juxtaposition of assimilated German Jews and authentic oriental Jews was also reflected in the work of Else Lasker-Schüler, the most notable female German Expressionist poet (who received the coveted Kleist Prize in 1932, less than a year before German students burned her writings and the Nazis forced her into exile). Like Wassermann, Lasker-Schüler had little sympathy for her German-Jewish contemporaries. In a letter to Stefan George, she wrote, "I hate the Jews, because they despise my language, because their ears are deformed and they listen to *Zwergerei* and *Gemauschel.*"[26] Her aversion to "the Jews" concentrated on Ashkenazic *Mauscheljuden* (Jews with Yiddish accents), whom she portrayed as a distortion of the genuine oriental Jews—that is, the proud Hebrews of the Bible—as depicted in her *Hebräische Balladen* (Hebrew ballads, 1913).

Her admiration for those biblical "Jewish Jews" led to a direct identification with oriental characters. Projecting herself into biblical times, Else Lasker-Schüler identified with the figure of Joseph, to whom she dedicated two poems in *Hebrew Ballads*. She signed her letters "Prince Jussuf of Thebes," painted portraits herself in oriental clothes, and constructed her own biography as an oriental. "I was born in Thebes (Egypt), although I came to the world in Elberfeld in the Rhineland. I went to school for eleven years, became Robinson, lived five years in the orient, and since then I have been vegetating," she wrote in a curriculum vitae of 1920.[27] In reality, however, she hardly ever left Berlin prior to her emigration in 1933.

Lasker-Schüler's identification with the characters of the Hebrew Bible culminated in her conviction that her native language was Hebrew, not

The image of the oriental Jew: Else Lasker-Schüler, *Jussuf and His Dear Brother Bulus in the Temple.* Courtesy Städtische Galerie im Lenbachhaus, Munich.

German. When the Hebrew poet Uri Zvi Greenberg offered to translate some of Lasker-Schüler's poems into Hebrew, she replied angrily, "What? But I am writing in Hebrew."[28] Greenberg, who lived in Berlin in 1922 and 1923, remained an admirer of the "black swan of Israel," as poet Peter Hille called her.[29] When Greenberg acclaimed the poet "of Judean blood" (another of Peter Hille's names for Lasker-Schüler) in the Hebrew newspaper *Davar* in 1925, he seemed convinced of her statement. "The non-Hebrew reader," Greenberg wrote about one of her poems, "will find original Hebrew in her poem. Living Hebrew of the twentieth century."[30]

In his Hebrew poems, Greenberg adopted a motif that frequently appeared in Lasker-Schüler's work: the depiction of oriental Jews as wild Jews, embodying everything the tamed European Jews were lacking.[31] Joshua represented such a wild Jew in Lasker-Schüler's *Hebrew Ballads* (see the poem "Moses and Joshua"), and in her novel *Der Malik* (1919) she portrayed herself as the belligerent emperor Jussuf Abigail I, who led seven other wild Jews to conquer Moscow. In that novel Lasker-Schüler revealed her idea of publishing a journal called *Wilde Juden* (Wild Jews).[32] For many of her Jewish contemporaries, she personified the new ideal of the oriental Jew. Not incidentally, she was characterized both by contemporaries and later critics as the typical representative of an oriental literary style, with flowery and decorative language.[33]

Like the novels and stories of Wassermann and Tucholsky, Else Lasker-Schüler's poetry was an expression of her personal struggle with her Jewish identity. Although depicting her own ancestors as rabbis and religious Jews in the drama *Arthur Aronymus und seine Väter* (Arthur Aronymus and his fathers, 1932), she was well aware of the gap separating her individual identification as a Jew from the collective Jewish life of her time. Her poem "Mein Volk" (My people), which was included in *Hebrew Ballads,* depicted her as emotionally tied to her ancestors but remote from their spiritual world:

So much I've streamed away
Of my blood's
Early fermentation
And always and again the echoing
In me,
When shuddering towards the East
The grumbling skeleton of stone,
My people
Cries to God.[34]

The appropriation of biblical characters in Else Lasker-Schüler's *Hebrew Ballads* was indicative of the enormous popularity of biblical motifs among contemporary German-writing Jewish authors. Two biblical dramas, both published in 1918, became a few years later the core productions of the two emerging Hebrew theaters. Richard Beer-Hofmann's *Jaákobs Traum* (Jacob's dream) was performed in Hebrew translation by the Moscow-based theater Habimah, and Stefan Zweig's *Jeremias* (Jeremiah) was adapted to the Hebrew stage by the Tel Aviv theater Ohel.[35] The literary adaptation of biblical motifs was not restricted to Jews: the most acclaimed author of a biblical novel in this period was Lübeck patrician Thomas Mann, who in 1933 published the first volume of his grandiose Joseph tetralogy.

Another ancient text was interpreted exclusively by Jewish writers. The Talmud, no longer studied but accessible to German Jews in a recent translation, presented Jewish writers with a unique opportunity to idealize the image of the oriental Jew. Moritz Heimann's drama *Das Weib des Akiba* (Akiba's wife, 1922) was an example of this thematic approach.[36] As chief editor of Germany's most prestigious publishing house, S. Fischer, Heimann enjoyed a certain celebrity in Germany's literary world. He made no secret of his Jewishness and often referred to it in his publications. Just as the planets had an "orbit with two centers," Heimann argued, German Jews could combine the two poles of their Jewishness and their Germanness.[37]

Those two poles were visible in Heimann's own life and work. Born in a village in Brandenburg, he remained tied to his rural origins all his life.[38] His comedy *Joachim von Brandt* (1908) tells the story of a typical Prussian *Junker* (squire), while his drama *Akiba's Wife* is a literary representation of various talmudic legends.[39] A wild Jew from the field, Akiba was persuaded by his wife, the daughter of a wealthy man who had been opposed to his daughter's marriage, to study Talmud. After many years of study, Akiba returned as a celebrated scholar, accompanied by thousands of students. He ended his life as a martyr who supported the Bar Kokhba revolt against the Romans and was killed by them because of his insistence on teaching Talmud, despite having been forbidden to do so.

In *Akiba's Wife* Heimann presented the story of a gradual reappropriation of Jewish knowledge, intended as a model for German-Jewish readers. Like many of Heimann's contemporaries, Rabbi Akiba grew up without Jewish knowledge but discovered Judaism as an adult. Akiba's wife, Jalta, was willing to accept him only if he decided to renounce his savage upbringing and "start to be who you are."[40] Akiba chose to identify with his Jewish origins and, ultimately, was ready to die for the ideals of his people. For contemporary German-Jewish critics he was the literary incarnation of the "Jew as a warrior and sage."[41] But more than that, Heimann used a new medium to continue the long tradition of interpreting ancient Jewish religious sources. Martin Buber praised Heimann as a modern *darshan* (interpreter of religious texts) and admitted that "only Heimann's drama explained this story [of Rabbi Akiba] and made it clear to me. . . . This work of a modern sage, who is a poet, . . . belongs to German literature, and it belongs to the Jewish people. The people should take possession of it."[42]

Whereas the Goldschmidt translation of the Talmud enabled the close study of this principal Jewish source for the few who could not read the original text but were willing to immerse themselves in the "sea of the

Talmud," Heimann presented a digest of some of the most popular talmudic legends, which were no longer preserved in the memory of most
German Jews. In addition to the legends about Akiba, Heimann's readers
learn about the quarrel between Rabban Gamliel and Rabbi Joshua about
the calendar calculation, the heresy of Elisha ben Abuya, and the dismissal
of patriarch Rabban Gamliel and the appointment of his successor, Eleazar.
Heimann further contributed to the spread of talmudic stories with various
publications in Siegfried Jacobsohn's journal *Die Weltbühne*.[43]

Through the medium of the modern stage, such dramas as *Akiba's Wife*
helped to integrate talmudic traditions into the consciousness of German
Jews who had grown up with Greek and Germanic myths and a few biblical stories as part of their educational baggage. They would have shown
little interest if an obscure East European rabbi had tried to tell them the
stories contained in Heimann's dramas. When the chief editor of the S. Fischer publishing house, however, wrote a drama on Rabbi Akiba, then the
Talmud became fit even for acculturated German Jews.

With his dramatization of talmudic tales, Heimann built on the ground
already established by his close friend Micha Josef Berdyczewski, a
Hebrew writer and scholar.[44] Born in 1865 in Ukrainian Medzibezh (the
home town of the Ba'al Shem Tov) and a descendant of a line of famous
Hasidic rabbis, Berdyczewski lived in Germany from 1890 until his death
in 1921. While most of his writings appeared in Hebrew, the twelve volumes of his Jewish legends and myths were published in German between
1913 and 1927.[45] One of the first volumes contained three different versions of the legends on Rabbi Akiba, and textual evidence suggests that
Berdyczewski's interpretation of those legends were a major basis for
Heimann's drama. Just as Martin Buber had made Hasidic tales available
to acculturated German Jews, Berdyczewski opened for them a new world
of mostly oriental premodern Jewish myths and legends.

The average reader did not know the true motive for Berdyczewski's
publication of Jewish legends and myths. Influenced by Nietzsche, Berdyczewski renounced the rabbinical traditions of his ancestors and called for
a transvaluation of Judaism. With his works he attempted to demonstrate
that the "Torah of Moses was a late, 'antinatural' imposition on the
Hebrews, whose real religion was founded on a prior, unexpressed experience of the sword and nature."[46] On the basis of his revolutionary interpretation of Jewish history, Berdyczewski came to believe that the "ancient
pagan myths and imaginations . . . reappeared among the Jews in their old
strength and gained a place in the Volksseele, no less than the teachings of

the Sinai."[47] The publication of *The Legends of the Jews* and *The Well of Judah* were systematic attempts to prove the existence of an allegedly authentic Jewish tradition that had been repressed by rabbinical authorities and could be revealed through folklore, legends, and myths.[48] For most German readers, especially German-Jewish ones, however, the twelve volumes of tales and legends constituted "nothing else than the reopened paradise of our youth," as Arnold Zweig wrote in a contemporary review.[49] Just as the Grimm brothers had fostered cultural nationalism among Germans with their treasure of German folk tales, Berdyczewski nourished the neo-Romantic notions among German Jews a century later.

Jewish institutions and organizations, whose goal was the revitalization of Jewish culture, spread the image of the authentic Jew as an oriental. Else Lasker-Schüler, always in financial difficulty, often recited her poems at meetings of Jewish organizations, and Richard Beer-Hofmann read excerpts of his unfinished work *Der junge David* (Young David) for the Berlin Women's Association for Palestine. Before Moritz Heimann's *Akiba's Wife* was staged at the Frankfurt Schauspielhaus, it was recited at the Stuttgart Jewish Lehrhaus. Stefan Zweig was present when amateur actors from Düsseldorf, who belonged to the Liberal Jewish youth movement, performed his *Jeremiah* at their annual conference of 1930 in Munich.[50]

Those plays and stories often substituted for the traditional Jewish sources. Siegfried Jacobsohn, the liberal editor of *Die Weltbühne*, spoke for many of his fellow German Jews when he praised Richard Beer-Hofmann's *Jacob's Dream* as *Bibel-Ersatz* (Bible substitute), and concluded with words alluding to the traditional prayer *Shema Yisra'el*: "We thank him [Beer-Hofmann] . . . with all our heart, with all our soul, and with all our might." Confronted with Beer-Hofmann's biblical drama, Jacobsohn, an acculturated German Jew, proclaimed, "I am enough of a Jew to perceive *Jacob's Dream* as a national poem and to admit that I was totally spellbound by it. . . . Especially in our time I welcome a kind of literature for which one has to be a Jew in order to understand it and sympathize with it."[51]

For many acculturated German Jews, the novels and dramas of German-Jewish writers were indeed a Bibel-Ersatz. They knew Jacob's dream only from Richard Beer-Hofmann's drama, learned about Rabbi Akiba only from Moritz Heimann, and were for the first time confronted with medieval Jewish legends when reading the collections of Micha Josef Berdyczewski. The idealized image of the "authentic" oriental Jew aimed at making "non-Jewish" German Jews aware of their roots and thus restoring to them a sense of authenticity, which was also expressed by the image of the East European Jew.

THE AUTHENTIC OSTJUDE

In their drive to become an integral part of German society throughout the nineteenth century, German Jews psychologically distanced themselves from the "barbarous" East European "ghetto Jews," who were an uncomfortable reminder of what they themselves had been only two or three generations earlier. While never entirely dissociating themselves from their East European brethren, they had little sympathy for what seemed to them to be backward lifestyle and rituals.[52] Despite an often nostalgic tone, such authors of nineteenth-century German-language accounts of ghetto life as Leopold Kompert, Karl Emil Franzos, and Aron Bernstein depicted Jews of East European "half-Asia" (the title of one of Franzos' novels) as culturally inferior.

The image of East European Jews underwent a profound transformation around the turn of the century. By the Weimar period, East European Jews were identified as the epitome of genuine Jewishness. For many German Jews, such an image helped to split the "identity of the Jew into polar opposites," as Sander Gilman remarked. According to his analysis, German Jews "discovered a new model for the 'good' Jew in those very qualities despised by the Enlightenment. Late-nineteenth-century German Jews created a new stereotype through which the anxiety of their self-definition was distanced, and called it the 'East European Jew.' This image became the new definition of the 'good' Jew, and it was contrasted with the assimilated or acculturated Jew, who became the prototypical 'bad' Jew."[53] Like the image of the oriental Jew, that of the East European Jew was an external Jewish model, but it was much less remote in place and time and was quite familiar to German Jews.

The image of East European Jews was essential in preserving a sense of Jewish distinctiveness among German Jews. Martin Buber played a seminal part in this process starting around the turn of the century, but the impact that Buber's idealization of the Hasidic world had on German-Jewish intellectuals did not become clear until the Weimar period. During and after World War I, many German Jews had experienced their first personal encounter with a world that they had previously known mostly from Buber's publications. The result was a massive glorification of East European Jewish life in war and travel accounts. The most vivid descriptions of

Jewish life in Eastern Europe as seen by German-Jewish soldiers were Arnold Zweig's *Das ostjüdische Antlitz* (The Eastern Jewish countenance, 1919), and Sammy Gronemann's *Hawdoloh und Zapfenstreich* (Havdalah and taps, 1924). Both Zweig and Gronemann belonged to the same administrative unit of the German army, the Bezirk Oberost in Lithuanian Kovno, as artist Hermann Struck, who illustrated Zweig's book. Their war accounts should be compared with two travel reports on the same subject, published a few years later.

When anti-Jewish riots occurred in the center of Berlin in 1923, German-Jewish writer Alfred Döblin felt the need to augment his minimal knowledge of Jews and Judaism.[54] Because he was not a Zionist, he rejected an offer by the Zionist Organization to travel to Palestine and instead chose Poland as his destination. Döblin presented his impressions of the trip in *Reise in Polen* (Journey in Poland, 1925), a book that was criticized by another Jewish writer, Joseph Roth. Roth, unlike the other authors mentioned here, was of East European background. Although he had lived long enough in Vienna and Berlin to consider himself a Westerner, this native Galician Jew found Döblin's book a product of the "arrogance of Western European civilization [*westeuropäischer Zivilisationshochmut*]."[55] Roth soon tried to make up for what, in his eyes, Döblin had failed to capture; in 1927 he published *Juden auf Wanderschaft* (Jews on wanderings), containing various sketches of East European Jews inside and outside their traditional setting.

The four authors varied not only in their religious and political views but also in their literary styles. Gronemann, a former editor of the satirical Zionist journal *Der Schlemiel,* composed a humorous book full of anecdotes and epigrams about his activities as a Yiddish interpreter for the German army in Russia during World War I. Zweig wrote with much pathos, and his character studies, accompanied by Hermann Struck's drawings, evoke the world of East European Jews with such sentimentality that they are reduced to caricatures. Döblin's account is in the style of a scientific or ethnographic study of an exotic tribe and even provides a short bibliography of the literature that he had read in preparation for his journey. Roth's Impressionist sketches are those of an insider who illuminated a setting familiar to him.

In spite of these substantial differences, all four accounts shared the same message: only in the East could one find "Jewish Jews." Döblin, who had grown up in a Jewish family, married a Jewish woman, and had mostly Jewish friends, declared, "I discovered I did not really know Jews. I could

The image of the East European Jew: Hermann Struck, drawing from *Das ostjüdische Antlitz*, 1919. Photograph by Jim Strong. Courtesy of the Leo Baeck Institute, New York.

not label my friends, who called themselves Jews, as Jews. . . . Thus, I asked myself and I asked others: Where are there Jews? I was told: in Poland. . . . Yes, I was there, and [it was there] for the first time I saw Jews."[56] Döblin had distanced himself from the acculturated Jews he knew by leaving the Jewish community in 1912 and raising his children as Protestants. In the Jews of the East, however, he did not find the negative traits he identified with German Jews: "I thought that those industrious people I had seen in Germany were Jews, those merchants reveling in their sense of family and slowly growing fat [*verfetten*], the nimble intellectuals, all those insecure, unhappy, fine people. Now I see: those are shabby exemplars, far away from the nucleus of the Jewish people that lives and works here [in Poland]."[57]

Döblin was the most radical in his juxtaposition of authentic East European Jews and "non-Jewish" German Jews. But similar sentiments are visible in all four travel accounts, which contrast the world of German Jews and that of the Ostjuden in the realms of Jewish self-definition (religion versus peoplehood), prayer service (*Tempel* versus *Schul*), character (materialism versus spirituality), and occupational structure (parasitism versus productivity).

All four authors agreed that the confessionalization of Judaism, as embodied by Western European Jews in Germany during the nineteenth century, was a hollow, superficial distortion of Jewish traditions. Only east of the German borders, where Jewish peoplehood had been preserved, were Jewish traditions still alive. Arnold Zweig and Sammy Gronemann used almost the same words to contrast Western and Eastern Jews. According to Zweig, "The Jew in the West was on his way to a torpid denomination, a feeble, desperate piety, . . . which threatened to decline daily and crumble away gradually. . . . The old Jew of the East, however, preserved his face."[58]

For Gronemann, the son of an Orthodox German rabbi, even Orthodox Jews in Germany practiced nothing more than a "stiff *Ersatzjudentum,*" whereas East European Jews "lived their particular life, just like Germans or Englishmen."[59] Likewise, Joseph Roth left no doubt about his sympathies. He praised East European Jews for displaying their Jewishness openly instead of being ashamed of it, which he regarded as typical of German Jews.[60]

A closer look at the place of prayer, the traditionally central mode of Jewish religious expression, revealed for all authors the significant differences between Judaism in the East and in the West. Joseph Roth mocked the Western Jews "who no longer pray in synagogues and prayer houses, but in boring temples, in which the service becomes as mechanical as in any Protestant church. They become *Tempeljuden,* which means: well-educated, clean-shaven gentlemen in frock coats and top hats. . . . The grandfathers still fought desperately with Jehova, . . . the grandchildren became Westernized."[61] A journey to Eastern Europe was also a journey back in time. There the traditions of the grandfathers were still practiced; there the *Shul* (the traditional prayer house) was still in use. All four authors described the Shul and its service reverentially. In the Shul, through prayers, the traditional Jew left his worldly affairs and came into contact with God. What for "superficial and Western ears and eyes made only an embarrassing and tasteless impression" was in fact a genuine expression of deep religiosity.[62]

Gronemann, the only one of the four who regularly went to Orthodox services in Germany, came to a similar conclusion after spending his war years in Lithuania: "Since I have got to know the synagogue of the East, I have been disgusted with the temple of the West and its service. This relates to many Conservative synagogues as well as to Liberal ones—seen from the perspective of a Lithuanian prayer house, there is only a minimal difference between the two."[63]

The religiosity of the East European Jew was, for Western European observers, part of a deep spirituality that was perceptible in other spheres. Study was the most obvious example: Gronemann and Zweig wrote long passages about Talmud study among the Ostjuden, and Roth and Döblin produced detailed descriptions of their visits to Hasidic rebbes and the spiritual life of the communities they saw. Zweig also recalled the spiritual leaders of secular East European Jews, such Hebrew and Yiddish poets as Hayim Nahman Bialik, Zalman Shne'ur, Mendele Mokher Seforim, and Sholem Aleichem, whose impact could be compared to only one figure in Western culture, Stefan George, though the status of the East European poets differed from his: "Here, however, it is the whole people including the poor and the common who adore their poets, and not only the few of high education and without close attachment to the nation [*volkhafte Verwurzelung*]."[64]

In Roth's idealized view, every East European Jew was a "spiritual man. One belongs to a people that for more than 2,000 years did not have any illiterates, a people with more periodicals than newspapers. . . . While the other peasants only now begin to learn writing and reading, the Jew behind his plough struggles with the problems of the theory of relativity."[65] This statement alludes to another typical characteristic that, according to Roth, distinguished East European Jews from their Western counterparts: in the West, Jews may develop the theory of relativity, but they would not stand behind a plough. Western European Jews were intellectuals or merchants but did not cultivate the land or work as artisans. Roth reported enthusiastically about the occupational variety among East European Jews, especially among the Jewish proletariat. He explained that many East European Jews lived as "rural people" in villages and small towns, tied to their soil (*Scholle*). "In Western Europe one does not know about their existence."[66] Similarly, Zweig, a socialist, regarded "work and land" as the two principal elements in the life of the Ostjude.[67]

In their glorification of the spirituality of East European Jewry, the four writers found a literary ally in one of the leading representatives of Germany's most observant Jewish community. Isaac Breuer, the grandson of the founder of separatist Orthodoxy, Samson Raphael Hirsch, and the son of the rabbi at the Frankfurt Israelitische Religionsgesellschaft, grew up in the inner circle of the Frankfurt separatist Orthodox community. After attending the school of the local Orthodox community (directed by his uncle) and the yeshivah (established by his father), he studied law and became a practicing attorney in Frankfurt am Main.[68] Although Breuer was never able to realize his dream of becoming a professional writer, his publications are more diverse than those of any other representative of Orthodox German Jewry in his generation. They include newspaper articles, political pamphlets, religious polemics, novels, children's literature, and an autobiography.

The two novels that Breuer wrote in the Weimar period, *Ein Kampf um Gott* (Struggling with God, 1920) and *Falk Nefts Heimkehr* (The return of Falk Neft, 1923), deal with the theme of alienation among young German Jews growing up in the atmosphere of a purely mechanical Orthodoxy in Germany. Heinrich Thorning, the hero of *Struggling with God,* becomes alienated from traditional Judaism during his high school years, and Falk Neft, the protagonist of Breuer's second novel, breaks decisively with tradition during the war. Breuer characterized the German Gymnasium and the army as institutions that furthered the assimilation of German Jews. The deeper cause of the young Jews' alienation from Judaism, however, was the superficial Orthodoxy practiced by their fathers. In particular, he singled out for attack the "pseudo-Orthodox" figures, the fathers and the rabbis, who fulfill the religious commandments but are not interested in the spiritual meaning behind them. These pseudo-Orthodox differed in behavior from the reformers but had essentially adopted their interpretation of Judaism as a religion only. Thus, Falk Neft cries out, "How can I turn Judaism into a religion, in the ways of the nations, . . . a decorative accessory for life. . . . The God of Zion is no God of the synagogue, no God of the Sabbath and the Holy Days and the Fast Days. The God of Zion and Yerushalayim is a God of the [whole] order of life, a God of economic order, of political order."[69]

The encounter with East European Jewry marked the turning point in both novels. In the end, both heroes find their way back to tradition with the help of East European Jews. Falk Neft joins a revolutionary group and is imprisoned. While in jail, he meets an East European rabbi who leads him to genuine Judaism through Torah study. As a Torah scholar, he returns to his home town and takes over his father's business. In *Struggling with God,* an East European dairyman instructs Heinrich Thorning in Talmud study. This dairyman embodies Jewish learning much more than the Orthodox German rabbi, who favors the eviction of the Galician Jew Freilich from Germany.[70]

Breuer's idealization of the East European shtetl cannot disguise the fact that he, like most of the other authors, did not belong to the world of East European Jewry. The German novel had become the ideal medium for presenting his ideas, and those of other Orthodox Jewish leaders in Germany. Thus, like Zionists and Liberals, the Orthodox encouraged the creation of a new tradition among German Jews. Whereas for an East European yeshivah student the reading of nonreligious texts was taboo, German Orthodox rabbis encouraged the writing of German-Jewish novels and praised them as the culmination of Jewish literature. As an Orthodox journal put it, "For Jewish pens there is no better task than the creation of such novels."[71]

At the other end of the religious spectrum, a different sort of German-Jewish literature was flourishing during the Weimar years. Many of those German Jews who could not identify with the ideals of traditional Judaism were inspired by literary depictions of some of Jewish history's more exotic figures, especially by stories of those branded as heretics.

THE HERETICAL IDEAL

Not one of the numerous historical novels written by German Jews in the Weimar period depicted the "hero" of nineteenth-century German Jewry, Moses Mendelssohn. Nor did the towering figures of Jewish tradition, such as Maimonides and Rashi, become topics of German-Jewish literature during this period. Instead, messianic and heretical characters of Jewish history figured prominently. Shabbetai Zevi, the seventeenth-century false messiah from Izmir, whose messianic claims and subsequent conversion to Islam split the entire Jewish world into believers and unbelievers—Shabbateans and anti-Shabbateans—was treated in at least five novels; the arch-heretic Spinoza received frequent literary attention, as did the tragic case of Uriel da Costa; and the Renaissance adventurer David Reubeni became the hero of a popular novel by the Prague writer Max Brod.

It was certainly no coincidence that Jewish heretics were rediscovered at about the same time by both Jewish scholarship and Jewish fiction. While German-Jewish writers published their novels about Shabbetai Zevi, Gershom Scholem wrote his first scholarly article on the Shabbatean movement. Beginning with his early writings during the 1920s, Scholem relentlessly critiqued the nineteenth-century depiction of Jewish mysticism as an aberration of Jewish history. Throughout his life, Scholem tried to integrate mystics and heretics into his definition of Judaism. For him, Shabbetai Zevi and his followers were proof that Judaism could not be confined to the religious sphere, as many nineteenth-century scholars had maintained. Although some in the Shabbatean movement may have switched allegiances to Islam, Shabbateanism's original value system was undoubtedly part of Judaism.[72]

Like Scholem, Jewish novelists were no longer content with the traditional definitions of Judaism. They were convinced that Judaism could not be reduced to a religious essence and that factors other than religion bound Jews together. By portraying Jewish figures outside or on the fringes of traditional Judaism—apostates, heretics, and false messiahs—they offered themselves and their fellow German Jews alternative role models that would suit their own situation outside Jewish tradition. Such characters as the Marrano Uriel da Costa, the apostate Spinoza, the adventurer David Reubeni, and the false messiah Shabbetai Zevi had long been ignored before Jews began to write about them. About the same time that Gershom Scholem went from Berlin to Jerusalem, Shabbetai Zevi made his literary journey from Izmir to Weimar.

Two of Germany's best-selling German-Jewish authors, Jakob Wassermann and Lion Feuchtwanger, used the theme of Shabbateanism. Wassermann introduced it in the prologue of his novel *The Jews of Zirndorf* (1897), which describes the mystical atmosphere in a nineteenth-century rural Franconian Jewish community in the context of the Shabbatean movement. Only in 1925, however, did the prologue, which addresses the direct effect of Shabbetai Zevi's appearance in the Jewish community of Fürth, appear as a separate account.

Like Wassermann, Feuchtwanger integrated the Shabbatean controversy into the context of German-Jewish history in his novel *Jud Süß* (Jew Süß, 1925), based on the tragic case of Joseph Süß Oppenheimer.[73] Feuchtwanger included the fictional character of Rabbi Gabriel and the famous Hamburg rabbi Jonathan Eybeschuetz, who were both known as followers of the false messiah, in order to discuss Shabbateanism in his novel. As John Milfull has suggested, Feuchtwanger's motive for this was his conviction that Shabbateanism symbolized a form of Jewish identity that had abandoned traditional Judaism and initiated the Jewish Enlightenment.[74] This thesis reflects Gershom Scholem's argument that the Shabbatean movement smoothed the way for modern forms of Judaism.

While Feuchtwanger used the Shabbatean movement only as background to his account of Jud Süß, Shabbetai Zevi and his adherents occupied a central role in a number of lesser-known novels by German-Jewish authors. In the chiliastic novel *Dein Reich komme!* (Your kingdom come) by Munich Zionist physician Felix Theilhaber, Shabbetai Zevi's shadow is always visible, although he never actually appears. One of the characters is

Sara, Shabbetai Zevi's mystical bride, who escaped from a Polish monastery, returned to Judaism, and wandered through Holland and Italy until she finally arrived in Cairo to marry Shabbetai Zevi. Also present is Elischa, the messiah's prophet, who arranged Sara's journey to Cairo and tried to convince Amsterdam Jews to accept Shabbetai Zevi as the messiah.

Theilhaber, who was famous for his pessimistic prognosis of German Jewry, which he published in 1911 as *Der Untergang der deutschen Juden* (The demise of German Jewry), did not concentrate solely on the Shabbateans. He also described Shabbetai Zevi's opponents: scientist Joseph Solomon Delmedigo, Orthodox rabbi Jacob Sasportas, and philosopher Baruch Spinoza. What emerges in this novel is a pluralistic Jewish community, deeply divided over questions of religion but united by its peoplehood. Spinoza is characterized as a proud, albeit heretical, Jew. When accused of denouncing his Judaism, he cries out, "How could I denounce my own blood, how could I curse my father's name?" and he goes on to say, "Have not all great Jews been stigmatized as traitors, apostates, and agnostics?"[75] Sara even decides that Spinoza is the messiah, before she is sent to Shabbetai Zevi.

Like Spinoza, the Shabbateans emerge as fully Jewish figures. Their heresy does not make them lesser Jews than the anti-Shabbateans. Theilhaber paid little attention to the religious system of the Shabbateans. What counted for him was that they formed a national Jewish movement ready to settle in Palestine. Those mystics had to be included in the broad framework of Judaism, as were pantheist philosophers, Orthodox rabbis, and rationalist scientists, because all were part of the Jewish people. Seen from this perspective, seventeenth-century Amsterdam may have seemed like the ideal backdrop for a Zionist writer whose aim was to characterize the broad spectrum of the Jewish people. That time and place was an apt metaphor for German Jewry, which was deeply divided along religious lines but could unite through Zionism. In 1902 Theodor Herzl had recognized the relevance of the Shabbatean movement for modern Zionist culture, when in his utopian vision of a Jewish state, *Altneuland* (Old-new land), he described the performance of an opera about Shabbetai Zevi as a major cultural event. And three decades later, the first publication of the Heine-Bund—a Jewish book club of the Zionist Welt publishing house—was a biography of Shabbetai Zevi.[76]

Shabbetai Zevi and Shabbateanism figured prominently in numerous other novels, novellas, plays, and travel reports written by German Jews. They included *Die Messiasbraut* (The messiah's bride, 1925), by Selig

Schachnowitz, the editor of the Orthodox German-Jewish periodical *Der Israelit* and author of a number of Jewish historical novels; *Der Reiter* (The horseman, 1930), by Martin Buber's son-in-law, Ludwig Strauss; Artur Sakheim's drama *Der Zadik* (The righteous one); and the collection of travel reports on "exotic" Jewish communities, among them the Shabbatean sect of Dönmehs, by Esriel Carlebach, the editor of the Hamburg-based *Israelitisches Familienblatt* and later founder of the Israeli daily *Ma'ariv*.[77]

Most successful among German literary depictions of Jewish pseudomessianic movements was, with an initial circulation of twenty thousand copies, Max Brod's novel on another messianic figure, the Renaissance adventurer David Reubeni. The success of Brod's *Reubeni* was matched only by a biography on Shabbetai Zevi published by the respected Rowohlt publishing company in 1930. Its author was Bremen lawyer Josef Kastein (the pen name of Julius Katzenstein), a Zionist follower of Martin Buber who was a contributor to Buber's journal, *Der Jude*. A lecture course by Buber on Jewish messianism, delivered in Switzerland at Ponte Tresa in 1928, had inspired Kastein to write *Sabbatai Zewi*. According to Kastein's biographer, the novel, which was translated into English, Spanish, and Hebrew, sold so well that it ensured his economic well-being and enabled him to build a house in Swiss Ascona.[78]

This success led to Kastein's career as a writer, and the Rowohlt publishing house solicited him to write a one-volume Jewish history, which he finished in only one year. In the preface, Kastein admitted that he had written his history from the Zionist point of view, characterizing the history of the Jewish people as a national history, not a religious one. *Eine Geschichte der Juden* (A history of the Jews) became a source of inspiration for many German Jews.[79]

In 1932 Rowohlt published another historical novel by Kastein about a different Jewish heretic.[80] *Uriel da Costa* dealt with the Marrano who found his way back to Judaism in early-seventeenth-century Portugal. Da Costa emigrated from Portugal to Amsterdam but was not willing to subscribe to the postbiblical tenets of Judaism. Growing up in a Christian world, he was convinced that the legal basis of Judaism could essentially be reduced to the Hebrew Bible. As a heretic who rejected the oral tradition and denied the immortality of the soul, he was banned and humiliated by the Amsterdam Jewish community and subsequently committed suicide.[81]

As Kastein revealed in the epilogue to his novel, his hero's search for *Gemeinschaft* represented the longings of many young German Jews, whom

Kastein described as modern Marranos: "Again, a generation of Marranos came into existence. . . . Those Marranos placed themselves not under the yoke of another religion but under the yoke of the world; a world that only wants . . . humanity and enlightenment and brotherliness, . . . without the knowledge of the burden of their own blood. As with those original Marranos, they begin to return home today, rejected by the strong resistance of the outside world."[82]

Moritz Goldstein's demands for a retreat of German Jews from German literature went largely unheeded during the Weimar period, when Jewish writers occupied a more conspicuous place in German literature than ever before. Yet Goldstein's call for the creation of a Jewish literary ideal was fulfilled to some extent by the end of the Weimar years. Although all the authors mentioned in this chapter remained firmly anchored in German literature, they increasingly depicted themes that were relevant to a particular Jewish experience and contained a specific message to their Jewish readers. Those contemporary accounts and historical novels have become historical documents themselves—witnesses to a changing spirit among many German Jews after World War I, and their search for new modes of self-definition.

At the same time, those writers signaled the limits of the cultural Jewish renaissance in Weimar Germany. Although they invented positive Jewish ideals in their works, they were not able to materialize them in their own lives. Roth sympathized openly with Catholicism, and Döblin actually converted to the Catholic religion when in exile in the United States. Arnold Zweig returned from Palestine to communist East Germany, deeply disappointed with life in the Jewish homeland dominated by the East European Jews he had formerly glorified, and Lasker-Schüler continued to live in her illusory oriental world even after emigrating to the real Jerusalem.

These writers, escaping from the often shallow remnants of Judaism they experienced at home, deeply deplored the image of the assimilated German Jew. In their works, their rejection of this image led to the creation of idealized non-German Jewish types, but in their lives it often meant a flight in the opposite direction, leading to complete assimilation. The desperate longing for Jewish heroes and ideals was thus an expression of their dual identity as Germans and Jews.

6

Authenticity and Modernism Combined: Music and the Visual Arts

The authentic work of art instructs us in our inauthenticity and adjures us to overcome it.

—Lionel Trilling, *Sincerity and Authenticity* (1972)

The words *Weimar* and *modernism* are used today almost synonymously. "When we think of Weimar, we think of modernity in art, literature, and thought," writes Peter Gay in his study of Weimar culture. For Gordon Craig, "Weimar culture was pre-eminently modern," and Walter Laqueur referred to Weimar Germany as the "first truly modern culture."[1] In the context of such cultural developments as Expressionist literature and art, Bauhaus architecture and *Neue Sachlichkeit* (New Objectivity), the Piscator theater, and Bertolt Brecht and Kurt Weill's *Threepenny Opera*, Weimar Germany's claim to modernity can hardly be doubted. Weimar was a unique laboratory for the development of those and other daring cultural experiments. Some had already been under way prior to the war, but the war experience and the political transformation of German society enabled their broad reception. In Weimar society, the radical break with traditional values and cultural expressions no longer bore the stigma of disgrace and infamy but attained official legitimation and the support of large segments—though not the majority—of the population.

Jewish writers, artists, composers, and critics were significant in the development of Weimar's modern culture. Expressionist literature without Ernst Toller's dramas and Alfred Döblin's novels, modern theater without Kurt Weill's music and Max Reinhardt's direction, and New Music without Arnold Schoenberg's compositions would have been substantially different. This is not the place to add to the controversy concerning the extent of the impact that German Jews had on German modernist culture.[2] I shall instead reverse this question by asking how Weimar modernism influenced the development of a distinctly modern Jewish culture in the realms of music and the visual arts. The impact of Weimar Germany's modernism was felt in almost all areas of Jewish cultural activity: music with extended modalities was introduced into synagogue liturgy, Expressionist art was used for illustrations in Jewish books, new Jewish community centers were built in the Bauhaus style, and ceremonial objects were designed in the fashion of New Objectivity.

To reduce either Weimar culture or Weimar Jewish culture to the aspect of modernity, however, would provide us with an incomplete picture. Most cultural historians have pointed to the coexistence of modernist and anti-modernist forces in German society between 1918 and 1933. With regard to the interrelation of culture, technology, and politics, Jeffrey Herf has introduced the term "reactionary modernism," elaborating on such thinkers as Ernst Jünger, Oswald Spengler, Werner Sombart, and Martin Heidegger. One might instead characterize the diverse tendencies in music and the visual arts during this period as a modernism in search of authenticity. With their frequent religious, mythical, and primitivist motifs, Expressionist artists shaped a style of art that, though modern, yielded to contemporary demands for a return to authentic forms of culture. Similarly, modern composers were interested in the revival of folk traditions, as popularized by the Youth Music Movement. The term *authenticity* represented for them the creation of art products that would be received not as modern inventions but as modern interpretations of long-established "genuine" religious or folk traditions.

For many Jewish artists and musicians, such a combination of modernism and alleged authenticity led to a preoccupation with their Jewish cultural heritage. But not all Jewish artists and musicians were in search of Jewish authenticity. Any attempt to define the creativity of Max Liebermann and Kurt Weill as "Jewish art" or "Jewish music," for example, would do them injustice. In this chapter, however, I will elucidate a cultural realm of Weimar Germany that historical research has previously ignored in the Jewish context: the development of a distinctive art and music within Jewish communities and cultural associations.

Many of Weimar Germany's Jews no longer found appealing the traditions of nineteenth-century Jewish art and music. Like Jewish scholarship and literature, Jewish music and visual arts in Germany changed fundamentally during the first three decades of the twentieth century. In the mid-nineteenth century, when Berthold Auerbach wrote his idyllic accounts of German-Jewish rural life and Leopold Zunz promoted the cause of Jewish emancipation by producing scholarly studies, Louis Lewandowski composed liturgical music according to the ideals of European Romanticism, while Moritz Oppenheim's genre paintings in the Biedermeier style depicted a sanitized version of traditional Jewish life.

Lewandowski's compositions were part of the movement toward a profound Westernization of the Jewish prayer service, in which synagogues were transformed into temples with organ music and choirs, and rabbis dressed as Protestant clergymen. Lewandowski's music and Oppenheim's paintings remained enormously popular throughout much of imperial Germany, but German Jews in the 1920s considered them increasingly old-fashioned. Instead, such artists as Jakob Steinhardt and Joseph Budko and such composers as Heinrich Schalit and Hugo Adler applied modern cultural styles—art nouveau, Expressionism, and New Objectivity, or Instructional Cantatas—when reshaping Jewish culture in Weimar Germany. Contemporary music critics characterized the changes in Jewish music of the nineteenth century century as a development "from Lewandowski to Schalit," and German-Jewish art historian Karl Schwarz juxtaposed what he considered the inauthentic Jewish art of Oppenheim with the authentic ornamental works of graphic artist Joseph Budko, who based his work on traditional Jewish motifs. Looking back on a century of modern Jewish art, Schwarz came to this conclusion: "Within one century, [Jewish] painting has come a long way from Moritz Oppenheim, who *believed* himself to be a Jewish painter with his depictions of Jewish family life, to Joseph Budko, who *is* a Jewish painter."[3]

Like the writers of this period, these artists and composers constructed a fictitious and allegedly authentic Jewish world of oriental and East European Jews as the basis for their own cultural identity. Jewish artists, influenced by the Zionist program, the establishment of Jewish ethnography, and the general search for an ethnically defined art, recovered the cultural expressions of the Jews of Eastern Europe and the Middle East. Composers of liturgy that used extended modalities beyond the traditional modes of the synagogue chant claimed to base their compositions on oriental Jewish music, artists depicted Ostjuden in book illustrations, and Jewish museums displayed Jewish folk art. On all levels, the rich cultural treasures of the Jewish past, unveiled by extensive ethnographic research, were combined with modernist art tendencies. The results were presented as both authentically Jewish and modernist.

JEWISH MUSIC IN A NEW KEY

On July 24, 1933, Louis-Germain Levy, rabbi of the Liberal Jewish congregation in the rue Copernic of Paris, received two celebrated visitors to carry out a rather unusual ceremony. Arnold Schoenberg, the Austrian composer and pioneer of modern music who had converted to Protestantism in 1898, had asked for a formal return to Judaism. As one of his witnesses he brought with him the Russian-Jewish avant-garde painter Marc Chagall.[4]

Since the early 1920s, Schoenberg had entertained the thought of returning to Judaism. The Nazi rise to power finally pushed him to do it. Like many Jewish intellectuals, he had rediscovered his Jewishness as a result of antisemitic attacks that he experienced after World War I. In the summer of 1921 he and his family were forced to leave an Austrian spa because it was restricted to Aryan guests. And when, a year later, Schoenberg sensed an antisemitic undertone in the letters of his friend Wassily Kandinsky, he stressed that he "would never again forget . . . that I am a Jew."[5] Shortly after moving to Berlin in 1926, he wrote his only drama, *Der biblische Weg* (The path of the Bible, 1926–1927), in which he elaborated on the idea of establishing a Jewish state by means of a magic weapon. The play (still unpublished except for an Italian translation) foreshadowed many aspects of his opera *Moses und Aron* (1928–1932). The creation of *Moses and Aron* was not only a pioneering attempt to produce an opera libretto according to the principles of twelve-tone music but also an exceptional example of setting central issues of Jewish existence to music.

Schoenberg was the most famous of a number of Jewish composers who renewed or strengthened their interest in Judaism after World War I. While numerous scholars have examined Schoenberg's "cult music without cult" (*kultische Musik ohne Kultus*), as Theodor Adorno called *Moses and Aron*,[6] musical developments within the framework of the Jewish community have been less studied. In the context of this book it is not Schoenberg's music but the influence of musical innovations on the development of Jewish liturgical music that shall interest us. Schoenberg's revolutionary use of expanded tonal and atonal music helped composers of Jewish liturgical music to solve a century-old dilemma. On one hand, they wanted to improve synagogue music along the lines of the general musical development, but on the other hand they did not want this improvement to blur the distinctiveness and authenticity of the music's Jewish setting.

By basing their compositions on a different tonal system, composers of synagogue music avoided the accusation that they were embracing traditional European music or church liturgy. As Arno Nadel, a composer and leading critic of Jewish music in Weimar Germany, remarked, the "new music (especially Schoenberg!) attempts to free itself from the harmonic basis and to proceed in new contexts in ways similar to what we assumed of the ancients."[7] Musicologist Hugo Leichtentritt called for the creation of a Jewish music that was authentically Jewish and modern at the same time:

> The renewal of Jewish synagogue music is one of the most important missions of modern Jewish composers. After half a century of the music of Lewandowski, its color has faded and its spirituality has become weak. What is needed today is music that has a strong, original note and religious meditation but that likewise satisfies our ears, which have become attuned to contemporary music. Conventionally soft and smooth euphony no longer pleases us. . . . Contemporary Jewish music must be Jewish as well as novel, simultaneously traditional and original.[8]

In postwar society there was a general feeling that in music, as in many other areas, an epoch had come to an end. What followed was a "period of intense search for means whereby to transform radically the face of music and lend it a new physiognomy."[9] Schoenberg, Alban Berg, and Anton von Webern composed New Music of expanded tonality, Paul Hindemith aimed at a New Objectivity, and Kurt Weill pursued a boldly experimental and Expressionist line with his *Zeitoper,* whereas Igor Stravinsky clung at that time to a neoclassicist style.

The diversity of styles and range of experiment were reflected in the development of modern Jewish music. Following Stravinsky and Bartók, folk melodies regained popularity among composers of Jewish music.[10] Hindemith's and Weill's experiments with political opera served as models for the Instructional Cantata of the Mannheim Jewish community, and other musical innovations of the period influenced Jewish liturgical compositions. In the 1920s a mutual influence of traditional Hebrew prayer motifs and modern music could be observed in other countries as well, as most prominently demonstrated in the works of Swiss composer Ernest Bloch and Italian composer Mario Castelnuovo-Tedesco.[11]

The most prolific representative of such an approach was the musical director of the Munich Jewish community, Heinrich Schalit (1886–1976). Like Schoenberg, he was born in Vienna and started his musical career without any connection to Jewish music. A friend of the renowned conductor Bruno Walter, he had lived and composed in Munich starting in 1907. He rediscovered Judaism as a result of increasing antisemitism in World War I, as he wrote in a letter to a friend: "The psychological experience of the war years and of the period after the war led to a decisive turning point in my creative work, and at the same time to the termination of my 'romantic' period. The conviction of my being Jewish penetrated my musical work more and more and reminded me of my responsibility."[12]

Schalit's Jewish compositions were nourished by three principal sources: East European, Spanish, and oriental Jewish folk music. His intensive study between 1920 and 1923 of Jewish folk songs resulted in the arrangements published under the title *Ostjüdische Volkslieder* (East European Jewish folklore songs). Some of them were performed at the Frankfurt International Music Fair in 1927 in front of more than twenty-five hundred listeners, an audience probably unprecedented for a concert of Jewish music.[13] Schalit, influenced by the publication of Franz Rosenzweig's German translation of Yehuda Halevi's poetry, turned from East European Jewish folk melodies to medieval Spanish-Jewish poetry. His first choral work, *In Ewigkeit*, set to music one of Yehuda Halevi's poems.[14] Most important for Schalit's third creative phase in the years before 1933 was the publication of Abraham Zvi Idelsohn's monumental ten-volume *Thesaurus of Hebrew Oriental Melodies* (1914–1932), the unsurpassed collection of ethnographic research of Jewish music and one of the major scholarly Jewish publishing projects in Weimar Germany.

Like Jewish writers, Schalit and other Jewish composers in Weimar Germany used both oriental and East European Jewish models in their search for authenticity. But Schalit was not content with copying traditional forms of Jewish music. His goal was its integration into modern music, thus meeting Hugo Leichtentritt's demand that contemporary Jewish music must be simultaneously traditional and original.

Hired as organist and musical director of the Munich Jewish community in 1927, Schalit began to transform this desideratum into reality. In Munich, his ideas were well-received by the community's longtime cantor, Emanuel Kirschner (1857–1938). Kirschner, a member of the transitional generation between Lewandowski and Schalit, was the "first to overcome the enormous prestige of Lewandowski" without, however, achieving a renewal of liturgical music, a task he left to his younger colleague.[15] Also in Munich was Paul Ben-Haim (then Paul Frankenburger), another composer of modern Jewish music, whose *Psalm 131* was performed at the prestigious Nuremberg Choral Festival in July 1931. Both Schalit's and Ben-Haim's works were characterized by the fusion of archaism, modality, and diatonic dissonant progressions.[16]

The climax of Schalit's career as composer of Jewish liturgy, and at the same time the conclusion to a creative phase of German-Jewish music, was the performance of *Eine Freitagabend Liturgie* (A Friday evening liturgy) in the Berlin Lützowstraße Synagogue in September 1932. In this work Schalit clearly distanced himself both from Western musical traditions, such as the German lied, and from the nineteenth-century classics of Jewish liturgy. Instead, his harmony was characterized by polyphonic choral and organ parts, which he related to the contemporary compositions of Schoenberg and to premodern oriental forms of Jewish music, as published by Idelsohn. The novelty of the work attracted a large audience, including many who would not attend an ordinary Sabbath service. As a press review stated, "The synagogue was packed with people, as during the High Holidays, which is an indication of the widespread interest in the revival of synagogue music."[17] Although the uncommon musical style provoked mixed reactions among the worshipers, most critics of Jewish music praised Schalit's reintegration of Jewish authenticity into the German synagogue, following Hugo Leichtentritt's conclusion that "these oriental Jewish melodies sound very authentic and Jewish, they appear to us as both strange and familiar."[18]

Performed four months before Hitler's accession to power, Schalit's *Freitagabend-Liturgie* concluded a period of experiment and renewal of Jewish music. Such technical innovations as the radio and the phonograph further contributed to significant changes in Jewish music and were used to promote various aspects of Jewish culture. Enthusiastic proponents of a Jewish Hour on Radio Cologne believed that broadcasts could help revitalize and modernize neglected religious traditions, such as the celebration of Rosh Hodesh, the first day of a new month. Broadcasted at the beginning of every Jewish month, such a Jewish Hour would have two aims: first, to remind non-Orthodox Jews about this much forgotten Jewish holiday, and second, to provide information on the upcoming events of the Jewish month.[19]

Although this plan proved to be too ambitious, more conventional Jewish programs became reality. They included lectures and discussions but most frequently concentrated on Jewish music. After protracted negotiations, an agreement was reached for Berlin Radio to broadcast Jewish liturgical music, introduced by Arno Nadel in October 1929.[20] Bavarian Radio contributed to the popularization of modern Jewish music by transmitting Heinrich Schalit's choral work *In Ewigkeit*.[21]

Like the introduction of the radio, the spread of records affected the course of modern Jewish music. A multitude of records of Jewish music had been distributed in Germany before World War I, many of them through the journal *Ost und West*. In 1928, the four largest record companies listed 1,325 titles of Jewish music in their catalogues.[22] During the 1920s, the general enthusiasm for the new technical possibilities of producing music was sometimes expressed radically. In their belief in the democratization and *Versachlichung* (objectivization) of music, some progressive music critics even advocated replacing live music with recorded music and advised parents to buy records for their children instead of sending them to piano lessons.[23] This mood was reflected in the initiative of the small Jewish Reform Congregation of Berlin to introduce recorded music into its services. The extremely liberal congregation "exported" to smaller Jewish communities its "recorded services," which contained compositions by the classic composers of Jewish liturgy and by Christian composers from Bach to Bruckner.[24]

Although liturgical music constituted the majority of Jewish music recordings, folk music by East European and Yemenite Jews was well represented, too. The popularity of nonliturgical Jewish music was expressed in lively theoretical debates in Jewish journals. Starting in the late 1920s, the *Jüdische Rundschau* contained regular supplements on Jewish music edited by pianist and music critic Alice Jacob-Loewenson, who arranged the music to Yemenite songs on the basis of Idelsohn's *Thesaurus*.[25] Like Schalit and Nadel, Jacob-Loewenson advocated a modern Jewish music that was clearly distinct from European traditions and based on a "return to authentic, old Jewish music." This included the replacement of European homophonic and polyphonic systems by oriental harmony.[26]

Jacob-Loewenson did not lack material for her regular columns on performances of Jewish music. When looking back on the Jewish musical events in Berlin during the winter of 1928–1929, she compiled an impressive list, containing concerts of the United Synagogue Choirs of Berlin, young Jewish composers from the United States, Yiddish and Hebrew lied recitals, programs on New Jewish Music, and Yiddish theater music from Russia, as well as courses on Jewish music at the Freie Jüdische Volkshochschule and the Schule der jüdischen Jugend.[27] In large Jewish communities, a number of Jewish musical associations and choirs were established during the 1920s, among them the Juwal Publishing Company for Jewish Music, the United Synagogue Choirs, and the Society of the Friends of Jewish Music, all in Berlin.[28]

The performance of Jewish music on records and on the radio as well as in concert halls characterized a decisive break with the traditional reception of Jewish music. Until the nineteenth century, Jewish music (including traditional cantoral chants, choral music, and East European Klezmer music) had been performed either during the prayer service or at Jewish family festivals. In Weimar Germany, however, an increasing number of German Jews experienced Jewish music by attending a Sunday matinee or turning on their radios. They listened to Klezmer music, Yemenite Jewish dances, and Lewandowski's and Schalit's versions of Jewish liturgy in the same way that they listened to Beethoven's symphonies and Wagner's operas: as a concert audience. Even if a program contained religious music, it had been transformed for many listeners into a secular experience.

The transformation of Jewish music was welcomed as a sign of revived interest in Jewish culture and a partial realization of Franz Rosenzweig's dream that secular German Jews would begin to reintegrate Jewish culture into their general interests. As one historian of Jewish music in Weimar Germany wrote,

> A new form of musical life arose within the urbanized Jewish communities, one which was somewhat removed from its more traditional roots, yet still embracing the characteristic and supportive culture of the community. This transformation, which gained increased impetus during the three decades before the Holocaust, was symbolic of a cultural consolidation that had begun to pervade virtually every segment of German-Jewish life and that had consequently succeeded in stimulating no less than a Jewish cultural renaissance in certain cities.[29]

At the same time, however, skeptics discerned the seeds of a contrary development. They warned that the detachment of Jewish music from religious Jewish life would lead to a purely passive appreciation of Judaism among German Jews. Some contemporary critics, aware of such a danger, attempted to involve the audience actively by transferring the newest invention of the German musical scene—the Instructional Cantata (*Lehrkantate* or *Lehrstück*)—to a distinctly Jewish context.

With the waning of the Golden Twenties, the concern for contemporary social problems in the music of Weimar Germany also reached its conclusion. The plots of new operas came to be determined not by the most recent "news of the day" (the title of an opera by Hindemith) but by the deep reservoir of the past. These operas aimed to re-create a strong sense of community by means of education and the creation of new myths.[30]

This quest for community among composers was expressed in two ways. First, a revival of religion, was significant not only in the life and oeuvre of Schoenberg but also among such contemporary Christian composers as Honegger, Bartók, and Stravinsky, who in 1926 returned to the Russian Orthodox church and composed his *Psalm Symphony*. Hindemith turned during those years increasingly to folk music as a source for his new *Gemeinschaftsmusik,* which was part of the Youth Music Movement.[31] Second, socialist intellectuals and composers tried to create a sense of community among the working class by creating the Instructional Cantata, whose main purpose was the active participation of a large number of people. The means of achieving this goal varied: the audience could change the text, a large choir was used, and the audience had to repeat simple phrases.[32] The Instructional Cantata—first conceived by Bertolt Brecht and set to the music of Kurt Weill and Paul Hindemith in 1929—thus aimed at educating all its participants.[33]

The performance of the Instructional Cantata *Das Wasser,* by Alfred Döblin and Ernst Toch, at the New Music Festival in Berlin in 1930 had special significance for the Jewish community. Toch, who taught at the Mannheim music academy between 1913 and 1929, was occasionally involved in the musical life of the local Jewish community and served as organist for its special concerts. The associate cantor of the Jewish community, Hugo Adler, was a student of Toch and was influenced by his concept of new music. Together with the youth rabbi of Mannheim, Max Grünewald, Adler immediately recognized the educational potential of the Instructional Cantata and transformed it for use in a Jewish context.

Before this endeavor, Adler and Grünewald had helped to make the Mannheim Jewish community of seven thousand one of the most active centers of Jewish culture outside Berlin. Hired as youth rabbi in 1925, Grünewald almost immediately established a Jugendgemeinde, where he could systematically coordinate all activities for Mannheim's Jewish youth. In 1929 he initiated the Lehrhaus, which was based on the Frankfurt model, though on a much smaller scale.[34] Music was an integral part of the Mannheim Lehrhaus from the beginning. Prior to the foundation of the

Lehrhaus, the Jewish community had organized several benefit concerts of traditional liturgical or folk music, but after the Lehrhaus was established, Jewish music took a more original form.[35] At the Franz Rosenzweig memorial concert in February 1930, compositions by the Renaissance Italian-Jewish composer Salomone Rossi and by Ernst Toch were performed along with two original works by members of the Mannheim Jewish community, one of which was Hugo Adler's arrangement of Rosenzweig's translations of Yehuda Halevi's medieval Hebrew poems.

The success of the Rosenzweig memorial concert paved the way for the presentation of the first Jewish Instructional Cantata, *Licht und Volk* (Light and people), by Max Grünewald and Hugo Adler. Performed during the celebration of Hanukkah in December 1930, it told "seven chapters of the history of the Maccabees." Grünewald and Adler combined the tradition of a Jewish *Hanukkah Shpil* (dramatization of the story of Hanukkah) with the latest trends in modern music. The significance of the performance of *Licht und Volk* was the active participation of many community members. More than 250 Mannheim Jews participated in the choir, and many others helped to plan and organize the event. Several hundred others listened to the performance staged at Mannheim's largest concert hall at the Rosengarten.

The local Mannheim newspaper was proud to report that "Mannheim is the first provincial city in Germany to join Berlin with such a performance."[36] Another non-Jewish newspaper rated the performance as a "musical extravaganza" (*musikalische Großtat*).[37] Despite the attention it received in non-Jewish circles, however, the performance was primarily directed at a Jewish audience. The program clearly stated the task of this musical experiment: "to form an interested, active community out of an indifferent mass . . . to strengthen the feeling of common bonds [*Zusammengehörigkeitsgefühl*] of the Jewish community."[38] As musicologist Philip V. Bohlman stated, "*Licht und Volk* was intended by its creators as a clear statement attesting that they were in the midst of a Jewish cultural renaissance and that there was no other effective vehicle for this renaissance than music."[39]

One of those for whom the Instructional Cantata marked the beginning of a strengthening of his bonds with Judaism was Paul Eppstein, the director of the general Mannheim Volkshochschule and a sociology professor. Grünewald convinced the twenty-nine-year-old Eppstein to lead the choir of the Instructional Cantata.[40] Through this involvement he became interested in Jewish culture and began a career as a Jewish politician. After

A performance of *Licht und Volk* in Mannheim Rosengarten, 1930. Courtesy Stadtarchiv Mannheim.

1933 he became a member of the executive committee of the central organization of German Jews, the Reichsvertretung der Juden in Deutschland. Later, he achieved notoriety as *Judenältester* in Theresienstadt and was shot in September 1944.[41]

One year after its initial staging in Mannheim, the Instructional Cantata was exported to Cologne, where the Jewish Lehrhaus organized a performance. Reviewing the event, in which three hundred participants performed before an audience of fourteen hundred in the famous Gürzenich Hall, the local Jewish news bulletin rejoiced, "Who of us, thirty or forty years ago, had thought that such a Renaissance would be possible?"[42] The beginning of a renaissance of Jewish music in Germany came only a few years before its premature conclusion. When Grünewald and Adler performed their second Instructional Cantata in 1934 (*Balak und Bilam*), the performance was just another episode in a story of a community forced back into its cultural ghetto. Praise in the non-Jewish press was no longer possible. Both Adler and Grünewald were soon forced to emigrate to the United States, where they lived to see an English adaptation of *Licht und Volk* by Rabbi Alexander Schindler, later the leader of the Reform movement.[43]

AESTHETICS AND THE JEWISH BOOK

The visual arts never played a central role in the religiously dominated premodern Jewish culture. Because the Bible prohibits the making of images, the development of European painting found little reflection among Jewish artists. Among the few exceptions were the rich and colorful illustrations in Jewish books. It is those illustrations—often painted by non-Jewish artists—that provide us with the only significant visual insight into medieval Jewish society.

Long before the disintegration of traditional Jewish society in Germany around the turn of the nineteenth century, the connection between books and art had disappeared. In a mostly rural Jewish community, characterized by economic insecurity and high mobility, the Jewish book continued to be a witness of divine revelation and a mediator of secular knowledge but ceased to be an object of art. In the 1920s poet Karl Wolfskehl juxtaposed the relation between the Jew and his book with modern bibliophilic principles: "There is a peculiar relationship between the Jew and the book. He loves it and appreciates it; he likes it, as one likes everything that is familiar . . . . For all of that, [the Jew] does not treat his beloved book with caution, tenderness, and care. Anyone who has to do with Jewish books . . . bemoans their condition: How overused, how spotted they are; how frequent binding cut the margins of the pages; how the fly-leaf has been scribbled on; and how scraped the cover has become."[44]

Wolfskehl's complaint about the lack of bibliophilic interests among Jewish readers revealed a new attitude among German Jews toward the book. With rapid urbanization, partial social integration, and the rise to prosperity in the second half of the nineteenth century, many German Jews became interested in the aesthetics of the book. By this time, however, most of them had lost their attachment to Jewish literature and expressed their bibliophilic interests as bourgeois Germans. A significant proportion of the members of the German bibliophilic associations, established around the beginning of the twentieth century, were Jews: almost 20 percent of the members of the Gesellschaft der Bibliophilen (founded in 1899), about 30 percent of the Maximilian-Gesellschaft (founded in 1911), and the majority of the Berlin Fontane-Gesellschaft (founded in 1926). Some of the leading figures in the bibliophilic movement in Germany were Jews, such as Georg Witkowski, the editor-in-chief of the Zeitschrift für Bücherfreunde; Aby Warburg, whose Hamburg library was one of the greatest treasures for bibliophiles; and Samuel Fischer, whose publishing house was the most prestigious for bibliophilic publications.[45]

Before World War I, only a handful of Zionists tried to channel this general bibliophilic interest among German Jews into an aesthetic improvement of the Jewish book. Around the turn of the century, the illustrations of Ephraim Mose Lilien and Hermann Struck and the publications of the *Jüdischer Verlag* reflected the first attempts to make not only the contents but also the exterior of Jewish books more attractive. By the end of the Weimar period, bibliophilic activities had become a distinct and well-organized field in the cultural landscape of German Jews.

The renewed aesthetic value of Jewish books was expressed on three different levels: in the private sphere, Jewish book lovers began to commission bookplates with Jewish motifs around the turn of the century; in the area of publishing, there was a new emphasis on book illustrations after World War I; in the institutional realm, the Soncino Society of the Friends of the Jewish Book was established in 1924.

Bookplates not only identify a book's owner but constitute an intimate link between book lovers and their books. They express concern for the aesthetics of a collection and point to the specific interests of the collector. Although Jews began to use bookplates in the eighteenth century, they did not employ Jewish themes until the beginning of the twentieth century, when Ephraim Mose Lilien created the first known Jewish bookplate for the Hebrew writer Reuben Brainin.[46] During the next three decades, bookplates with Jewish motifs became an integral part of Lilien's oeuvre, and that of many other Jewish artists, including Hermann Struck, Joseph Budko, Jakob Steinhardt, and Uriel Birnbaum. Those artists received many of their commissions from German Jews—mostly Zionists—who adorned their books with the images of Jerusalem, biblical figures, or East European Jews, and thus connected their bibliophilism to a cultural Jewish identity in a modern context.[47]

Jewish bibliophilism became more popular with the publication of Jewish books for small circles of book lovers during and after World War I. The production of bibliophilic printings in limited numbers within Germany's large publishing houses was soon adopted by such Jewish publishers as Löwith in Vienna and the Zionist Welt-Verlag in Berlin. The renowned (non-Jewish) publishing house Fritz Gurlitt established the Verlag für jüdische Kunst und Kultur in 1920.[48] One of the results of growing bibliophilic activities in general, as well as in Jewish publishing houses, was a renaissance of book illustration in Germany. Originally inspired by the British arts-and-crafts movement, German book illustrations developed a distinctive character around World War I with the productions of such Expressionist artists as Ernst Barlach, Ernst Ludwig Kirchner, and Oskar Kokoschka.

In contrast to the realm of literature, in the visual arts there were few Jewish representatives of Expressionism and New Objectivity. When painter Karl Hofer informed a Nazi official in 1933 that "next to the army no field was as judenrein as the visual arts," this statement contained a grain of truth.[49] Although art historians have noted the lack of prominent Jewish Expressionist artists, they have not acknowledged that their only two representatives of renown, Ludwig Meidner and Jakob Steinhardt, both contributed to the revival of Jewish art in general and book illustration in particular.

Meidner's and Steinhardt's fame dated back to 1912, when they— together with non-Jewish artist Richard Janthur—organized a small group of Expressionist artists that called itself Die Pathetiker. Their paintings, soon displayed in Herwarth Walden's famous avant-garde art gallery Der Sturm, were characterized by religious ecstasy and apocalyptic visions. The parallels between Meidner and Steinhardt went beyond the artistic. Born in the eastern provinces of Prussia, they both moved to Berlin at a young age and were temporarily separated from the traditional Jewish life they had experienced in Posen and Silesia, respectively. Both were influenced by the general religious revival in Expressionist circles during World War I before renewing their identification with Judaism in the Weimar period. During the first stage of their creativity, depictions of biblical prophets were prominent in their works. Those prophets, in their mystical ecstasy, were reminiscent of El Greco's masterpieces and of the wild oriental Jews in Else Lasker-Schüler's contemporary poems and drawings.

Steinhardt's encounter with East European Jews during his military service in World War I was one of the most decisive experiences of his life. According to him, in the faces of East European Jews he sought to discover his own ancestors. He noted in his war diary that he "recognized" his great-grandmother in an old Jewish woman in the streets of Lithuania.[50]

Meidner, too, was deeply influenced by the war and increasingly expressed his religious experiences in Jewish Orthodox terms. His gradual adoption of an Orthodox style of life was reflected in both his poems and his drawings. In 1918 he confessed that he had been an atheist and "far from the

Ludwig Meidner, *Self-Portrait with Prayer Shawl*, 1918, ink on paper. Courtesy D. Thomas Bergen, London.

faith of my fathers," but by then he had returned to their religion.[51] A decade later, one of his poems began with a moving call for religious steadfastness:

> Jew, don't waver
> Hold firm to your precious possession
> the Holy God
> and the eternal Torah[52]

In his poems and drawings, Meidner depicted himself wrapped in a *talit* (ritual prayer shawl) as a "Hebrew poet." According to a friend, Meidner indeed received visitors in his talit and covered his walls with huge Hebrew excerpts from psalm texts.[53]

Meidner's friend and colleague Jakob Steinhardt had become one of the premier artists of Jewish motifs in the postwar period, with his illustrations of the stories by Yiddish writer Yitzhak Leib Peretz, his portfolio on Lithuanian Jews, and depictions of his trip to Palestine in 1925. When new bibliophilic Jewish books appeared after World War I, both Meidner and Steinhardt contributed illustrations to poems of Arno Nadel.[54] Nadel, in turn, referred to the two artists as representing a "totally new type of contemporary art."[55]

One of Steinhardt's most notable illustrations was his Passover Haggadah of 1923. Steinhardt's version of the traditional collection of prayers, benedictions, and midrashic comments for the Passover Eve reflected a

Jakob Steinhardt, the motif of the four sons, from Steinhardt's Passover Haggadah, 1923. Photograph by Jim Strong. Courtesy of the Leo Baeck Institute, New York.

society marked by war, economic crisis, and social misery. If there is one characteristic illustration in this Haggadah, which Yosef Hayim Yerushalmi has called "one of the most truly distinguished Haggadahs published in modern times, a milestone in Hebrew book production," it is the depiction of the wicked son as a soldier dressed in Prussian uniform with a spiked helmet on his head.[56] Like the apocalyptic depictions of the *Had Gadya* story at the end of the Haggadah, the soldier brings to mind the sufferings of World War I.

The illustrations of this Haggadah do not attempt to reveal an imaginary past, with Egyptian pyramids and oriental desert scenes. They plainly depict postwar Germany, a time of social grievances and personal tragedy. The characters of Steinhardt's Haggadah, and of his later illustrations in the Book of Jesus ben Sira, represented in a Jewish context the world of Otto Dix's distorted soldiers, Käthe Kollwitz's starving children, George Grosz's stout war profiteers, and Christian religious motifs in the works of Max Beckmann and Karl Schmidt-Rottluff. They also reflected the style of contemporary Expressionist book illustrations, with their edged and pointed, often bizarre forms that made them so different from contemporary French artists. Steinhardt took seriously the talmudic dictum according to which members of every generation must feel as if they themselves took part in the Exodus from Egypt.[57] German Jews could indeed identify with this Haggadah as a document reflecting their own era and experience.

This connection becomes even more manifest on examination of the history of the Steinhardt Haggadah. Its publication was initiated by Erich Goeritz, a Jewish textile manufacturer and one of the most important art collectors in Weimar Germany. Goeritz, who lived around the corner from Steinhardt's studio, supported the painter by purchasing, for a number of years, every print that he produced. After Steinhardt had published ten linocuts depicting the Ten Plagues (1920), Goeritz commissioned the artist to illustrate a modern German-Jewish Haggadah.[58]

Steinhardt's Haggadah was a typical product of German Expressionism in style and in topic. During and after World War I, many Expressionist artists turned to religious motifs, sometimes ironically but mostly in genuine religiosity.[59] Karl Schmidt-Rottluff's *Ist Euch nicht Kristus erschienen* (1918) must be singled out as a direct influence on Steinhardt's book illustrations. The parallels between Schmidt-Rottluff's *Kristus* and Steinhardt's Jewish faces are visible not only in the similar technique of their woodcuts but also in the gestures and facial expressions of their characters.

In Steinhardt's Haggadah, Jewish authenticity is represented less by the artist's illustrations than by the design of the text. The text of this otherwise so conspicuously German Haggadah is in Hebrew with no accompanying German translation, a rather unusual innovation at a time when most German Jews could hardly read the Hebrew and certainly could not understand it. Steinhardt's Haggadah was clearly an art book, rather than a liturgical book, in which the text was less significant than the illustrations. Even the Hebrew characters, drawn by the well-known calligraphic artist Franzisca Baruch and executed by Steinhardt in wood, constituted a work of art.[60]

Expressionism was not the only style in which modern Jewish book illustrations were created. Art nouveau inspired Russian-born graphic artist Joseph Budko, who was considered the artistic heir to Ephraim Mose Lilien. It seemed natural for Budko to provide the illustrations for a second edition of Münchhausen's *Juda,* originally illustrated by Lilien.[61] Budko's etchings had an ornamental, filigreed style and used motifs adapted from Jewish folk art. His book illustrations relied heavily on motifs from rural wooden synagogues in Germany, thus reminiscent of the expedition taken by Russian avant-gardist artists to wooden synagogues along the Dnieper in 1917. Budko's departure from Expressionism during the mid-1920s coincided with the relative political and economic stabilization that characterized those years in Germany, which saw the decline of Expressionist art.

Neue Sachlichkeit (New Objectivity) dominated art during the concluding period of Weimar. Like Expressionism, New Objectivity was not a clearly defined art style, but its various manifestations were discernible as post-Expressionist. Instead of showing revolution, pathos, and religious ecstasy, the new style returned to more naturalist and classicist forms. The Geismar Haggadah, published in Berlin in 1927, was a radical expression of the new search for simplicity, with its "essentially black-and-white drawings that depict their themes in deceptively simple strokes." Yosef H. Yerushalmi's description of the Geismar Haggadah reveals striking parallels with the traditions of Neue Sachlichkeit, which were connected with the Bauhaus movement: "Everything is reduced to bare essentials, as it were, and yet all is present, in a virtuoso display of sheer inventiveness and wit."[62]

The most outstanding example of the new aesthetic taste among Jews and non-Jews in the second half of the 1920s was the Offenbach Haggadah of 1927, which appeared in a bibliophilic edition of three hundred copies. Offenbach, a suburb of Frankfurt am Main, was a center of arts and crafts. Here the brothers Klingspor established their famous print shop, in which Rudolf Koch developed his German typefaces. The contributions of the Offenbach school to Jewish art grew out of the personal friendship between Rudolf Koch and Siegfried Guggenheim, a local Jewish lawyer and collector of Jewish art.[63] Beginning in 1919, Guggenheim had commissioned artists, most of whom were not Jewish, to create a range of domestic Jewish art products, including huge tapestries with psalm texts, a specially designed wooden Seder plate, and other ritual objects for the Passover celebration.[64] The Offenbach Haggadah was the culmination of his attempt to provide traditional Jewish festivals with new aesthetic value.

In contrast to most of the bibliophilic Jewish books mentioned so far, Zionists were not involved in the production of the *Offenbach Haggadah*. Its commissioner, Siegfried Guggenheim, was a Liberal Jew, and the Passover Haggadah closely resembles the 1913 Haggadah of Liberal rabbi Caesar Seligmann. In his preface, Guggenheim underlined that his Haggadah was intended to be accessible to those who were unable to read Hebrew letters;

he provided not just translations but also transliterations of the most important parts. He wanted to inspire assimilated German Jews who usually would not celebrate the Passover Seder to do so, with a Haggadah that provided explanations for the Passover service and appealed to the highest aesthetic standards.[65]

At the end of the Haggadah, Guggenheim expressed his distance from Zionism and his close ties with his German surroundings by inserting versions deviating from the traditional conclusion, *Le-shanah ha-ba'ah bi-yerushalayim* (Next year in Jerusalem). He quoted a fifteenth-century Haggadah, in which the Moravian author had added the words "or in Brünn" (Brno) to the traditional conclusion, and recalled that his own family in Worms used to replace it altogether by the sentence "Next year in Worms-on-the-Rhine, our *Heimat.*"

It is not surprising that the Liberal Jewish press praised the new Haggadah as a unique "sign of solidarity [*Verbundenheit*] between German Jewry and German culture."[66] More remarkable was that the Orthodox chief rabbi of Altona, Joseph Carlebach, believed, in spite of his reservations concerning deviations from the traditional text, that "with the help of this Haggadah many a German Jew will find access to the genuine Seder celebration." Carlebach promised to read the Offenbach Haggadah with his children the next Passover.[67]

Indeed, the Offenbach Haggadah cannot be considered simply an additional sign of the growing assimilation among German Jews, or just another Liberal Haggadah. For the first time a layperson, who was neither Orthodox nor Zionist, had compiled a German-Jewish Haggadah, which points to the increasing interest in Judaism among mainstream Liberal German Jews. More significant, Guggenheim expanded the traditional text with appropriate additions designed to encourage its readers to reflect on the Passover story—as has become usual in modern American Haggadot. The principal merit of this Haggadah, however, was not the text but the artistry. Fritz Kredel's modern, colorful, naive illustrations may be regarded as part of the New Objectivity and constituted a pointed contrast to Rudolf Koch's antiquated typeface of *Bibelgothisch,* which a few years later was exploited by the Nazis as a prototype for a distinctly German script.[68]

The Offenbach Haggadah was welcomed by German-Jewish book lovers. They admired the high standard of the print and the illustrations, and the "especially tasteful book cover made of precious material."[69] For some bibliophiles, however, this standard was not sufficient. The Dessau Staatsrat Hermann Cohn, for example, ordered an additional copy—

The *Had gadya* motif: *Offenbacher Haggadah*, 1927. Courtesy of the Leo Baeck Institute, New York.

bound in calfskin and with handmade paper—for his collection of biblio-philic books.[70] Cohn, an activist of the CV and a Liberal member of the Anhalt parliament, represented a certain type of Liberal upper-middle-class Jews who thought it fashionable to create a Jewish corner in their libraries with modern bibliophilic editions bound in calf leather and published in limited numbers.

Three years before the publication of the Offenbach Haggadah, German-Jewish bibliophiles had founded the Soncino Society of the Friends of the Jewish Book, the first Jewish bibliophilic association. The society was ini-tiated by three young Jews—Herrmann Meyer, Moses Marx, and Abraham Horodisch—who had been involved in bibliophilic activities for several years.[71] Originally limited to five hundred members, the society soon had to be expanded to eight hundred because of strong interest. Taking into account that the largest German bibliophilic association had only twelve hundred members, this was a considerable number.[72] Almost half its members lived in Berlin, and another quarter came from seven large communities.[73] Among its active members were Zionists (such as Heinrich Loewe and Sammy Gronemann), Orthodox (such as Rabbi Meier Hilde-sheimer), and Liberals (such as writer Martin Beradt and Gershom

Scholem's brother Reinhold).[74] Rabbi Leo Baeck, Hebrew poet Hayim Nahman Bialik, and writers Arnold Zweig, Richard Beer-Hofmann, and Max Brod sat on the honorary committee of the society.[75]

The Soncino Society, named after the sixteenth-century Italian-Jewish family of printers, institutionalized the new aesthetic taste of urban bourgeois Jews, who demanded the revival of the "beautiful Jewish book." In practice, this included the reprint of rare Jewish books, the modern creation of outstanding book illustrations, and the improvement of Hebrew characters. The society published an internal news bulletin and the journal *Soncino-Blätter,* containing important scholarly articles on the history of the Jewish book and bibliographies of contemporary Jewish publications. During its fourteen years of existence, eighty-two books and booklets appeared in the name of the Soncino Society. They included reprints—such as Süßkind of Trimberg's medieval German poems, the seventeenth-century *Sefer Meschalim,* and David Friedländer's *Lesebuch für jüdische Kinder*—and such modern publications as a drama by Arnold Zweig and translations of works by Shmu'el Yosef Agnon and the contemporary Yiddish novelist Samuel Levin.[76]

Jewish bibliophilic activities resembled parallel efforts in the field of music. The Soncino Society presented German Jews with publications that claimed to be authentically Jewish, while at the same time fulfilling the highest modern aesthetic demands. The two most remarkable publications of the society, Jakob Steinhardt's woodcuts to selected verses from the Book of Jesus ben Sira (1929) and the complete Pentateuch edition (1930–1933), exemplify this twofold task.

The Book of Jesus ben Sira was an interesting choice for the society's first publication. The wisdom literature of Jesus ben Sira was not part of the Jewish biblical canon and therefore had not been studied by Jews. Until the discovery of the Cairo Geniza around the beginning of the nineteenth century, the only known versions of the book were the Greek ones preserved by Christians; a Hebrew original was not known to exist. The re-publication of excerpts of a text that for many centuries had not been part of Jewish tradition and that was unknown and irrelevant to Orthodox Jews indicates that German Jews were searching their ancient roots for new self-definitions. Unlike Reform Jews, however, Jewish bibliophiles were not interested in redefining the traditional canon of holy Jewish books or prayers. The text of the Book of Jesus ben Sira (Hebrew with German translation) was thus limited to a few selected verses, and Jakob Steinhardt's woodcuts constituted the center of this publication.

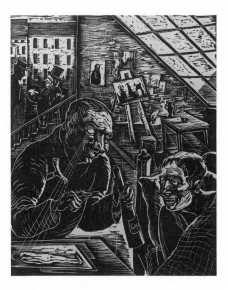

Jakob Steinhardt, woodcut from *Jesus ben Sira,* 1929. Photograph by Jim Strong. Courtesy of the Leo Baeck Institute, New York.

Because the ancient Hebrew source of this text had been discovered only three decades before, it was authentic in a profoundly different way from the traditional Jewish texts. Steinhardt's illustrations combined an allegedly authentic Jewish setting and modern social criticism. With this book readers possessed a work that established a new relation of Jews and their literature, a relation in which the aesthetic element constituted the central attraction. According to Abraham Horodisch, who was responsible for the typographical design, "This book was probably the first bibliophilic Hebrew print that met the standards of Western European book art."[77]

The Book of Jesus ben Sira was the prologue for the society's most ambitious project of Hebrew printing. By the time it appeared, the members of the society had decided to revolutionize Hebrew printing by creating new Hebrew letters that would look antique but would meet the highest modern bibliophilic standards. Only the most representative Jewish text, the Hebrew Bible, could be the basis for this task. One of the leading German calligraphers of the time, Marcus Behmer, created the letters, which according to Horodisch constituted the "first Hebrew script since 1700 that satisfied aesthetic demands."[78] In contrast to the then-common bibliophilic Hebrew printings, Behmer did not choose prototypes from the Italian or Sephardic regions but leaned toward an Ashkenazic model. This choice emphasized a German-Jewish heritage and revealed a predilection for a script close to Expressionist design.[79]

The five books of the Pentateuch, published between 1930 and 1933, marked the culmination of a series of modern bibliophilic Bible publications that appeared in Germany during the first decades of the twentieth century, all of which had been produced thanks to the collaboration of Jewish artists and scholars. On the eve of World War I, the pioneer of Jewish book illustration, Ephraim Mose Lilien, began with a Bible illustration that was to "serve primarily the artistic pleasure" of its readers.[80]

These bibliophilic Bible translations not only elicited enthusiastic approval but also engendered critical reactions among the Jewish public. The expensive Bible translation by Lazarus Goldschmidt—known for his Talmud translation—in which the only Hebrew letter appeared in the watermark, was ridiculed by a Zionist reviewer as a purely aesthetic product not intended for practical use:

> The Bibles of our ancestors were large folios, well and carefully printed and bound—to correspond with the dignity of the work. But because of their frequent use through generations, they were so well-thumbed that they appeared to reflect the spirit of their readers. The Bible of today—and especially the Jewish Bible—looks different. Today one uses it for different reasons; one has not religious but bibliophilic needs. Therefore it is necessary that such a volume be printed on the finest handmade paper and bound in expensive leather, so that the respected text is adorned with all sorts of hand-colored letters. Thus, such a work graces the bookshelves of the nouveaux riches, together with other richly splendorous editions and bibliophilic erotica. Herr Lazarus Goldschmidt fulfilled this "urgent need" by supplying such a Bible.[81]

Although the Soncino Society's Hebrew Bible differed substantially from Goldschmidt's translation, significantly entitled *The Holy Books of the Old Covenant,* it was subject to the same criticism: did aestheticism replace religious spirituality as the major motive for the purchase of Jewish books? This may indeed have been the case for certain people. Still, one should be careful not to dismiss Jewish bibliophily as "book snobbery" (*Bücherprotzertum*), as the Zionist critic did. The founders of the Soncino Society, like the initiators of Jewish adult education, the editors of the *Jüdisches Lexikon,* and the composers of modern liturgical Jewish music, were confronted with the question of how to make Jewish knowledge and culture attractive to a group of bourgeois Jews who were alienated from traditional Judaism.

When the Soncino Society celebrated its first anniversary, Joseph Budko designed the dinner menu. Like all the society's creations, Budko's ornamental decorations aimed at meeting the highest aesthetic demands. The dinner prepared by the strictly kosher Restaurant Vienna, under supervision of the Orthodox Adass Jissroel community of Berlin, however, sounded rather *haymish* (familiar and quaint): chicken soup, pickled tongue, and Viennese apple strudel.[82] Perhaps it was this combination of aestheticism and the remnants of a popular Jewish culture that made enterprises like the Soncino Society viable.

THE PUBLIC PRESENTATION OF JEWISH ART

One week before Adolf Hitler was appointed chancellor of the German Reich, German state officials and Jewish community leaders were reunited for the last time in celebrating a major Jewish cultural endeavor. On 24 January 1933, the Berlin Jewish Museum opened its doors with a solemn ceremony. When a Prussian governmental delegation visited the museum on March 2, it was already an epilogue to a bygone chapter of German-Jewish coexistence. This visit took place only a few blocks away from the burnt-down Reichstag, and a few days before Hitler's final election victory. The head of the delegation, Ministerialdirektor Trendelenburg of the Prussian Department of Culture, "expressed his enthusiasm about the establishment of the museum and its riches of outstanding Jewish artifacts."[83] Two weeks later Max Liebermann, the honorary chairman of the Jewish Museum Association and grand old man of German Impressionism, resigned as the honorary president of the Prussian Academy of Arts.

Although the official opening of the Jewish museum coincided with the waning days of the Weimar Republic, its roots reach back to World War I. Based on the estate of the Dresden Jewish art collector Albert Wolf, the Art Collection of the Jewish Community of Berlin first became accessible to the public in 1917. Stored in two small rooms of the Jewish community library and administered by its chief librarian, Moritz Stern, the collection was ignored until art historian Karl Schwarz became the collection's director in 1927.

Owing to Schwarz's activities, the collection was enlarged considerably. Between 1928 and 1932 the number of paintings grew from 18 to 80, and that of ceremonial objects from 227 to 348. According to a contemporary art critic, the problem of insufficient space had become so evident that the art collection resembled a peddler's storage room.[84] In search of adequate exhibition halls, Schwarz initiated the foundation of a Jewish Museum Association and persuaded Max Liebermann to serve as honorary chairman, and many other Jewish notables and art connoisseurs to be board members.[85] When the Jewish hospital (*Siechenheim*) moved to a new location in 1932, the Jewish art collection finally obtained a permanent and dignified home next to the Oranienburger Straße Synagogue and officially adopted the name Jewish Museum.

The notion of a Jewish museum is a modern one, possible only in a highly secularized Jewish society. In a traditional society there was little interest in the display of ceremonial objects, which were used in the synagogue or at home. If they could no longer be used, their place was the *geniza,* the storage room for old books and ritual objects in the synagogue. Although a certain aesthetic value had always been attached to those ceremonial objects, it would never have occurred to Jews in traditional societies to create ceremonial objects for the exclusive purpose of public display.

Formerly restricted to ceremonial use, the displayed objects obtained an autonomous function as objects whose worth was determined by their aesthetic attractiveness rather than their ritual value. In this respect, the visitors to Jewish museums were closely related to collectors of Jewish books and the audiences who attended Jewish concerts. In search of their group identity, they were especially attracted to everything that seemed authentically Jewish, not despite their feeling that they no longer lived authentically, but because of it. The objects displayed in the museum became for them the bearers of a vicarious authenticity, and they believed that they could attain a modicum of this authenticity by associating with these objects in a public space or by placing them in their homes.

The emphasis on the aesthetic value of Jewish ceremonial objects does not contradict the notion of a revitalization of Jewish culture. Jewish secular society longed for new approaches to guarantee its survival. The public display of ceremonial objects, like the recitals of Jewish liturgy and the establishment of a Jewish bibliophilic association, were answers to the dilemma of modern Judaism, torn between the cultural ideals of the larger society and the determination to express its cultural distinctiveness.

The entrance hall of the Jewish Museum in Berlin was itself a programmatic statement. Two busts of prominent German Jews, Moses Mendelssohn and Abraham Geiger, reminded visitors of their German-Jewish heritage, and four works depicted biblical motifs through the eyes of contemporary German-Jewish artists: a sculpture of David by Arnold Zadikow, Lesser Ury's famous depictions of Jeremiah and Moses, and

Entrance hall of the Jewish Museum, Berlin, January 1933. Courtesy Bildarchiv Abraham Pisarek, Berlin.

Jakob Steinhardt's painting of 1912, *Prophet,* which had established his fame as an Expressionist artist. The emphasis on contemporary Jewish painting and sculpture constituted a distinct contrast to the contents of Albert Wolf's original art collection, which consisted mainly of antiquities, coins, old ceremonial objects, portraits, and prints.[86]

The contrast was intended by Schwarz, who regarded a Jewish museum as a means to revitalize Jewish artistic creativity. In the guide to the museum created for its opening, Schwarz stressed his conviction that the aim of such a place was the depiction of Jewish art and culture as *living* history.[87] He saw one of his main tasks to be inspiring artists to create modern ceremonial objects. Recalling his role in the modernization of Jewish ceremonial art, Schwarz wrote, "The department of modern ritual objects . . . was a totally new enterprise, which no Jewish collection before had dared to initiate. The collector appeared here at the same time as direct commissioner of the artists. In long discussions I talked to them about the preparation of those objects, developed my ideas about the use of symbols and the reshaping of old forms." Partly under Schwarz's guidance, Jewish artists developed modern designs for ceremonial art, such as kiddush cups and Seder plates.

A second stimulus for the production of modern Jewish ceremonial art in Weimar Germany was the general interest among all religious groups in

the modernization of religious objects. Led by progressive Protestant theologians, the Berlin Museum of Applied Arts organized an exhibit called
Kult und Form in 1931. Protestants, Catholics, and Jews displayed rich
selections of ceremonial objects, with a special emphasis on contemporary
art. This exhibit was only the first in a series of similar enterprises in many
large German cities that lasted until the end of the Weimar period.
According to Karl Schwarz, who was a member of the exhibit's organization committee, this forum of interfaith dialogue stimulated the creation of
numerous modern Jewish ceremonial objects.[88]

Sculptor Ludwig Yehuda Wolpert figured most prominently among the
contemporary artists whose ceremonial objects were displayed in the Berlin
Jewish museum. Raised in a religious, Zionist family near Heidelberg,
Wolpert studied at the School of Arts and Crafts in Frankfurt am Main
under the guidance of Bauhaus teachers. When he began to develop an
interest in Jewish ceremonial objects in the mid-1920s, he was deeply influenced by Bauhaus theory. His creations were characterized by a simple and
functional purity and thus contrasted sharply with the profusely ornate ceremonial objects of the nineteenth century. In the Berlin Jewish Museum a
room was dedicated to modern Jewish ceremonial objects, housing
Wolpert's three-tiered Passover Seder plate and Hanukkah lamp.[89]

Like most of his colleagues, Wolpert integrated traditional artistic
models into New Objectivity, thus fulfilling Schwarz's demands. It was
this combination of authenticity and modernity that made Wolpert and
other artists extremely popular among their contemporaries: "The quest
for modern ceremonial objects alone is proof of a Jewish spiritual renaissance. One wants the old familiar objects as decoration in one's home but
is not content with antiquities and traditional family pieces; instead, one
tries to revitalize them by reshaping them in accordance with the modern
sense [of art]."[90]

The Berlin Jewish Museum was preceded by a number of smaller Jewish
museums and art collections with similar goals. The first association dedicated to the collection of Jewish artifacts was constituted in Vienna in
1895; in Germany, Jewish art associations and collections followed in a
number of cities, such as Hamburg (1898–1900), Frankfurt am Main
(1901), Kassel (1927), Breslau (1928), and Munich (1931). Permanent
contact between those institutions was established during the Weimar years
by annual conventions of the various Jewish Museum Associations in Germany.[91]

After a visit through museums of Germany and Austria in 1907, Russian-

Jewish anthropologist Samuel Weissenberg had been "disappointed and shattered" by the lack of Jewish art collections.[92] Had he returned twenty-five years later, he would have encountered rich and growing Jewish art collections housed in independent institutions or larger museums. Although this development represented a significant change from the apparent lack of interest in Jewish art objects before World War I, its ambivalent character must be noted.

According to ethnographer Christoph Daxelmüller, this "accumulation of foundations of Jewish museums within a few decades" was a sign of further consolidation of the Jewish cultural renaissance.[93] Indeed, as a contemporary Jewish teacher wrote, a Jewish museum had the potential of becoming a "source of new strength" for the revival of Jewish culture.[94] Karl Schwarz's attempt to use the Berlin Jewish Museum as a basis for modern artistic creativity was proof of such an attitude in Weimar Germany. The creation of museums, however, always implies a distance between the observer and the objects. Far removed from their original purpose, ritual objects in museums were no longer used but merely displayed. Like Jewish liturgical recitals, or Haggadot produced specifically as artworks, museums encourage passive admiration, not active involvement. Their increasing popularity thus points to both the achievements and the limits of the renaissance of Jewish culture in Weimar Germany.

BAUHAUS AND NEW SYNAGOGUE ARCHITECTURE

Perhaps even more than other areas of the visual arts, the architecture of Weimar Germany was conceived not just as another innovation but as an entirely new approach, a *Neues Bauen*.[95] With their emphasis on simplicity, utility, and the synthesis of different fields of art to create one harmonious whole, such architects as Walter Gropius, Bruno Taut, Mies van der Rohe, and Erich Mendelsohn were part of the New Objectivity movement. The Bauhaus, founded in Weimar and continued in Dessau, was their major institutional base. Established amid the revolutionary disorder of 1919, the Bauhaus aimed to create art that proved useful to society, rather than aesthetically attractive art.

Erich Mendelsohn, though not associated with the Bauhaus movement, was the most prominent Jewish architect among the representatives of Neues Bauen. He designed strikingly modern facades for the Schocken chain of department stores and the Mosse publishing house. His outstanding project was Albert Einstein's extravagant laboratory tower near

Berlin. He was also active in Palestine long before his emigration in the 1930s. Jewish organizations and communities turned to him in their eagerness to provide Jewish venues for modern architectural expression. Mendelsohn, who never designed any non-Jewish sacral objects, constructed a Jewish lodge in East Prussian Tilsit (1925), the Jewish cemetery in Königsberg (1927), and the Jewish youth center in Essen (1929–1930). The choice of such a renowned architect as Mendelsohn for Jewish institutions amplifies the significance of the changing face of German-Jewish communities.[96] Although Mendelsohn designed his first synagogue only when he was in exile in the United States after having lived in Palestine during the 1930s, synagogue architecture expressed most clearly the penetration of Neues Bauen into Jewish communities. A recurrent topic in *Menorah* and other Jewish art journals was the demand for modern synagogue architecture.[97]

There has never been a distinct architectural style for the construction of synagogues, and when in the nineteenth century ostentatious temples were built in all large German cities, they usually were designed in a mixture of neoclassical, neo-Gothic, and neo-Islamic styles. The economic crisis after World War I, as well as the decline in need for new large synagogues, halted the boom of expensive synagogue constructions.

The few synagogues built between 1918 and 1933 were not exclusively dedicated to religious service but had a number of additional functions. These synagogues, which were community centers rather than temples, indicated the growing social and cultural tasks of the Jewish community. While the first two, constructed during World War I in Essen and Augsburg, were built in the art nouveau style and reflected the exterior splendor of imperial times, the republic's synagogues were far more modest, partly because of financial necessity and partly for ideological reasons.

Austerity and utility became the leitmotifs for contemporary synagogue architecture. Influenced by the Bauhaus style, such European Jewish communities as Vienna, Amsterdam, and Zurich experimented with this new simplicity.[98] In Germany, the synagogues of Plauen (1930) and Hamburg-Oberstraße (1931) used most clearly the ideas of Neues Bauen.

When Fritz Landauer, the architect of the Augsburg synagogue, was commissioned with the construction of a new synagogue in Plauen (Thuringia) in the late 1920s, his concept differed decisively from his earlier art nouveau model. Three factors led him on this new path. First, economic necessity forced the consolidation of the synagogue with other Jewish institutions. Second, ideological reasons contributed to the construction of a

Plauen synagogue, 1928–1930. Courtesy Vogtlandmuseum Plauen.

community center instead of a synagogue. With the increasing secularization of the Jewish community and its extension to areas of culture and social welfare, assembly halls, theater stages, and office space were as necessary as traditional prayer rooms. Third, the new aesthetic, as developed most radically by the Bauhaus movement, pledged simplicity and utility instead of pomp and representation.

Landauer believed that "modern sacral art is only possible by the symbiosis of sacral-ceremonial traditions with the art-language of the time."[99] The Plauen synagogue, an elongated cube with bands of small windows, would not have been recognizable as sacral from outside, were it not for a small Star of David. Although the exterior was modernism proper, the interior reflected the longing for authenticity that we have observed in many other areas of Jewish art. The graffito paintings adorning the interior of the synagogue depicted "authentic" biblical landscapes of the Middle East. As Landauer noted, the building served various aspects of Jewish community life. This unification of "cult and culture" under one roof, emphasized by the massive block structure, was for him both a sign of the "wholeness of our new lives"—thus reflecting Bauhaus ideology—and a return to the medieval Jewish community, where cultural and religious expressions of Jewish life had been unified.[100]

The synagogue in the small town of Plauen with a Jewish community of eight hundred was followed by a similar modernist construction in the large Jewish community of Hamburg. Here, the Reform Jewish congregation was in need of a new building because most of its members had moved to a different part of the city during the previous decades. The predilection for a distinctly modern construction was reflected in most contributions to the architectural competition, and in the jury's visit to the exhibition *Contemporary Sacral Buildings*. Certainly the congregation's self-definition as progressive contributed to the modernist predilections. At the same time, however, the new building marked an architectural parallel to the return to traditions in the Hamburg Reform congregation. In the modern Bauhaus-style temple, German was again replaced by Hebrew as the major language for services, and the prayers for a return to Zion were reintroduced. For the first time, special youth services were established.[101]

The Hamburg and Plauen synagogues both bore a certain resemblance to contemporary church projects, but churches never went as far in their adaptation of the Bauhaus style. Modern church constructions in Weimar Germany still had traditional stepped roofs with gables and clock tower, but some modern synagogues in no way resembled sacral architecture.

The same combination of modernism and claimed authenticity was thus perceptible in the areas of Jewish music, Jewish book illustration, and Weimar's synagogue architecture. In their drive to express a cultural Jewish distinctiveness, a group of acculturated German Jews recovered East European and oriental musical traditions, and produced Hebrew books and their translations. For Jewish musicians and artists, as for Jewish writers, East European Jewish traditions, as well as Hebrew and Yiddish, represented the ultimate expression of Jewish authenticity. Few of them, however, were aware that for a short period during the early 1920s they lived in the midst of the creative center of both Hebrew and Yiddish literature and scholarship. Those Hebrew and Yiddish writers, and their relation to German-Jewish culture, will be discussed in the next chapter.

7

Authenticity Revisited: Jewish Culture in Jewish Languages

For the first time after leaving Russia, I felt myself in the midst of my
people, in a warm and living Hebrew atmosphere. In all the countries I
have been so far, I felt estranged, as if there was a barrier [*mehitza*],
because there was no Hebrew spoken there. Only here in Berlin did this
barrier fall.

—Hayim Nahman Bialik to a gathering at the Beth ha-va'ad ha-ivri
be-Berlin (1922)

One of the factors that made oriental and East European Jews
look authentic to German Jews was their use of distinctly Jewish languages.
During and after World War I, German Jews had various opportunities to
encounter Hebrew and Yiddish cultures. Most German Jews were neither
willing nor able to immerse themselves in those cultures. For a small elite
group, however, Jewish culture expressed in Jewish languages constituted
the culmination of a Jewish renaissance. Their attitude was reflected on
several cultural levels, from the admiration of Yiddish theater troupes to
the study of modern Hebrew.

At the same time, the small circle of East European Jewish intellectuals
in Weimar Germany did not live in a cultural vacuum. Although their presence was unnoticed by the average German Jew, they left their mark on the
Jewish cultural renaissance. The encounter between poet and publisher
Hayim Nahman Bialik and the leading representatives of Wissenschaft des
Judentums resulted in the publication of the Hebrew journal *Devir*, an
important forum for the Hebrew-language scholarly study of Judaism

(*Hokhmat Israel*). Writer Shmu'el Yosef Agnon was active in Weimar's Jewish cultural renaissance in several ways. During his twelve-year stay in Germany he gave readings at Franz Rosenzweig's Lehrhaus, worked on a scholarly project with Martin Buber, and became one of the forces behind the establishment of the Schocken publishing house. Another representative of the Hebraist colony in Berlin, philosopher Simon Rawidowicz, was actively engaged both in the revival of Hebrew and in German-Jewish culture. He established the Hebrew World Union in Berlin in 1931, worked as a librarian in the Berlin Jewish community, and collaborated on one of German Jewry's most prestigious scholarly enterprises, the jubilee edition of Moses Mendelssohn's writings.

In 1931, Rawidowicz summarized the short-lived blossoming of Hebrew culture in Germany after World War I: "In those times, the Hebrew word went forth from Germany to Palestine and to all countries of the diaspora. . . . Future literary historians of Hebrew will certainly speak of a 'German period' when modern Hebrew literature flourished."[1] While Rawidowicz was certainly right concerning the Weimar period, his prognosis for future historiography proved wrong. When the skies over German Jewry darkened, the short but fascinating episode of Hebrew culture in Germany was largely forgotten and has been by-and-large neglected by scholars. If at all remembered, it is considered merely a "temporary asylum" (*miklat le-sha'ah*) for Hebrew and Yiddish writers, without further implications.[2]

GERMAN JEWS' ENCOUNTER WITH HEBREW AND YIDDISH CULTURE

The migration of tens of thousands of East European Jews, who arrived in Germany as refugees or forced laborers during World War I, offered German Jews the possibility of meeting what appeared to them to be the incarnation of Martin Buber's literary characters. In search of an encounter with the purveyors of authentic Judaism, Zionist physician and pedagogue Siegfried Lehmann founded, in 1916, the Jüdisches Volksheim in Berlin's East European Jewish quarter, the Scheunenviertel.

The Volksheim was modeled on the English settlement system, which provided an educational framework for a mainly proletarian population. It aimed to provide practical training for East European Jewish immigrants and education for their children, based on modern pedagogical principles. According to the first annual report of the Volksheim, its paternalistic objective was to "gather the children and youth in the streets near the Volk-

sheim, which are populated mostly by East European Jews, within Gemein-
schaften . . . in order to gain cultural influence on the growing generation."[3]
The influence of the ideals of the German youth movement and the desire
for community can be clearly identified in the activities of the Volksheim.
Its main educational goal was to create a sense of Gemeinschaft among the
East European Jewish youth.

The educational process in the Volksheim was not unidirectional, however. The educators, mostly young German Zionists, sought among the
youth of the Scheunenviertel what they could not find in themselves: Jewish
authenticity. For Lehmann, Yiddish songs recited by a German concert
singer, or Jewish festivals celebrated by acculturated German Jews, lacked
the spirit of genuine Judaism, which could be regained only through the
intervention of East European Jews: "A Jewish popular culture in Germany
remains an artificial, not a genuine . . . creation, as long as it is cultivated
by an intellectual elite, and as long as we do not . . . experience this popular
culture together with its true bearers."[4]

Some of the educators moved to the Volksheim in order to live in the
East European Jewish atmosphere of the Scheunenviertel. Others came
only for the regular lectures and discussion groups. Audiences at the Volk-
sheim could hear Gustav Landauer (who in 1919 became the leader of the
short-lived Bavarian Soviet Republic) speak on Judaism and socialism,
Martin Buber read from his unpublished writings, or Volksheim director
Siegfried Lehmann lecture on Franz Werfel. Franz Kafka was among those
Jewish intellectuals who were peripherally connected with the Volksheim.
Shortly after its opening in summer 1916, he encouraged his fiancée, Felice
Bauer, to continue her active involvement in the Volksheim as a social
worker and assured her that "there is no better way of spending the little
time you have" than with Lehmann in the Volksheim. At the same time he
realized that the Central European Jewish educators profited more from
the Volksheim's activities than the East European children who supposedly
were to be educated: "It is one of the most self-interested of occupations.
One is not helping, but seeking help." And a few weeks later he emphasized
his own spiritual involvement in the Volksheim through Felice's work: "I
can think of no closer spiritual bond between us than that created by this
work. . . . As far as I can see, it is positively the only path, or threshold to
it, that can lead to spiritual liberation."[5]

In her letters to Kafka, Felice mentioned the provocative comments by a
young student, named Gerhard Scholem, in one of the Volksheim discussions. The still unknown Scholem criticized the "aesthetic ecstasy" of the

Volksheim and demanded that "people learn Hebrew and go to the sources" instead of listening to "literary twaddle."[6] Although Kafka was less critical of the Volksheim's activities, he concurred with Scholem's sentiment. Both Scholem and Kafka had begun to study Hebrew around the same time, although their paths led them in different directions. In 1923— just after Scholem had left Berlin, convinced that genuine Jewish life would be possible only in Palestine—Kafka moved to Berlin, where he immediately immersed himself in Jewish culture. As he reported in the letters to his friend Robert Klopstock, he spent most of his time translating Yosef Hayim Brenner's Hebrew novel *Shekhol ve-kishalon* (Loss and stumble) into German, and studying at the Hochschule für die Wissenschaft des Judentums, the Liberal rabbinical seminary.[7] Kafka complained about the difficulty of the Hebrew language but learned it more successfully than other German-Jewish intellectuals, including Walter Benjamin, who dedicated a few months in 1920 and 1929 to the study of Hebrew.

Robert Alter has aptly described Kafka's attraction to the Hebrew language, which he began to study with a private teacher in Prague, as a search for authenticity:

> Here was a language that reached back to a world in every respect antithetical to the realm of Hermann Kafka's shop and bourgeois apartment and his thin veneer of Prague German. . . . To follow the original words of the creation story, the Psalms, the prophecies of Isaiah, to make a first tentative foray into the dialectical labyrinth of the Talmud, to ponder the modern literary articulation of the millennia-old language—all this could provide neither intellectual solutions nor spiritual redemption for the dying Kafka, but it did put him in touch with something he could feel was authentic.[8]

When Scholem and Kafka began to teach themselves Hebrew before and during World War I, they represented isolated cases in German-speaking Jewish intellectual circles. After the war, however, Scholem's demand that people learn Hebrew was met by German Zionists, who established a network of Hebrew schools and courses in large German cities.

The Jüdischer Schulverein (Jewish School Association) in Berlin was a pioneering example. In 1919 it initiated a Hebrew language school, and until the mid-1920s four preschools and two elementary schools with a strong emphasis on the study of modern Hebrew were under its control.[9] After initial resistance, the study of modern Hebrew was also encouraged by the Liberal-dominated Jewish community board, and in 1925, when about three hundred students attended nineteen courses in the Jüdischer

Schulverein, the Hebrew language school was integrated into the framework of the Jewish community. The Berlin example soon found imitators elsewhere. By 1927, fourteen hundred students were enrolled in Zionist-sponsored evening courses of modern Hebrew in more than thirty Jewish communities.[10]

The study of modern Hebrew formed the core of all Jewish adult education institutions and assumed increasing importance in Jewish high schools and in the less intensive programs of Jewish religious education.[11] In some big cities young German Jews went beyond the purely theoretical study of Hebrew by publishing their own typewritten periodicals, performing Hebrew plays, and producing Hebrew card games and parlor games for Jewish children.[12]

Because the systematic study of modern Hebrew was a new phenomenon in the German-Jewish community, appropriate teaching material was lacking. One of the most urgent tasks of the Cultural Committee of the Zionist Federation of Germany, established in 1916, was to produce a Hebrew textbook for German-Jewish students. The work was begun during the war, but owing to the initial author's death and the inflation, its publication was delayed for almost a decade. When the book appeared in 1927, it gave new impetus to the growing network of Hebrew schools.[13]

Additional signs indicated an increasing recognition of Hebrew in the German-Jewish community. A Hebrew Convention of German-Jewish rabbis and teachers, and Hebrew writers, in June 1922 symbolized the interest in the study of modern Hebrew as well as a process of decentralization. By meeting in Essen, in the Ruhr region, the participants aimed to prove that Hebrew culture was not restricted to Berlin.[14] The study of modern Hebrew spread geographically and ideologically. A growing number of Liberals and Orthodox joined the struggle for the revitalization of the Hebrew language. Only a few months after the Essen convention, the rabbinical assembly of Rhineland and Westphalia passed a resolution welcoming the increasing importance of the Hebrew language and demanding that it be taught in more schools.[15]

For most German Jews, however, Hebrew remained a foreign language. The majority of German Jews did not study Hebrew, but many of them were fascinated by its revival as a spoken language and as a means of modern cultural expression. The enthusiastic reception that German Jews gave the Hebrew theater group Habimah illustrates this phenomenon. Founded in Moscow in 1917 as the first professional Hebrew theater company, Habimah was heavily influenced by contemporary Russian avant-garde theater. The founders of Habimah solicited help from Constantin Stanislavsky, the director of the Moscow Art Theater, who agreed to work with the Hebrew troupe and appointed his best student, Eugene Vakh-tangov, as Habimah's first director. Between 1926 and 1931 the troupe toured several times through Germany and other countries, until it finally settled down in Palestine, where it went on to become Israel's National Theater.

In Eastern Europe, Habimah's performances were celebrated as national events of foremost importance. When Habimah first toured Germany in 1926, however, they expected hardly anyone to understand the spoken text. It came as a surprise to organizers and actors when a broad spectrum of German Jews (and non-Jews) raved about their performance. Albert Einstein wrote to the members of Habimah, "Your performance was of truly monumental greatness and made the greatest impression on me I have ever experienced at the theater."[16] For Alfred Kerr, Germany's leading theater critic, the performances of Habimah remained an "unforgettable experience," and Max Reinhardt, the stage director of Berlin's prestigious Deutsches Theater, found the productions of the Hebrew theater thrilling.[17]

When the two leading Yiddish theater troupes of Eastern Europe, the Vilna Troupe and the Moscow Jewish Academic State Theater, toured Germany during the Weimar years, they enjoyed similar success. Much of the praise from German-Jewish critics was certainly due to the companies' incontestable artistic creativity and dramatic skills. But this does not explain the unusual enthusiasm of the German-Jewish audience. Only a few years before, hardly any German Jew in an influential position would have praised cultural products presented in languages that were considered debased or simply antiquated. On the eve of World War I, Franz Kafka was derided because of his enthusiasm for a touring Yiddish theater company.[18] Although such derogatory voices could still be heard in Weimar Germany, they were no longer in vogue.

Instead, the most noted German-Jewish critics, playwrights, and stage directors emphasized their admiration for Yiddish culture, which, like Hebrew, was perceived as an authentic expression of Jewish culture. In the plays of Habimah and the Vilna and Moscow Yiddish theaters, the "anti-quated" and "debased" languages had become symbols of a renewal of Jewish authenticity that was no longer reduced to a mere nostalgic longing for the world of yesterday. Those performances in Jewish languages combined folk tales of dybbuks or golems, for example, with avant-garde stage design and direction. This blend allowed German-Jewish critics to express their emotional attachment to the cultural products of their East European kin while expressing their preference for modernism.[19]

Typical of such a perspective were Alfred Kerr's reviews, which combined admiration for a rediscovered Jewish authenticity with regret for his linguistic shortcomings. In a review of the Vilna Troupe, which settled in Berlin between September 1921 and March 1923, Kerr displayed both distance from and familiarity with their performances. He admitted that the Yiddish language was entirely strange to him, but he was enthusiastic about a popular (*volkstümlich*) Jewish theater of high quality, which he compared to Bavarian folk theater.[20]

Kerr characterized the actors of Habimah's Hebrew performance of Richard Beer-Hofmann's *Jaákobs Traum* as *Bibel-Bauern* (Bible peasants) who "use the same old tone, the tone of the Bible, which unfortunately has become strange to me, although . . . our cousins have probably been archangels and *Heerscharen* [heavenly hosts], and so on."[21] He emphasized that in spite of his lack of understanding he felt a special "family relationship" with the bearers of this culture.

In praise for the performance, the critic was joined by the playwright. Richard Beer-Hofmann, who, like Kerr, did not understand Hebrew, nevertheless regarded Habimah's performance as a perfection of his literary model, and saw a "tender, almost loving hand trying to transform my work. . . . Here were people who expressed their sorrow and hope with my words, who stood before God to pray in my words. . . . I am grateful that I was given such a rare [honor]." Again, both linguistic nonunderstanding and emotional attachment characterized Beer-Hofmann's reception of the Hebrew translation of his play: "It sounded strange, in a language which I do not understand, but in some way seemed to be familiar, a part of me."[22]

German-Jewish intellectuals were impressed by the artistry of the modern Jewish theater, which they juxtaposed with what they perceived to be the rudimentary quality of traditional Yiddish theater. When the only permanent Berlin Yiddish theater company, the Herrnfeld Theater in the Kommandantenstraße, was replaced by the Vilna Troupe in 1921, Alfred Döblin praised the new troupe as one of the two best theaters in town. Instead of the "unworthy *Gemauschel*" of the Herrnfeld Theater, Döblin continued, one could now see "authentic Jewish theater, . . . the spontaneous artistic achievements of a living people." And Max Reinhardt was so enthusiastic about the Vilna Troupe's guest performance that he invited its leading actor to play in two of his own Shakespeare stagings.[23]

The replacement of the popular Herrnfeld Theater by the avant-garde

Vilna Troupe was representative of the development of Yiddish culture in Weimar Germany. The theater of the Herrnfeld brothers may have possessed no great artistic value, but it enjoyed enormous success among the masses of the Scheunenviertel. The Vilna Troupe (*Jüdisches Künstlertheater*), in contrast, succeeded in attracting a German-Jewish audience and was celebrated even by segments of the non-Jewish public, but its plays were a departure from popular Yiddish theater, as it was known to the average East European Jewish immigrant.[24] Not incidentally, it was a German Zionist, Sammy Gronemann, who had discovered the Vilna Troupe during World War I and who, together with *Ost und West* editor Leo Winz, helped bring the ensemble to the West in 1921.[25]

The Jewish Theater Association—established by Winz, Gronemann, and Arnold Zweig—did not succeed, however, in maintaining a permanent Jewish theater company. After the Vilna Troupe left Berlin in March 1923, Yiddish theater in Berlin was reduced to a few guest performances.[26] The most prominent was by the Moscow Jewish State Theater (GOSET), founded in Petrograd in 1918 by Alexander Granovsky, a student of the leading theater directors in Russia and Germany, among them Vsevolod Meyerhold and Max Reinhardt.[27] Like Habimah and the Vilna Troupe, the Moscow Jewish State Theater aimed at a synthesis of traditional folk motifs and avant-garde technique, but it had a stronger emphasis on the socialist art ideals represented in the emerging Soviet state theaters. Marc Chagall, Nathan Altman, and other Russian-Jewish avant-garde artists created stage designs, costumes, and paintings for the theater walls.

When the troupe began touring Europe in 1928, it was enthusiastically welcomed by German Jews. For a broad range of critics, the Moscow Jewish State Theater represented both Gemeinschaft and Jewish authenticity. Marxist economist Alfons Goldschmidt, for example, identified in its performances the "play of a genuine community."[28] He explained this sense of community only partly by the impact of the Russian Revolution and its emphasis on the collective spirit in the arts. The specific Gemeinschaft of the Moscow Jewish State Theater was nourished by its Jewish authenticity, which Joseph Roth underlined by using images of East European and oriental Jews: "It seemed to me as though the Jewishness portrayed here is more oriental than what one usually encounters. . . . They are Jews of a higher degree, more Jewish Jews. . . . All standards which I bring with me from Western culture to this theater are insufficient to measure it."[29]

The Hebrew and Yiddish troupes, conceived as authentically Jewish in the West, were considered modern European art theater in the East.

Anchored in the tradition of the art theater established all over Europe since the late nineteenth century, those Yiddish and Hebrew theaters constituted the Jewish counterparts of a general European trend of retheatralization of the theater. Their language and repertoire were specifically Jewish, but their creativity came from such non-Jewish Russian stage directors as Constantin Stanislavsky, Eugene Vakhtangov, and Vsevolod Meyerhold. The founder of the Moscow Jewish State Theater, Alexander Granovsky, stated at the occasion of the theater's opening performance, "We do not agree with those who claim that a Jewish theater needs certain specific Jewish laws. . . . We maintain that the tasks of our theater are the tasks of world theater, and only in language does it differ from other theaters."[30] The main characteristics of Granovsky's troupe were those of other European avant-garde theaters during the first third of the twentieth century: radical deliterarization (one play had fewer than a thousand spoken words), unity of stage and audience, and an emphasis on grotesque aesthetics. Although Jewish folk motifs and shtetl life constituted the thematic background for the troupe's performances, Jewish tradition was viewed rather critically, if not altogether negatively. The dominant socialist ideology of the Jewish State Theater made it an ardent advocate of a profound transformation of traditional Jewish life. It was an intriguing misperception when Joseph Roth called the actors of the Moscow Jewish State Theater "more Jewish Jews"; a misperception that can be explained only by the search for an alternative Jewish identity among Jews estranged from Judaism. As Delphine Bechtel observed, "While the Yiddish theater troupes wanted to modernize, to become avant-garde, German Jews wanted to be spellbound back into the archaic and magic world of the ghetto."[31] Like the German-Jewish novels and plays discussed in Chapter 5, Yiddish and Hebrew theater offered an aesthetic affirmation of Judaism, with the additional authentic touch of Jewish languages.

When Berlin again boasted a resident Jewish theater in 1930, Maxim Sakaschansky's Kaftan cabaret, the Yiddish-language sketches that kept many acculturated German Jews away contributed to its popularity among a minority of mostly Zionist German Jews. Some of them were actively involved, such as Alfred Döblin's brother, who played an East European Jew carrying a heavy burden across the stage, a sack with the inscription "107." This was one of the increasingly frequent references to the changing political climate in Germany; the NSDAP had raised its number of seats from 12 to 107 at the Reichstag elections of 1930.[32]

Better known than Sakaschansky's Kaftan was Walter Mehring's German-language play *Der Kaufmann von Berlin* (The merchant of Berlin), which Erwin Piscator's famous experimental theater performed in September 1929. The drama tells of the economic and social rise and fall of the Yiddish-speaking protagonist Simon Chajim Kaftan, an East European Jew, in Berlin at the height of the inflation of 1923. Like Shakespeare's Shylock, Kaftan was both perpetrator and victim, as Piscator wrote, a "capitalist who is ruined by capitalism."[33]

The author of the play, Walter Mehring, was a highly acculturated German Jew, who, under the influence of Yiddish theater troupes touring Berlin, began to study Yiddish. In creating the part of the Ostjude Kaftan, Mehring decided not to make the character speak German with a Yiddish accent (a traditional way to represent East European Jews in German theater) but to allow him to speak Yiddish. When Piscator brought the play to the stage, he imported a native Yiddish speaker from New York, Paul Baratoff, to play Kaftan. Some theater critics praised *Der Kaufmann von Berlin,* and one remarked that "never before has 'the street' been so clearly depicted on a stage."[34] Most reviews, however, were negative, focusing on the chaos and confusion on stage. Critics complained about the stage design by Bauhaus artist Moholy-Nagy, which featured ever moving elevators, and about the actors' use of different dialects. After a few performances, the play was canceled, mainly because of the conservatives' allegation that the play contained anti-patriotic sentiments.

Most German-Jewish critics felt hurt by Mehring's overt depiction of the antagonism between German Jews and East European Jews.[35] The same critics who had welcomed the use of Yiddish in the "authentic" East European theater companies thought it inappropriate when integrated into a German play written by a German-Jewish author for a German audience. Alfred Kerr, for example, the admirer of the visiting Yiddish theater troupes, criticized the play because the audience would not understand the Yiddish spoken on stage.[36]

The Yiddish word was not confined to the stage in Weimar Germany. Berlin became a center of Yiddish publishing activities in the early 1920s, when at least 187 Yiddish books and seventeen periodicals were printed there.[37] The most notable journals were Uri Zvi Greenberg's literary periodical, *Albatros* (founded in Warsaw), and the art and literature journal *Milgroyim* (a simultaneous Hebrew edition appeared under the name *Rimon*). Edited by Mark and Rachel Wischnitzer between 1922 and 1924, this was the most beautiful Yiddish art journal ever to appear, containing illustrations and contributions of Russian-Jewish avant-garde artists living in Berlin, among them Marc Chagall, Nathan Altman, and El Lissitzky. It also published Yiddish and Hebrew translations of notable contemporary essays on art and art history. *Milgroyim-Rimon* was both the vehicle of avant-garde Jewish art in the 1920s and the center of the East European Jewish artist colony in Berlin.[38]

When, by the middle of the twenties, *Milgroyim* and *Albatros* ceased to appear and most Russian-Jewish artists had already left Berlin, the German capital became the center of another major enterprise of Yiddish culture. The Yidisher Visnshaftlekher Institut (YIVO, Institute of Jewish Research) was established in Berlin in 1925.

Vilna, called the Jerusalem of the East, is often identified as the birthplace of YIVO, the foremost research institute of East European Jewish history and culture.[39] As a short account of the early history of YIVO reveals, this honor actually goes to Berlin, which in the early 1920s was home to numerous leading Yiddish scholars, among them historians Simon Dubnow, Elias Tcherikower, and Nahum Shtif, as well as demographer Jacob Lestschinsky and the former minister of justice in Lenin's revolutionary government, Isaac Nahman Steinberg. They had all fled Eastern Europe after World War I and found shelter in the German capital. Their primary interest was the scholarly study of the immediate past. As a precursor to YIVO, a group of Jewish intellectuals led by Tcherikower, who had just come to Berlin from Kiev, founded the East European Jewish Historical Archives to collect and analyze material concerning the anti-Jewish pogroms that took place in the Ukraine between 1917 and 1921.[40] In 1924, the leading East European Jewish intellectuals in Berlin gathered at the house of Isaac Nahman Steinberg to set up a commission to establish a Yiddish-language academy of higher learning.[41] Although this plan was not realized, another meeting in Berlin a year later proved to be the decisive breakthrough for the establishment of a systematic research center on East European Jewish history and culture.

In August 1925, YIVO was officially founded in Berlin, and its future activities were divided into three sections: a historical section led by Elias Tcherikower in Berlin, a socioeconomic section led by Jacob Lestschinsky in Berlin, and a philological section directed by Max Weinreich in Vilna. A fourth (pedagogical) section was added later. The main discussion at the Berlin conference concerned where the secretariat of the new institute should be located. The supporters of Vilna spoke of the need for close contact with the Jewish masses, while the defenders of Berlin believed that the presence of the most important intellectuals and close connections to the non-Jewish world were more important. In the end a compromise was reached: the central office was to be established in Berlin, and Vilna was to be responsible for activities in the countries of Eastern Europe. This proved to be no more than an interim solution. With the departure from Berlin of Nahum Shtif (for the Soviet Union) and Elias Tcherikower (for France), Vilna became the undisputed center of YIVO only a year later.[42]

Berlin, however, remained the seat of the sections occupied with economic and historical research. Although the object of research was Eastern Europe, German Jewry occupied an important role in the work of those YIVO activists who lived in Berlin. Thus, the first collection of essays on Jewish economics and statistics by YIVO—published in Berlin—contained several contributions on German Jewry.[43] And the Zentralwohlfahrtsstelle der deutschen Juden commissioned YIVO's economic historian Jacob Lestschinsky to be the author of a study on recent economic trends among German Jews that it published in 1932.[44]

The Berlin branch of YIVO also developed various public relations activities in German, aiming for the interest and material support of German Jews. A special committee for friends and sponsors of the Berlin YIVO issued a bulletin in German (*Mitteilungen der Auslandszentrale des Jiddischen Wissenschaftlichen Instituts*) and, after 1930, organized weekly lectures in German on East European Jewry.[45] Those activities were the cause of a dispute with the central office in Vilna. Fearing a loss of control over the Berlin branch, the Vilna secretariat admonished the German office to restrict its activities to scholarship and not to waste too much energy on public lectures.[46]

Although YIVO received some material help from the Berlin Jewish community, such as rooms for YIVO's public lectures and financial subsidies, the interest among German-Jewish scholars in YIVO's activities was negligible. Shortly after the opening of the institute, the founders sought to make contact with the luminaries of Wissenschaft des Judentums. They were encouraged by Ismar Elbogen, who provided them with a list of the movement's leading representatives. But after YIVO sent them several invitations to lectures, only one of them appeared (and even Elbogen himself stayed away), so the directors of the institute gave up their initial hope of cooperation, remarking bitterly that "either the scholars of Wissenschaft des Judentums know what we want and do not want it, or they do not even wish to know. In any case, we will no longer put our hopes in them."[47]

The fruitless attempts of YIVO scholars to win the recognition of their German-Jewish colleagues were not entirely emblematic of the interactions between East European Jewish intellectuals and German-Jewish intellectuals. The relations between East European Hebraists and the representatives of the German-Jewish cultural renaissance were quite different.

THE HEBRAIST COLONY AND THE GERMAN-JEWISH RENAISSANCE

Eighteenth-century Germany was the cradle of modern Hebrew literature. The *Haskalah*, the Jewish counterpart to the European Enlightenment, not only opened the doors of *German* culture to German Jews but also produced the first modern *Hebrew* literary journal (*Ha-me'assef,* Königsberg, 1784) and secular Hebrew poetry. However, the seeds planted by the *Maskilim* (Enlighteners) of Berlin and Königsberg did not develop on German soil during the nineteenth century. Although representatives of Wissenschaft des Judentums, such as Leopold Zunz, laid the foundation for the scholarly study of Hebrew literature, its creative center shifted to Eastern Europe. It was there, a century after the pioneering work of the *Me'assefim,* that Eliezer Ben-Yehuda resuscitated Hebrew as a spoken language and such writers as Peretz Smolenskin and Ahad Ha'am launched the most significant modern journals of Hebrew literature. Germany became a major center of modern Hebrew literature again only in the twentieth century, when many East European Jewish intellectuals moved westward.

The first Conference of Hebrew Language and Culture was convened in Berlin in 1909. Political reasons certainly figured in the decision to call for a gathering of Hebrew writers outside Eastern Europe, but there was an additional motive. The German capital had become a major center for Hebrew writers who had left their homes in Eastern Europe as a result of political repression and antisemitic outbursts.[48] At the heart of the organizational activities of this group was critic and publisher Saul Israel (Shai Ish) Hurwitz, who in 1907 had founded the Hebrew journal *He-Atid* in Berlin and figured among the organizers of the Hebraists' gathering. At the meeting, the Hebraists' reaction to the first Yiddishist conference, which had been held in Czernovitz a year earlier, left no doubt that Hebrew, not Yiddish, was the national language of the Jewish people. Their original plan to extend the Berlin convention to an official congress with the participation of all important Hebraists failed, but even the small conference attracted about 150 delegates, who established the Histadrut la-safah vela-tarbut ivrit (Association for Hebrew Language and Culture).[49]

The group of Hebrew writers in Berlin grew steadily in the years after the conference. In 1910 the general-secretary of the newly founded religious Zionist Mizrahi movement, Meir Berlin (Bar-Ilan), established the central organ of his organization, the journal *Ha-Ivri,* in Berlin and made it clear that one of the journal's purposes was to strengthen the presence of Hebrew in Germany.[50] A year later, writer Micha Yosef Berdyczewski—who had lived in Breslau for about twenty years—moved to Berlin. For the rest of his life he lived in the Friedenau quarter, which for him and his friends became known as Neveh-Shalom.[51] Other Hebraists were attracted to Berlin when the World Zionist Organization moved there in 1911. In 1912, Shmu'el Yosef Agnon, who half a century later would become the first Hebrew writer to receive the Nobel Prize, returned to Europe from a five-year stay in Jaffa and chose Berlin as his permanent domicile.

Many memoirs bear witness to the close contacts among those Hebrew writers who used to meet regularly at the Café Monopol and Café des Westens. Ittamar Ben-Avi, son of the creator of modern Hebrew, Eliezer Ben-Yehuda, recalls from his student days in Berlin the existence of a Hebrew-speaking corner in the Café Monopol.[52] When Gershom Scholem was thrown out of his parents' home during World War I for his pacifism and Zionism, he lived among a group of Hebrew intellectuals centered around the later president of Israel, Zalman Rubaschoff (Shazar), in the Berlin Villa Struck.[53]

The flourishing intellectual life of Hebrew writers in Berlin on the eve of World War I was, however, only the prologue to a stronger community in the Weimar period. With the influx of about seventy thousand East European Jews during and after the war, the colonies of Hebrew and Yiddish intellectuals in Germany grew significantly. Before World War I Berlin was one center of Hebrew culture, but it became *the* center between 1920 and 1924.[54] The concentration of mostly Russian-Jewish Hebraists in Weimar Germany was part of a broader movement of Russian intellectuals attracted by Berlin's flourishing cultural life. Among the 230,000 Russian emigrés in Weimar were many writers, artists, and publishers, including Maxim Gorky, Vladimir Mayakovsky, Sergeij Eisenstein, Boris Pasternak, and Ivan Puni. For a few years Berlin was the cultural capital of "Russia Abroad."[55]

More than any other event, the arrival in 1921 of the most celebrated Hebrew poet, Hayim Nahman Bialik, underlined the new position of the German capital as the center for Hebrew culture. One of the young Hebrew writers living in Berlin at that time recalled the enthusiasm: "The

Leonid Pasternak, painting of Hayim Nahman Bialik (right) and David Frischmann (left) in Berlin, 1920. Courtesy of the Leo Baeck Institute, New York.

young Hebraists in the German metropolis perceived his coming as a festive event, with a true sense of spiritual elevation [*aliyat neshamah*]."[56] Bialik, in turn, emphasized in one of his first speeches the leading role of Berlin as a center for Hebrew culture.[57] One of the most impressive demonstrations of Berlin's role as the center of Hebrew literature was the illustrious celebration of Bialik's fiftieth birthday in January 1923 at the Berlin Philharmonic, attended by leading Zionist politicians and Hebrew writers, such as Nahum Sokolow, Vladimir Jabotinsky, Saul Tchernikhowsky, and Zalman Shne'ur, and by German-Jewish notables.[58] Bialik was an occasional guest at the Beth ha-va'ad ha-ivri (meeting place for Hebrew speakers), the intellectual center of the Hebrew colony in postwar Berlin. The Beth ha-va'ad organized public readings and concerts, and provided a platform for informal contacts among Hebrew speakers.[59] According to its founder, S. Hermoni, "first and foremost among [our goals] is the propagation of Hebrew among our German brethren."[60] Although the Beth ha-va'ad fell short of accomplishing this goal, the statement underlines the intention of the Berlin Hebrew colony to enter into an active relationship with local German Jews, instead of secluding themselves culturally.

Berlin was not the only center of Hebrew literature in Weimar Germany, however. During the years of his stay in Germany (1921–1924), Bialik commuted between Berlin and the small resort town of Bad Homburg near Frankfurt, where Agnon and other Jewish writers were living. Bad Homburg proved attractive to Hebrew writers for its parks and cafés and because Shoshana Persitz, a Russian-Jewish publisher (who later became an Israeli politician), opened her home to them. It became a literary salon, like those of Rahel Varnhagen and Henriette Herz a century earlier, albeit with the opposite ideological orientation. The salons of the famous German-Jewish women had been part of the process of acculturation, but the salon of the wealthy Persitz symbolized the national reawakening among European Jews.[61]

The most visible sign marking Germany as a center for the development of Hebrew culture during those years was the extent of its Hebrew-language publishing. Together with her husband, Shoshana Persitz reestablished in Bad Homburg the Omanut publishing house, which the two had originally founded in Moscow in 1917, mainly for children's literature. In Berlin, Bialik established the Devir publishing house, Jakob Klatzkin founded Eschkol as a platform for his encyclopedia and other scholarly works, Yehezkel Kaufmann edited the periodical *Atidenu* of the Tarbut publishing company in Berlin, Simon Rawidowicz published important Hebrew texts in his journal *Ayanot,* and in 1926–1927 Abraham J. Stybel moved the most important Hebrew publishing house, Stybel, from Warsaw to Berlin.[62] From January 1923 to May 1924, *Ha-Olam,* the official Hebrew organ of the World Zionist Movement, appeared in Berlin, as did other journals of international Jewish organizations.

There was a direct connection between the economic misery in Germany during those postwar years and the blossoming of Hebrew and Yiddish culture. In addition to the appeal of Weimar culture and the similarity between Yiddish and German, the tremendous inflation rate attracted publishers and writers. If paid for with foreign currency, publishing endeavors in Germany were exceptionally cheap in the early 1920s. At the height of the inflation in 1923, the value of the mark dropped dramatically. In July one dollar was worth 353,412 marks, in September 98,860,000, and in November 4,200,000,000,000 marks. One of the Hebrew publishers noted in his diary in June 1923 that his monthly salary was a million German marks, at the time seven U.S. dollars.[63] A few weeks later, he could not even buy a loaf of bread for a million marks, and seven dollars amounted to a small fortune. At the end of the same year, the appointment of Hjalmar Schacht as the president of the Reichsbank and the introduction of the *Rentenmark* as the new German currency brought the rapidly galloping inflation, and the most fruitful period of Hebrew and Yiddish publishing activities in Weimar Germany, to an end. With the stabilization of the German currency, most of those publishers and writers left Germany.

By 1922 the Hebrew colony in Berlin had lost three of its most prominent representatives, when Berdyczewski, Frischmann, and Hurwitz were buried at the Weißensee cemetery within a few months of each other. Agnon's stay in Bad Homburg from 1921 to 1924 was brought to a tragic end when a fire destroyed his house, consuming his private library and many manuscripts. Agnon took this as a sign to leave Germany and settle in Israel, thus embarking on the same journey Bialik had chosen only a few months earlier. Agnon's emigration marked the dusk of the most productive phase of Hebrew writers on German soil.

In the words of Bialik's young friend Simon Rawidowicz, "It was Dr. Schacht who 'banished' [*higlah*] Bialik to *Eretz Yisrael*."[64] The causes of the exodus of East European Jewish intellectuals from Germany cannot, however, be reduced to the recovery of the German economy, following Schacht's appointment. Political reasons were significant as well. In November 1923, Hitler—who, ten years later, would appoint Schacht as his first minister of economics—undertook his ill-fated Beer Hall Putsch in Munich. His march to Berlin was stopped shortly after his supporters had gathered at the Munich Feldherrenhalle, but the tide of antisemitism could no longer be dammed. While Hitler was arrested in Munich, anti-Jewish riots took place in the streets of the Scheunenviertel. Back in Munich, the Bavarian government detained and expelled a number of East European Jews only a few days after Hitler's failed coup attempt.[65] These deportations were no singular case. During the Weimar years, Ostjuden lived in constant fear of deportation to their countries of origin. From Prussia alone, about four thousand East European Jews were transferred to Eastern Europe between 1922 and 1932.[66] The Reichstag elections of 1924 gave further cause for unease, with Hitler's Nazi party celebrating its first major success.

An additional reason for Hebrew and Yiddish writers and publishers to leave Germany was their growing realization of the gulf between a flourishing elite culture, on one hand, and the absence of an audience for cultural products in Jewish languages, on the other. Although Berlin became the home of the most important Hebrew and Yiddish writers and publishers, their audience remained in the East, or had emigrated to Palestine and the United States. Most of the journals and books printed in Germany were commissioned and sold outside the country. The Wostok publishing house, for example, founded in Dresden in 1921, specialized in Yiddish textbooks mainly for the new Jewish schools of Eastern Europe, and the Klal-Farlag—probably financed by the German publishing firm Ullstein—published in 1922 more than fifty books in a series of small paperbacks of original Yiddish literature and translations into Yiddish and Hebrew for East European Jewish readers.[67]

"They lived in the West, but told about the East and wrote for the East" is how one scholar summarized the situation of the Yiddish writers in Weimar Germany, and similar words could be used for most Hebraists.[68] The position of Berlin as the center of Hebrew and Yiddish literature in the 1920s stood in conspicuous contrast to the city's lack of a vibrant East European culture.[69] Although one could hear Yiddish, see Hebrew letters above bakeries and bookstores, and find kosher restaurants and Talmud schools, Berlin's Scheunenviertel was not comparable to London's Whitechapel, Paris' Pletzl, or New York's Lower East Side. The differences were visible both in the numbers of immigrants and in their cultural activities. In Great Britain, France, and the United States, recently immigrated East European Jews were the majority of the Jewish population in the 1920s, whereas in Weimar Germany they were a minority of less than 20 percent. Their periodicals, theaters, and political organizations never became as important as similar institutions in the other cities. Comparing the Scheunenviertel to those other centers of East European Jewish life, the writer Joseph Roth stated that "Berlin has no ghetto. It has a Jewish quarter."[70]

Most Hebraists of Weimar Germany had little contact with or interest in their German surroundings. Simon Rawidowicz was so stunned by Bialik's lack of interest in his German environment that he noted in his diary, "He lives in Germany, and he has no idea what is going on in the flourishing intellectual atmosphere of the Weimar days."[71] Similarly, historian Simon Dubnow considered his Berlin years a period of seclusion and immersion in his research and private life. As a friend recalled, Dubnow stuck to a precisely arranged daily schedule. After reading the two local newspapers, the *Berliner Tageblatt* and the *Vossische Zeitung,* he took an extensive walk in

Simon Dubnow packing his library in Petrograd before his departure to Berlin in 1922.
Courtesy YIVO Institute for Jewish Research, New York.

the nearby Grunewald and dedicated the rest of the day to his work. Only on Sundays would he receive visitors, who included both East European and German-Jewish intellectuals.[72]

In spite of their isolation from their (non-Jewish) German surroundings, neither Bialik nor Dubnow lived in a social and cultural vacuum. Like other East European intellectuals in Weimar Germany, they were connected with leading representatives and institutions of the cultural renaissance among German Jews. Before his arrival in Berlin in 1922, Dubnow noted in his Petrograd diary, "Berlin is the only point in the universe where I might conclude my literary work in a few years' time."[73] Indeed, far from the political turmoil and violent pogroms of Eastern Europe, Dubnow not only completed his most important Hebrew work, a two-volume history of Hasidism, but also arranged for its publication in German translation by the Jüdischer Verlag. A few years earlier, the German edition of Dubnow's magnum opus, his ten-volume *World History of the Jewish People* (1925–1929), had been published by the same firm, thus preceding the publication of the Russian original by almost a decade. It soon became the best-selling product of the Jüdischer Verlag, with one hundred thousand individual copies sold.[74]

Whereas Dubnow's publications were the product of cooperation between an East European Jewish author and a German-Jewish publisher, just the opposite was the case with Bialik. It was Bialik the publisher, not Bialik the poet, who was involved with the leading scholars of Wissenschaft des Judentums in Berlin. When the circle of Hebrew writers in Berlin organized a welcome banquet for Bialik in the popular Aschinger restaurant in late October 1921, Bialik used the occasion, at which almost all prominent Hebrew writers were present, to campaign for his new publishing house, Devir.[75] Bialik regarded the foundation of Devir—replacing his well-established Moriah company and organized as a cooperative enterprise—as his primary mission during his stay in Berlin: "I see my principal work, besides my literary productions as a writer, in my activities as a publisher. I could not emigrate directly from Russia to the Land of Israel. The working conditions there were not comfortable, the conditions for publishing very hard. . . . We were here in Berlin to found the Devir publishing company and to work. We were successful, and now I am moving on to the Land of Israel."[76]

One of the first activities of Bialik's new publishing firm was the publication of a scholarly journal, also called *Devir*. It was edited by the luminaries of Wissenschaft des Judentums at the Liberal Berlin rabbinical seminary, German-born Ismar Elbogen, Galician-born Harry Torczyner (Tur-Sinai), and Russian-born Jacob Nahum Epstein. Although their collaboration constituted a personal encounter of East and West, their project marked a clear departure from traditional German Wissenschaft des Judentums. For example, Elbogen recognized in a contribution to *Devir* the influence of contemporary developments, such as the revival of the Hebrew language and the movement to establish a Hebrew University in Palestine, on the future course of Jewish studies: "With this change of status, the question for Jewish studies of using the Hebrew language becomes a question of survival. Only in it [Hebrew] can the proper expression for the development of each and every discipline and science be found; and only through its aid can a natural connection to living Judaism be found."[77]

In postwar Berlin, as David Myers noted, the "paths of German and Hebrew scholarship . . . [reached] a portentous intersection." No contemporary expressed this encounter more eloquently than Bialik: "Many of the bearers of Hebrew culture [from the East] found their way to Berlin, the same Berlin which was the birthplace of "Haskalah" and the seat of

Hokhmat Yisra'el in its Western dress. At this great and decisive hour, relatives who had been separated by force happened onto the same inn. Is it conceivable that their meeting will be for naught? Already, there are signs of [mutual] influence in certain areas."[78]

Those signs could be observed in most major German-Jewish cultural achievements of the Weimar period. East European Jewish intellectuals were represented prominently among the teachers of Jewish adult education institutions and the rabbinical seminaries of Berlin and Breslau. Nowhere was the encounter between East and West more visible than in the publication of intellectual journals.

As the title of Germany's first truly modern illustrated Jewish journal, *Ost und West* (1901–1923), suggests, the deepening of this encounter was the foremost goal of its editors. During World War I and the Weimar period, other journals, such as *Die Freistatt,* the *Neue Jüdische Monatshefte,* and *Der Jude* further promoted this encounter. They contained many contributions by and about East European Jews. Translations and transliterations of Hebrew and Yiddish texts in the journals aimed at exposing German-Jewish readers to literature written in Jewish languages.

Der Jude, edited by Buber—who grew up in Galicia but was part of German-Jewish intellectual circles—in particular provided a forum where East European writers and German-Jewish readers could meet on neutral ground. We find works of many Hebraists of Weimar Germany in the pages of *Der Jude.* The first volume, for example, includes articles in which Dubnow reflects on the course of contemporary Jewish history, Shmu'el Abba Horodetzky ponders Hasidism, Yehezkel Kaufmann writes on the significance of the revival of Hebrew, and Jacob Lestschinsky addresses problems of Jewish economic life.[79]

The manifold interrelations of the German-Jewish community and Hebrew writers are best illustrated by the case of Shmu'el Yosef Agnon, who became an integral part of the Galician colony in Leipzig, the East European intellectual circles in Berlin, and the small group of Hebrew writers in Bad Homburg, while also tied to the German-Jewish community.[80] Agnon's entire family was in Germany during most of his twelve-year sojourn. Although his parents were no longer alive, his four siblings moved to Germany before or during World War I, and two of them remained there until 1939.[81] His wife, Esther Marx (whom he married in Berlin in 1920), was the daughter of a German-Jewish banker from Königsberg, and their two children were born in Königsberg in 1921 and in Frankfurt in 1922, respectively. His brother-in-law was publisher Moses

Marx, a cofounder of the Soncino Society. In 1925 the society published Agnon's short stories, "The *Schass* of my Grandfather" and "The Tale of Rabbi Gadiel, the Infant," initially translated by Gershom Scholem in 1920.[82]

Agnon soon became known among German Zionists, for whom this Hebrew writer was the embodiment of East Jewish spirituality, as Gershom Scholem recalled: "For us . . . every Eastern Jew was a carrier of all the mysteries of Jewish existence, but the young Agnon appeared to us as one of its most perfect incarnations."[83] Two East European Jews, well established in Berlin's Jewish society, helped elevate Agnon's name to modest fame. Martin Buber, in a literary collection published by the Federation of Zionists in Germany, praised Agnon as "one of those few who have holy authority regarding Jewish life."[84] In the 1920s, Buber and Agnon were to join ranks to publish a four-volume work on Hasidic lore and literature in Bialik's Devir publishing house. This grandiose project was brought to an abrupt end when the first volume, which Buber and Agnon had already prepared, was consumed in the fire that destroyed Agnon's house in 1924.

The initial assistance of Ahron Eliasberg, Buber's close friend and owner of the *Jüdischer Verlag,* proved decisive for Agnon's early reception among German Jews. Eliasberg employed Agnon for editorial work in his publishing company, and during World War I the two jointly edited *Das Buch von den polnischen Juden,* a collection of tales and legends about the Jews of Poland.[85] More important, Eliasberg's *Jüdischer Verlag* made Agnon's work accessible to German readers. The first German version of Agnon's work was his story "Agunot," translated by Ernst Müller, which appeared in 1910. But it was the 1918 edition of "And the Crooked Shall Be Made Straight," translated by Max Strauss, that marked a breakthrough in Agnon's literary recognition among German Zionists, as well as the beginning of a wave of modern Hebrew publications in Germany, both in the original and in German translation.[86]

Agnon's most important patron was a German Jew. Salman Schocken — co-owner of a chain of department stores, Zionist leader, bibliophile, and autodidact — paid him a regular salary throughout the last ten years of his stay in Germany (and even after his move to Palestine) and published his collected stories. The relationship between the businessman from an assimilated German milieu and the East European Jewish intellectual remains one of the most intriguing personal encounters of East and West in Weimar Germany.[87] Schocken provided Agnon with money, food, clothes, and insight into European literature, and in turn Agnon helped Schocken to become acquainted with Jewish culture and Hebrew literature, and to acquire books for what was to become one of the most impressive private collections of Judaica in Germany. Schocken had found his way back to Judaism under the influence of Buber's Hasidic writings on the eve of World War I. He immediately established a local chapter of the Zionist organization in his home town of Zwickau and was elected chairman of the newly established cultural commission of the Zionist Federation for Germany in 1916. About the same time, he became close to Agnon, resulting in the establishment of the Schocken Publishing Company and the first publication of Agnon's collected writings.

Some of their cooperative plans, such as the *Aleph-Beth* reader for German-Jewish children, with texts by Agnon and illustrations by Sigmund Freud's niece, Tom Seidmann-Freud, were initiated by the German Zionist cultural commission, which Schocken chaired.[88] Schocken's interest, however, went deeper than children's literature. Disappointed with the inactivity of the German Zionists' cultural commission, he resigned from his post as chairman in December 1927 and decided to "found a Jewish publishing house that will publish Hebrew and German books," as he wrote to Agnon a few months later.[89] After three years of preparations, he established the Schocken Verlag, which became better known after 1933 for its Judaica series, the Schocken Bücherei. In the Weimar period, the four volumes of Agnon's *Collected Stories* (in Hebrew) represented the core of Schocken's publications. The only other original publication before 1933 was the "Jewish reader" *Sendung und Schicksal* (1931), edited by Nahum Glatzer and Ludwig Strauss, Buber's son-in-law. Containing German translations of essential Jewish texts from the Talmud and Midrash up to the medieval Jewish philosophers and Hasidic tales, this volume was initiated by the Zionist cultural committee, headed by Schocken, in order to provide German Jews with a representative anthology of Jewish classic texts. Most of the other early publications of the Schocken Verlag were new editions of Buber's and Rosenzweig's works, originally published by Lambert Schneider (who became the director of the Schocken Verlag) and centering around the Buber-Rosenzweig Bible translation. Schocken also established the Research Institute for Hebrew Poetry in 1932, directed by the former chief rabbi of Prague, Heinrich (Hayim) Brody. The institute issued its own journal in German and after 1933 continued its existence in Palestine.

All the facets of Agnon's involvement in German-Jewish life were reflected in his later literary oeuvre. Whereas the Hebrew writers of the previous generation living in Germany, such as Berdyczewski and Frischmann, never attempted to portray German Jews, some of the most fascinating accounts of German Jewry came from Agnon's pen.[90] Many of his works focus on the life of German Jews—such as his unfinished novel *Shirah,* in which he vividly depicted the life of German Jews, or the short story *Merutsat ha-sus* (The horse race), in which he delineated premodern rural German Jewish life, reflecting his own experiences during a short stay in Lower Franconia after World War I—and even stronger autobiographical traces can be found in his accounts of the lives of East European Jewish immigrants in German cities, as presented in the novella *Ad henah* (Until now) and the posthumously published novel *Be-hanuto shel mar Lublin* (In the store of Mister Lublin).

In contrast to most German-Jewish authors, Agnon abstained from both stigmatizing German Jews as assimilated "non-Jewish Jews" and idealizing "authentic" East European Jews. Although concentrating mostly on the family conflicts and the intricate social situation of a highly assimilated minority, Agnon demonstrated his respect for the multifaceted achievements of German Jews. As Dan Miron has commented, "He strove consciously to destroy the stereotype of the German Jew, and to appreciate the positive aspects of German-Jewish life."[91] Agnon's sentences about German Jews in *Ad Henah* stand in stark contrast to the rather critical self-portrait of most German-Jewish authors:

> All our traditional notions of German Jews are nonsensical; and if we praise the Jews of other countries for their knowledge of the Torah, their reverence, their righteousness, their piety, their innocence, we should praise German Jews for their integrity, their keenness of mind, their sense of responsibility, their faithfulness in keeping their word. Also . . . most of the knowledge we have in Jewish studies is nothing but the sawdust which fell from the tools of the great craftsmen, that is, the German-Jewish scholars.[92]

About the time when such German-Jewish writers as Alfred Döblin and Arnold Zweig went East in search of authentic Jews, East European Jewish intellectuals like Agnon moved westward, attracted by the flourishing cultural life in Germany. The encounter with local Jews was as much a part of Agnon's experiences in Germany as it was for Döblin on his trip to Poland. Unlike Döblin, who remarked that he never met "real Jews" in Germany, Agnon experienced German Jews as Jews. To him, the rural Franconian Jews, the scholars of Wissenschaft des Judentums, and the sponsors of a Jewish cultural renaissance were different, but no less Jewish, than the population of his native shtetl. Nothing of the negative character-ization of Kurt Tucholsky's Herr Wendriner can be found in Agnon's depiction of German Jews. It took an East European Jew to accomplish what German-Jewish writers failed to achieve: a portrayal of the varieties of Jewish life in Germany, without bias.

A few years after the departure of Bialik, Agnon, and other Hebrew writers, the German capital saw a short revival of Hebrew culture: in 1926, Polish-Jewish publisher Abraham Stybel moved his Hebrew publishing firm and its journal *Ha-tekufah* to Berlin. One of its editors, Simon Rawidowicz, became the central figure of the Hebraist circle in Berlin during the last years of Weimar. Rawidowicz had come to Berlin from Poland as a student in 1919 and subsequently founded his own publishing house, Ayanot. The Hebrew writers still living in Germany were the main authors of his publications.[93] In 1929, Rawidowicz established a Beth ha-am ha-ivri as the new meeting place for Hebraists. His greatest organizational achievement was the convening of a Hebrew Conference in Berlin in 1931. For the first time since 1909, the German capital was home to an international conference on Hebrew language and culture, and as in 1909, there were vigorous discussions as to whether this was to be a real congress or merely a preparatory conference. When, as an outcome of the meeting, the newly established Brit ivrit olamit (Hebrew World Union) chose Berlin as its first center and Rawidowicz as its president, the discussions concerning the organization's ideology continued.[94]

Rawidowicz' life and work were deeply interwoven with the fate of German Jewry. Shortly after he came to Berlin in 1919, he began to teach at the fledgling Hebrew language school in Berlin. There the mostly East European Jewish teachers encountered mainly German-Jewish students. Like Agnon, whose wife had been his student, Rawidowicz met his future wife, Esther Klee, when she was a pupil in one of his Hebrew classes. Her father, Alfred Klee, was a leading German Zionist and vice-president of the Prussian Federation of Jewish Communities. Through his father-in-law Rawidowicz became closely associated with the community of German Zionists.[95] But his involvement in German-Jewish life reached far beyond the Zionist circles. A few years before the Nazi rise to power, he was appointed librarian of the Jewish community library. Further, Rawidowicz, together with the luminaries of Wissenschaft des Judentums, became one of the editors of the ambitious edition of the collected writings of Moses Mendelssohn, which began to be published on the two hundredth anniversary of Mendelssohn's birth, in 1929.

Although Rawidowicz was an ardent supporter of the spread of the

Hebrew language and the establishment of a Jewish homeland in Palestine, he envisioned an equal role for the diaspora in the future development of Jewish culture. In his opening speech to the Hebrew Conference in Berlin in 1931, Rawidowicz presented his own vision of the future of Zionism. He borrowed the major principle from Ahad Ha'am's cultural Zionism but went further in his emphasis on Jewish culture in the diaspora. In contrast to Ahad Ha'am, who regarded the Land of Israel as the spiritual center of the Jewish people and the diaspora as the periphery, Rawidowicz spoke of two equally important centers. The task of Hebrew culture in the diaspora was not *hikui* (imitation) of the activities in the center but independent *yet-zirah* (creativity); the relation between the two was not to be one of *telut* (dependence) but one of *shutafut* (cooperation). This was a highly provocative concept for mainstream Zionists and caused a deep division among the supporters of the Brit ivrit olamit, some of whom accused Rawidowicz of a Hebrew version of diaspora nationalism.[96]

Rawidowicz's notion also contradicted the official position of German Zionism, which, under the leadership of Kurt Blumenfeld, was to demand the emigration of every Zionist to Palestine. Still, other German Jews advocated Jewish cultural autonomy in the diaspora: the Jüdische Volkspartei (JVP), led by Rawidowicz's father-in-law, Alfred Klee, regarded its main task to be the control of Jewish communities and the strengthening of Jewish and Hebrew culture in Germany. Klee hoped to transform the Jewish communities in Germany into Volksgemeinden. On the JVP's lists of candidates for the Prussian Federation of Jewish Communities were a number of leading East European intellectuals of Weimar Germany, including Simon Dubnow. On several levels, leading representatives of the Jüdische Volkspartei and the Brit ivrit olamit had the same objective—the foundation of independent centers of creative Jewish life in the diaspora and support for the establishment of a Jewish homeland.

Agnon's and Rawidowicz's contacts with leading representatives of the German-Jewish cultural renaissance signaled a new tendency of the encounter between East and West in Jewish culture. Before World War I, the Hebraists were profoundly isolated in German and German-Jewish society.[97] Zionism was still a marginal phenomenon, and even the most prolific German-speaking Zionist at the time, Martin Buber, had to address the Berlin Conference of Hebrew Language and Culture in 1909 in German because, as he had to admit, he was "not able to think in Hebrew."[98] An East European Jew living in Berlin and attending the same conference described the situation of the Hebrew writers in the capital: "We are lost here amidst the city's multitudes and tumult; no one pays attention to us."[99]

This was no longer the case after World War I, when German Jews possessed a highly developed Jewish cultural framework, in which the East European Hebraists could find their place. In such an atmosphere, Jakob Klatzkin and Nahum Goldmann published their German-language *Encyclopaedia Judaica,* Bialik initiated a scholarly Hebrew journal together with the professors of the Hochschule für die Wissenschaft des Judentums, Agnon taught at the Frankfurt Lehrhaus and collaborated with Salman Schocken, and Rawidowicz became involved in the expanding network of Jewish community libraries.

Some Hebraists decided to stay in Germany and affirm their presence by acquiring Prussian citizenship. When Rawidowicz did so in 1930, he expressed his mixed feelings in a letter to his brother, who had settled in Palestine: "Yesterday, I received my citizenship diploma. Now I am a Prussian! . . . Actually, I did not leave any country and did not embrace a new one. . . . When the German officer who handed me the diploma yesterday said: 'Jetzt sind Sie Preusse,' [now you are a Prussian], it gave me the shivers."[100]

Within three years, the German citizenship held by Jews was meaningless. Together with his German-born wife, Rawidowicz left Germany and, after failed attempts to find a suitable position in Palestine, settled in England. At this time of crisis, German Jews and the colony of East European Jewish intellectuals were united by their fate. When the last Hebrew and Yiddish writers and scholars fled from Germany, the exodus of German Jews had begun as well.

Epilogue

Like a horrible nightmare the abrogation of equal rights weighs upon us all, but especially upon those Jews who, like me, had surrendered themselves to the dream of assimilation. . . . As difficult as it has been for me, I have awakened from the dream that I dreamed my whole life long.

—Max Liebermann to Hayim Nahman Bialik and Meir Dizengoff (8 June 1933)

During their years of agony, German Jews experienced a remarkable flurry of Jewish cultural activities. In Nazi Germany they expanded their adult education programs, restructured their publishing activities, and established their own theater. Although the writings of Jewish authors were burned publicly and purged from German libraries, Jewish publishing houses were able to print Kafka, and the Jewish theater in Nazi Germany was the only place where Lessing's *Nathan the Wise* could be performed. This last flare-up of Jewish cultural activities in a time of persecution might seem paradoxical. It was, however, the logical consequence of the Nazi policy of separation of Jews from non-Jews. Nazi authorities were willing to tolerate, and to some degree even support, Jewish culture, as long as it promoted the segregation of Jewish and non-Jewish Germans. Jewish culture in Nazi Germany thus must not be mistaken for a direct continuation of Weimar's Jewish cultural renaissance. It developed under entirely different conditions. Weimar Jews, no matter how strongly they felt the existence of antisemitism, were an integral part of non-Jewish culture and society. After 1933, they were confined to a cultural ghetto and gradually excluded from all facets of German society.

Jewish cultural activities in Nazi Germany did not develop in a vacuum, however. They were constructed on the solid foundation that had been created in the Weimar years—partly out of a profound hope for a fruitful German-Jewish coexistence, partly out of a deep fear of hatred's triumph. The three most important institutions of Nazi Germany's Jewish cultural life had their roots in Weimar Germany. The Central Agency for Jewish Adult Education, under the leadership of Martin Buber, was an expansion of the already existing Lehrhaus framework; the Schocken publishing house, whose Schocken Library enjoyed enormous popularity, was founded in 1931; and the theater productions on Jewish topics in the Jewish Culture League were based in some instances on plays written in the Weimar period.

In November 1933 the Frankfurt Jewish Lehrhaus reopened its doors, but the basic assumption of its founder, Franz Rosenzweig, was no longer valid. The Lehrhaus of Nazi Germany was not the center of a Jewish community that coexisted with the participation of German Jews in the larger non-Jewish culture. Instead, many German Jews attended the new Lehrhaus because of their isolation from German culture. The concluding words of Franz Rosenzweig's opening speech of 1920 attained a new meaning thirteen years later: "Turn into yourself, return home to your innermost self and to your innermost life."[1] The teachers of the Lehrhaus, by strengthening communal bonds and cultural forms of expression in times of relative comfort, had helped prepare German Jews to endure their forced retreat into cultural and social isolation.

The reopening of the Frankfurt Lehrhaus was only a small part of the reorganization of Jewish adult education in Germany after the Nazis assumed power. In many cities, similar institutions were founded, and—with the establishment of the Mittelstelle für Jüdische Erwachsenenbildung (Central Agency for Jewish Adult Education)—there existed for the first time a Germany-wide network for Jewish adult education. Initiated by Martin Buber in the spring of 1933, the Central Agency organized seminars on Jewish learning (*Lerntage*) for Jewish teachers and for the leaders of the Jewish youth movement, and cooperated closely with the Hochschule für die Wissenschaft des Judentums (which now was called Lehranstalt). One of the main tasks of the Central Agency was to coordinate among the various local Lehrhaus branches.[2] Although the conditions and tasks of the Jewish adult education movement in Nazi Germany differed

Martin Buber lecturing at the Jüdisches Lehrhaus Berlin, 17 January 1935. Courtesy Bildarchiv Abraham Pisarek, Berlin.

considerably from those of the Weimar period, its achievements would have hardly been possible without a preexisting structure. The founders of the Central Agency were the leaders of the old Lehrhaus movement, most prominently Martin Buber and Ernst Simon, who returned from Palestine to Nazi Germany for this task. Such local Lehrhaus leaders as Eduard Strauss in Frankfurt, Karl Adler in Stuttgart, and Paul Eppstein in Mannheim remained active after 1933.

Another cultural institution of the Jews in Nazi Germany that had its roots in Weimar was the Schocken publishing house. Founded in 1931, Schocken initially concentrated almost exclusively on the writings of Shmu'el Yosef Agnon and Buber. In 1933, the publishing house adopted a new profile with the introduction of an enormously popular series, the Schocken Library (Bücherei des Schocken-Verlags). Under the guidance of Lambert Schneider (the non-Jewish publisher who had initiated the Buber-Rosenzweig Bible translation) and Moritz Spitzer (who had directed the Schule der jüdischen Jugend in Berlin), this series issued a rich array of Jewish literature in affordable paperback copies. Modeled after the widely read German Insel-Bücherei, the Schocken Library was published in monthly

installments, like a journal. According to the initial plans, two volumes—
each costing 1.25 marks—were to appear every month. Although this
ambitious goal could not be achieved throughout the series' existence, the
Schocken Library produced ninety-two volumes between 1933 and 1938,
presenting German Jews with a rich selection of Jewish literature, philosophy, and religion.[3]

According to Ernst Simon, the Jewish literature produced by Schocken
on the topics of suffering and consolation constituted a New Midrash—an
internal discourse among the oppressed, which was not accessible to the
hostile community surrounding them. The first volume of the Schocken
Library, for example, was entitled *Consolation of Israel* and contained
verses from Jeremiah, translated by Buber and Rosenzweig. In the face of
their own tragedy, those lamentations on the destruction of the first Temple
attained a new meaning for German Jews.

The New Midrash was also expressed on the stage, when German Jews
formed their own cultural association. As a result of the "Aryanization" of
German theaters and orchestras, thousands of Jewish actors and musicians
became unemployed in 1933. While many of them emigrated in search of
a brighter future, others were unable or unwilling to leave Germany. In July
1933, only a few months after Hitler's appointment as chancellor of the
German Reich, they founded the Cultural League of German Jews (Kulturbund deutscher Juden or, after 1935, Jüdischer Kulturbund). The concerts, theater performances, and lectures of the Kulturbund were performed only by Jews and attended by an exclusively Jewish audience (and
the omnipresent Nazi agents). In Nazi Germany, non-Jews were thus not
permitted to attend the performances of some of the most acclaimed actors
and musicians of Germany.

Most of the organizers of the Kulturbund were acculturated German
Jews without much Jewish background. Their goals in creating a Jewish
cultural organization were to provide jobs for unemployed Jewish artists
and to offer the German-Jewish public a forum for entertainment outside
the increasingly hostile atmosphere of German public life. From its very
beginnings, however, the Kulturbund had to face an ideological dilemma:
Was it possible and desirable for those artists, who had just been thrown
out of the official institutions of German culture, to continue to spread
their old values? Or should they turn to their Jewish tradition?

In staging *Nathan the Wise* as its first production, the Kulturbund provided an ambivalent response to this dilemma. Lessing's Nathan was a
symbol of tolerance in a time of intolerance. Therefore, to perform this

Kurt Katsch as Nathan the Wise in the opening performance of the Jüdischer Kulturbund, 1 October 1933. Courtesy Bildarchiv Abraham Pisarek, Berlin.

play was to produce a moral and intellectual outcry against the injustice and discrimination outside the theater hall. But Karl Loewenberg's direction of Nathan contained an additional message, which deviated considerably from Lessing's intent. Loewenberg emphasized Nathan's Jewishness by having him enter the stage with a Hasidic melody on his lips and begin his German speech with the Hebrew greeting *Barukh haba!* (Welcome!). Further, in contrast to Lessing's idea of universal tolerance, Loewenberg's Nathan remained in the end a lonely and isolated figure on one side of the stage, while the non-Jewish characters merrily celebrated their family reunion. Liberal Jews criticized the "Judaization" of the play and demanded a rendering closer to Lessing's universalist tone. Some Zionists, in contrast, were not happy with the choice of this Enlightenment drama for the opening event of the Kulturbund. They would have preferred a contemporary play expressing "conscious Jewishness."[4]

The question whether the Kulturbund should concentrate mainly on Jewish culture, and what such a Jewish culture was, occupied much of the internal debates of the Kulturbund in the following years. Some Liberal Jews regarded the Kulturbund as a stronghold of European culture in the midst of barbarism and believed that its mission was to preserve the "good" side of the cultural German heritage. Such a mission became increasingly difficult, however, after the performance of "Aryan" German authors and composers was forbidden. Austrians were still allowed, until the Nazis declared Haydn and Schubert to be Germans with the *Anschluss* of 1938. What remained were plays and compositions by German Jews and non-Germans.

In contrast to the Liberals, the growing minority of German Zionists regarded the Kulturbund as a means of making acculturated German Jews aware of their Jewish heritage. For Rabbi Joachim Prinz, the only task of the Kulturbund theater was to "build a bridge to Jewish life for the de-Judaized German Jews." Therefore, Prinz continued, the Kulturbund had to educate its actors as "conscious Jews."[5] The director of the Kulturbund, musician Kurt Singer basically adopted such a point of view. In summarizing the first five years of the Kulturbund, he emphasized the importance of awakening the Jewish spirit "in the midst of our depression and isolation."[6] Part of this awakening was the staging of plays with Jewish content, mainly by East European Jewish authors. The Yiddish classics, by Sholem Aleichem and Yitshak Leib Peretz, finally were performed in German translation, as were plays about the Golem and Shabbetai Zevi. At the same time, the Kulturbund theater produced plays on Jewish topics written by German-Jewish authors between the First World War and the rise of the Nazis, including Stefan Zweig's *Jeremias* and Richard Beer-Hofmann's *Jaákobs Traum*. Max Brod's novel *Reubeni* was adapted for the stage as well. In the Kulturbund's music program, Heinrich Schalit's modern liturgy figured prominently, as did other Jewish religious compositions.

Neither those who sought to defend the classical tradition of European culture nor those who aimed at a deeper immersion within Jewish culture gained the support of the majority of the Kulturbund's audience. After years of discrimination, most German Jews sought in literature and theater a short, albeit illusory, escape from the struggles of everyday life and longed simply for entertainment. German-Jewish author Gerson Stern summarized this view in early 1938: "What does the Jew in Germany read? Recently, a gentleman told me: 'You would like to know what I really want to read? Well, you will laugh: I want to laugh.' "[7]

There was indeed little cause for laughter. In 1938 the situation of the Jews in Germany began to deteriorate rapidly. In November, Jewish synagogues were burning and Jewish men all over Germany were deported to concentration camps, but Goebbels ordered the Kulturbund to continue its plays. Kulturbund actors and assistants were released from concentration camps to perform comedies and operas. And the show went on, even after the outbreak of the war and the beginnings of the deportations.

The Nazis dissolved the Kulturbund on 11 September 1941—ten days after the order obliging every German Jew to wear the yellow star was issued. Nevertheless, the last chapter of the Kulturbund was not over. In the Nazi camp of Westerbork in Holland, some of the Kulturbund's activists continued to perform as late as August 1944. Among the audience was the seventy-year-old Georg Hermann, the once celebrated German-Jewish author of *Jettchen Gebert*. When he was deported from Westerbork to a death camp in Poland in 1943, he might have remembered the lines he had written in 1919: "We experienced a great disappointment with the Germans and we still experience it today, every hour. Let me say openly a harsh word, why conceal it or hush it up?! The Germans proved to be bad keepers of the seal of humanity."8

The Kulturbund had an ambiguous role in Nazi Germany. On one hand, it offered consolation to the many desperate German Jews who had become social outcasts. On the other hand, the creation of such an island of peaceful illusion may have prevented some Jews from recognizing the extent of their tragedy. But whatever its function, it never established a creative Jewish culture. Most "Jewish plays" that it performed were written in Eastern Europe or Weimar Germany, and even they were poorly attended by a Jewish audience, which largely wanted light entertainment.

Although times of oppression may strengthen the feeling of solidarity and community, they do not allow for cultural creativity. The ghetto of the Jews in Nazi Germany lacked the basic condition for the development of a cultural renaissance: a democratic and pluralistic setting, where minorities can participate in the larger society while being granted the right to develop their own cultural framework. In Weimar, at least the illusion of such a society existed.

Thus it was Weimar, and not the Third Reich, in which German Jews set out to explore new and creative modes of Jewish culture within a non-Jewish environment. By establishing publishing houses and journals, adult education systems and libraries, schools and youth activities, museums and music associations, they prepared a new tradition, a mostly (though not exclusively) secular Jewish culture, one with which many highly acculturated German Jews could and did identify. The number of Jews who adopted this new tradition differed in each section of cultural activity. Probably most German Jews read a Jewish newspaper, and about every third young German Jew was a member of a Jewish youth organization, but the institutions of adult education and the concerts of Jewish music attracted a much smaller number. There can be no doubt, however, that the Jewish cultural renaissance signaled a trend recognized by most German Jews, even if they did not entirely identify with it.

When Franz Rosenzweig died in 1929, he had achieved one of his major goals. In the Weimar period, like a generation before, most German Jews knew no Hebrew and had a rather superficial knowledge of traditional Jewish texts. But in contrast to their parents and grandparents, who were often ashamed of their remaining connections to traditional Judaism, an increasing number of German Jews felt ashamed of knowing so little. Jewish learning, Yiddish theater, avant-garde Haggadah illustrations, and modern Bible translations had become fashionable among many acculturated Jews of Weimar Germany. The new curiosity about their cultural heritage did not mean that these Jews were profoundly immersed in Jewish culture, but it marked a first step toward a renewal of Jewish knowledge.

We will never know how this story might have continued in a pluralistic and democratic society. The renaissance of Jewish culture in Weimar Germany constituted a particular response to the challenge of expressing Jewish distinctiveness while participating in a modern secular society. The answer that German Jews provided was restricted to their place and time, but the challenge has remained for Jews throughout the diaspora.

Abbreviations

JGBB   *Jüdisches Gemeindeblatt Breslau*
JJB   *Jüdisches Jahrbuch für Groß-Berlin*
JJGL   *Jahrbuch für jüdische Geschichte und Literatur*
JLZ   *Jüdisch-Liberale Zeitung*
JNUL   Jewish National and University Library, Jerusalem
JR   *Jüdische Rundschau*
JVP   Jüdische Volkspartei
JVZ   *Jüdische Volkszeitung,* Breslau
JWuS   Jüdische Wohlfahrtspflege und Sozialfürsorge
LBI-AR   Leo Baeck Institute Archives, New York
LBIB   *Bulletin des Leo Baeck Instituts*
LBIYB   *Year Book of the Leo Baeck Institute*
MB   *Mitteilungsblatt der Hitachduth Olej Germania we Olej Austria*
MGWJ   *Monatsschrift für Geschichte und Wissenschaft des Judentums*
NJM   *Neue Jüdische Monatshefte*
SchA   Schocken Archives, Jerusalem
YIVO   YIVO Institute for Jewish Research Archives, New York
ZVfD   Zionistische Vereinigung für Deutschland

Notes

Unless otherwise noted, all translations are my own.

INTRODUCTION

1. Stern, *Dreams and Delusions,* p. 99. The list of publications on contributions of German Jews to German culture is exceedingly long. Kaznelson's *Juden im deutschen Kulturbereich* was one of its first products and remains a classic. A later interpretation of Weimar German Jewry in the context of assimilation is Bolkosky, *Distorted Image.* A more popular introduction to this topic is Grunfeld, *Prophets Without Honour.* The phrase "German Jews beyond Judaism" is borrowed from George Mosse, who, however, used it only for a certain segment of German Jewry.

2. Cohen, "German Jewry," p. xx. In striking contrast, scholars produced a range of path-breaking studies on Jews in imperial Germany in the 1970s, 1980s, and 1990s, including Aschheim, *Brothers and Strangers;* Breuer, *Jüdische Orthodoxie;* Kaplan, *Making of the Jewish Middle Class;* Reinharz, *Fatherland or Promised Land;* Schorsch, *Jewish Reactions to German-Antisemitism;* Tal, *Christians and Jews;* and Wertheimer, *Unwelcome Strangers.*

3. The only monograph devoted exclusively to Weimar Jewry, Donald Niewyk's *Jews in Weimar Germany,* does not discuss the development of Jewish culture. A brief account of the renaissance of Weimar's Jewish culture can be found in Hans Bach's *German Jew,* pp. 227–243. On Weimar culture in general see Gay, *Weimar Culture;* Laqueur, *Weimar;* and Hermand and Trommler, *Kultur der Weimarer Republik.*

4. Rosenzweig, *On Jewish Learning,* p. 28.

5. Schorsch, "German Judaism," p. 68.

6. On the gender-specific characteristics of this generational conflict see Brenner, "Tale of Two Families."

7. Kafka, *Letter to His Father,* p. 81.

8. Arendt, *Jew as Pariah,* p. 92.

9. Thomas Mann to Heinrich Mann, 27 February 1904, in *Briefwechsel, 1900–1949,* p. 27.

10. Martin Buber, "Jüdische Renaissance," *Ost und West* 1 (1901), pp. 7–10.

11. Kaplan, in *Making of the Jewish Middle Class,* asserts that Jewish women were especially responsible for keeping Jewish traditions alive.

12. Hobsbawm and Ranger, *Invention of Tradition,* pp. 1–14. For a related

attempt at deconstructing nations and nationalism see Anderson, *Imagined Communities.*

13. Shulamit Volkov pointed to the relevance of such an approach for modern German-Jewish history. See her article "Erfindung einer Tradition."

14. Nora, *Lieux de mémoire,* vol. 1, pp. xvii–xlii.

15. I follow here the definition used by Marc Raeff for a different minority culture in interwar Europe. See his *Russia Abroad,* p. 10. There are, of course, other possible and more inclusive definitions. See, e.g., Löwy, *Redemption and Utopia,* and Rabinbach, "Between Enlightenment and Apocalypse."

16. For a critical assessment of this tendency in Jewish historiography see Todd Endelman, "Legitimization of the Diaspora Experience in Recent Jewish Historiography."

CHAPTER ONE: PRE-WEIMAR ORIGINS

1. 1. Hobsbawm, *Age of Revolution,* p. 17.

2. For a more detailed analysis of this process see Volkov, "Erfindung einer Tradition," and Wertheimer, *Uses of Tradition.*

3. On the Verein see Meyer, *Origins of the Modern Jew,* pp. 144–182, and Schorsch, "Emergence of Historical Consciousness."

4. Yerushalmi, *Zakhor,* p. 86. The quote from Zunz can be found in Meyer, *Origins of the Modern Jew,* p. 181.

5. Meyer, *Origins of the Modern Jew,* p. 175.

6. Wolf, "On the Concept of a Science of Judaism," p. 204.

7. Zunz, *Zur Geschichte und Literatur,* p. 21.

8. Wolf, "On the Concept of a Science of Judaism," p. 194.

9. Quoted in Meyer, *Origins of the Modern Jew,* p. 170.

10. One of the first works to use this definition was Marcus Brann, *Geschichte der Juden und ihrer Litteratur* (Beslau: W. Jacobsohn, 1896–1899), pp. 449–450. Gustav Karpeles, in *Geschichte der jüdischen Literatur* (Berlin: R. Oppenheim, 1886), too, restricted the Zunzian definition of Jewish literature to the pre-modern period (p. 1). For a modern discussion of the definition of German-Jewish literature see Horch, "Heimat und Fremde."

11. On the institute see Horch, *Auf der Suche nach der jüdischen Erzählliteratur,* pp. 153–161.

12. One of the first examples of the Sephardic genre was Phoebus Philippson's *Marranen* (1837), which glorified the steadfastness of the Abrabanel family in the face of persecution, and a novel by Eugen Rispart (Isaac Ascher Francolm), *Die Juden und die Kreuzfahrer in England unter Richard Löwenherz* (1841), juxtaposed the "narrow-minded" talmudic study of medieval German Jews with the philosophical inclinations of their Sephardic contemporaries. See also Schorsch, "Myth of Sephardic Supremacy."

13. See Philippson's introduction to *Saron,* vol. 5, p. viii.

14. Schorsch, "Art as Social History," pp. 52–56.

15. Quotation from the Stuttgart Rabbi and CV representative Paul Rieger. See Reichmann, "Bewußtseinswandel," p. 567.

16. On the Catholic milieu see Spael, *Katholische Deutschland,* and Heitzer, *Volksverein für das katholische Deutschland.* On the subculture of German workers see Guttsmann, *Workers' Culture in Weimar Germany,* and Lidtke, *Alternative Culture.* On Polish immigrant workers see Kleßmann, *Polnische Bergarbeiter im Ruhrgebiet.*

17. Rosalie Perles, "Unsere Großväter," *JJGL* 22 (1919), pp. 129–131.

18. On the Verband see Borut, *Ruah Hadash,* pp. 237–259. On regional and local VJGL activities see Alexander Margolius, "Der Verein für jüdische Geschichte und Literatur in Berlin, 1892–1927," *JJGL* 28 (1927), pp. 166–185; Aschoff, "Westfälischen Vereine für jüdische Geschichte und Literatur;" and Samuel Echt, "Der Danziger Verein für jüdische Geschichte und Literatur," manuscript, Samuel Echt Collection, LBI-AR 7016.

19. "Mitteilungen," *JJGL* 12 (1909), p. 3.

20. "Bericht über die Tätigkeit des Vereins für Geschichte und Literatur des Judentums für die Jahre 1902 bis 1904," BA, Gesellschaft zur Förderung der Wissenschaft des Judentums, 75 C, Ve 5/2, p. 4. The libraries of the Vereine in Danzig and Bochum contained six hundred volumes, that in Dortmund three hundred, and small Vereine usually possessed only a few dozen books. The Verband actively initiated the establishment of similar Jewish libraries in smaller cities. In 1903 the yearbook published a list of 152 scholarly works and 203 titles of belles lettres that should constitute the basis of any Jewish library in a local association. See Wilhelm Bacher, "Altjüdische Schulwesen," *JJGL* 6 (1903), pp. 47–56.

21. "Bericht über die Tätigkeit des Vereins," p. 4. The Essen VJGL organized a particularly successful course program, which was attended by a third of the local Jewish population. See "Mitteilungen," *JJGL* 7 (1904), p. 14.

22. This number refers to the winter of 1898–1899. See "Zur Geschichte des Verbandes," *JJGL* 3 (1900), p. 282. With a membership of fifteen thousand in 1904, the Verband was among the largest Jewish organizations in imperial Germany, and was still growing. The number of local branches rose to 107 in 1908 and to 229 in 1912. See "Mitteilungen," *JJGL* 7 (1904), p. 6.

23. Schorsch, "German Judaism."

24. On Achad Ha'am's impact on German Jewry see Reinharz, "Achad Ha-am und der deutsche Zionismus."

25. Buber, "Jüdische Renaissance," *Ost und West* 1 (1901), pp. 7–10.

26. See Gelber, *"Jungjüdische Bewegung."*

27. The Fifth Zionist Congress constituted the climax of the discussion of Jewish culture within the Zionist movement. Buber tried without success to organize a conference on Jewish culture on the eve of the Sixth Zionist Congress in 1903. See his letter to Israel Zangwill, 22 April 1903, in Buber, *Briefwechsel,* vol. 1, p. 189.

28. *Stenographisches Protokoll der Verhandlungen des V. Zionisten-Congresses* (Vienna: Eretz Israel, 1901), p. 156. Another Zionist, Theodor Zlocisti, echoed Buber when he wrote one year later, "Jewish art contains the seeds, out of which

our nationality (*Volkstum*) will blossom to new strength and beauty and freedom." See *Ost und West* 2 (April 1902), p. 234.

29. For a discussion of a national German art see Belting, *Die Deutschen und ihre Kunst,* pp. 33–39.

30. Among the publications on Lilien are Gelber, "E. M. Lilien und die jüdische Renaissance," and Finkelstein, "E. M. Lilien, Das Werden eines Künstlers." See also Berkowitz, *Zionist Culture,* pp. 119–143.

31. Heyd, "Lilien and Beardsley," pp. 58–69.

32. For a discussion of this motif in the context of the Jewish renaissance see Bertz, *"Eine neue Kunst für ein altes Volk,"* p. 12.

33. See Le Rider, "Sionisme et Antisemitisme." Münchhausen's relation to Jews and Judaism always remained ambivalent. Although a German nationalist, he viewed Jewish nationalism favorably, without being a philosemite. In the mid-1920s he favored the exclusion of Jews from such German associations as the Alpenverein (see *Jüdisch-Politische Nachrichten,* 7 February 1925, p. 11, GStA Merseburg, MU Rep. 76 III, Sekt. 1, Abt. XIIIa, No. 36, Bd. 2, Bl. 38). On Münchhausen's ambivalent relationship to Judaism see Brenner, " 'Gott schütze uns vor unseren Freunden,' " pp. 185–188.

34. Börries von Münchhausen, "Wie das Buch Juda entstand," *Die Welt* (3 April 1901), pp. 21–22.

35. Theodor Zlocisti, "Juda," *Ost und West* 1 (1901), p. 63.

36. Herzl's letter was reprinted as a facsimile in *Die Welt,* no. 15 (1901), p. 358.

37. Quotes are from Zweig, *E. M. Lilien,* p. 21.

38. Börries von Münchhausen, "Lieder des Ghetto," *Ost und West* 2 (1902), p. 760.

39. Quote from Gronemann, "Erinnerungen," vol. 1, p. 32.

40. See Berkowitz, "Art in Zionist Popular Culture."

41. Berthold Feiwel, "Geleitwort zur ersten Auflage," in *Jüdischer Almanach,* p. 16.

42. Simon, "Martin Buber and German Jewry," p. 13. Liberal Jews, in contrast, viewed the Jüdischer Verlag as a superfluous institution demonstrating only Jewish particularism and thus hampering German Jews' complete integration into German society: "Why a Jewish publishing house? Why a Jewish almanac? Those are, to put it mildly, anachronisms. . . . To found a Jewish publishing house in order to publish belles lettres—this is more than superfluous. Or should Germany, which has enough denominational tensions and splits, receive an additional one?" *Berliner Tageblatt,* 7 February 1903, quoted in *Jüdischer Almanach, 1902–1964,* p.7.

43. The first volume was supposed to contain contributions by Thomas Masaryk, Eduard Bernstein, Gustav Landauer, Ahad Ha'am, Solomon Schechter, Simon Dubnow, and Theodor Lessing. Martin Buber to Efraim Frisch, 14 April 1903, 29 April 1903, Efraim Frisch Collection, LBI-AR 2523.

44. "Ost und West," *Ost und West* 1 (1901), p. 2. See Brenner, "Promoting the *Ostjuden.*"

45. Graetz, *Geschichte der Juden,* vol. 11, p. 94.

46. On Grunwald and Jewish folkloristics in Germany see the publications of Christoph Daxelmüller, especially "Jüdische Volkskunde in Deutschland vor 1933."

47. Langbehn, *Rembrandt als Erzieher,* p. 43. For Burckhardt see Mosse, *Germans and Jews,* p. 58.

48. Max Grunwald, "Kapitlekh fun an Oytobiografye," p. 246.

49. "Erster Jahres-Bericht der Gesellschaft zur Förderung der Wissenschaft des Judentums (1903)," BA, Gesellschaft zur Fîrderung der Wissenschaft des Judentums, 75 C Ge 4, folder 4. The center of the society's activities was the "Outline of *Wissenschaft des Judentums*" consisting of thirty-six monographs on various aspects of Judaism. Among the works inspired by the outline were Leo Baeck's *Das Wesen des Judentums,* Ismar Elbogen's *Geschichte des jüdischen Gottesdienstes,* Julius Guttmann's *Die Philosophie des Judentums,* and Hermann Cohen's *Die Religion der Vernunft aus den Quellen des Judentums.*

50. Buber, "Jüdische Wissenschaft," *Die Welt,* 17 January 1901. Reprinted in Buber, *Jüdische Bewegung,* p. 53.

51. Max Weber to his sister Lilli, 8 September 1914. English translation is cited in Mitzman, *Iron Cage,* p. 224. Hermann Cohen, "Deutschtum und Judentum," *Jüdische Schriften* 2 (1916), pp. 275–277.

52. See the contemporary account in *JJGL* 18 (1915), pp. 6–7, and the memoirs by Elias Auerbach, *Pionier der Verwirklichung,* pp. 350–366.

53. See Simon, *Entscheidung zum Judentum,* p. 30. For a systematic analysis of this issue see Reichmann, "Bewußtseinswandel," pp. 512–613.

54. Arnold Zweig, "Judenzählung vor Verdun," *Die Schaubühne* 13, no. 1 (1917), pp. 117–119. The best account of the Jews' census is in Angress, "Deutsche Militär."

55. Georg Hermann, "Zur Frage der Westjuden," *NJM* 3 (1919), p. 400.

56. Simon, *Brücken,* p. 22.

57. Maurer, *Ostjuden,* p. 95.

58. Fritz Mordechai Kaufmann, "Zum Programm der Freistatt," *Die Freistatt* 1 (1913–1914), pp. 3–5.

59. Buber, "Die Losung," *Der Jude* 1 (1916–1917), pp. 1–3.

60. *NJM* 1 (1916), p. 1.

61. Buber, "Die Losung," *Der Jude* 1 (1916–1917), p. 2.

CHAPTER TWO: GEMEINSCHAFT AND GEMEINDE

1. Martin Buber, "Die Losung," *Der Jude* 1 (1916), pp. 1–2.

2. For a stimulating interpretation of community see Anderson, *Imagined Communities,* p. 6.

3. For a discussion of German Zionists' view of a Jewish race see Efron, *Defenders of the Race,* pp. 123–174.

4. Reinharz, *Fatherland or Promised Land,* p. 227. On the concept of ethnicity see Smith, *Ethnic Origin of Nations.*

5. In a letter to the German nationalist Wilhelm Schwaner, Walther Rathenau wrote on 18 August 1916, "Mein Volk sind die Deutschen, niemand sonst. Die Juden sind für mich ein deutscher Stamm, wie Sachsen, Bayern oder Wenden." Rathenau, *Briefe,* vol. 1, p. 220.

6. On the concept of an "invisible subculture" among nineteenth-century German Jews see Sorkin, *Transformation of German Jewry,* pp. 6–7.

7. Toury, *Politischen Orientierungen,* pp. 110–169.

8. Hamburger and Pulzer, "Jews as Voters in the Weimar Republic."

9. Mosse, "German Jews and Liberalism in Retrospect," p. xxiv. The main source for Mosse's analysis of Liberal German Jews is the radical Reformgemeinde of Berlin. See also Mosse, *German Jews Beyond Judaism,* pp. 72–73. Similarly, Donald L. Niewyk maintains that German Jews "attached themselves to the liberal movement, and they retained that association until well into the Weimar years." See Niewyk, *Jews in Weimar Germany,* p. 3.

10. This development is recognized in Schorsch, *Jewish Reactions to German Anti-Semitism.* A history of the CV in Weimar Germany, however, remains a desideratum. Bolkosky's *Distorted Image,* p. 16, presents a rather distorted image of the CV, identifying it with assimilation and not taking into account its internal development. Similarly, Donald L. Niewyk subtitled his chapter on Liberal German Jews "The Search for an Assimilationist Identity." See Niewyk, *Jews in Weimar Germany,* p. 96.

11. Fuchs, *Um Deutschtum und Judentum,* pp. 236–237.

12. The German word *Stamm* literally means "tribe" or "race" and was often used as self-identification by German Jews who disliked the terms *nation* and *religion.* It is related to *Abstammung* (descent) and *Stammesgemeinschaft* (community of common descent). The popularity of its use can be partly explained by its vagueness. Assimilationists interpreted it in the sense of a German *Stamm* analogous to Bavarians or Saxons, but for Zionists it became a synonym for a Jewish *Volk.*

13. Fuchs, *Um Deutschtum und Judentum,* p. 242.

14. See Baumgartner, *Sehnsucht nach Gemeinschaft,* p. 40.

15. I shall mention only a few of the numerous lectures, essays, and studies discussing the renewal of Gemeinschaft. See, for example, Paul Natorp, *Individuum und Gemeinschaft* (Jena, Germany: E. Diederichs, 1921); Erich Stern, *Über den Begriff der Gemeinschaft* (Langensalza, Germany: Beyer and Söhne, 1921); Hans Pichler, *Zur Logik der Gemeinschaft* (Tübingen, Germany: J. C. B. Mohr, 1924); and Franz Wilhelm Jerusalem, *Gemeinschaft und Staat* (Tübingen, Germany: J. C. B. Mohr, 1930). The motto of the 1928 conference of the German Philosophical Society was *Philosophie der Gemeinschaft.*

16. Plessner, *Grenzen der Gemeinschaft,* p. 26.

17. For a discussion of Tönnies and his reception by the German academic community see Ringer, *German Mandarins,* pp. 164–172.

18. Holländer, *Deutsch-jüdische Probleme der Gegenwart,* p. 14.

19. For a discussion of this essay see Ringer, *German Mandarins,* pp. 358–359.

20. Erich von Kahler, "Juden und Deutsche," *Europäische Revue* 6 (1930), pp. 744–756.

21. Werner Cahnmann to Erich von Kahler, 27 November 1930, 31 December 1930, Erich von Kahler Collection, LBI-AR, 3890.

22. Werner Cahnmann, "Judentum und Volksgemeinschaft," *Der Morgen* 2 (1926), pp. 291–298; Werner Cahnmann, "The Nazi-Threat and the Central-Verein: A Recollection," manuscript, Werner Cahnmann Collection, LBI-AR, 556,

p. 6. Two of the younger CV leaders who argued against a purely religious definition of Judaism were Ludwig Tietz and Friedrich Brodnitz. The participation of such Liberal German Jews as Leo Baeck and Julius Blau in the enlarged Jewish Agency created by the World Zionist Organization in 1928 was a further indication of the CV's shift in attitude.

23. Seligmann, *Erinnerungen*, pp. 119–120. See also the contemporary statement of another Liberal German rabbi, Felix Goldmann of Leipzig, who characterized the last remnants of nineteenth-century radical reform congregations in Germany as "able neither to live nor to die." Felix Goldmann, "Das liberale Judentum," in *Deutsche Judentum*, pp. 19–20.

24. Some of the most popular products of the "new thinking" in Jewish theology were reactions to the contemporary debates in Bible scholarship that attacked the most important source of Judaism. Franz Delitzsch's *Babel und Bibel* (Leipzig: J. C. Hinrichs, 1902) questioned the originality of many central concepts of the Hebrew Bible, and Adolf Harnack's *Wesen des Christentums* (Leipzig: J. C. Hinrichs, 1900) called for Christians to remove themselves further from the Old Testament.

25. Krueger, *Philosophie der Gemeinschaft*, p. 155.

26. On the *Star of Redemption* see Moses, *System und Offenbarung*, and Mendes-Flohr, *Philosophy of Franz Rosenzweig*.

27. Scholem, *From Berlin to Jerusalem*, p. 150. Bloch, one of the most learned and respected Liberal rabbis in Germany and longtime president of the Liberal rabbinical association, was in fact the author of several essays on Kabbalah.

28. Meyer, *Response to Modernity*, pp. 207–208. Baeck's biographer, Albert Friedlander, expresses a similar view when he calls the changes from Baeck's earlier writings to his later ones the "move from essence to existence." Friedlander, *Leo Baeck*, p. 103.

29. Friedlander, *Leo Baeck*, p. 101.

30. Baeck's new interest in nonrational aspects of Judaism was best expressed in his essay "Geheimnis und Gebot," in *Wege im Judentum*, pp. 33–48. On this subject see also Alexander Altmann's important essay "Leo Baeck and the Jewish Mystical Tradition."

31. Leo Baeck, "Nehemias Anton Nobel zum Gedenken," in *Korrespondenzblatt für die Gründung und Erhaltung einer Akademie der Wissenschaft des Judentums* 3 (1922), pp. 1–3.

32. For Goldmann see *Deutsche Judentum*, pp. 19–20; for Graetz, see *Geschichte der Juden*, vol. 11, p. 94.

33. Max Dienemann, "Über die Bedeutung des Irrationalen für das Liberale Judentum," *Liberales Judentum* 13, nos. 4–6 (1921), p. 29.

34. Ibid., p. 32.

35. "Verhandlungen und Beschlüsse der Versammlung der Liberalen Rabbiner Deutschlands," *Liberales Judentum* 14, nos. 1–3 (1922), pp. 5–9.

36. Schine, *Jewish Thought Adrift*, pp. 109–120.

37. Their critical view toward the rational traditions of Liberal Judaism was shared by numerous other Liberal rabbis. Cologne rabbi Isidor Caro rejected the elevation of reason to the ultimate ideal of Judaism (*GBH*, 10 January 1927, p. 1),

and rabbi Max Elk of Stettin held rationalism responsible for the long passivity of Liberal Jews (*BIGZ,* 13 December 1927, p. 373).

38. Rosenzweig, *Briefe,* p. 980.

39. In three pamphlets entitled "Die blau-weiße Brille," Scholem demanded that the Zionist youth take emigration to Palestine more seriously and promote the knowledge of Hebrew and Judaism. The essence of Scholem's criticism appeared in his essay "Jüdische Jugendbewegung," *Der Jude* 1 (1917), pp. 822–825 (translated in Scholem, *On Jews and Judaism in Crisis,* pp. 49–53). See also Rinott, "Major Trends in Jewish Youth Movements in Germany," pp. 87–90.

40. See Schatzker, "Martin Buber's Influence on the Jewish Youth Movement in Germany."

41. BA, Wanderbund Kameraden 75 C Wa 1, folder 16.

42. Sharfman, "Jewish Youth Movement," p. 436.

43. Maoz, "Werkleute," p. 167.

44. Leo Baeck, "Gemeinde in der Großstadt," *Der Morgen* 5 (1929), pp. 583–590.

45. See Noam, "Erinnerung und Dialog," p. 70, and Nussbaum, "Weg und Schicksal eines deutschen Juden," p. 8. On a radical rejection of urban Jewish life and its materialism, see Alfred Lemm [Lehmann], "Großstadtkultur und Juden," *Der Jude* 1 (1916–1917), pp. 316–317.

46. Fritz Kahn, "Neue Wege jüdischer Kultur," *Festnummer zum Ordenstag: Großloge für Deutschland VIII.U.O.B.B.* (October 1921), pp. 93–95. Kahn's distinction between civilization and culture reflected one aspect of a transformation of the German B'nai Brith lodges in the Weimar period. By the end of the 1920s, the lodge was for many members no longer a place for sociability and charity but an *Erlebnisbund* (association of common experience). See, e.g., Fritz Wieluner, "Der Weg der Loge von der Gesinnungsgemeinschaft zum Erlebnisbunde," *Der Orden Bne Briss* (June–July 1928), pp. 77–80.

47. Siegfried Bernfeld Collection, YIVO, RG 6, folder 41: "Die jüdischen Jugendvereine und die Gemeinden: Leitsätze von Landesrabbiner Dr. Rieger" (n.d.). See also Max Grünewald, "Jüdische Jugend und jüdische Gemeinde," *JWuS* 2 (1931), pp. 65–72.

48. See, e.g., Max Grünewald, "Zur Einrichtung der Jugendgemeinde," *Die Jugendgemeinde: Beilage zum Israelitischen Gemeindeblatt Mannheim,* 25 February 1926, p. 1. On Hamburg: Lorenz, *Juden in Hamburg,* pp. 869–893. On Breslau: *JGBB,* vol. 8, no. 2 (February 1931), appendix.

49. The rise of the Jewish Youth Movement in Germany was parallel to the development of interwar French Jewry. See Hyman, *From Dreyfus to Vichy,* pp. 179–198.

50. See Wilhelm, "Jewish Community in the Post-Emancipation Period."

51. See Ma'ayan, *Ha-behirot be-kehilat Berlin, 1901–1920,* and Ma'ayan, *Ha-behirot be-kehilat Köln, 1900–1921.*

52. On Prussia see Birnbaum, *Staat und Synagoge, 1918–1938.*

53. The fight for universal suffrage took many years and encountered considerable resistance in most communities.In Leipzig, Chemnitz, and a few other places with a high percentage of Ostjuden, German immigrants who were not citizens

never attained equal voting rights, and neither did women in Cologne. See Kaplan, *Jewish Feminist Movement*, p. 271.

54. *Jüdisches Jahrbuch für Gross-Berlin auf das Jahr 1926*, pp. 115–116.

55. Both quotes are from CZA, Alfred Klee Collection, A 142/87/2.

56. Simonsohn, *Jüdische Volksgemeinde*, p. 29.

57. *JR*, 2 December 1930, p. 639.

58. For more details see Brenner, "Jüdische Volkspartei."

59. For Hamburg see CAHJP, AHW 348; for Cologne see Ma'ayan, *Ha-behirot be-kehilat Köln*, pp. 117–118.

60. *Jüdische Zeitung für Ostdeutschland*, 7 November 1930, n.p.

61. *JLZ*, 8 June 1928, n.p.

62. On the community budget and synagogue attendance see Niewyk, *Jews in Weimar Germany*, pp. 102–105. A similar decline in involvement in religious life could be observed in rural areas. See Jacob Borut, "Hayei ha-dat be-kerev yehudei ha-kefarim veha-ayarot be-ma'arava shel Germaniah bi-tekufat Weimar," in Heilbronner, *Yehudei Weimar*, pp. 90–107. On election turnout see Brenner, "Jüdische Volkspartei," p. 223.

63. Kober, "Jewish Communities in Germany," p. 220.

64. See Strauss, "Jewish Press in Germany," pp. 350–351.

65. *GJGB* 1, no. 1 (1 July 1909).

66. Winz had recognized the importance of local Jewish newspapers long before his employment in Berlin. When still editing *Ost und West*, he proposed the creation of an illustrated Jewish weekly that would contain a main section and different local section for each Jewish community, to be published with an average circulation of two thousand in the sixteen largest Jewish communities. Leo Winz Collection, CZA, A 136/39.

67. Leo Winz Collection, CZA, A 136/42. On circulation numbers and advertising strategies see Leo Winz Collection, CZA, A 136/46.

68. In 1928 the largest Gemeindeblätter other than the one in Berlin were in Breslau (with a circulation of 8,700), Hamburg (8,000), and Frankfurt (6,000). Leo Winz Collection, CZA, A 136/49.

69. On the *BIGZ* see Grünewald, "Critic of German Jewry."

70. Georg Herlitz, "Jüdische Gemeindebibliotheken," *Orden Bne Briss: Festschrift zum Ordenstage* (October 1928), pp. 171–172.

71. Josef Lin, "Die Berliner Jüdische Lesehalle in ihrem neuen Heim," *Ost und West* (November 1908), pp. 683–690; Johannes Giskala, "Zum zehnten Stiftungstage des Vereins Jüdische Lesehalle und Bibliothek," *Ost und West* (February 1905), pp. 137–142.

72. *JJB*, 1926, pp. 151–152.

73. *Verwaltungsbericht des Vorstandes der Jüdischen Gemeinde zu Berlin*, pp. 26–27.

74. Scholem, *From Berlin to Jerusalem*, p. 91.

75. Rosenzweig, *Zweistromland*, pp. 511–512.

76. *JE*, 24 December 1920. An incomplete list of community libraries can be found in the *Führer durch die jüdische Gemeindeverwaltung 1932/33*, pp. 527–528.

77. Synagogenausschuß of the Israelitische Kultusgemeinde Speyer to community members, 28 February 1919, CAHJP, PF XII 21. On Neuwied see CAHJP, Rh/Nw 75. The library of the Jewish community of Cologne had three thousand volumes in 1932. See *GBJK*, no. 2 (22 January 1932), p. 17.

78. Jüdische Lesehalle und Bibliothek to Gemeindevorstand, 7 December 1922, CAHJP, AHW 887.

79. Gemeindevorstand to JOINT, 19 March 1923, CAHJP, AHW 887.

80. *GBH*, 10 July 1930, p. 5, and *GBH*, 25 January 1932, pp. 1–2.

81. *GBH*, 25 January 1932, pp. 1–2.

82. See Schatzker, *Jüdische Jugend*, p. 37, and *Führer durch die jüdische Gemeindeverwaltung 1932/33*, p. 522.

83. In Breslau, for example, there were only five *Simultanschulen*, compared to more than one hundred conspicuously Christian schools. See *Jüdische Zeitung für Ostdeutschland*, 27 March 1931, n.p.

84. *Jüdische Zeitung für Ostdeutschland*, 27 March 1931, n.p. See also Schatzker, *Jüdische Jugend*, pp. 83–89.

85. *Statistisches Handbuch der Stadt München 1928*, p. 261.

86. Prestel, *Jüdisches Schul- und Erziehungswesen in Bayern*, pp. 135–139. In Nuremberg's neighboring city of Fürth, a young Henry Kissinger was among the pupils of the local Jewish high school, the only one left in Bavaria. Ibid., p. 262.

87. On Breslau see *Jüdische Zeitung für Ostdeutschland*, 27 March 1931, n.p. The Duisburg school had about two hundred pupils in 1930; see *Gemeinde-Zeitung Duisburg*, 17 February 1930, n.p. On Berlin see *Jüdisches Jahrbuch Berlin 1932*, p. 142.

88. For 1913 see *Handbuch der jüdischen Gemeindeverwaltung und Wohlfahrtspflege 1913*; for 1930 see *GJGB* 20, no. 10 (October 1930), p. 459; for 1932 see *Führer durch die jüdische Gemeindeverwaltung 1932–33*, pp. 512–515. See also Schiratzki, "The Rykestraße School in Berlin," and Kochavi, "Beyn Tsionim le-Liberalim be-Berlin 1929–1932," p. 69.

89. *GJGB*, October 1930, p. 462. See also Sinasohn, *Adass Jisroel Berlin*, p. 58. On Prussia see the numbers provided in Levinson, *Ha-tenu'ah ha'ivrit ba-golah*, p. 70.

90. *Jüdische Zeitung für Ostdeutschland*, 27 March 1931, n.p.

91. Fürst, "Höheren jüdischen Schulen," pp. 57–58.

92. Lorenz, *Juden in Hamburg*, vol. 2, pp. 413–414.

93. On Cologne see Carlebach, *Adass Yeshurun of Cologne*, pp. 100–102.

94. *Führer durch die jüdische Gemeindeverwaltung 1932–33*, pp. 516–517. See also the statistics in Arnsberg, *Geschichte der Frankfurter Juden*, vol. 2, pp. 502–505. On the Philantropin see Schlotzhauer, *Philanthropin*, p. 90.

95. Fürst, "Höheren jüdischen Schulen," pp. 54–56.

96. On Carlebach's pedagogical principle see Gillis-Carlebach, *Hinukh ve-emunah*.

97. *Jüdische Zeitung für Ostdeutschland*, 27 March 1931, n.p.

98. Eliav, *Ha-hinukh ha-yehudi*, p. 238.

99. Among the sons were Nahum Glatzer and Jacob Katz, who later became important scholars. See Katz's recollections in Horwitz, *Yitshak Breuer: Iyunim be-*

mishnato, pp. 39–49. There was another small yeshivah in Frankfurt, directed by the Orthodox rabbi of the mainstream community, Marcus Horovitz. See Breuer, *Jüdische Orthodoxie im Deutschen Reich,* p. 111.

100. *Der Israelit,* 25 March 1922, p. 3.

101. On Berlin see *Führer durch die jüdische Gemeindeverwaltung 1932–33,* pp. 51–52; on Hamburg see *GBH,* no. 7 (10 July 1926) pp. 1–2, and Lorenz, *Juden in Hamburg,* pp. 776, 792–808; on the Cologne yeshivah on St. Apern Street see Carlebach, "Orthodoxie in der Kölner jüdischen Gemeinde der Neuzeit," p. 353; on Nuremberg see Prestel, *Jüdisches Schul- und Erziehungswesen,* p. 135. On Leipzig see *Der Israelit,* 16 February 1922, p. 12, and Kreutner, *"Mein Leipzig,"* pp. 49–59. In Lübeck a yeshivah had been established in 1920. See Carlebach, *Adass Yeshurun,* p. 121.

102. *GBH,* 11 July 1926, p. 7.

103. Quoted in Eisner, "Reminiscences of the Berlin Rabbinical Seminary," p. 41.

104. Fritz Bamberger, "Julius Guttmann: Philosopher of Judaism," *LBIYB* 5 (1960), p. 11.

105. Kafka, *Letters to Friends, Family, and Editors,* pp. 402–403.

106. Rothschild, "Geschichte des Seminars,", pp. 145–156.

107. At the same time systematic attempts were under way to improve Jewish education in afternoon schools and Sunday schools. In Stuttgart, for example, sixty pupils attended a *Talmud-Tora-Schule* with supplementary Hebrew lessons. *JE,* 9 May 1919, pp. 214–215.

108. *Jüdisches Gemeindeblatt: Mitteilungsblatt der Israelitischen Gemeinde Bremen,* 1 April 1930, n.p.

CHAPTER THREE: A NEW LEARNING

1. Koch, "Freie Jüdische Lehrhaus," p. 119.

2. Circular letter to Stuttgart Jewish community members, Stuttgart and Cannstatt, September 1925, Karl Adler Collection, LBI-AR, 7276.

3. Quotation is from Kafka, *Letter to His Father,* p. 81.

4. The literature on Jewish adult education in Weimar Germany concentrates almost exclusively on the Frankfurt Lehrhaus and is based mainly on accounts written by its teachers. These accounts include Simon, "Franz Rosenzweig und das jüdische Bildungsproblem"; Koch, "Freie Jüdische Lehrhaus"; and especially Glatzer, "Frankfort Lehrhaus." Among the later accounts, the most detailed are Bühler, *Erziehung zur Tradition;* Kern, "Franz Rosenzweig's Jüdisches Lehrhaus in Frankfurt"; and Schivelbusch, "Auf der Suche nach dem verlorenen Judentum."

5. Salzberger, "Zwischen zwei Weltkriegen," p. 98.

6. Siegfried Kracauer and Leo Löwenthal were members of this circle; they also contributed to *Gabe, Herrn Rabbiner Dr. Nobel zum 50.* See also Heuberger, "Orthodoxy Versus Reform."

7. Among Rabinkow's students were Nahum Goldmann (who was later president of the World Jewish Congress), Zalman Rubaschoff (Shazar) (later president of Israel), mathematician Abraham Fraenkel, Erich Fromm, and Ernst

Simon. See Honigmann, "Jüdische Studenten zwischen Orthodoxie und moderner Wissenschaft."

8. Scholem called the institute *Torapeutikum* in *From Berlin to Jerusalem,* p. 156. Among its participants were Leo Löwenthal, Ernst Simon, and Erich Fromm (who later married Reichmann). For an account of the institution see Blomert, "Vergessene Sanatorium."

9. Voigts, *Oskar Goldberg,* pp. 153–172. On the *Volksheim* see Chapter 7 of this book.

10. See Rosenzweig's letter to Nahum Glatzer, 30 June 1929, a few months before Rosenzweig's death: "Enough has been published about my relations toward Zionism. . . . I regard myself as a Liberal." Rosenzweig, *Briefe,* p. 1220.

11. Rosenzweig, *On Jewish Learning,* p. 64.

12. Ibid., p. 59.

13. Rosenzweig's "return to Judaism" has been described elsewhere. See, e.g., Glatzer, *Franz Rosenzweig,* pp. 23–31.

14. An English translation of this essay, titled "Towards a Renaissance of Jewish Learning," is found in Rosenzweig, *On Jewish Learning,* pp. 55–71.

15. Rosenzweig, *On Jewish Learning,* p. 98.

16. See the letter from D. Minden to Dr. Nathan, 10 November 1930, CAHJP, AHW 833a, "Franz Rosenzweig Gedächtnis-Stiftung": "Die Anstellung für den jüdischen Schulverein kam zustande. . . . Die Unterzeichnung der Verträge unterblieb, weil die Frankfurter Gemeinde im letzten Augenblick Franz Rosenzweig die Stellung einräumte, die er hoffte sich in Hamburg verschaffen zu können."

17. At one point Rosenzweig was proposed as the head of a Frankfurt branch of the Akademie für die Wissenschaft des Judentums, which had been established in Berlin in 1918 on Rosenzweig's initiative. The Frankfurt branch, however, was never opened. Rosenzweig, *Briefe,* p. 667. A slightly different version of Rosenzweig's visit to Nobel appears in his later letter to Rudolf Hallo, in which he did not mention the Akademie project. See Rosenzweig, *Briefe,* p. 850.

18. Rosenzweig himself taught the only four courses in this program: belief and knowledge, Hebrew language, Jewish history, and the biblical book Numbers. The list of participants and Rosenzweig's original notes are kept in the Franz Rosenzweig Collection, LBI-AR, 3003 IV.

19. *AZJ,* 29 September 1893, p. 457.

20. Of the 90 lecture courses and 180 study groups of the Lehrhaus, 42 dealt with the introduction to the Hebrew language and the basic books, 40 with the Hebrew Bible (not counting the regular Bible-reading class of Eduard Strauss), 30 with talmudic-midrashic literature, 30 with theology and mysticism, 25 with Jewish history, and 15 with Jewish liturgy. The remaining courses were dedicated to Hebrew and Yiddish literature, contemporary Jewish issues, and all kinds of general discussion ranging from such topics as "sickness and health" to "political movements in the contemporary Western world." For an approximate statistical analysis see Glatzer, "Frankfort Lehrhaus," p. 119. A detailed list of all courses and lecturers can be found in the Nahum Glatzer Collection, Brandeis University Archives, folder 24.

21. Rosenzweig, *Briefe,* p. 675.

22. Weber, "Science as a Vocation," p. 143.

23. Ringer, *Decline of the German Mandarins*, p. 416.

24. Ibid., p. 281.

25. An English translation of "It Is Time," titled "Concerning the Study of Judaism," is found in Rosenzweig, *On Jewish Learning*, pp. 25–54. The quotation is from Rosenzweig, *On Jewish Learning*, p. 68.

26. Meinecke was never able to understand Rosenzweig's move toward Judaism. He wrote, in an obituary of Rosenzweig, "The World War led him astray from the way he originally entered upon, the exploration of the heights of German Protestant culture, therefore he fled into the world of his blood. But with his book on Hegel he left behind a work of enduring value to German intellectual history." *Historische Zeitschrift* 142 (1930), p. 220.

27. Rosenzweig, *On Jewish Learning*, p. 68.

28. Ibid., p. 63.

29. Ibid., p. 55.

30. Langewiesche, "Freizeit und 'Massenbildung,'" p. 124.

31. For a general survey on the development of modern adult education with an emphasis on Germany see Pöggeler, *Geschichte der Erwachsenenbildung*.

32. Rosenzweig went so far as to use the term Volkshochschule as a shibboleth to distinguish whom to hire as teachers: "People who called the Lehrhaus a Volkshochschule are people who want to speak only once, or only want to earn money, or both; the others speak of the Lehrhaus, and those are our teachers." Rosenzweig, *Briefe*, p. 855.

33. Rosenzweig, *Briefe*, p. 851. The reference was to Werner Picht, *Die deutsche Volkshochschule der Zukunft* (Leipzig: Quelle and Meyer, 1919).

34. Herrmann, *"Neue Erziehung,"* p. 147. See also the concepts of such leading representatives of the Volkshochschule as Eduard Weitsch, Werner Picht, and Georg Koch, reprinted in Tietgens, *Erwachsenenbildung*, pp. 45, 56, 73–76. For a detailed discussion on this issue see Tuguntke, *Demokratie und Bildung*, pp. 51–78.

35. Tuguntke, *Demokratie und Bildung*, pp. 32–49. A similar approach was chosen by the Protestant institutions of adult education in Weimar Germany. See Ahlheim, *Zwischen Arbeiterbildung und Mission*.

36. Wunsch, *Idee der "Arbeitsgemeinschaft."*

37. Eduard Strauss, "Volksbildungsarbeit," in *Aufsätze und Anmerkungen, 1919–1945*, n.p. Rosenzweig's first publication on educational questions was also outside the specific Jewish realm. See his essay "Volksschule und Reichsschule" (1916), in *Zweistromland*, pp. 371–411.

38. At the sixth conference of the Hohenrodter Bund in 1928 Buber delivered a speech on philosophical and religious weltanschauung, and in the following year he participated—together with Karl Jaspers, Ernst Kantorowicz, Eugen Rosenstock, Alfred Weber, and many other prominent scholars—in the Heidelberg conference Universität und Volkshochschule. See Sandt, *Martin Bubers bildnerische Tätigkeit*, pp. 122–144. The minutes of the Heppenheim conference can be found in the Martin Buber Archives, Zayin 44, Jewish National and University Library, Jerusalem.

39. The role of Jews in the development of the Volkshochschule movement in Weimar Germany has not yet been analyzed. Numerous Volkshochschulen had Jewish directors; among them were the philosopher Theodor Lessing in Hanover and Alfred Mann in Breslau, who until 1933 served as the chairman of the Reichsverband der deutschen Volkshochschulen, the Germany-wide organization of independent adult education institutions. See Pöggeler, "Erwachsenenbildung in der Weimarer Republik," p. 346. See also Simon, *Aufbau im Untergang,* pp. 30–31.

40. The percentage of male Volkshochschule students who were workers rose from 58 percent to 64 percent between 1925 and 1930. Another 30 percent were white-collar workers (*Angestellte*). See Pöggeler, *Geschichte der Erwachsenenbildung,* p. 118.

41. Rosenzweig, *On Jewish Learning,* p. 69. In later years, when advising his successor, Rudolf Hallo, how to run the Lehrhaus, Rosenzweig demanded that in every program there be at least one complete *am-ha'arets* (ignoramus). See Rosenzweig, *Briefe,* p. 861.

42. Rosenzweig, *On Jewish Learning,* pp. 98–100.

43. Simon, "Franz Rosenzweig und das jüdische Bildungsproblem," p. 399.

44. Rosenzweig, *Briefe,* p. 855. Of the sixty-five teachers of the Lehrhaus, only nine were rabbis, and none of them belonged to the Lehrhaus' inner circle.

45. Rosenzweig, *Briefe,* p. 857. As Rudolf Stahl, later secretary of the Lehrhaus, jokingly recalled, the Gesellschaft was the "enemy number one" for Rosenzweig because its leaders, Rabbi Salzberger and Paula Nassauer, considered the Lehrhaus the "naughty child which had declared its independence." They wanted the Lehrhaus to depend strongly on the Jewish community and the Gesellschaft, whereas Rosenzweig wanted to keep the Lehrhaus as independent as possible. Rudolf Stahl, interview by the author, New York, 2 July 1991.

46. Kafka, *Letter to His Father,* pp. 77–85.

47. Rosenzweig and Scholem have been the subjects of a number of essays. See, e.g., Alter, *Necessary Angels;* Moses, *L'ange de l'histoire;* and Brenner, "A Tale of Two Families."

48. Quotation from Moses, "Scholem and Rosenzweig," pp. 102–103.

49. Bühler, *Erziehung zur Tradition,* p. 20; Richard Koch, untitled memoirs, LBI-AR, ME 735, pp. 212–219; Rudolf Stahl, interview by the author, New York, 2 July 1991.

50. See Hallo, "Hallos and Rubensohns," LBI-AR, ME 251, p. 31.

51. Rudolf Stahl, interview by the author, New York, 2 July 1991; Richard Koch, "Einzelne Erinnerungen an Franz Rosenzweig," Franz Rosenzweig Papers, Vanderbilt University, Divinity Library, folder 65, p. 1.

52. Rosenzweig, *Briefe,* p. 677.

53. Scholem, *From Berlin to Jerusalem,* p. 154.

54. Altogether, Strauss taught thirty classes, the most popular of which was his Bible-reading course. This course was the only class to continue after the dissolution of the Lehrhaus, into the time of the new Lehrhaus after 1933. After Strauss's emigration to America, the course was even continued in New York among a circle of German-Jewish emigrants of the congregation Habonim. The name *Habonim*

(Builders) was inspired by Rosenzweig's essay "Die Bauleute." I am grateful to Carola Trier (née Strauss) and Ludwig Boettigheimer for information on Strauss and his activities in New York. See also Tramer, "Eduard Strauss und seine Freundschaft mit Franz Rosenzweig und Martin Buber."

55. "Rede auf der 21. ordentlichen Sitzung der Grossloge VIII.U.O.B.B. 1920," p. 2, Eduard Strauss Collection, LBI-AR 7077, box 1, folder 7.

56. Eduard Strauss, "An die Jugend," *Kameraden,* vol. 1 (June–August 1920), p. 2.

57. Franz Rosenzweig to Eduard Strauss, 14 November 1919, Edith Scheinmann Collection, LBI-AR, 5043, box 1. See also Strauss, "Der Deutsche Jude Franz Rosenzweig," pp. 30–32.

58. Other than Martin Buber's and Nobel's crowded lectures, Strauss's Bible-reading course was the best-attended class of the Lehrhaus, "composed mainly of ladies." Nahum N. Glatzer, "The Frankfurt Lehrhaus," lecture delivered in Kassel, 1986, Nahum Glatzer Collection, Brandeis University Archives, folder 24, p. 14.

59. "Eduard Strauss—60 Jahre," *CVZ,* 13 February 1936, n.p.

60. Scholem, *From Berlin to Jerusalem,* p. 154. See also Ahrens, "Reminiscences," pp. 252–253.

61. I am grateful to Anne Glatzer for the information on Nahum Norbert Glatzer, provided to me in a personal interview on 21 April 1991. See also Paul Mendes-Flohr, "Knowledge as Service." Glatzer's early admiration is documented in an unpublished letter of the seventeen-year-old Glatzer to Buber, kept in the Siegfried Bernfeld Collection, YIVO Institute Archives, RG 6, folder 51.

62. Rosenzweig, *Briefe,* pp. 865–866.

63. Rosenzweig recalled that even on cold winter days 150 people would attend Nobel's class, some of them with toboggans or skis. Rosenzweig, *Briefe,* p. 867.

64. Friedman, *Martin Buber's Life and Work,* p. 31.

65. Rosenzweig, *Briefe,* pp. 861, 869.

66. Glatzer, "Frankfort Lehrhaus," p. 120.

67. Simon, "Franz Rosenzweig und das jüdische Bildungsproblem," p. 401.

68. Scholem, *From Berlin to Jerusalem,* p. 140.

69. As his wife, Gertrude Hallo, later recalled, "In reality Franz did not only demand this issue but tried to force its realization with the cruelty which was the back side of his greatness. Thus he forbade us, after we had found an apartment of our own, to visit him on Friday nights etc. etc." Gertrude Hallo to Nahum Glatzer, 1 June 1956, Glatzer Collection, Brandeis University Archives, folder 25.

70. Rosenzweig, *Briefe,* p. 862.

71. The prices rose to six hundred marks per class in the time of inflation and settled at a price range of between 50 pfennigs and 1.50 marks in 1925.

72. Rosenzweig, *Briefe,* pp. 851–852.

73. Ibid., p. 763.

74. On Hallo see the letter by Gertrude Hallo to Nahum Glatzer, 6 May 1954, Glatzer Collection, Brandeis University Archives, folder 25. Simon explained his decision in a letter to the four other leaders of the Lehrhaus, citing the personal conflicts among the new "council" and their different approaches to teaching. Simon suggested that Kassel physician Joseph Prager become director, with the assistance of Erich Fromm, and proposed the restriction of the Lehrhaus courses to Arbeits-

gemeinschaften. Ernst Simon to Rosenzweig, Buber, Strauss, and Koch, 22 July 1923, Franz Rosenzweig Collection, LBI-AR, Varia, V 10/7, F.

75. Buber, *Briefwechsel,* vol. 2, pp. 172–177. See also Nahum Glatzer's recollection of this case: "One lady shamelessly 'revealed her heart,' expecting Buber to respond in kind. He overdid it. . . . Some of the students left the hall, others waited to see what would happen." Glatzer, "The Frankfurt Lehrhaus," lecture delivered in Kassel, 1986, Nahum Glatzer Collection, Brandeis University Archives, folder 24, p. 10. In his summary of the Lehrhaus, Glatzer referred to "the ubiquitous *nudnik,* male and female, who could not find rest unless all his profoundly persistent questions were adequately answered." See Glatzer, "Frankfort Lehrhaus," p. 121.

76. Erich Fromm's great-grandfather was the Würzburger Rav, Seligmann Baer Bamberger, one of the leading figures of nineteenth-century German Jewish Orthodoxy. Erich's father, Naftali Fromm, represented the Orthodox in the council of the Frankfurt Jewish community. On Fromm see Funk, *Erich Fromm.*

77. Löwenthal, *Critical Theory and Frankfurt Theorists,* p. 240.

78. This was the number of students during academic year 1923–1924. The actual number of Lehrhaus attendants during its six years of existence was certainly much higher, as different people registered every year.

79. For a statistical account of the attendants of the Volkshochschulen in Leipzig and Dresden see Langewiesche, "Freizeit und 'Massenbildung,'" pp. 124, 137.

80. Koch, "Freie Jüdische Lehrhaus," p. 116.

81. Rosenzweig, *Briefe,* p. 887.

82. "If Fräulein Levy of the Westendstraße were to marry [a Christian], it would be as tragic as if she were to marry a Chinese. . . . It would lead to a happy divorce and she would marry Herr Pinkowitz from Lodz, be happy with him and they would leave their numerous children a nice estate. Herr Pinkowitz is a university lecturer. He writes in *Der Morgen* on the 'Customs of the Jews in Poland.' Grandmother Levy reads it and thinks: just like at our parents' in the Ostendstraße. Just like there." Richard Koch to Julius Goldstein, Julius Goldstein Collection, LBI-AR, 7167.

83. Rosenzweig, *Briefe,* pp. 444–445.

84. *JR,* 13 July 1926, p. 395.

85. Ismar Freund to the board of the Jewish community of Berlin, 3 June 1918. Ismar Freund Collection, CAHJP, P 2 D/5. Freund's first initiative dated from 1915.

86. *JE,* 28 February 1919, p. 112.

87. Rosenzweig, *Briefe,* pp. 668–669.

88. *GJGB,* 11 March 1921, p. 27; *GJGB,* 26 January 1925, p. 9. At the general Berlin Volkshochschule, between 1,300 and 4,200 students were registered in the 1920s. See Pöggeler, *Geschichte der Erwachsenenbildung,* p. 117.

89. Scholem, *From Berlin to Jerusalem,* p. 152.

90. See Krüger, "Für die Verbreitung jüdischen Wissens," pp. 385–387.

91. See Leopold Marx, "Das Stuttgarter Jüdische Lehrhaus," newspaper clipping, Karl Adler Collection, LBI-AR, 7276, box 2, folder 18, p. 25.

92. Ibid.

93. Circular letter to Jewish community members, Stuttgart and Cannstatt, September 1925, Karl Adler Collection, LBI-AR, 7276, box 2, folder 18.

94. In later years, however, Chief Rabbi Paul Rieger supported the Lehrhaus actively and was one of its regular teachers. Marx, "Stuttgarter Jüdische Lehrhaus," p. 25.

95. Leopold Marx, "Zur Errichtung des jüdischen Lehrhauses Stuttgart: Rede gehalten in der Gründungsversammlung am 10. Februar 1926" (Stuttgart, 1926); partly reprinted in *GIGW,* 16 March 1926, p. 641.

96. Other examples of this approach that come to mind are the works by Protestant theologians Emil Felden (*Die Sünde wider das Volk* [Berlin: Oldenburg, 1921]) and Eduard Lamparter (*Das Judentum in seiner kultur—und religionsgeschichtlichen Erscheinung* [Gotha, Germany: Leopold Klotz, 1928), and the Berlin Institutum Judaicum's new approach toward mission under its director Hugo Gressmann. See also Siegele-Wenschkewitz, "Relationship Between Protestant Theology and Jewish Studies During the Weimar Republic," and Greive, *Theologie und Ideologie.*

97. On *Die Kreatur* see Friedman, *Buber: Middle Years,* pp. 95–119.

98. *IFM,* 3 December 1931, n.p.

99. Buber's talk with Hauer was originally planned as part of the public discussion series but took place as a private lecture in front of invited guests. See *GIGW,* 1 October 1928, p. 157. See also Zelzer, *Weg und Schicksal der Stuttgarter Juden,* pp. 114–123.

100. Quoted in Mendes-Flohr, "Ambivalent Dialogue," p. 131.

101. In his opening address (on 9 November 1919, one year before Rosenzweig created the Lehrhaus in Frankfurt), Marcus Brann characterized the Jewish Volkshochschule as a "modern form of the old beth midrash." See *JVZ,* 14 November 1919, p. 5; see also A. Lewkowitz, *Festrede zur Eröffnung der Freien Jüdischen Volkshochschule zu Breslau* (n.p., n.d.).

102. The special events organized by the Volkshochschule also included concerts of Jewish music and performances of Jewish plays. *JVZ,* 8 April 1921, p. 4.

103. *JVZ,* 16 April 1920, p. 5.

104. *JE,* 7 November 1919, p. 547; Max Elk, "Ein jüdisches Lehrhaus," *BIGZ,* 6 November 1925, pp. 188–189; the regular program was stimulated by special events, such as Karl Wolfskehl's reading of his drama *Saul.* See *BIGZ,* 8 November 1926, pp. 282–283; 9 February 1927, p. 44; 1 July 1930, pp. 202–203; and 15 January 1931, p. 23.

105. Emil Schorsch, "Zwölf Jahre vor der Zerstörung der Synagoge in Hannover, Germany. Persönliche Erinnerungen," manuscript, LBI-AR, ME 575, p. 48.

106. *GSGK,* 11 December 1931, p. 1.

107. This plan never materialized, however. See "Arbeitsausschuß für das Jüdische Lehrhaus Stuttgart. Verhandlungsbericht vom 26. Januar 1928," Karl Adler Collection, LBI-AR, box 2, folder 18. Of the more prominent teachers, Gershom Scholem taught in both Frankfurt and Berlin, and Erich Fromm had ties to the Frankfurt Lehrhaus and the Munich Lehrhaus.

108. *BIGZ,* 15 November 1929, p. 370; *GSGK,* 7 August 1931, p. 44.

109. Rudolf Hallo to Martin Buber, 31 October 1924, Buber Archives, Het 2 289.

110. Rudolf Stahl to Franz Rosenzweig, 24 December 1926, Edith Scheinmann Collection, LBI-AR, 5043, V 10/4, box 1.

111. Lazarus, *Jüdische Gemeinde Wiesbaden,* p. 20.

112. *JR,* 9 March 1928, p. 142.

113. See *GJGB,* January 1931, p. 27.

CHAPTER FOUR: TOWARD A SYNTHETIC SCHOLARSHIP

1. For a detailed discussion of this debate in the German academic community see Ringer, *Decline of the German Mandarins,* pp. 305–366.

2. For a review of the prevailing tendencies in Jewish historiography during this period see Hofmann, "Jüdische Geschichtswissenschaft in Deutschland, 1918–1938."

3. Rosenzweig, *On Jewish Learning,* pp. 27–54.

4. For a study on the academy see Myers, "Fall and Rise of Jewish Historicism."

5. The idea for this proposal originated in the CV. The Ismar Elbogen Collection in the Archives of the Leo Baeck Institute (LBI-AR 7209, box 4, folder 8) contains questionnaires sent by the Jewish community of Berlin to nineteen rabbis and scholars of Jewish studies in 1911. Fifteen of them supported the proposal; they believed that an amount between three hundred thousand marks and one million marks would be necessary to initiate the project. The question whether "there is any way to secure that the person chosen for the chair is a Jew" was met with skepticism among the respondents. See also Elbogen, *Century of Jewish Life,* p. 418.

6. For more details see Brenner, "Unknown Project of a World Jewish History in Weimar Germany," pp. 250–251.

7. On the Institute for Jewish Studies at the Hebrew University see Myers, "From Zion." On YIVO see Chapter 7 of this book.

8. Although the Frankfurt chair was established in 1921, Buber began teaching only in 1924. The first incumbent of the chair, Nehemias Anton Nobel, died before delivering his first lecture, and his successor, Franz Rosenzweig, was already ill when appointed in December 1922. Liberal members of the Frankfurt Jewish community board tried extremely hard to prevent the appointment of Buber, a Zionist. See Ernst Auerbach to Ismar Elbogen, Elbogen Collection, LBI-AR, 7209, and Eduard Strauss's comment on a newspaper clipping, Eduard Strauss Collection, LBI-AR, 7077. On Buber's activities as lecturer see Sandt, *Martin Bubers bildnerische Tätigkeit,* pp. 86–94, and Willy Schottroff, "Martin Buber an der Universität Frankfurt am Main (1923–1933)," in Licharz and Schmidt, *Martin Buber (1878–1965),* vol. 1, pp. 19–95. On other lectureships see Jospe, "Study of Judaism."

9. In 1931 Rabbis Ignaz Maybaum of Frankfurt an der Oder and Max Grünewald of Mannheim, together with the young philosopher Fritz Bamberger, conceived a "Jewish theological quarterly," the main purpose of which was to "retain new inspirations for the practical Jewish theology" and to "point to new ways in the future." See outline by Max Grünewald and letter from Kurt Wolff Verlag to Grünewald, 26 November 1932, Max Grünewald Collection, LBI-AR, box 2, folder 4.

10. In addition to the works mentioned, complete or partial Bible translations into German during the nineteenth century included those made by Moses J. Landau (1831), Josef Johlson (1831–1836), Gotthold Salomon (1837), Julius Fürst (1874), and Simon Bernfeld (1902). On German-Jewish Bible translations see Weintraub, *Targumei ha-torah;* Mach, "Jüdische Bibelübersetzungen ins Deutsche"; and Ben-Chorin, "Jüdische Bibelübersetzungen in Deutschland." For Goethe's pronouncement see Johann Wolfgang von Goethe, *West-östlicher Divan: Goethes Werke,* 9th ed. (Munich: C. H. Beck, 1972), vol. 2, p. 256.

11. See Schneider, "Beginnen." This translation has been the subject of several studies. All secondary accounts are based largely on Buber, "Aus den Anfängen unserer Schriftübertragung," in *Schrift und ihre Verdeutschung,* pp. 316–329.

12. Gershom Scholem, "At the Completion of Buber's Translation of the Bible," in *Messianic Idea in Judaism,* p. 315.

13. Rosenzweig, *Arbeitspapiere zur Verdeutschung der Schrift.* Vol. 4, part 2 of *Mensch und sein Werk,* p. 1.

14. Steiner, *After Babel,* p. 324. On parallels between early-nineteenth-century German Romantics and early-twentieth-century Jewish Romantics see Schocken, "Gershom Scholem und die deutsch-jüdische Romantik."

15. Benjamin, *Illuminationen,* p. 67.

16. Buber and Rosenzweig did not address their translation exclusively to a Jewish audience. Still, they intended to lead only the Jewish audience back to the Hebrew original, and they wanted Christian readers to return to the Luther translation. See Buber, *Schrift und ihre Verdeutschung,* p. 346.

17. Martin Buber, "Über die Wortwahl in einer Verdeutschung der Schrift," in *Schrift und ihre Verdeutschung,* pp. 140–141.

18. On the translation of *ruah* and the tetragrammaton see Buber, *Schrift und ihre Verdeutschung,* p. 160–161. See also Fox, "Technical Aspects," pp. 88–91.

19. See Friedmann, *Buber: Middle Years,* p. 70.

20. Margarete Susman, "Eine neue Übersetzung der Heiligen Schrift," *Basler Nachrichten,* 18–19 February 1928 (literary supplement to no. 49), n.p.

21. "Deutsche Bibelübersetzungen," *JLZ,* 20 May 1927, n.p.

22. On recitals see *JLZ,* February 1927, n.p., and *Jüdische Wochenzeitung für Kassel, Hessen und Waldeck,* November 1926, n.p.; on usage in schools see ibid., November 1931, n.p.; on Hanukkah recommendation see ibid., April 1929, n.p.

23. *Frankfurter Zeitung* (Abendblatt), 7 June 1927, no. 415, p. 4. See also Hermann Gerson, "Jüdisches Leben im Bunde," *Der Bund* (1928), n.p.

24. Ernest M. Wolf, "Martin Buber and German Jewry," *Judaism* 1 (1952), p. 350. Quoted in Friedmann, *Buber: Middle Years,* p. 71.

25. Siegfried Kracauer, "Die Bibel auf Deutsch," *Frankfurter Zeitung,* 27 April 1926, pp. 1–2, and 28 April 1926, p. 1. See also Jay, "Politics of Translation." Emanuel Bin Gorion, "Bubers Bibel," *Das Tagebuch,* 18 June 1927, pp. 992–996.

26. Joseph Wohlgemuth, "Die neue Bibelübersetzung," *Jeschurun,* nos. 1–2 (February 1926), pp. 1–16. For a straightforwardly positive review by an Orthodox rabbi see Joseph Carlebach, "Buber-Rosenzweig und der massoretische Text," *Der Israelit,* 5 February 1931, n.p.

27. *Der Israelit,* 7 April 1927, pp. 3–4.

28. Ernst Simon, "Die neue deutsche Bibel," *BIGZ*, 15 September 1929, pp. 289–292.

29. See Bertha Badt-Strauß, "Die deutsche Bibel," *JR*, 9 February 1926, p. 83.

30. Buber, *Zu einer neuen Verdeutschung der Schrift*, p. 7. On the influence of Jewish sources and German Romanticism on Buber's translation see Maren Ruth Niehoff's thought-provoking article "Buber-Rosenzweig Translation." See also Shapira, "Buber's Attachment to Herder and German 'Volkism.' " It was the anti-semitic press that stressed the alleged use of Hebraized German in the Buber-Rosen-zweig translation. Pastor Bubitz wrote in Theodor Fritsch's journal *Hammer,* "We can be grateful to Buber, for he shows us that a real translation of the Old Testa-ment into the German mode of speech, thought, and feeling is impossible. Just as it is impossible to translate the Edda and Goethe into Hebrew, one cannot translate the 'Scripture' into German." *Der Hammer,* 15 March 1927, pp. 158–160.

31. The Jüdischer Verlag sold more than one hundred thousand individual vol-umes of the Talmud, which became one of its main sources of income. See *Alman-ach 1902–1964,* p. 21. A nine-volume version of Goldschmidt's Talmud translation also existed.

32. One of the people known to have owned a complete Goldschmidt Talmud set was Sigmund Freud. See Trosman and Simmons, "Freud Library," p. 660.

33. Quoted in Lenz, *Kleine Geschichte großer Lexika,* p. 9.

34. National encyclopedias were published in Yugoslavia starting in 1925, in Latvia starting in 1927, and in Lithuania starting in 1931.

35. Letter of 7 June, 1894. Quoted in Brisman, *History,* p. 9.

36. On early attempts to write a Jewish encyclopedia in Germany see Brisman, *History,* pp. 4–7.

37. On the *Jewish Encyclopedia* see Schwartz, *Emergence of Jewish Scholarship in America.*

38. On the life of Herlitz and the initial phase of the *Jüdisches Lexikon* see Her-litz, *Mein Weg nach Jerusalem,* pp. 100–127; Franz Meyer, "Georg Herlitz. Zum 80. Geburtstag," *MB,* 12 March 1965, pp. 5–6; Georg Herlitz, "Zum Gedenken Dr. Bruno Kirschner," *MB,* 24 April 1964, p. 6; for Kirschner's description see his letter to Rabbi Posner, 12 May 1929, Bruno Kirschner Collection, CZA, A 369, no file number. In this letter, Kirschner minimized the role that Herlitz played in the conception of the plan: "I drew the program, Dr. Herlitz signed it with his name, just as he only signed with his name under the preface written by me for the first edition. This information, of course, remains among the two of us."

39. Circular letter by Georg Herlitz and Bruno Kirschner, 6 May 1921, Georg Herlitz Collection, CZA, A 198/17; see also their letter of March 1922, CZA, A 198/54, in which both still expressed their intention to publish the work by summer 1922.

40. The six expert editors—Ismar Elbogen, Josef Meisl, Max Soloweitschik, Felix Theilhaber, Robert Weltsch, and Max Wiener—began work early in 1925. A seventh editor, Aron Sandler, was recruited later. See letter of the expert editors to the contributors of the *Jüdisches Lexikon,* 11 March 1929, Bruno Kirschner Col-lection, CZA, A 369, no file number.

41. See Kirschner's letter to the *Mitarbeiter* of 8 February 1929, Georg Herlitz

Collection, CZA, A 198/7 (also in CAHJP, P/2 P 23). In a second letter, of 29 March 1929, Kirschner concluded his involvement in the project after almost a decade, with deep disappointment: "Herausdrängung aus der eigenen Schöpfung, nachdem sie für den Unternehmer einträglich zu werden beginnt, ehrengerichtliche Klagen wegen angeblicher, natürlich niemals erfolger 'Beleidigungen'—das ist das Fazit der Hingabe von neun Jahren mühevollster Arbeit an das Jüdische Lexikon." (Bruno Kirschner Collection, CZA, A 369, no file number). Herlitz never resigned, but he shared much of Kirschner's disappointment. He wrote to Kirschner, after the completion of the *Jüdisches Lexikon,* "Von dem Stolz, mit dem ich einst gemeinsam mit Dir auszog, dieses Werk zu schaffen, und mit dem ich noch den ersten Band erscheinen sah, ist nicht viel geblieben." (Herlitz to Kirschner, 16 November 1930, Bruno Kirschner Collection, CZA, A 369, no file number.)

42. See Brisman, *History,* p. 110.

43. Goldmann, *Autobiography,* pp. 74–83.

44. Goldmann's uncle Abraham Szalkowitz owned a Hebrew publishing house in Warsaw, which he intended to transfer to Berlin around 1920. He died before he could realize his plan, and Nahum Goldmann was asked by his family to carry out his uncle's initiative. Goldmann, *Autobiography,* p. 84.

45. Program of Eschkol publishing house, n.d., SchA, 517/222. Of the eleven members of the committee, eight lived in Berlin.

46. Program of Eschkol publishing house, n.d., SchA, 517/222.

47. Goldmann, *Autobiography,* p. 84.

48. Klatzkin's letter to Bialik of 27 April 1925 (in Hebrew), Klatzkin Collection, CZA, A 40/59/2. For the story of Goldmann's adventures in search of financial support, see Goldmann, *Autobiography,* p. 87.

49. Goldmann, *Autobiography,* p. 89.

50. Entries beginning with the letters *M* and *N* were ready for the printer but were never published. According to Goldmann, the Nazis destroyed more than forty thousand copies of the printed volumes that had not been sold. Ibid., p. 89.

51. There was a certain competition between the two projects. The editors of the *Encyclopaedia* believed that their creation was the only scholarly work of the two, and Bruno Kirschner regarded the *Encyclopaedia* as a superfluous enterprise. See Kirschner's letter to the participants of the *Lexikon,* 8 February 1929, Georg Herlitz Collection, CZA, A 198/17.

52. Because of the coincidence of the publication of the two encyclopedic works, their publishers composed a common note clarifying the difference between the two compendia. See *GJGB,* 2 September 1927, p. 220.

53. *Encyclopaedia Judaica* 5, cols. 1022–1034. The article appeared in a significantly adulterated version, because of major changes by editors Nahum Goldmann and Rabbi Benno Jacob. Benjamin's handwritten comment on the editing is reprinted in his *Gesammelte Schriften,* vol. 2, part 2, pp. 807–813. See also Scholem, *Walter Benjamin,* p. 160.

54. Scholem contributed several articles for the *Encyclopaedia,* among them a long entry on his dissertation topic, the Book of Bahir.

55. After securing Goldschmidt's initial help, the *Encyclopaedia* was supported by a sponsoring committee that consisted of a number of German-Jewish financiers,

among them the directors of Germany's largest banks, Wilhelm Kleemann of the Dresdner Bank and Oskar Wassermann of the Deutsche Bank, who also belonged to the sponsoring committee of the Akademie für die Wissenschaft des Judentums. The sponsoring committee of the *Encyclopaedia* was supposed to supply about one-third of the projected expenditure of 3.3 millions marks, and the sales proceeds were to make up for the remaining two-thirds. See the notes on a discussion between Jakob Klatzkin and Siegfried Moses, 6 November 1930, SchA, 517/222. The major Zionist Maecenas Salman Schocken initially refused to grant any financial aid, on the basis that the *Encyclopaedia* was a general Jewish project that should be funded mainly by non-Zionists. When work was in progress, however, Schocken did support the *Encyclopaedia*. See Schocken's letter to Klatzkin of 8 July 1925, SchA, 517/222.

56. Hans Kohn, "Assimilation," *Jüdisches Lexikon* 1, cols. 521–522; Ludwig Holländer, "Central-Verein deutscher Staatsbürger jüdischen Glaubens," *Jüdisches Lexikon* 1, col. 1292.

57. Each of the five volumes of the *Lexikon* had a printing of ten thousand. See *Almanach 1902–1964*, p. 21. The initial print run of the first two volumes of the *Encyclopaedia* was three thousand each. They were almost sold within three years, and in 1930 a second edition was prepared. See the notes on a discussion between Klatzkin and Siegfried Moses, 6 November 1930, SchA, 517/522.

58. *JR*, 12 October 1928.

59. *Der Morgen* 4 (1928), p. 290.

60. For a moderate Orthodox criticism of the *Encyclopaedia*'s depiction of the Bible and its alleged preference of Hebrew over Yiddish, see *IFM*, 14 April 1932, n.p.

61. *JLZ*, 28 October 1927, n.p. As with all reference works, the encyclopedias were criticized by scholars who complained of the insufficient treatment of their area of interest. See, e.g., Berthold Rosenthal's criticism concerning the entries on Baden Jewry in both encyclopedias. Berthold Rosenthal Collection, LBI-AR, 638, box IA.

62. Bruno Kirschner, "Nachwort zum Jüdischen Lexikon," *MGWJ* 76 (1932), pp. 246–262.

63. Ringer, *Decline of the German Mandarins*, p. 387.

64. Among the most important are Martin Philippson's *Neueste Geschichte des jüdischen Volkes* (1907–1911), Georg Caro's *Sozial- und Wirtschaftsgeschichte der Juden im Mittelalter und der Neuzeit* (1908), Ismar Elbogen's *Der jüdische Gottesdienst in seiner geschichtlichen Entwicklung* (1913), Eduard Mahler's *Handbuch der jüdischen Chronologie* (1916), and Hermann Cohen's *Die Religion der Vernunft aus den Quellen des Judentums* (1919), all of which were commissioned by the society and published in Leipzig by G. Fock. On the original outline of thirty-one volumes see *Erster Jahres-Bericht der Gesellschaft zur Förderung der Wissenschaft des Judentums* (1903).

65. The *Germania Judaica* was initiated in 1903. It contains an alphabetical collection of information on Jewish life in every part of Germany where Jews have been living from the Middle Ages until the nineteenth century. The first volume (places from *A* to *L* before 1238) appeared in 1917.

66. Elbogen, along with some other Jewish historians, was also troubled by Dubnow's methodology. Besides numerous specific issues, he found fault with Dubnow's title, *World History of the Jewish People,* "because no single people . . . has a *world* history." See Ismar Elbogen, "Zu S. Dubnows Geschichtswerk," *MGWJ* 70 (1926), p. 145. Elbogen's colleague Selma Stern had earlier criticized Dubnow's concentration on intellectual history and his neglect of social, economic, and legal factors. See her review "S.M. Dubnows 'Neueste Geschichte des jüdischen Volkes,'" *MGWJ* 63 (1920), pp. 200–210.

67. Ismar Elbogen to "Sehr geehrter Herr Kollege" (unknown), 12 May 1924, Elbogen Collection, LBI-AR, 7209. Among the scholars who agreed to participate were talmudist Samuel Krauss, Breslau rabbi and historian Hermann Vogelstein, folklorist Max Grunwald, historian Yitshak Fritz Baer, and Elbogen himself.

68. Ismar Elbogen to "Sehr geehrter Herr Kollege" (unknown), 12 May 1924, Elbogen Collection, LBI-AR, 7209. Elbogen mentions the strong objections of the Graetz family in his letter concerning the new edition. Two decades later Elbogen published his last book, *A Century of Jewish Life,* which he called a continuation of Graetz's history. For more details see Brenner, "Unknown Project of a World Jewish History in Weimar Germany."

69. The only comparable project, the *World History of the Jewish People,* was started many decades later, mostly by scholars at the Hebrew University in Jerusalem. Whereas the twelve volumes edited by Elbogen were to have appeared simultaneously, the first volumes of the Jerusalem *World History* were published over several decades, and the series ceased to appear when the publisher ran out of money.

70. Elbogen Collection, LBI-AR, 7209.

71. Cecil Roth to Ismar Elbogen, 5 April 1929, Elbogen Collection, LBI-AR, 7209.

72. Peter Reinhold to Ismar Elbogen, 3 January 1930, Elbogen Collection, LBI-AR, 2709, box 4, folder 10.

73. Peter Reinhold to Ismar Elbogen, 12 January 1930, Elbogen Collection, LBI-AR, 2709, box 4, folder 10.

74. Freud, *Letters of Sigmund Freud and Arnold Zweig,* pp. 103–105. The book was expanded and translated into Hebrew between 1957 and 1962 (*Ha-midbar ve-eretz ha-behirah*). By that time Auerbach had also written a biography of Moses.

75. Ismar Elbogen to Cecil Roth, 16 January 1933, Elbogen Collection, LBI-AR, 1179.

76. Cecil Roth to Hermann Z. Elbin (son of Ismar Elbogen), 29 June 1962, Elbogen Collection, LBI-AR, 1179.

77. Goebel, *Kurt Wolff Verlag,* p. 918 n. 24.

78. Scholem, "The Science of Judaism," in *Messianic Idea,* p. 307.

79. Elbogen, *Ein Jahrhundert Wissenschaft des Judentums,* p. 44.

80. Elbogen, "Zum Begriff 'Wissenschaft des Judentums,'" p. 34.

81. Salman Rubaschoff, "Erstlinge der Entjudung," *Der jüdische Wille: Zeitschrift des Kartells jüdischer Verbindungen* 1 (1918–1919), pp. 36–42, 108–121, 193–203. For the term *re-Judaization* see *JR,* 12 October 1928.

CHAPTER FIVE: THE INVENTION OF THE AUTHENTIC JEW

1. Goldstein, "Deutsch-jüdischer Parnaß," p. 283. See also Goldstein, *Begriff und Programm einer jüdischen Nationalliteratur.* Goldstein later published his own account of this stirring controversy in "German Jewry's Dilemma."

2. Goldstein, "Deutsch-jüdischer Parnaß," pp. 293–294.

3. Although much has been written on the role of Jews in modern German literature, how German-Jewish writers viewed Jews and Judaism has not been discussed systematically. See, e.g., Grimm and Bayerdörfer, *Im Zeichen Hiobs;* Moses and Schöne, *Juden in der deutschen Literatur;* and Shaked, *Shadows Within.*

4. See, e.g., Hermann Hesse's *Zarathustras Wiederkehr* (1919) and *Siddharta* (1922), Eduard Stucken's *Die weißen Götter* (1918–1922), and Alfred Döblin's *Die drei Sprünge des Wang-Lun* (1915) and *Manas* (1927). Martin Buber's editions of Chuang Tse's parables (1910) and of Chinese ghost stories and love stories (1911) must be seen as part of this overall interest in Eastern culture. On Exoticism see Reif, *Zivilisationsflucht und literarische Wunschräume,* and Koebner and Pickeroth, *Die andere Welt.*

5. Mendes-Flohr, "Fin-de-Siècle Orientalism, the Ostjuden and the Aesthetics of Jewish Self-Affirmation," p. 120.

6. *AZJ* 75 (1911), pp. 101–102, quoted in Horch, *Auf der Suche,* p. 207.

7. Feuchtwanger, *Centum Opuscula,* p. 511. On Feuchtwanger and Judaism see Wolf, "Lion Feuchtwanger und das Judentum."

8. Isaac Deutscher, "The Non-Jewish Jew and Other Essays" (London: Oxford University Press, 1968).

9. Bettauer, *Stadt ohne Juden,* p. 76. On Bettauer see Hall, *Fall Bettauer,* and Spielmann, "German-Jewish Writers on the Eve of the Holocaust," pp. 61–65.

10. Tucholsky, *Gesammelte Werke,* vol. 8, pp. 237–240.

11. In five years the circulation of *Der Fall Maurizius* reached 112,000. See Richards, *German Bestseller in the Twentieth Century,* p. 239.

12. Lessing, *Jüdische Selbsthaß.* On Trebitsch see also Gilman, *Jewish Self-Hatred,* pp. 248–250.

13. Tucholsky officially left Judaism in 1914 (not, as he later stated, in 1911), and joined the Protestant church two years later. See Ackermann, "'Wir andern—auch wir suchen'" p. 167.

14. Wassermann, *My Life,* pp. 137–138, 148.

15. Ibid., pp. 226–227.

16. Lessing, *Jüdische Selbsthaß,* p. 42.

17. Scholem, *On Jews and Judaism in Crisis,* p. 85. Unlike Scholem, the *Jüdische Rundschau,* the official organ of German Zionism, praised Tucholsky's criticism of assimilated German Jews. See *JR,* 22 March 1929, p. 148. See also Hiller, "Kurt Tucholsky und der Selbsthaß," pp. 8–10.

18. Kurt Tucholsky to Fritz Tucholsky, 5 December 1935, in Tucholsky, *Politische Briefe,* pp. 109–110. Tucholsky's view was shared by Siegfried Jacobsohn, the editor of the *Weltbühne,* who expressed his special dislike for *German* Jews when he reported to Tucholsky (12 July 1925), "Even the Jews are nicer in other countries than in Germany." Jacobsohn, *Briefe an Kurt Tucholsky, 1915–1926,* p. 314.

19. In *Etzel Andergast*, the second volume of Wassermann's Maurizius trilogy, antisemitism was an even more prominent motif. In this novel, the Jewish secretary Hermann Mewer committed suicide after being excluded from a student association because he was Jewish. Wassermann intended to elaborate further on the problem of antisemitism in two projects that never materialized. In 1926 he conceived a novel on the "eternal Jew" *Ahasver,* and in 1932 he wrote down notes for a novella on the anti-Jewish riots in Alsace in 1338. Wassermann's notes for the two projects are reprinted in Wassermann, *Deutscher und Jude,* pp. 249–255.

20. "Die beiden Brüder H.," *Schaubühne,* no. 2 (1913), p. 50. Tucholsky's different judgments of German Jews and East European Jews can also be seen in his review of Arnold Zweig's novel *Grischa.* See Tucholsky, *Gesammelte Werke,* vol. 2, pp. 975–982.

21. Wassermann, *Deutscher und Jude,* p. 23.

22. For an English translation of this speech see Buber, *On Judaism,* pp. 56–78.

23. Wassermann, *Deutscher und Jude,* p. 31.

24. Shaked, *Shadows Within,* p. 66. On the same page, Shaked equated Wassermann's oriental Jews with East European Jews, a thesis for which I do not see any basis. Wassermann deliberately linked oriental Jews with Middle Eastern traditions, whereas his designation of the "Jew as European" clearly includes East European Jews.

25. *JR,* no. 94, 27 November 1928, p. 660.

26. Lasker-Schüler, *Lieber gestreifter Tiger,* vol. 1, p. 112.

27. Lasker-Schüler, *Sämtliche Gedichte,* p. 291.

28. Hever, *Uri Zvi Greenberg,* n.p.

29. See Lasker-Schüler, *Sämtliche Gedichte,* p. 332.

30. *Davar (Musaf le-shabatot ve-lemo'adim),* 12 Adar (8 March) 1925, p. 21. Greenberg introduced Lasker-Schüler not only to a Hebrew-reading audience, but also to Yiddish speakers. When he published the avant-garde Yiddish journal *Albatros,* first in Warsaw and later in Berlin, Lasker-Schüler made a short contribution. See *Albatros* 3 (1923), p. 29. Lasker-Schüler wrote, "I dedicate the seal of my city Thebes to Albatros."

31. See *JR,* 27 March 1928, p. 184.

32. Lasker-Schüler, *Prosa und Schauspiele,* p. 402.

33. Meir Wiener, "Else Lasker-Schüler," in Krojanker, *Juden in der deutschen Literatur,* pp. 179–192. Lasker-Schüler was also depicted as a representative of oriental spirit in Hegglin, *Else Lasker-Schüler und ihr Judentum,* pp. 88–93. For a different view see Gay, *Freud, Jews, and Other Germans,* p. 145.

34. Lasker-Schüler, *Your Diamond Dreams,* p. 247. The *Hebrew Ballads* were dedicated to her friend Karl Kraus, the Austrian-Jewish writer, who distanced himself from Judaism. One might argue that this dedication was more than an act of friendship, namely, an invitation to Kraus to get to know a positive sort of Jew through her poems.

35. Levy, *Habimah,* p. 152. On *Jeremias* see Shoham, "Jeremias—Prophet für jede Gelegenheit."

36. The talmudic stories on Rabbi Akiba were also the basis for a short story by Emil Bernhard Cohn, contained in his volume *Legenden.* As early as 1902, Walter

Rathenau had published five talmudic tales in his collection *Impressionen*, pp. 101–120.

37. Heimann, *Prosaische Schriften*, vol. 1, p. 202.

38. Literary critic Julius Bab described Heimann as a *märkischer Dorfbewohner* and a pious Jew. See Bab, "Moritz Heimann," in Krojanker, *Juden in der deutschen Literatur*, p. 261.

39. See especially Ketubot 62b and 63a, and Nedarim 50a.

40. Heimann, *Weib des Akiba*, p. 16.

41. Julius Bab, "Jüdische Dramen," *Festnummer zum Vereinstage der Großloge für Deutschland* (August 1929), p. 195.

42. Martin Buber, "Hinweis auf ein Werk," *Der Jude* 6 (1922–1923), p. 767. Another review of Heimann's play in a Jewish newspaper expressed the hope that "*Das Weib des Akiba* shall become *the* Jewish drama." *GIGW*, 16 April 1927, p. 56.

43. See, e.g., Heimann's poem on Rabbi Shimon ben Lakish, published as "Der Rabbi und der Räuber" in *Die Weltbühne* 20, no. 1 (1924), p. 272.

44. On the friendship between the two writers, see the memoirs of Berdyczewski's son, Emanuel Bin Gorion, *Reshut ha-yahid*, pp. 70–73.

45. Berdyczewski's legends on biblical topics appeared in chronological order as *Die Sagen der Juden: Jüdische Sagen und Mythen* in six volumes between 1913 and 1927. During the same period the renowned Leipzig Insel Verlag published his collection of Jewish legends from talmudic times until Hasidism, which were arranged thematically under the title *Der Born Judas* (6 vols., 1916–1922).

46. Aschheim, *Brothers and Strangers*, p. 123.

47. Berdyczewski, *Sinai und Garizim*, p. xv. A similar statement appears in the preface to *Sagen der Juden*, vol. 1, p. xii.

48. Berdyczewski [Bin Gorion, pseud.], *Born Judas*, vol. 1, pp. 15–16.

49. Arnold Zweig, "Der Born Judas," *JR*, 9 September 1924, p. 516. Even the Orthodox initially praised Berdyczewski's work, misjudging his intention to create a countertradition to rabbinical Judaism. See *Jüdische Presse*, 22 January 1915, p. 43.

50. On Lasker-Schüler see, e.g., *JR*, 23 February 1923, p. 88 (on a recitation she gave for the Berlin Zionist Organization), and *GIGW*, 16 October 1929, p. 192 (on a recitation in Berthold-Auerbach-Verein Stuttgart); on Beer-Hofmann see *JR*, 26 October 1928, p. 598; on Heimann see *GIGW*, 16 April 1927, pp. 53–56; on Zweig see *BIGZ*, 1 July 1930, pp. 209–210.

51. Siegfried Jacobsohn, "Bibel-Ersatz," *Die Weltbühne* 15, no. 2 (1919), p. 641.

52. On this ambivalent heritage see Aschheim, *Brothers and Strangers*, pp. 32–57.

53. Gilman, *Jewish Self-Hatred*, pp. 270–271.

54. Döblin, *Autobiographische Schriften*, p. 211.

55. Roth, *Werke*, p. 533. All four accounts (Zweig's, Gronemann's, Döblin's, and Roth's) were reprinted during the 1980s. Literature on them can be found in Bernd Hüppauf, "I Have Travelled to the Jews"; Hans-Peter Bayerdörfer, "Ghettokunst"; and Gelber, "'Juden auf Wanderschaft.'"

56. Döblin, *Autobiographische Schriften,* p. 211.

57. Döblin, *Reise in Polen,* p. 137.

58. Zweig, *Ostjüdische Antlitz,* p. 14.

59. Gronemann, *Hawdoloh und Zapfenstreich,* p. 134.

60. Roth, *Juden auf Wanderschaft,* p. 13.

61. Ibid., p. 21.

62. Zweig, *Ostjüdische Antlitz,* p. 46.

63. Gronemann, *Hawdoloh und Zapfenstreich,* p. 60.

64. Zweig, *Ostjüdische Antlitz,* p. 52.

65. Roth, *Juden auf Wanderschaft,* p. 71. Similarly, Zweig equated the Jew with the spiritual person. See Zweig, *Ostjüdische Antlitz,* p. 40.

66. Roth, *Juden auf Wanderschaft,* pp. 15, 36.

67. Zweig, *Ostjüdische Antlitz,* p. 158.

68. On Breuer see Horwitz, *Yitshak Breuer: Iyunim be'mishnato,* and Mittleman, *Between Kant and Kabbalah.*

69. Breuer, *Falk Nefts Heimkehr,* p. 182.

70. Breuer, *Kampf um Gott,* p. 75.

71. *Jüdische Monatshefte* 1 (1914), p. 436. On Orthodox Jewish writers in Weimar see also Brenner, "East and West in Orthodox German-Jewish Novels."

72. Scholem's first major publication on Shabbateanism was "Über die Theologie des Sabbatianismus im Lichte Abraham Cardozos," in a special issue of *Der Jude,* called *Sonderheft zu Martin Bubers fünfzigstem Geburtstag* (1928), pp. 123–139.

73. For his principal sources see Feuchtwanger, *Centum Opuscula,* pp. 388–391. In 1918 Feuchtwanger had written a drama about Jud Süß. Another contemporary Jewish author, Paul Kornfeld, wrote a play about Jud Süß that was performed for the first time in the Berlin Theater am Schiffsbauerdamm in October 1930.

74. Milfull, "Juden, Christen und andere Menschen," pp. 214–217.

75. Theilhaber, *Dein Reich komme!* pp. 139–140. On Theilhaber see Efron, *Defenders of the Race,* pp. 141–153.

76. This was S. Poljakoff's *Sabbatai Zewi,* originally written in Russian. Poljakoff's novel was reviewed by Georg Hermann in *CVZ,* 18 November 1927, pp. 645–646. A number of Yiddish novels and plays about the Shabbatean movement were written outside Germany in the first third of the twentieth century. See, e.g., Scholem Asch's *Sabbatai Zewi,* which appeared in a German translation in 1908 (Berlin: S. Fischer); Aron Zeitlin's *Yakov Frank* (Vilna: B. Kletskim, 1929); and Isaac Bashevis Singer's *Der Sotn in Goray* (Warsaw: Bibliotek fon Yidishn P.E.N. Klub, 1935).

77. Like Theilhaber's novel, *Die Messiasbraut* told of a triangular relationship between Rembrandt, Spinoza, and Shabbetai Zevi. Ludwig Strauss's *Der Reiter* (originally in *JR,* nos. 34–38 [October–November 1928]) focuses mainly on the Frankfurt rabbi Naftali Hacohen and alludes to the Shabbatean allegiances of his father. For reviews see *BIGZ,* 1 May 1931, p. 131, and *GIGW,* 1 July 1929, p. 103. Sakheim's drama *Der Zadik* is about the 1648 pogroms in Poland and is deeply mystical.

78. Dreyer, "Josef Kastein—Schöpferische Jahre," p. 34. This statement is sup-

ported by Mayer (*Ernst Rowohlt,* p. 100), who recalled the "unexpected success" of Kastein's novel.

79. Writer Schalom Ben-Chorin, who characterized Kastein as the "historian of the Jewish soul," is one of those inspired by Kastein's work. See Schalom Ben-Chorin, "Josef Kastein, der Historiker der jüdischen Seele: Zum 30. Todestag am 13. Juni 1976," *Israel-Nachrichten,* 11 June 1976, p. 9. Another is philosopher Michael Landmann, who recalled that Kastein's writings convinced him that "Judaism did not only mean belonging to a religious community, but also to a people." Landmann, *Jüdische Miniaturen,* S. 211.

80. As in his earlier works, Kastein provided an impressive bibliography at the end of this novel. It is obvious, however, that he drew most of his historical information for *Uriel da Costa* from a scholarly work that had appeared only a few years earlier: Carl Gebhardt, *Die Schriften des Uriel da Costa, mit Einleitung, Übertragung und Regesten* (1922).

81. Uriel da Costa's story had been the topic of a well-known drama by the nineteenth-century German writer Karl Gutzkow and was in the 1920s frequently adopted by such modern Jewish theater troupes as the Moscow Jewish State Theater and the Hebrew Habimah.

82. Kastein, *Uriel da Costa,* pp. 327–328.

CHAPTER SIX: AUTHENTICITY AND MODERNISM COMBINED

1. Gay, *Weimar Culture,* p. viii; Craig, *Germany,* p. 470; Laqueur, *Weimar,* pref.

2. For two diverging views see Gay, *Freud, Jews, and Other Germans,* pp. 93–168, and Klein, "Assimilation and Dissimilation."

3. Hugo Leichtentritt, "Von Lewandowski zu Schalit," *GSGK,* 16 November 1932, p. 226. Schwarz, *Juden in der Kunst,* p. 216.

4. The document of reconversion with Chagall's signature is reprinted in Stuckenschmidt, *Schönberg,* p. 335. See also Ringer, "Arnold Schoenberg and the Politics of Jewish Survival."

5. Schoenberg and Kandinsky, *Letters, Pictures, and Documents,* p. 88. The translation used here is from Ringer, *Arnold Schoenberg,* p. 4. See also Mäckelmann, *Arnold Schönberg und das Judentum,* pp. 12–49.

6. Adorno, "Sakrales Fragment," p. 457.

7. Arno Nadel, "Jüdische Musik," *Der Jude* 7 (1923), p. 235. Translation is from Ringer, *Arnold Schoenberg,* p. 194.

8. Hugo Leichtentritt, "Über die Erneuerung der jüdischen Kultmusik," *GJGB,* September 1932, p. 213.

9. Carner, "Music in the Mainland of Europe," p. 210.

10. See Bohlman, "Volksmusik," and Bohlman, "Folk Music in the Urban German-Jewish Community."

11. Heskes, *Passport to Jewish Music,* pp. 283–291.

12. The letter was written to Gerhard Herz and is quoted in Hirshberg, "Heinrich Schalit," p. 135. On the same page Hirshberg quotes a note from the private list of Schalit's compositions that determines as his turning point the year of the

Jews' census in the German army: "1916—Beginning of the creative period of music with Jewish contents and character."

13. Seven thousand people attended the four concerts of the Jewish Music Days at the Frankfurt exhibition, which constituted one of the most successful events of Jewish music in Germany. See *BIGZ*, 24 August 1927, pp. 248–249. On Schalit's study of Jewish folk music see Schalit, *Heinrich Schalit*, p. 31.

14. Hirshberg, "Heinrich Schalit," pp. 137–138.

15. Ibid., p. 131.

16. Ibid., p. 146.

17. Quoted in ibid.

18. Leichtentritt, *GJGB*, September 1932, p. 213. Schalit was not the only composer who set himself the task of modernizing Jewish liturgy. In fact, two choirmasters of Berlin synagogues—Arno Nadel and Leo Kopf—arranged modern Friday evening liturgies at about the same time as Schalit.

19. *IFM*, 7 January 1932, p. 9.

20. On a series of lectures on intellectual Jewish history see *GSGK*, 24 July 1931, p. 31. For a radio discussion on antisemitism see *CVZ*, 27 May 1932. Arno Nadel's introduction on Jewish music was followed by cantor Leo Gollanin and the choir of the Lützowstraße synagogue. See CAHJP, P I/16. Reviews of the program can be found in *Tempo* (Berlin), 11 October 1929, and *IFM*, 17 October 1929.

21. *BIGZ*, July 1932, p. 214. On plans for the Frankfurt radio to perform Schalit's music see the letters from Franz Rosenzweig to Schalit, 31 July 1929 and 7 August 1929, in Franz Rosenzweig Papers, Vanderbilt University, Divinity Library, folder 98. Orthodox Jews were shocked by the plan to transmit regular Sabbath services on the Sabbath and by the general idea of promoting the Liberal Jewish service with organ and mixed choir. See "Die deutschen Juden und der Hörfunk," *IFM*, no. 46, 12 November 1931.

22. On records of Jewish liturgy see Alice Jacob-Loewenson, "Synagogale Musik auf der Schallplatte," *JR*, 28 September 1928, p. 546. In November 1929 Jacob-Loewenson delivered a lecture on recordings of Jewish music in the Freie Jüdische Volkshochschule. Fred Lachmann Collection, LBI-AR, 5256.

23. Hermand and Trommler, *Kultur der Weimarer Republik*, p. 326.

24. Hermann Schildberger, "Die Schallplatte im Dienste des jüdischen Gottesdienstes," *Jüdisches Jahrbuch für Berlin 1931*, pp. 66–71.

25. Hirshberg, "Heinrich Schalit," p. 137.

26. Alice Jacob-Loewenson, "Zur alten und neuen liturgischen Musik," *JR*, 28 September 1928, p. 546. On Jacob-Loewenson see *MB*, 27 October 1967, p. 10, and *IGBM* 8, no. 1, p. 4.

27. Alice Jacob-Loewenson, "Die Saison hat begonnen! Jüdische Musik in Berlin," *Berliner Jüdische Zeitung*, 13 October 1929, pp. 2–3.

28. Idelsohn, *Jewish Music*, p. 464; *GJGB*, 4 June 1926, p. 139. In many other large Jewish communities, preexisting societies for Jewish music increased their activities in the Weimar period. The Days of Jewish Music at the 1927 International Music Fair in Frankfurt am Main, which included performances of Munich and Frankfurt Jewish choirs, characterized this development. See *BIGZ*, 24 August 1927, pp. 248–249.

29. Bohlman, "Resurgence of Jewish Musical Life," p. 34.

30. See Rudolf Stephan, "Die Musik der Zwanzigerjahre," and Thomas Koebner, "Die Zeitoper in den zwanziger Jahren: Gedanken zu ihrer Geschichte und Theorie," both in Rexroth, *Erprobungen und Erfahrungen,* pp. 9–14, 60–115.

31. In 1927 Hindemith cooperated in the production of a collection *Das neue Werk: Gemeinschaftsmusik für Jugend und Haus* for the Youth Music Movement that grew out of the German Youth Movement. See Hermand and Trommler, *Kultur der Weimarer Republik,* p. 336.

32. Brecht, "Zu den Lehrstücken," *Gesammelte Werke,* vol. 17, p. 1022. For a general development of leftist music in Weimar Germany, see Fuhr, *Proletarische Musik in Deutschland, 1928–1933.*

33. The first Instructional Cantata of 1929 was entitled *Der Lindbergh Flug.* It was followed by a number of other Instructional Cantatas, such as *Der Jasager* by Brecht and Weill (1929) and *Das Unaufhörliche* by Gottfried Benn and Paul Hindemith (1931).

34. On the first semester of the Mannheim Lehrhaus see *IGBM,* 13 December 1929, p. 16.

35. Bohlman, in "Resurgence of Jewish Musical Life," p. 38, lists more than ten Jewish choirs and orchestras in Mannheim during the 1920s and 1930s.

36. *Badisches Landesblatt,* 17 December 1930.

37. *Volksstimme,* 18 December 1930 (no. 342).

38. *IGBM,* 9 December 1930, supplement *Licht und Volk,* p. 4.

39. Bohlman, "Resurgence of Jewish Musical Life," p. 46.

40. On Eppstein and the Mannheim Volkshochschule see Wendling, *Mannheimer Abendakademie,* pp. 77–94. In a letter to me on 12 June 1991, Rabbi Max Grünewald remarked about Eppstein, "I had something to do with his renewed interest in Judaism. He had a leading part in the 'Sprechchor' which I organized. . . . He became an active member in the Lehrhaus movement."

41. Two diverging opinions on Eppstein's last years can be found in Adler, *Theresienstadt,* p. 29, and Simon, *Aufbau im Untergang,* p. 93.

42. Fritz Neulaender, "Erziehung zur Gemeinschaft," *GSGK,* 16 October 1931, p. 103. See also *GSGK,* no. 14, 22 December 1931, p. 176.

43. Max Grünewald, *Bearers of Light: A Cantata,* trans. Alexander M. Schindler (Worcester, Mass., private printing, 1954). The original German text was published in 1930 as a private printing by Hugo Adler.

44. Karl Wolfskehl, *Gesammelte Werke,* vol. 2 (Hamburg: Claassen, 1960), pp. 336–337.

45. Homeyer, *Deutsche Juden als Bibliophilen und Antiquare,* pp. 62–76.

46. David Friedländer and Isaak Euchel were among the eighteenth-century *Maskilim* who used bookplates, but these plates had non-Jewish motifs. See Weiss, "Jewish Book-Plate," and Simon, "Jüdische Exlibris."

47. Budko created fifty-one Jewish bookplates between 1911 and 1927, most of them for German Zionists. See Abraham Horodisch, "Joseph Budkos jüdische Exlibriskunst," *Soncino-Blätter* 3 (1929–1930), pp. 73–79. On Lilien see "The Bookplate Designs of E. M. Lilien," *The Bookplate Journal* 4, no. 2 (September 1986). On Birnbaum see Horodisch, *Exlibris des Uriel Birnbaum.*

48. Löwith's Jüdische Liebhaber-Bibliothek issued three limited publications: J. L. Perez, *Die Nacht auf dem alten Markt* (1915), *Proverbia Judaeorum erotica et turpia* (1918), and Gottlieb von Leon, *Rabbinische Legenden* (1919). Gurlitt's series "The Beautiful Jewish Book" emphasized illustrations. The four books that appeared before the series' end in 1921 were illustrated by Jakob Steinhardt and Joseph Budko. Steinhardt illustrated Arno Nadel's poems *Rot und glühend ist das Auge des Juden* (1920) and J.L. Perez's *Musikalische Novellen* (1920), and Budko provided etchings and lithographs for Nadel's poems *Das Jahr des Juden* (1920) and a new edition of Mendelssohn's German translation of the psalms (1921). Gurlitt's Verlag für jüdische Kunst und Kultur established a Jewish Library with a total of twenty-three publications, including new editions of precious Jewish printings and portraits of Jewish writers and painters.

49. Quoted in Laqueur, *Weimar*, p. 182.

50. Quoted in Behrens, *Jakob Steinhardt*, p. 10.

51. Meidner, *Septemberschrei*, p. 66.

52. Meidner, *Gang in die Stille*, p. 20. See also p. 22.

53. Tau, *Land, das ich verlassen mußte*, pp. 169–171. See also Meidner, *Gang in die Stille*, p. 22.

54. Meidner provided the frontispiece to *Der Sündenfall: sieben biblische Szenen* (1920) and illustrations to a selection of Nadel's poems in *Der Anbruch*, vol. 2, nos. 4–5, and Steinhardt illustrated *Rot und glühend ist das Auge des Juden* (1920).

55. Nadel, *Jakob Steinhardt*, p. 7. For Meidner, Steinhardt's merit lay in the authenticity of his Ostjuden. He contrasted his work with Hermann Struck's Ostjuden, who "radierte betende Juden, zwar Ostjuden, jedoch sehr reinliche, edle, unauffällige und acceptabel auch vom liberalsten Berliner Haus. Er macht sie so wie Pechstein die Polynesier: als ein fernes Volk mit altertümlichen Bräuchen." Letter from Meidner to Franz Landsberger, 29 January 1934, quoted in Breuer and Wagemann, *Ludwig Meidner*, vol. 1, p. 115.

56. Yerushalmi, *Haggadah and History*, plates 130 and 134. Yerushalmi called Budko's Haggadah the "first notable illustrated *Haggadah* of the twentieth century."

57. Mishna Pesahim 10, 5. During the Weimar period, Steinhardt became religious but not strictly Orthodox. His precious Haggadah, like many Jewish bibliophilic publications, was bound in pigskin, which is forbidden according to religious Jewish law. Horodisch, "Aus den Erinnerungen," pp. 251–252.

58. See Gilam, "Erich Goeritz," p. 68.

59. Emil Nolde was perhaps the best known but certainly not the only Expressionist artist to depict religious Christian motifs. One might think also of Max Beckmann's *Kreuzabnahme* (1917) and Lovis Corinth's *Der rote Christus* (1922). In the area of book illustration, Max Pechstein's *Das Vaterunser* was a prominent example.

60. On Franzisca Baruch see Howes and Paucker, "German Jews and the Graphic Arts," p. 462.

61. Budko's works in the Weimar period included illustrations for a *Haggada schel Pessach* (Berlin and Vienna: R. Löwith, 1921) and Hayim Nahman Bialik's collected writings, *Kitvei Hayim Nahman Bialik u-mivhar tirgumav* (Berlin: Hotsa'at hovevei ha-shirah ha-ivrit, 1923). Budko and Steinhardt rose to fame as art

teachers after their emigration to Palestine in 1933, where they served subsequently as directors of the New Bezalel art school. Budko directed the Bezalel between 1934 and his death in 1940, Steinhardt between 1953 and 1957. See Bertz, *"Eine neue Kunst für ein altes Volk,"* pp. 17–22.

62. Quotes from Yerushalmi, *Haggadah and History,* plates 147–150.

63. Siegfried Guggenheim, "Rudolf Koch and the Offenbach Workshop," *Print: A Quarterly Journal of the Graphic Arts* 5, no. 1 (1947), pp. 7–42.

64. Martha Wertheimer, "Ein Sedertisch in unseren Tagen: Betrachtungen zu der Sammlung von Dr. Guggenheim, Offenbach a.M.," *JLZ* (Unterhaltungsblatt Breslau), April 1932, n.p. See also Georg Haupt, "Rituelle Kunst," *Soncino-Blätter* 2 (1927), pp. 117–143, and Fritz Kredel, "Jahre mit Rudolf Koch," *Imprimatur,* new series 7 (1972), p. 213.

65. Advertising brochure for the Offenbach Haggadah, Siegfried Guggenheim Collection, C VII, LBI-AR, 180.

66. *CVZ,* 16 December 1927, pp. 702–703.

67. Joseph Carlebach to Siegfried Guggenheim, 9 March 1928, Siegfried Guggenheim Collection, C VII, LBI-AR, 180.

68. Georg Kurt Schauer, "Die Legende von Rudolf Koch," *Imprimatur* 12 (1954), p. 169.

69. *Der Orden Bne Briss,* no. 2 (February 1928), p. 31.

70. " . . . in Halbfranzband, Kalbleder mit Handdruckpapier. Es paßt so am besten in meine Bibliothek." Hermann Cohn to Siegfried Guggenheim, 28 May 1928, Siegfried Guggenheim Collection, C VII, LBI-AR, 180.

71. On Horodisch, see "Bibliophile Porträts: Abraham Horodisch," *Börsenblatt für den deutschen Buchhandel (Frankfurter Ausgabe),* no. 91 (12 November 1963), pp. 2018–2020. Horodisch had established the bibliophilic Euphorion Verlag in 1920. Together with Marx in 1923 he initiated a publishing house dedicated to the reprinting of bibliophilic Jewish books, which was unproductive. The breakthrough was reached after law student Herrmann Meyer called for the foundation of a bibliophilic Jewish association in 1924.

72. Besides the Gesellschaft der Bibliophilen, all other bibliophilic societies in Germany were smaller. The third largest, the Maximilian-Gesellschaft, counted only three hundred members. See Homeyer, *Deutsche Juden als Bibliophilen,* pp. 62–64.

73. Horodisch, "Ein Abenteuer im Geiste," p. 185.

74. Reinhold Scholem's membership is remarkable because his brother portrays him as a staunch representative of assimilation. Scholem, *From Berlin to Jerusalem,* pp. 57–59.

75. Horodisch, "Abenteuer im Geiste," p. 196.

76. An almost complete list of publications can be found in ibid., pp. 198–208.

77. Ibid., p. 187.

78. Ibid., p. 195. On Behmer see Eyssen, *Buchkunst in Deutschland,* pp. 23–24.

79. In 1924, another Hebrew type—the Frank-Rühl Hebrew—was created by the Berthold printing office in Berlin. Based on sixteenth-century Venetian prints, the Frank-Rühl letters became the dominant Hebrew characters for almost all pub-

lications in modern Hebrew in subsequent years. See Schütz, "Kunst aus jüdischen Verlagen," p. 157, and Jacques Adler, "Die Renaissance des Hebräischen," in Frank, *Über hebräische Typen und Schriftarten,* n.p.

80. Brieger, *E. M. Lilien,* p. 210.

81. "Auch eine Bibelausgabe!" *JR,* 7 April 1922, p. 180.

82. CAHJP, INV 1409.

83. Karl Schwarz, "Berliner Jüdisches Museum (Aus den Memoiren von Karl Schwarz)," Robert Weltsch Collection, LBI-AR 7185, box 10, folder 15, p. 21.

84. Max Osborn, "Das Berliner 'Jüdische Museum,'" *CVZ,* 3 April 1931, p. 173. See also Schwarz's description: "Als ich meine Arbeit begann, befand sich die ganze Sammlung in einem fast hoffnungslosen Zustand der Unordnung." Schwarz, "Berliner Jüdisches Museum," p. 3.

85. Simon, *Berliner Jüdische Museum,* pp. 17–19.

86. Ibid., p. 11.

87. Quoted in Schwarz, "Berliner Jüdisches Museum," p. 18.

88. Ibid., p. 10. See also Will Pleß, "Neuzeitliche jüdische Kultgeräte," *Menorah* (March–April 1931), pp. 149–150.

89. *Ludwig Yehuda Wolpert,* n.p.

90. Schwarz, *Juden in der Kunst,* pp. 219–220.

91. The art collection in Hamburg was part of the Gesellschaft für jüdische Volkskunde. See Daxelmüller, "Max Grunwald and the Origins of Jewish Folkloristics in Hamburg." The Frankfurt Gesellschaft zur Erforschung jüdischer Kunst-Denkmäler was initiated by the (non-Jewish) director of the Düsseldorf Museum of Arts and Crafts, Heinrich Frauberger. It issued its own journal and news bulletin. On its beginnings, see *Ost und West* 2 (1902), pp. 115–116. On Kassel see *GBH,* 10 July 1927, p. 2. The Breslau Jewish Museumsverein also organized excursions to Jewish sites, such as Krakow and Dyhernfurt, the home of the first German-Jewish print. See *Breslauer Jüdisches Gemeindeblatt (BJG)* (June 1930), p. 102, and *BJG* (August 1930), p. 135. The Verein für jüdische Museen in Bayern had organized its first exhibition in Munich in 1930. See *BIGZ,* 1 May 1931, p. 134. On conventions see *BJG* (April 1929), p. 66.

92. Samuel Weissenberg, "Jüdische Museen und Jüdisches in Museen," *Mitteilungen zur jüdischen Volkskunde* 10, no. 23 (1907), p. 88.

93. Daxelmüller, "Jüdische Museen," p. 16.

94. E. Badrian, "Kulturaufgaben der Gemeinde Hamburg," *Gemeindeblatt der Deutsch-Israelitischen Gemeinde Hamburg,* 10 July 1927, p. 3. See also the affectionate account of Jewish ceremonial objects by German-Jewish writer Georg Hermann, "Von Bsombüchsen [sic] und alten Hagaden," *CVZ,* 10 February 1928, pp. 77–78.

95. Huse, *"Neues Bauen,"* p. 10.

96. Whittick, *Eric Mendelsohn,* pp. 76, 205; Zevi, *Erich Mendelsohn,* pp. 122, 128. Another modern Jewish cemetery construction was the Ehrenfeld of the huge Berlin-Weissensee cemetery by Alexander Beer. See Schwarz, *Juden in der Kunst,* p. 218.

97. Max Eisler, the leading art critic of *Menorah,* emphasized that synagogues were the most important and most interesting objects of Jewish art. *Menorah* 8 (1930), p. 541.

98. Hammer-Schenk, *Synagogen in Deutschland,* pp. 508–509.
99. Ibid., p. 532.
100. Max Eisler, "Neue Synagogen," *Menorah* 8 (1930), p. 544.
101. Eschwege, *Synagoge in der deutschen Geschichte,* p. 147.

CHAPTER SEVEN: AUTHENTICITY REVISITED

1. *BIGZ,* 1 June 1931, p. 166.
2. Shaked, *Ha-sifrut ha-ivrit, 1880–1980,* vol. 1, p. 37.
3. *Das Jüdische Volksheim Berlin,* p. 5. On the Volksheim see Aschheim, *Brothers and Strangers,* pp. 193–197.
4. Salomon Lehnert (Siegfried Lehmann), "Jüdische Volksarbeit," *Der Jude* 1 (1916–1917), p. 110.
5. Kafka, *Letters to Felice,* p. 481 (30 July 1916), p. 500 (12 September 1916).
6. Scholem, *From Berlin to Jerusalem,* p. 79.
7. Kafka, *Letters to Friends, Family, and Editors,* p. 402 (19 December 1923).
8. Alter, *Necessary Angels,* p. 42.
9. *JR,* 28 May 1925, pp. 380–381.
10. "Bericht über hebräische Unterrichtstätigkeit Wintersemester 1926/27," SchA, 537/311, pp. 14–16.
11. In Mannheim, for example, the teaching of modern Hebrew became an obligatory part of Jewish religious education in 1922 and was financially supported by the Jewish community. *IGBM,* 17 September 1922, p. 4.
12. A Hebrew biweekly in Breslau was *Ha-gesher: Du-shevu'on le-mishtalmim be-ivrit.* Forty-five editions appeared before July 1932. A similar periodical was *Ha-moreh ha-ivri,* produced in Berlin (1926–1928). On a Hebrew theater evening by the Munich Hebrew language school see *BIGZ,* 15 March 1929, p. 87. On Hebrew games see *JR,* 17 August 1920, p. 446.
13. SchA, 537/163, 164.
14. *JR,* 9 June 1922, p. 302.
15. *JR,* 8 November 1922, p. 478.
16. Letter from Einstein to the members of Habimah, 18 December 1929. Published in Kreis der Freunde des Habimah, *Habimah,* n.p.
17. For Kerr see *JR,* 29 October 1926, p. 608; For Reinhardt see *JR,* 29 September 1926, p. 545. The "Friends of Habimah" included German-Jewish writers—such as Lion Feuchtwanger, Alfred Döblin, Arnold Zweig, and Franz Werfel—publisher Samuel Fischer, painter Max Liebermann, actors Elisabeth Bergner and Ernst Deutsch, the Liberal president of the Frankfurt Jewish community, Julius Blau, and non-Jews, most famous among them Thomas Mann. See Kreis der Freunde des Habimah, *Habimah,* n.p.
18. Between October 1912 and February 1913 Kafka attended at least fifteen performances of a Yiddish theater troupe in Prague. See Beck, *Kafka and the Yiddish Theater,* pp. 214–215.
19. See Hemmerle, "Jiddisches Theater im Spiegel deutschsprachiger Kritik."
20. "Ein koscherer Exl? Schlierseer aus Tarnopol . . . der Rickudl (nicht ganz ein

mosaischer Fox; halt ein ritueller Schuhplattler)," *Berliner Tageblatt,* 7 August 1921.

21. Quoted in *JR,* 29 October 1926, p. 608.

22. *JR,* 29 September 1926, p. 545.

23. Döblin, *Kleine Schriften,* vol. 1, pp. 365–366; Reinhardt, *JR,* 24 November 1922, p. 613.

24. See, e.g., the description of the Truppe Surokin in Joseph Roth's *Juden auf Wanderschaft,* pp. 51–54.

25. Leo Winz Collection, CZA, A 136/52. The trip of the Vilna Troupe had already been planned in 1919, but it had to be postponed repeatedly because of organizational and financial complications. See also Gronemann, *Hawdoloh und Zapfenstreich,* pp. 182–187, and Maurer, *Ostjuden,* pp. 730–732.

26. See Maurer, *Ostjuden,* pp. 732–733. There were Yiddish theater groups in a few other German cities, such as the Frankfurt Jüdisches Theater im Löwenhof. See *Der Israelit,* 9 February 1922.

27. Adler, "Alexander Granovskij," pp. 27–42.

28. Alfons Goldschmidt, "Das jüdische Theater in Moskau," in *Moskauer Jüdische Akademische Theater,* p. 20.

29. Joseph Roth, "Das Moskauer Jüdische Theater," in *Moskauer Jüdische Akademische Theater,* pp. 11–13. In similar terms, Arnold Zweig linked the oriental descent of the Jews to their talents as actors. See his *Juden auf der deutschen Bühne.*

30. Cited in Fischer-Lichte, "Retheatrilisierung," p. 245.

31. Bechtel, "'Primordial Worlds of Exorcism.'"

32. Klinger, *Frau im Kaftan,* p. 98.

33. "Ein Stadt-Zeit-Bild: Zu Walter Mehrings 'Kaufmann in Berlin,'" *Theater heute* (October 1979), p. 22.

34. Bernhard Diebold in *Frankfurter Zeitung,* 11 September 1929.

35. In Mehring's play, East European Jews in the Berlin Scheunenviertel live in constant fear of German Jews, whom they believe to assist the state authorities in preparing their expulsion. Mehring, *Kaufmann von Berlin,* p. 162.

36. *Berliner Tageblatt,* 7 September 1929.

37. Fuks and Fuks, "Yiddish Publishing Activities," pp. 427–434.

38. Some of the most important works on Jewish art by those artists were published during their Berlin stay, such as Boris Aronson's *Modern Jewish Graphics,* Marc Chagall's *My Life,* Nathan Altman's *Jewish Graphics,* and illustrations for Jewish children books by Joseph Tchaikow and Issachar Ber Ryback. On the Russian-Jewish artists in Berlin see Bertz, *"Eine neue Kunst für ein altes Volk,"* pp. 38–44.

39. See, e.g., Dawidowicz, *From That Place and Time,* pp. 25, 79–81; and Mendelsohn, *Jews of East Central Europe,* p. 64.

40. Two volumes of this projected seven-volume oeuvre actually appeared. See Meisel, "Hayei Shimon Dubnow," p. 55.

41. Zosa Szajkowski, "Der YIVO un zayne grinders," *YIVO-Bleter,* Jubilee Volume 46 (1980), p. 25.

42. Ibid., pp. 31–32.

43. *Jüdisches Wissenschaftliches Institut,* vol. 1. See especially pp. 117–132.

44. YIVO also intended to publish a comprehensive study called "The Jewish Population in Germany During the Years 1910–1925." Jiddisches Wissenschaftliches Institut, Letter by the Komitée in Berlin to Vorstand der Jüdischen Gemeinde Berlin, 9 February 1930. In Tcherikower Collection, YIVO, file 2295, p. 144894.

45. "Vorlesungs-Verzeichnis," Tcherikower Collection, YIVO, file 2295, p. 144912. See also *Jiddische Wissenschaftliche Institut,* p. 15.

46. General Board of Yiddish Scientific Institute to Gesellschaft "Fraynde fun YIVO" Berlin, 12 June 1930, Tcherikower Collection, YIVO, file 2293, p. 144871.

47. Tcherikower and Shtif to the Vilna executive, 5 March 1926, *YIVO-Bleter,* Jubilee Volume 46 (1980), pp. 33–34.

48. On the circle of Hebrew writers in Berlin on the eve of World War I see Nash, *In Search of Hebraism.*

49. *JR,* 24 December 1909, p. 582. See also the minutes of the conference, *Din ve-heshbon shel ha-ve'idah la-safah ve-la-tarbut ha-ivrit be-Berlin.* Nash, *In Search of Hebraism,* pp. 285–294, speaks of eighty participants.

50. *Ha-Ivri,* 2 December 1910, p. 1. *Ha-Ivri* was published in Berlin between 1910 and 1916.

51. Keshet, *M.Y.Berdyczewski,* pp. 166–172.

52. Ben-Avi, *Im shahar atzma'utenu,* p. 147.

53. Scholem, *From Berlin to Jerusalem,* pp. 85–87.

54. Among the numerous East European Jewish refugees who made the Hebrew colony their intellectual home in Berlin were Hayim Nahman Bialik, David Frischmann, Saul Tchernikhovsky, Uri Zvi Greenberg, Moshe Kleinmann, Hayim Tchernovitz, Shmu'el Abba Horodetzky, Jacob Klatzkin, Benzion Katz, Jakob Fichmann, Benzion Dinaburg, Yehezkel Kaufmann, and Simon Rawidowicz. Whereas the prewar circle used to meet in the eastern part of the city near Café Monopol, the postwar Hebrew circles moved westward to the Charlottenburg Romanisches Café. See Horodetzky, *Zikhronot,* p. 125.

55. On Russian-Jewish culture in Weimar see Williams, *Culture in Exile;* Raeff, *Russia Abroad;* and Mierau, *Russen in Berlin.* See also Congdon, *Exile and Social Thought.*

56. Rawidowicz, *Sihotai im Bialik,* p. 28.

57. See *Beth va-ad: Kli-mabato shel beth ha-va'ad ha-ivri be-Berlin,* no. 1 (April 1922), p. 5.

58. *JR,* 19 January 1923, p. 26. Bialik's fiftieth birthday was also the occasion of a laudatory article in the *Berliner Tageblatt* (17 January 1923, p. 2), which compared the Jewish "national poet" with intellectual representatives of other nations, such as Maxim Gorki and Rabindranath Tagore.

59. In March 1924, a farewell party for Bialik was organized in the Beth ha-va'ad. See invitation card in Benjamin Ravid Private Archives. On the *Beth va'ad ivri* see *JR,* 23 June 1922, pp. 329–330.

60. *Beth va-ad. Kli-mabato shel beth ha-va'ad ha-ivri be-Berlin,* no. 1 (April 1922), p. 6.

61. When he stayed in Bad Homburg, Bialik organized every Shabbat afternoon

an Oneg Shabbat in the home of the Persitzes. The event was attended by young local and East European Jews who listened to short lectures, discussed Zionist politics in Hebrew, and got together to sing and dance. See Herz, *Meine Erinnerung,* pp. 256–257. See also Grosche, *Geschichte der Juden in Bad Homburg,* pp. 38–42.

62. Other Hebrew publishing houses in Berlin during those years included Jalkut, Jiwne, Juwal (for Jewish music), and Choreb (mainly for religious literature).

63. Rawidowicz, *Sihotai,* p. 58.

64. Ibid., p. 73.

65. See Pommerin, "Ausweisung von 'Ostjuden' aus Bayern 1923."

66. Maurer, *Ostjuden,* p. 398.

67. Fuks, "Yiddish Publishing Activities," pp. 422–423. See also Krüger, "Buchproduktion im Exil: Der Klal-Verlag."

68. Bechtel, "Les revues modernistes yiddish," p. 165.

69. On popular East European Jewish culture in Weimar see Maurer, *Ostjuden,* pp. 717–741; Heid, "Ostjüdische Kultur im Deutschland der Weimarer Republik"; and Geisel, *Im Scheunenviertel.*

70. Roth, *Juden auf Wanderschaft,* p. 47.

71. Rawidowicz, *Sihotai,* p. 46.

72. Meisel, "Hayei Shimon Dubnow," p. 54. See also Horodetzky, *Zikhronot,* p. 134.

73. Hurwicz, "Shai Ish Hurwicz," p. 99.

74. *Almanach: 1902–1964,* p. 21.

75. After a lengthy laudation by the old Odessa rabbi Hayim Tchernovitz, Bialik "turned the banquet into an organizational session of Devir." Rawidowicz, *Sihotai,* p. 39.

76. Rawidowicz, *Sihotai,* p. 78.

77. Ismar Elbogen, "Hokhmat Yisra'el: Sekirah," *Devir* 2 (1923), p. 15. See Myers, "Reinventing the Jewish Past," pp. 35–36.

78. *Devir* 1 (1923), p. xii, quoted in Myers, "Reinventing the Jewish Past," pp. 35–36.

79. *Der Jude* 1 (1916–1917).

80. For an overall assessment of Agnon's German years see Laor, "Agnon in Germany."

81. See Band, *Nostalgia and Nightmare,* pp. 7–8.

82. Horodisch, "Abenteuer im Geiste," pp. 198–202.

83. Scholem, "Agnon in Germany: Recollections," in Scholem, *On Jews and Judaism in Crisis,* p. 119.

84. Martin Buber, "Über Agnon," in Hermann, *Treue,* p. 59.

85. Other editorial works by Agnon for the *Jüdischer Verlag* included *Chad Gadja: Das Pessachbuch* (The book for Passover) and *Maus Zur: Ein Chanukkabuch* (A book of Hanukkah). On the friendship between Agnon and Eliasberg see Agnon's recollections at the occasion of Eliasberg's funeral, in Agnon, *Mi-atsmi el atsmi,* pp. 255–256.

86. Ahron Eliasberg's *Jüdischer Verlag* published several of Agnon's stories, as

well as writings by Bialik and Ahad Ha'am, and in 1922 the renowned (non-Jewish) Insel publishing house surprised Hebrew readers with an anthology of Hebrew poetry in the original: *Anthologia Hebraica: Poemata selecta a libris ex Hispania expulsionem,* edited by Heinrich Brody and Max Wiener (1922). For a list of German translations of Agnon's writings see Band, *Nostalgia,* pp. 552–553.

87. The encounter is well documented in their extensive exchange of letters: Agnon and Schocken, *Hilufei igerot.*

88. The manuscript was completed but, because of financial problems, was never published. The masks of Seidmann-Freud's illustrations are preserved by the Schocken Archive in Jerusalem. Seidmann-Freud also cooperated with Hayim Nahman Bialik. See Murken, "Tom Seidmann-Freud," p. 174.

89. See Dahm, *Jüdische Buch im Dritten Reich,* vol. 2, pp. 438–439.

90. See Miron's essays, "German Jews in Agnon's Work," and "Ashkenaz."

91. Miron, "German Jews in Agnon's Work," p. 269.

92. Agnon, *Kol sipurav,* vol. 7, p. 93. English translation in Miron, "German Jews in Agnon's Work," p. 269.

93. Ayanot published Dubnow's *Pinkas* of the Lithuanian Jewish communities and Horodetzky's sources of Hasidism, and Rawidowicz himself edited the first complete critical works of Nahman Krohmal (*Kitvei Ranak*).

94. On the activities of the Brit see *Yediot ha-brit ha-ivrit ha-olamit,* nos. 6–7 (1932). This typewritten bulletin can be found in the library of YIVO, New York.

95. For a biography of Rawidowicz see Ravid, "Le-hayav u-likhtevav shel Shimon Rawidowicz." A shortened English version is Ravid, "Life and Writings of Simon Rawidowicz."

96. Ravid, "Le-hayav u-likhtevav shel Shimon Rawidowicz," pp. xxxiv–xxxix; Levinson, *Ha-tenu'ah ha'ivrit ba-golah,* pp. 104–111.

97. Wertheimer, *Unwelcome Strangers,* p. 106.

98. Martin Buber, "Die hebräische Sprache und der Kongreß für hebräische Kultur," *JR,* 14 January 1910, p. 13.

99. Quoted in Nash, *In Search of Hebraism,* pp. 169–170.

100. Ravid, "Le-hayav u-likhtevav shel Shimon Rawidowicz," pp. xxxii–xxxiii.

EPILOGUE

1. Rosenzweig, *On Jewish Learning,* p. 102.

2. Simon, *Aufbau im Untergang,* pp. 55–66.

3. Dahm, *Jüdische Buch im Dritten Reich,* vol. 2, pp. 515–522.

4. Gronius, "Klarheit, Leichtigkeit und Melodie," pp. 68–69.

5. *IFM,* 7 October 1936, n.p.

6. Kurt Singer, "Jüdisches Kulturbundtheater," Kurt Singer Collection, LBI-AR, 2947.

7. Freeden, "Jüdischer Kulturbund," p. 64.

8. *NJM,* 10./25.7.1919, p. 400.

Bibliography

ARCHIVAL SOURCES

Brandeis University Archives, Waltham, Mass. Nahum Glatzer Collection.
Bundesarchiv, Potsdam. Society for the Promotion of Wissenschaft des Juden-
    tums, 75 C Ge 4.
———. Wanderbund Kameraden, 75 C Wa 1.
Central Archives for the History of the Jewish People, Jerusalem. Altona-Ham-
    burg-Wandsbek Jewish Community Archives, AHW.
———. Ismar Freund Collection, P 2.
———. Georg Kareski Collection, P 82.
———. Neuwied Jewish Community Archives, Rh/Nw 75.
———. Society for the Promotion of Wissenschaft des Judentums, M 22/1.
———. Soncino Society, INV 1409.
———. Speyer Jewish Community Archives, PF XII 21.
Central Zionist Archives, Jerusalem. Harry Epstein Collection, A 101.
———. Georg Herlitz Collection, A 198.
———. Bruno Kirschner Collection, A 369.
———. Jakob Klatzkin Collection, A 40.
———. Alfred Klee Collection, A 142.
———. Heinrich Loewe Collection, A 146.
———. Aron Sandler Collection, A 69.
———. Leo Winz Collection, A 136.
Geheimes Staatsarchiv Preußischer Kulturbesitz, Merseburg (now Berlin). Jewish
    Community, MU Rep. 77, Tit. 416, Nos. 54 and 55.
———. Jewish Press, MU Rep. 76-III, Sekt. 1, Abt. XIIIa, No. 36
———. Wissenschaft des Judentums, MU Rep. 76, Vc Sekt. 2, Tit. 16.
Jewish National and University Library, Jerusalem. Martin Buber Archives,
    Hebrew Language Congress (Berlin, 1909), Bet 135.; Letters, Files Het 2/194,
    2/289, 140.80, 610.I3, 705.44.; Academy for *Wissenschaft des Judentums,* Hey
    44.; Zionist Cultural Activities Committee, Wav 13; Frankfurt University, File

Yud 11; Disputation at Stuttgart Lehrhaus, Zayin 43; Conference for the Renewal of Education, Zayin 44.

Leo Baeck Institute, New York. Karl Adler Collection, AR 7276.

———. Julius Bab Collection, AR 2887.

———. Werner Cahnmann Collection, AR 556.

———. Samuel Echt Collection, AR 7016.

———. Ismar Elbogen Collection, AR 7209.

———. Efraim Frisch Collection, AR 2523.

———. Julius Goldstein Collection, AR 7167.

———. Max Grünewald Collection, AR 7204.

———. Siegfried Guggenheim Collection, AR 180.

———. Jewish Theater Collection, AR 678.

———. Erich von Kahler Collection, AR 3890.

———. Fred Lachmann Collection, AR 5256.

———. Berthold Rosenthal Collection, AR 638.

———. Franz Rosenzweig Collection, AR 3003.

———. Edith Scheinmann Collection, AR 5043.

———. Kurt Singer Collection, AR 3100.

———. Eduard Strauss Collection, AR 7077.

———. Robert Weltsch Collection, AR 7185.

Private Archives, Benjamin Ravid, Newton, Mass. Simon Rawidowicz Collection.

Schocken Institute Archives, Jerusalem. Encyclopaedia Judaica, File 517/222.

———. Hebrew Language Activities, Files 537/22, 51, 16, 164, 312, 431, 4412, 4413.

———. Jewish Communities in Germany, Files 512/221, 222, 224, 231.

———. Jewish Museum Berlin, File 517/212.

———. Jewish Museum Breslau, File 517/213.

———. Soncino Society, File 517/227.

Stadtarchiv Leipzig. Jewish Cultural Associations: Files PP-V 644, 1040, 3070, 4231, 4381, 4455

Vanderbilt University, The Divinity Library, Nashville, Tenn. Nahum N. Glatzer Special Collection, Franz Rosenzweig Papers.

YIVO Institute Archives, New York. Siegfried Bernfeld Collection, RG 6.

———. Elias Tcherikower Collection: Files 2293, 2295.

BOOKS AND ARTICLES

Ackermann, Irmgard. "'Wir andern—auch wir suchen': Kurt Tucholsky und das Christentum." In *Tucholsky heute: Rückblick und Ausblick,* by Irmgard Ackermann and Klaus Hübner, pp. 165–193. Munich: Judicum, 1991.

Adler, Hans Günther. *Theresienstadt, 1941–1945: Das Antlitz einer Zwangsgemeinde. Geschichte. Soziologie.* Tübingen, Germany: J.C.B. Mohr, 1960.

Adler, Lois. "Aexander Granovskij and the Jewish State Theatre of Moscow." *Drama Review* 24 (1987), pp. 27–42.

Adler-Rudel, Shalom. *Ostjuden in Deutschland, 1880–1940.* Tübingen, Germany: J. C. B. Mohr, 1959.

Adorno, Theodor W. "Sakrales Fragment. Moses und Aron." In *Gesammelte Schriften,* vol. 16. Frankfurt: Suhrkamp, 1978.

Agnon, Shmu'el Yosef. *Kol sipurav shel Sh.Y. Agnon.* 11th ed., vol. 7. Jerusalem and Tel Aviv: Schocken, 1966.

———. *Mi-atsmi el atsmi.* Tel Aviv: Schocken, 1976.

Agnon, Shmu'el Yosef, and Salman Schocken. *Hilufei igerot.* Jerusalem: Schocken, 1991.

Ahlheim, Klaus. *Zwischen Arbeiterbildung und Mission: Beispiele und Probleme protestantischer Erwachsenenbildung und ihrer Theorie in der Weimarer Republik und nach 1945.* Stuttgart: Alektor, 1982.

Ahrens, Erich. "Reminiscences of the Men of the Frankfurt Lehrhaus." *LBIYB* 19 (1974), pp. 245–253.

Alexander, Gabriel. "Die Entwicklung der jüdischen Bevölkerung in Berlin zwischen 1871 und 1945." *Tel Aviver Jahrbuch für deutsche Geschichte* 20 (1991), pp. 287–314.

Almanach: 1902–1964. Berlin: Jüdischer Verlag, 1964.

Almog, Shmuel. *Zionism and History: The Rise of a New Jewish Consciousness.* Jerusalem: Magnes Press and St. Martin's Press, 1987.

Alter, Robert. *Necessary Angels: Tradition and Modernity in Kafka, Benjamin and Scholem.* Cambridge: Harvard University Press, 1991.

Altmann, Alexander. "Leo Baeck and the Jewish Mystical Tradition." *Leo Baeck Memorial Lecture* 17 (1973).

Altmann, Alexander. *Moses Mendelssohn: A Biographical Study.* University: University of Alabama Press, 1973.

Amishai-Maisels, Ziva. "The Art of German Jews." In *The Jewish Legacy and the German Conscience: Essays in Memory of Rabbi Joseph Asher,* ed. Moses Rischin and Raphael Asher, pp. 249–275. Berkeley: Judah L. Magnes Museum, 1991.

Anderson, Benedict. *Imagined Communities: Reflections on the Origin and Spread of Nationalism.* Rev. ed. London: Verso, 1991.

Angress, Werner T. "Das deutsche Militär und die Juden im Ersten Weltkrieg." *Militärgeschichtliche Mitteilungen* 1 (1976), pp. 77–146.

Apter-Gabriel, Ruth, ed. *Tradition and Revolution: The Jewish Renaissance in Russian Avant-Garde Art, 1912–1928.* Jerusalem: The Israel Museum, 1987.

Arendt, Hannah. *The Jew as Pariah: Jewish Identity and Politics in the Modern Age,* ed. Ron H. Feldman. New York: Grove Press, 1978.

Arnsberg, Paul. *Die Geschichte der Frankfurter Juden seit der Französischen Revolution.* Vol. 2. Frankfurt: Eduard Roether, 1983.

Aschheim, Steven E. *Brothers and Strangers: The East European Jew in German and German Jewish Consciousness, 1800–1923.* Madison: University of Wisconsin Press, 1982.

Aschoff, Diethard. "Die westfälischen Vereine für jüdische Geschichte und Literatur im Spiegel ihrer Jahrbücher (1899–1920)." In *Gedenkschrift für Bernhard Brilling,* ed. Peter Freimark and Helmut Richtering, pp. 218–245. Hamburg: Hans Christians, 1988.

Auerbach, Elias. *Pionier der Verwirklichung: Ein Arzt aus Deutschland erzählt vom Beginn der zionistischen Bewegung und seiner Niederlassung in Palästina kurz nach der Jahrhundertwende.* Stuttgart: Deutsche Verlags-Anstalt, 1969.

Der babylonische Talmud, trans. Lazarus Goldschmidt. 12 vols. Berlin: Jüdischer Verlag, 1929–36.

Bach, Hans I. *The German Jew: A Synthesis of Judaism and Western Civilization, 1730–1930.* Oxford: Oxford University Press, 1984.

Baeck, Leo. *Wege im Judentum. Aufsätze und Reden.* Berlin: Schocken, 1933.

Bamberger, Fritz. "Julius Guttmann—Philosopher of Judaism." *LBIYB* 5 (1960), pp. 3–34.

Band, Arnold. *Nostalgia and Nightmare: A Study in the Fiction of S. Y. Agnon.* Berkeley: University of California Press, 1968.

Baumgartner, Alois. *Sehnsucht nach Gemeinschaft: Ideen und Strömungen im Sozialkatholizismus.* Munich: Ferdinand Schöningh, 1977.

Bayerdörfer, Hans-Peter. "'Ghettokunst. Meinetwegen, aber hundertprozentig echt.' Alfred Döblins Begegnung mit dem Ostjudentum." In *Im Zeichen Hiobs: Jüdische Schriftsteller und deutsche Literatur,* by Gunter E. Grimm and Hans-Peter Bayerdörfer, pp. 161–177. Frankfurt: Athenäum, 1986.

Bayerdörfer, Hans-Peter, ed. *Theatralia Judaica: Emanzipation und Antisemitismus als Momente der Theatergeschichte. Von der Lessing-Zeit bis zur Shoah.* Tübingen, Germany: Max Niemeyer, 1992.

Bechtel, Delphine. "'Primordial Worlds of Exorcism.'" In *Proceedings of the Eleventh World Congress of Jewish Studies,* Div. C, vol. 3, pp. 39–46. Jerusalem: World Union of Jewish Studies, 1994.

———. "Les revues modernistes yiddish à Berlin et à Varsovie de 1922 à 1924: La quête d'une nouvelle Jérusalem?" *Etudes germaniques* 46 (1991), pp. 161–177.

Beck, Evelyn Torton. *Kafka and the Yiddish Theater: Its Impact on His Work.* Madison: University of Wisconsin Press, 1971.

Beer-Hofmann, Richard. *Jaákobs Traum: Ein Vorspiel.* Frankfurt: S. Fischer, 1918.

Behrens, Stefan, ed. *Jakob Steinhardt: Das graphische Werk.* Berlin: Kunstamt Wedding, 1987.

Beller, Steven. *Vienna and the Jews, 1867–1938: A Cultural History.* Cambridge: Cambridge University Press, 1989.

Belting, Hans. *Die Deutschen und ihre Kunst: Ein schwieriges Erbe.* Munich: C. H. Beck, 1992.

Ben-Avi, Ittamar. *Im shahar atsma'utenu: Zikhronot shel ha-yeled ha-ivri ha-rishon.* Tel Aviv: Mayer, 1961.

Ben-Chorin, Schalom. "Jüdische Bibelübersetzungen in Deutschland," *LBIYB* 4 (1959), pp. 311–331.

Benjamin, Walter. *Gesammelte Schriften,* Edited by Rolf Tiedemann and Hermann Schweppenhäuser. Vol. 2, part 2. Frankfurt: Suhrkamp, 1977.

———. *Illuminationen.* Frankfurt: Suhrkamp, 1969.

Berdyczewski, Micha Josef [Bin Gorion, pseud.]. *Der Born Judas.* 6 vols. Leipzig: Insel, 1916–1922.

———. *Die Sagen der Juden: Jüdische Sagen und Mythen.* 6 vols. Frankfurt: Ruetten and Loening, 1913–1927.

———. *Sinai und Garizim: Forschungen zum Alten Testament auf Grund rabbinischer Quellen.* Berlin: Morgenland Verlag, 1925–1926.

Berkowitz, Michael. "Art in Zionist Popular Culture and Jewish National Self-Consciousness, 1897–1914." *Studies in Contemporary Jewry* 6, pp. 17–42.

———. *Zionist Culture and West European Jewry before the First World War.* Cambridge: Cambridge University Press, 1993.

Bertz, Inka. *"Eine neue Kunst für ein altes Volk": Die jüdische Renaissance in Berlin 1900 bis 1924.* Museumspädagogischer Dienst Berlin, Ausstellungsmagazin No. 28. Berlin: Berlin Museum, 1991.

Bettauer, Hugo. *Die Stadt ohne Juden: Ein Roman von übermorgen.* Reprint. Berlin: Ullstein, 1988.

Biale, David. *Gershom Scholem: Kabbalah and Counter-History.* Cambridge: Harvard University Press, 1982.

Bin Gorion, Emanuel. *Reshut ha-yahid: Mikha Yosef Berdyczewski (Bin-Gorion) be-esrim shenotav ha-aheronim.* Jerusalem: Reshafim, 1980.

Birnbaum, Max P. *Staat und Synagoge, 1918–1938: Eine Geschichte des Preußischen Landesverbands Jüdischer Gemeinden.* Tübingen, Germany: J. C. B. Mohr, 1981.

Blomert, Reinhard. "Das vergessene Sanatorium." In *Jüdisches Leben in Heidelberg: Studien zu einer unterbrochenen Geschichte,* ed. Norbert Giovannini, Jo-Hannes Bauer, and Hans-Martin Mumm, pp. 249–263. Heidelberg: Wunderhorn, 1992.

Bohnke-Kollwitz, Jutta, ed. *Köln und das rheinische Judentum: Festschrift Germania Judaica, 1959–1984.* Cologne: J. P. Bachem, 1984.

Bohlman, Philip V. "Folk Music in the Urban German-Jewish Community, 1880–1939." *Musica Judaica* 9 (1986–1987), pp. 22–34.

————. *"The Land Where Two Streams Flow": Music in the German-Jewish Community of Israel.* Urbana: University of Illinois Press, 1989.

————. "The Resurgence of Jewish Musical life in an Urban German Community: Mannheim on the Eve of World War II," *Musica Judaica* 7 (1984–1985), pp. 34–53.

————. "Die Volksmusik und die Verstädterung der deutsch-jüdischen Gemeinde in den Jahrzehnten vor dem Zweiten Weltkrieg." *Jahrbuch für Volksliedforschung* 34 (1989), pp. 25–40.

Bolkosky, Sydney M. *The Distorted Image: German-Jewish Perceptions of Germans and Germany, 1918–1935.* New York: Elsevier, 1975.

Borut, Jacob. "Ruah hadashah be-kerev ahenu be-Ashkenaz: Temurot be-Yahadut Germanyah le-nokhah tahalikhei shinui kalkali, hevrati ve-politi ba Raikh be-sof ha-meah ha-19." Ph.D. dissertation, Hebrew University, Jerusalem, 1991.

Brecht, Bertolt. *Gesammelte Werke: Schriften zum Theater 3.* Vol. 17. Frankfurt: Suhrkamp, 1967.

Brenner, David Allen. "Promoting the *Ostjuden*: Ethnic Identity, Stereotyping, and Audience in the German-Jewish Cultural Review *Ost und West* (Berlin, 1901–1923)." Ph.D. dissertation, University of Texas at Austin, 1993.

Brenner, Michael. "East and West in Orthodox German-Jewish Novels (1912–1934)." *LBIYB* 37 (1992), pp. 309–323.

————. " 'Gott schütze uns vor unseren Freunden': Zur Ambivalenz des Philosemitismus im Kaiserreich." *Jahrbuch für Antisemitismusforschung* 2 (1993), pp. 174–199.

————. "The Jüdische Volkspartei—National-Jewish Communal Politics during the Weimar Republic." *LBIYB* 35 (1990), pp. 219–243.

————. "A Tale of Two Families: Franz Rosenzweig, Gershom Scholem and the Generational Conflict Around Judaism." *Judaism* 42 (1993), pp. 349–361.

————. "Tarbut ivrit be republikat Weimar." In *Proceedings of the Eleventh World Congress of Jewish Studies,* Div. B, vol. 2 (Hebrew section), pp. 69–74. Jerusalem: World Union of Jewish Studies, 1994.

————. "An Unknown Project of a World Jewish History in Weimar Germany: Reflections on Jewish Historiography in the 1920s." *Modern Judaism* 13 (1993), pp. 249–268.

————. "Zurück ins Ghetto? Jüdische Autonomiekonzepte in der Weimarer Republik." *Trumah: Jahrbuch der Hochschule für Jüdische Studien Heidelberg* 3 (1992), pp. 101–127.

Breuer, Gerda, and Ines Wagemann, eds. *Ludwig Meidner: Zeichner, Maler, Literat, 1884–1966.* 2 vols. Stuttgart: Gerd Hatje, 1991.

Breuer, Isaac. *Ein Kampf um Gott.* Frankfurt: Sänger und Friedberg, 1920.

————. *Falk Nefts Heimkehr.* Frankfurt: I. Kauffmann, 1923.

———. *Die Messiasbraut: Die Geschichte einer verlorenen Hoffnung.* Frankfurt: Hermon, 1925.

Breuer, Mordechai. *Jüdische Orthodoxie im Deutschen Reich, 1871–1918: Sozialgeschichte einer religiösen Minderheit.* Frankfurt: Athenäum, 1986.

Brieger, Lothar. *E. M. Lilien: Ein Künstlerleben um die Jahrhundertwende.* Berlin and Vienna: Benjamin Harz, 1922.

Brisman, Shimeon. *A History and Guide to Judaic Encyclopedias and Lexicons.* Cincinnati: Hebrew Union College Press, 1987.

Brod, Max. *Reubeni: Fürst der Juden.* Munich: Kurt Wolff, 1925.

Buber, Martin. *Briefwechsel aus sieben Jahrzehnten,* ed. Grete Schaeder. 3 vols. Heidelberg: Lambert Schneider, 1972–1975.

———. *Die jüdische Bewegung: Gesammelte Aufsätze und Ansprachen, 1900–1915.* Berlin: Jüdischer Verlag, 1916.

———. *On Judaism,* ed. Nahum N. Glatzer. New York: Schocken, 1967.

———. *Reden über Erziehung.* Heidelberg: Lambert Schneider, 1962.

———. *Die Schrift und ihre Verdeutschung.* Berlin: Schocken, 1936

———. *Zu einer neuen Verdeutschung der Schrift. Beilage zum ersten Band: Die fünf Bücher der Weisung.* Heidelberg: Lambert Schneider, 1981.

Buber, Martin, ed. *Jüdische Künstler.* Berlin: Jüdischer Verlag, 1903.

Bühler, Michael. *Erziehung zur Tradition—Erziehung zum Widerstand: Ernst Simon und die jüdische Erwachsenenbildung in Deutschland.* Berlin: Selbstverlag Institut Kirche und Judentum, 1986.

Carlebach, Alexander. *Adass Yeshurun of Cologne: The Life and Death of a Kehilla.* Belfast: W. Mullon and Sons, 1964.

———. "Die Orthodoxie in der Kölner jüdischen Gemeinde der Neuzeit." In *Köln und das rheinische Judentum: Festschrift Germania Judaica, 1959–1984,* ed. Jutta Bohnke-Kollwitz, pp. 341–358. Cologne: J. P. Bachem, 1984.

Carlebach, Esriel. *Exotische Juden: Berichte und Studien.* Berlin: Welt-Verlag, 1932.

Carner, Mosco. "Music in the Mainland of Europe: 1918–1939." In *New Oxford History of Music: The Modern Age,* ed. Martin Cooper, pp. 208–386. London: Oxford University Press, 1974.

Cohen, Arthur A., ed. *The Jew: Essays from Martin Buber's Journal "Der Jude," 1916–1928.* University: University of Alabama Press, 1980.

Cohen, Gerson D. "German Jewry as Mirror of Modernity." *LBIYB* 20 (1975), pp. ix-xxxi.

Cohn, Emil Bernhard. *Legenden.* Berlin: Siegfried Scholem, 1933.

Cohn-Wiener, Ernst. *Die Jüdische Kunst: Ihre Geschichte von den Anfängen bis zur Gegenwart.* Berlin: Martin Wasservogel, 1929.

Congdon, Lee. *Exile and Social Thought: Hungarian Intellectuals in Germany and Austria, 1919–1933.* Princeton: Princeton University Press, 1991.

Craig, Gordon. *Germany, 1866–1945.* New York: Oxford University Press, 1980.

Dahm, Volker. *Das jüdische Buch im Dritten Reich.* 2 vols. Frankfurt: Buchhändler-Vereinigung, 1982.

Dawidowicz, Lucy S. *From That Place and Time: A Memoir, 1938–1947.* New York: W. W. Norton, 1989.

Daxelmüller, Christoph. "Jüdische Museen—Jüdisches in Museen: Anmerkungen zur Geschichte der jüdischen Museologie." In *Dokumentation und Darstellung der Geschichte und Kultur der Juden im Museum,* ed. Bernward Deneke, pp. 15–26. Nuremberg: Germanisches Nationalmuseum, 1989.

———. "Jüdische Volkskunde in Deutschland vor 1933." In *Volkskunde als akademische Disziplin,* ed. Wolfgang Brückner, pp. 117–142. Vienna: Österreichische Akademie des Wissenschaften, 1983.

———. "Max Grunwald and the Origins of Jewish Folkloristics in Hamburg." In *Proceedings of the Ninth World Congress of Jewish Studies,* Division D, vol. 2, pp. 73–80. Jerusalem, 1986.

Déak, Istvan. *Weimar Germany's Left-Wing Intellectuals: A Political History of the Weltbühne and Its Circle.* Berkeley: University of California Press, 1968.

Deleuze, Gilles, and Felix Guattari. *Toward a Minor Literature,* trans. Dana Polan. Minneapolis: University of Minnesota Press, 1986.

Das deutsche Judentum: Seine Parteien und Organisationen. Eine Sammelschrift. Berlin: Verlag der Neuen Jüdischen Monatshefte, 1919.

Din ve-heshbon shel ha-ve'idah la-safah vela-tarbut ha-ivrit be-Berlin, ed. S. Hurwitz. Warsaw, 1910.

Döblin, Alfred. *Autobiographische Schriften und letzte Aufzeichnungen.* Olten and Freiburg: Walter, 1980.

———. *Kleine Schriften,* ed. W. Riley. Vol. 1. Olten: Walter, 1985.

———. *Reise in Polen.* Reprint. Munich: Deutscher Taschenbuchverlag, 1987.

Dreyer, Alfred. "Josef Kastein—Schöpferische Jahre in der Schweiz." *LBIB* 60 (1981), pp. 21–50.

Efron, John M. *Defenders of the Race: Jewish Doctors and Race Science in Fin-de-Siècle Europe.* New Haven: Yale University Press, 1994.

———. "Scientific Racism and the Mystique of Sephardic Racial Superiority," *LBIYB* 38 (1993), pp. 75–96.

Eisner, Isi Jacob. "Reminiscences of the Berlin Rabbinical Seminary." *LBIYB* 12 (1967), pp. 32–52.

Elbogen, Ismar. *A Century of Jewish Life.* Philadelphia: Jewish Publication Society, 1944.

———. *Ein Jahrhundert Wissenschaft des Judentums.* Berlin: Philo Verlag, 1922.

Elbogen, Ismar. "Zum Begriff 'Wissenschaft des Judentums,'" in *Zum 60-jährigen Bestehen der Hochschule für die Wissenschaft des Judentums.* Berlin, 1932.

Eliav, Mordechai. *Ha-Hinukh ha-yehudi be-Germaniah bi-yamei ha-Haskalah veha-Imantsipatsiah.* Jerusalem: Jewish Agency, 1960.

Eloni, Yehuda. *Zionismus in Deutschland: Von den Anfängen bis 1914.* Gerlingen: Bleicher, 1987.

Endelman, Todd M. "The Legitimization of the Diaspora Experience in Recent Jewish Historiography." *Modern Judaism* 11 (1991), pp. 195–209.

Eschwege, Helmut. *Die Synagoge in der deutschen Geschichte: Eine Dokumentation.* 2nd ed. Wiesbaden: Fourier, 1988.

Eyssen, Jürgen. *Buchkunst in Deutschland: Vom Jugendstil zum Malerbuch.* Hanover: Schlütersche Verlagsanstalt, 1980.

Feuchtwanger, Lion. *Centum Opuscula: Eine Auswahl,* ed. Wolfgang Berndt. Rudolstadt: Greifenverlag, 1956.

———. *Jud Süß.* Munich: Drei Masken, 1925.

Finkelstein, Haim, "E. M. Lilien: Das Werden eines Künstlers." *LBIB* 87 (1990), pp. 55–66.

Fischer-Lichte, Erika. "Retheatrilisierung des Theaters als Emanzipation: das 'Staatliche Jüdische Theater' in Moskau, 1920–1928." In *Theatralia Judaica: Emanzipation und Antisemitismus als Momente der Theatergeschichte. Von der Lessing-Zeit bis zur Shoah,* ed. Hans-Peter Bayerdörfer. Tübingen, Germany: Max Niemeyer, 1992.

Foucault, Michel. *The Archaeology of Knowledge and the Discourse on Language,* trans. A. M. Sheridan Smith. New York: Pantheon, 1972.

Fox, Everett. "Technical Aspects of the Translation of Genesis of Martin Buber and Franz Rosenzweig." Ph.D. dissertation, Brandeis University, 1975.

Frank, Rafael. *Über hebräische Typen und Schriftarten.* Berlin: H. Berthold, 1926.

Freeden, Herbert. "Jüdischer Kulturbund ohne 'Jüdische' Kultur." In *Geschlossene Vorstellung: Der Jüdische Kulturbund in Deutschland, 1933–1941,* ed. Akademie der Künste, pp. 55–66. Berlin: Edition Hentrich, 1992.

Freud, Ernst L., ed. *The Letters of Sigmund Freud and Arnold Zweig.* New York: New York University Press, 1970.

Friedberg, Haya. "The Unwritten Message—Visual Commentary in Twentieth-Century Haggadah Illustration." *Journal of Jewish Art* 16–17 (1990–1991), pp. 157–171.

Friedeberger, Hans. *Joseph Budko.* Berlin: Verlag für jüdische Kunst und Kultur, 1920.

Friedlander, Albert H. *Leo Baeck: Teacher of Theresienstadt.* New York: Holt, Rinehart and Winston, 1968.

Friedlander, Albert H., ed. *Georg Salzberger, Leben und Lehre.* Frankfurt: Waldemar Kramer, 1982.

Friedman, Maurice. *Martin Buber's Life and Work: The Early Years, 1878–1923.* New York: Dutton, 1981.

———. *Martin Buber's Life and Work: The Middle Years, 1923–1945.* Detroit: Wayne State University Press, 1988.

Fuchs, Eugen. *Um Deutschtum und Judentum,* ed. Leo Hirschfeld. Frankfurt: Kauffmann, 1919.

Fuhr, Werner. *Proletarische Musik in Deutschland, 1928–1933.* Göppingen: Alfred Kümmerle, 1977.

Führer durch die jüdische Gemeindeverwaltung und Wohlfahrtsplege in Deutschland 1932/33. Berlin: Zentralwohlfahrtsstelle der deutschen Juden, 1932.

Fuks, Leo, and Renate Fuks. "Yiddish Publishing Activities in the Weimar Republic, 1920–1933." *LBIYB* 33 (1988), pp. 417–434.

Funk, Rainer. *Erich Fromm.* Reinbek: Rowohlt, 1983.

Fürst, Adolf. "Die höheren jüdischen Schulen Deutschlands." *MGWJ* 75 (1931), pp. 48–67.

Gabe, Herrn Rabbiner Dr. Nobel zum 50. Geburtstag dargebracht. Frankfurt, 1922.

Gay, Peter. *Freud, Jews, and Other Germans: Masters and Victims in Modernist Culture.* New York: Oxford University Press, 1978.

———. *Weimar Culture: The Outsider as Insider.* New York and Evanston: Harper and Row, 1968.

Geisel, Eike. *Im Scheunenviertel: Bilder, Texte und Dokumente.* Berlin: Severin und Siedler, 1981.

Gelber, Mark H. "E. M. Lilien und die jüdische Renaissance." *LBIB* 87 (1990), pp. 45–53.

———. " 'Juden auf Wanderschaft' und die Rhetorik der Ost-West-Debatte im Werk Joseph Roths." In *Joseph Roth: Interpretation—Kritik -Rezeption,* ed. Michael Kessler and Fritz Hackert, pp. 127–135. Tübingen, Germany: Stauffenburg, 1990.

———. "The *Jungjüdische Bewegung*: An Unexplored Chapter in German-Jewish Literary and Cultural History." *LBIYB* 31 (1986), pp. 105–119.

Gilam, Abraham. "Erich Goeritz and Jewish Art Patronage in Berlin During the 1920s." *Journal of Jewish Art* 11 (1985), pp. 60–72.

Gillis-Carlebach, Miriam. *Hinukh ve-emunah.* Tel Aviv: Moreshet, 1979.

Gilman, Sander. *Jewish Self-Hatred: Anti-Semitism and the Hidden Language of the Jews.* Baltimore: Johns Hopkins University Press, 1986.

———. "The Rediscovery of Eastern Jews: German Jews in the East, 1890–1918." In *Jews and Germans from 1860–1933: The Problematic Symbiosis,* ed. David Bronsen, pp. 338–342. Heidelberg: Winter, 1979.

Glatzer, Nahum N. "The Frankfort Lehrhaus." *LBIYB* 1 (1956), pp. 105–122.

———. *Franz Rosenzweig: His Life and Thought.* New York: Schocken, 1961.

Glatzer, Nahum N., and Ludwig Strauss, eds. *Ein jüdisches Lesebuch. Sendung und Schicksal. Aus dem Schrifttum des nachbiblischen Judentums.* Berlin: Schocken, 1931.

Goebel, Wolfram. *Der Kurt Wolff Verlag, 1913–1930: Expressionismus als verlegerische Aufgabe.* Frankfurt: Buchhändler-Vereinigung, 1977.

Goldmann, Nahum. *The Autobiography of Nahum Goldmann: Sixty Years of Jewish Life*. New York: Holt, Rinehart and Winston, 1969.

Goldscheider, Calvin, and Alan S. Zuckerman. *The Transformation of the Jews*. Chicago: University of Chicago Press, 1984.

Goldstein, Moritz. *Begriff und Programm einer jüdischen Nationalliteratur*. Berlin: Jüdischer Verlag, 1913.

———. "Deutsch-jüdischer Parnaß." *Der Kunstwart* 25 (March 1912), pp. 281–294.

———. "German Jewry's Dilemma Before 1914: The Story of a Provocative Essay." *LBIYB* 2 (1957), pp. 236–254.

Grab, Walter, and Julius H. Schoeps. *Juden in der Weimarer Republik*. Stuttgart and Bonn: Burg, 1986.

Graetz, Heinrich. *Geschichte der Juden von den ältesten Zeiten bis auf die Gegenwart*. Vol. 11. Leipzig: Oskar Leiner, 1900.

Greive, Hermann. *Theologie und Ideologie. Katholizismus und Judentum in Deutschland und Österreich, 1918–1935*. Heidelberg: Lambert Schneider, 1969.

Grijn Santen, W. B. van der. *Die "Weltbühne" und das Judentum*. Würzburg, Germany: Königshausen und Neumann, 1994.

Grimm, Gunter E., and Hans-Peter Bayerdörfer, eds. *Im Zeichen Hiobs: Jüdische Schriftsteller und deutsche Literatur im 20. Jahrhundert*. Frankfurt: Athenäum, 1986.

Grochowiak, Thomas. *Ludwig Meidner*. Recklinghausen: Aurel Bongers, 1966.

Gronemann, Sammy. "Erinnerungen." *LBI-AR*, ME 203.

———. *Hawdoloh und Zapfenstreich: Erinnerungen an die ostjüdische Etappe, 1916–1918*. Reprint. Königstein: Jüdischer Verlag Athenäum, 1984.

Gronius, Jörg W. "Klarheit, Leichtigkeit und Melodie. Theater im Jüdischen Kulturbund Berlin." In *Geschlossene Vorstellung: Der Jüdische Kulturbund in Deutschland, 1933–1941*, pp. 67–94. Berlin: Edition Hentrich, 1992.

Grosche, Heinz. *Geschichte der Juden in Bad Homburg vor der Höhe 1866 bis 1945*. Frankfurt: Waldemar Kremer, 1991.

Grünewald, Max. "Critic of German Jewry: Ludwig Feuchtwanger and his Gemeindezeitung," *LBIYB* 17 (1972), pp. 75–92.

Grunfeld, Frederic V. *Prophets Without Honour: A Background to Freud, Kafka, Einstein, and Their World*. New York: Holt, Rinehart and Winston, 1979.

Grunwald, Max. "Kapitlekh fun an Oytobiografie," in *YIVO-Bleter* 36 (1952), pp. 241–251.

Guggenheim, Siegfried. "Rudolf Koch and the Offenbach Workshop." *Print: A Quarterly Journal of the Graphic Arts* 5, no. 1 (1947), pp. 7–42.

Guggenheim, Siegfried, ed. *Offenbacher Haggadah*. Offenbach: Private printing, 1927.

Guttsmann, W. L. *Workers' Culture in Weimar Germany: Between Tradition and Commitment*. New York: Berg, 1990.

Habima: Hebräisches Theater. Berlin: Heinrich Keller, 1928.

Hall, Murray G. *Der Fall Bettauer.* Vienna: Loecker, 1978.

Hallo, Gertrude. "The Hallos and Rubensohns: Three Centuries of Jewish Family Life in Germany." Manuscript. *LBI-AR, ME* 251.

Hamburger, Ernest. *Juden im öffentlichen Leben Deutschlands.* Tübingen, Germany: J. C. B. Mohr, 1966.

Hamburger, Ernest, and Peter Pulzer. "Jews as Voters in the Weimar Republic." *LBIYB* 30 (1985), pp. 3–66.

Hammer-Schenk, Harold. *Synagogen in Deutschland: Geschichte einer Baugattung im 19. und 20. Jahrhundert (1780–1933).* 2 vols. Hamburg: Hower, 1981.

Handbuch der jüdischen Gemeindeverwaltung und Wohlfahrtspflege 1913. Berlin: Deutsch-Israelitischer Gemeindebund and Zentralwohlfahrtsstelle der deutschen Juden, 1913.

Hegglin, Werner. *Else Lasker-Schüler und ihr Judentum.* Zurich: Iuris Druck, 1966.

Heid, Ludger. "Ostjüdische Kultur im Deutschland der Weimarer Republik." In *Juden als Träger bürgerlicher Kultur in Deutschland,* ed. Julius H. Schoeps, pp. 329–355. Stuttgart and Bonn: Burg, 1990.

Heilbronner, Oded. *Yehudei Weimar: Hevrah be-mashber ha-moderni'ut, 1918–1933.* Jerusalem: Magnes Press, 1994.

Heimann, Moritz. *Prosaische Schriften in drei Bänden* 1. Berlin: S. Fischer, 1918.

———. *Das Weib des Akiba.* Berlin: S. Fischer, 1922.

Heinemann, Manfred. *Sozialisation und Bildungswesen in der Weimarer Republik.* Stuttgart: Ernst Klett, 1976.

Heitzer, Horstwalter. *Der Volksverein für das katholische Deutschland, 1890–1918.* Mainz: Matthias-Grünewald-Verlag, 1979.

Hemmerle, Joachim. "Jiddisches Theater im Spiegel deutschsprachiger Kritik. Von der Jahrhundertwende bis 1928. Eine Dokumentation." In *Beter und Rebellen: Aus 1000 Jahren Judentum in Polen,* ed. Michael Brocke, pp. 277–311. Frankfurt: Deutscher Koordinierungsrat der Gesellschaften für christlich-jüdische Zusammenarbeit, 1983.

Herf, Jeffrey. *Reactionary Modernism: Technology, Culture, and Politics in Weimar and the Third Reich.* Cambridge: Cambridge University Press, 1984.

Herlitz, Georg. *Mein Weg nach Jerusalem: Erinnerungen eines zionistischen Beamten.* Jerusalem: Rubin Mass, 1964.

Hermand, Jost, and Frank Trommler. *Die Kultur der Weimarer Republik.* Munich: Nymphenburger, 1978.

Herrmann, Leo, ed. *Treue: Eine jüdische Sammelschrift.* Berlin: Jüdischer Verlag, 1916.

Herrmann, Ulrich, ed. *"Neue Erziehung"—"Neue Menschen": Ansätze zur Erziehungs- und Bildungsreform zwischen Kaiserreich und Diktatur.* Weinheim: Beltz, 1984.

Herz, Yitzhak Sophoni. *Meine Erinnerung an Bad Homburg und seine 600 jährige jüdische Gemeinde (1335–1942).* Rehovoth: Private printing, 1981.

Heskes, Irene. *Passport to Jewish Music. Its History, Traditions, and Culture.* Westport, Conn.: Greenwood, 1994.

Heuberger, Rachel. "Orthodoxy Versus Reform: The Case of Rabbi Nehemiah Anton Nobel of Frankfurt a. Main." *LBIYB* 37 (1992), pp. 45–58.

Heuberger, Rahel, and Helga Krohn, eds. *Hinaus aus dem Ghetto: Juden in Frankfurt am Main, 1800–1950.* Frankfurt: S. Fischer, 1988.

Hever, Hannan, ed. *Uri Zvi Greenberg. Be-melot lo shemonim.* Jerusalem: Bet ha-sefarim ha-le'umi ve-ha'universita'i, 1977.

Heyd, Milly. "Lilien and Beardsley: 'To the Pure All Things Are Pure.'" *Journal of Jewish Art* 7 (1980), pp. 58–69.

Hiller, Kurt. "Kurt Tucholsky und der Selbsthaß." *Text und Kritik: Zeitschrift für Literatur* 29 (June 1985), pp. 6–8.

Hirshberg, Jehoash. "Heinrich Schalit and Paul Ben-Haim in Munich." *Yuval* 4 (1982), pp. 131–149.

Hobsbawm, Eric. *The Age of Revolution: 1789–1848.* New York: Mentor, 1962.

Hobsbawm, Eric, and Terence Ranger, eds. *The Invention of Tradition.* Cambridge: Cambridge University Press, 1984.

Hofmann, Christhard. "Jüdische Geschichtswissenschaft in Deutschland, 1918–1938. Konzepte, Schwerpunkte, Ergebnisse." In *Wissenschaft des Judentums, Anfänge der Judaistik in Europa,* ed. Julius Carlebach, pp. 132–152. Darmstadt: Wissenschaftliche Buchgemeinschaft, 1992.

Holländer, Ludwig. *Deutsch-jüdische Probleme der Gegenwart: Eine Auseinandersetzung über die Grundfragen des Central-Vereins deutscher Staatsbürger jüdischen Glaubens.E.V.* Berlin: Philo-Verlag, 1929.

Homeyer, Fritz. *Deutsche Juden als Bibliophilen und Antiquare.* 2nd ed. Tübingen, Germany: J. C. B. Mohr, 1966.

Honigmann, Peter. "Jüdische Studenten zwischen Orthodoxie und moderner Wissenschaft. Der Heidelberger Talmudistenkreis um Salman Baruch Rabinkow." *Menora* 3 (1992), pp. 85–96.

Horch, Hans Otto. *Auf der Suche nach der jüdischen Erzählliteratur: Die Literaturkritik der "Allgemeinen Zeitung des Judentums," (1837–1922).* Frankfurt: Peter Lang, 1985.

———. "Heimat und Fremde: Jüdische Schriftsteller und deutsche Literatur oder Probleme einer deutsch-jüdischen Literaturgeschichte." In *Juden als Träger bürgerlicher Kultur in Deutschland,* ed. Julius H. Schoeps, pp. 41–65. Stuttgart and Bonn: Burg, 1990.

Horodetzky, Shmu'el Abba. *Zikhronot.* Tel Aviv: Devir, 1957.

Horodisch, Abraham. "Ein Abenteuer im Geiste: Die Soncino-Gesellschaft der Freunde des jüdischen Buches." In *Bibliotheca Docet: Festgabe für Carl Wehmer,* pp. 181–209. Amsterdam: Erasmus, 1963.

————. "Aus den Erinnerungen eines Berliner bibliophilen Verlegers der zwanziger Jahre," *Imprimatur* Neue Folge 8 (1976), pp. 243–254.

————. *Die Exlibris des Uriel Birnbaum: Gefolgt von einer Selbstbiographie des Künstlers.* Amsterdam: Erasmus Antiquariat, 1957.

Horwitz, Rivka, ed. *Yitshak Breuer: Iyunim be-mishnato.* Ramat Gan: Bar Ilan University, 1988.

Howes, Justine, and Pauline Paucker. "German Jews and the Graphic Arts." *LBIYB* 34 (1989), pp. 443–473.

Hunt, Lynn. *The New Cultural History: Essays.* Berkeley: University of California Press, 1989.

Hüppauf, Bernd. "'I have travelled to the Jews': Encounters of German Writers with Eastern Jews." In *From the Emancipation to the Holocaust: Essays on Jewish Writers,* ed. Konrad Kwiet, pp. 103–126. Kensington: University of New South Wales, 1987.

Hurwicz, Elias. "Shai Ish Hurwicz and the Berlin *He-Atid.*" *LBIYB* 12 (1967), pp. 85–103.

Huse, Norbert. *"Neues Bauen" 1918 bis 1933: Moderne Architektur in der Weimarer Republik.* Munich: Heinz Moos, 1975.

Hyman, Paula. *From Dreyfus to Vichy: The Remaking of French Jewry, 1906–1939.* New York: Columbia University Press, 1979.

Idelsohn, Abraham Z. *Jewish Music in Its Historical Development.* New York: Schocken, 1967.

Jacobsohn, Siegfried. *Briefe an Kurt Tucholsky, 1915–1926,* ed. Richard von Soldenhoff. Munich and Hamburg: Albrecht Knaus, 1989.

Jay, Martin. "Politics of Translation: Siegfried Kracauer and Walter Benjamin on the Buber-Rosenzweig Bible." *LBIYB* 21 (1976), pp. 3–24.

Das Jiddische Wissenschaftliche Institut. Berlin: Lutze und Vogt, 1928.

Jospe, Alfred. "The Study of Judaism in German Universities Before 1933." *LBIYB* 27 (1982), pp. 295–309.

Das Jüdische Volksheim Berlin: Erster Bericht Mai/Dezember 1916. Berlin, 1916.

Jüdischer Almanach. 2nd ed. Berlin: Jüdischer Verlag, 1904.

Jüdischer Almanach, 1902–1964. Berlin: Jüdischer Verlag, 1964.

Jüdisches Wissenschaftliches Institut, Sektion für Wirtschaft und Statistik: Schriften für Wirtschaft und Statistik. Vol. 1. Berlin: n.p, 1928.

Kafka, Franz. *Letter to His Father: Brief an den Vater,* trans. Ernst Kaiser and Eithene Wilkins. New York: Schocken, 1953.

————. *Letters to Felice,* ed. Erich Heller and Juergen Born. New York: Schocken, 1973.

————. *Letters to Friends, Family, and Editors,* trans. Richard Winston and Clara Winston. New York: Schocken, 1977.

Kahn, Lothar. *Mirrors of the Jewish Mind: A Gallery of European Jewish Writers of Our Time.* New York: Thomas Yoseloff, 1968.

Kaplan, Marion. *The Jewish Feminist Movement in Germany: The Campaigns of the Jüdischer Frauenbund, 1904–1938*. Westport, Conn.: Greenwood Press, 1979.

———. *The Making of the Jewish Middle Class: Women, Family, and Identity in Imperial Germany*. New York: Oxford University Press, 1991.

Kareski, Georg. *Der neue Gemeindehaushalt. Rede in der Repräsentantenversammlung vom 30.1.1930*. Berlin, 1930.

Kastein, Josef. *Eine Geschichte der Juden*. Berlin: Rowohlt, 1931.

———. *Sabbatai Zewi. Der Messias von Ismir*. Berlin: Rowohlt, 1930.

———. *Uriel da Costa oder die Tragödie der Gesinnung*. Berlin: Rowohlt, 1932.

Katz, Jacob. *Out of the Ghetto: The Social Background of Jewish Emancipation, 1770–1870*. Cambridge: Harvard University Press, 1973.

Kaznelson, Siegmund. *Die Juden im deutschen Kulturbereich: Ein Sammelwerk*. Berlin: Jüdischer Verlag, 1959.

Kern, Brigitte. "Franz Rosenzweig's Jüdisches Lehrhaus in Frankfurt: A Model for Jewish Adult Education." *Judaism* 30 (1990), pp. 202–214.

Keshet, Yeshurun. *M. Y. Berdyczewski (Bin-Gurion): Hayav u-fo'alo*. Jerusalem: Magnes Press, 1958.

Kirschner, Emanuel. "Erinnerungen aus meinem Leben, Streben und Wirken." LBI-AR, ME 361.

Klein, Dennis. "Assimilation and Dissimilation: Peter Gay's Freud, Jews and Other Germans." *New German Critique* 19 (1980), pp. 151–165.

Kleßmann, Christoph. *Polnische Bergarbeiter im Ruhrgebiet, 1870–1945*. Göttingen: Vandenhoeck und Ruprecht, 1978.

Klinger, Ruth. *Die Frau im Kaftan: Lebensbericht einer Schauspielerin*, ed. Ludger Heid. Gerlingen: Bleicher, 1992.

Knütter, Hans-Helmuth. *Die Juden und die deutsche Linke in der Weimarer Republik, 1918–1933*. Düsseldorf: Droste, 1971.

Kober, Adolf. "Jewish Communities in Germany from the Age of Enlightenment to Their Destruction by the Nazis." *Jewish Social Studies* 9 (1947), pp. 195–238.

Koch, Richard. "Das Freie Jüdische Lehrhaus in Frankfurt am Main." *Der Jude* 7, 1923, pp. 116–120.

———. Memoirs. LBI-AR, ME 735.

Kochavi, Jehojakim. "Beyn Tsionim le-Liberalim be-Berlin 1929–1932: ma'avakim tsiburi'im be-kehilat Berlin uva-yahadut Germaniah ba-shanim shekadmu le 'reich ha-shlishi.'" Manuscript, CZA.

Koebner, Thomas, and Gerhart Pickeroth, eds. *Die andere Welt: Studien zum Exotismus*. Frankfurt: Athenäum, 1987.

Kolb, Leon, ed. *The Woodcuts of Jakob Steinhardt*. Philadelphia: Jewish Publication Society, 1961.

Kollenscher, Max. *Jüdisches aus der deutsch-polnischen Übergangszeit: Posen, 1918–1920*. Berlin: Ewer, 1925.

Krapf, Thomas. *Yehezkel Kaufmann: Ein Lebens- und Erkenntnisweg zur Theologie der Hebräischen Bibel.* Berlin: Institut Kirche und Judentum, 1990.

Kreis der Freunde des Habimah, ed. *Habimah.* Berlin: Aldus, n.d.

Kreutner, S. J. *Mein Leipzig: Gedenken an die Juden meiner Stadt.* Jerusalem: Rubin Mass, 1992.

Krojanker, Gustav, ed. *Juden in der deutschen Literatur: Essays über zeitgenössische Schriftsteller.* Berlin: Welt-Verlag, 1922.

Krueger, Felix, ed. *Philosophie der Gemeinschaft: 7 Vorträge, gehalten auf der Tagung der Deutschen Philosophischen Gesellschaft vom 1.-4. Oktober 1928 in Leipzig.* Berlin: Junker und Dünnhaupt, 1929.

Krüger, Maren. "Buchproduktion im Exil: Der Klal-Verlag." In *Juden in Kreuzberg,* ed. Berliner Geschichtswerkstatt, pp. 421–426. Berlin: Edition Hentrich, 1991.

———. "Für die Verbreitung jüdischen Wissens: Das Büro der 'Freien Jüdischen Volkshochschule e.V.'" In *Juden in Kreuzberg,* ed. Berliner Geschichtswerkstatt, pp. 385–387. Berlin: Edition Hentrich, 1991.

Kulka, Otto Dov, and Paul R. Mendes-Flohr, eds. *Judaism and Christianity under the Impact of National Socialism.* Jerusalem: Historical Society of Israel and Zalman Shazar Center for Jewish History, 1987.

Künzl, Hannelore. "Die Frage der jüdischen Identität in den Werken des späten 19. und 20. Jahrhunderts." *Kairos* Neue Folge 30–31 (1988–1989), pp. 188–217.

———. *Jüdische Kunst: Von der biblischen Zeit bis in die Gegenwart.* Munich: C. H. Beck, 1992.

Landmann, Michael. *Jüdische Miniaturen.* Bonn: Bouvier, 1982.

Langbehn, Julius. *Rembrandt als Erzieher.* Leipzig: Hirschfeld, 1909.

Langewiesche, Dieter. "Freizeit und 'Massenbildung': Zur Ideologie und Praxis der sozialdemokratisch-gewerkschaftlichen Volksbildung in der Weimarer Republik." In *"Neue Erziehung"—Neue Menschen: Ansätze zur Erziehungs- und Bildungsreform zwischen Kaiserreich und Diktatur,* ed. Ulrich Herrmann. Weinheim: Beltz, 1984.

Laor, Dan. "Agnon in Germany, 1912–1924: A Chapter of a Biography." *AJS Review* 18 (1993), pp. 75–93.

Laqueur, Walter. *Weimar: A Cultural History, 1918–1933.* New York: G. P. Putnam's Sons, 1974.

Lasker-Schüler, Else. *Lieber gestreifter Tiger: Briefe,* ed. Margarete Kupper. Munich: Kösel, 1969.

———. *Prosa und Schauspiele.* Munich: Kösel, 1962.

———. *Sämtliche Gedichte.* Munich: Kösel, 1977.

———. *Your Diamond Dreams: Cut Open My Arteries,* trans. Robert P. Newton. Chapel Hill: University of North Carolina, 1982.

Lavski, Hagit. *Be-terem puranut: Darkam ve-yihudam shel Tsiyonei Germaniah, 1918–1932.* Jerusalem: Magnes Press, 1990.

Lazarus, Paul. *Die jüdische Gemeinde Wiesbaden, 1918–1942. Ein Erinnerungs-buch.* New York: I. Kauffmann, 1949.

Le Rider, Jacques. "Sionisme et antisemitisme: Le prège des mots." In *Karl Kraus et son temps,* ed. Gilbert Krebs and Gerald Stieg, pp. 66–73. Paris: Institut d'Allemand, 1989.

Lenz, Werner, ed. *Kleine Geschichte großer Lexika.* Gütersloh: Bertelsmann Lexikon Verlag, 1990.

Lessing, Theodor. *Der jüdische Selbsthaß.* Berlin: Jüdischer Verlag, 1930.

Lestschinsky, Jacob. *Das wirtschaftliche Schicksal des deutschen Judentums: Auf-stieg, Wandlung, Krise, Ausblick.* Berlin: Zentralwohlfahrtsstelle der deutschen Juden, 1933.

Levinson, Abraham. *Ha-tenu'ah ha'ivrit ba-golah.* Warsaw: Brith Ivrith Olamith, 1935.

Levy, Emanuel. *The Habimah: Israel's National Theater, 1917–1977.* New York: Columbia University Press, 1979.

Licharz, Werner, and Heinz Schmidt, eds. *Martin Buber (1878–1965): Interna-tionales Symposium zum 70. Geburtstag.* Frankfurt: Haag und Herchen, 1989.

Lidtke, Vernon L. *The Alternative Culture: Socialist Labor in Imperial Germany.* New York: Oxford University Press, 1985.

Liptzin, Solomon. *Germany's Stepchildren.* Cleveland: Meridian, 1961.

Lorenz, Ina. *Die Juden in Hamburg zur Zeit der Weimarer Republik: Eine Doku-mentation.* Hamburg: Hans Christians, 1987.

Löwenthal, Leo. *Critical Theory and Frankfurt Theorists: Lectures—Correspon-dence—Conversations.* New Brunswick and Oxford: Transaction Publishers, 1989.

Löwy, Michael. *Redemption and Utopia: Jewish Libertarian Thought in Central Europe: A Study in Elective Affinity.* Stanford: Stanford University Press, 1992.

Ludwig Yehuda Wolpert: A Retrospective. New York: Jewish Museum, 1976.

Ma'ayan, Shmu'el. *Ha-behirot be-kehilat Berlin ba-shanim 1901–1920.* Givat Haviva: Zvi Lurie Institute for the Study of Zionism and Diaspora, 1977.

———. *Ha-behirot be-kehilat Köln ba-shanim 1900–1921.* Givat Haviva: Zvi Lurie Institute for the Study of Zionism and Diaspora, 1979.

Mach, Dafna. "Jüdische Bibelübersetzungen ins Deutsche." In *Juden in der deutschen Literatur,* ed. Herbert Strauss and Christhard Hofmann, pp. 54–63. Munich: Deutscher Taschenbuch Verlag, 1985.

Mäckelmann, Michael. *Arnold Schönberg und das Judentum: Der Komponist und sein religiöses, nationales und politisches Selbstverständnis nach 1921.* Hamburg: Karl Dieter Wagner, 1984.

Manger, Itsik, Yonas Turkov, and Moyshe Perenson, eds. *Yidisher teater in Eyrope tsvishn beyde velt-milhomes: Materyaln tsu der geshikhte fun Yidish teater.* New York: Congress for Jewish Culture, 1968.

Mann, Heinrich, and Thomas Mann. *Briefwechsel, 1900–1949.* Frankfurt: S. Fischer, 1968.

Mannheim, Karl. "The Problem of a Sociology of Knowledge." In *Essays on the Sociology of Knowledge,* ed. Paul Kecskemeti. London: Routledge and Kegan Paul, 1952.

Maoz, Eliyahu. "The Werkleute." *LBIYB* 4 (1959), pp. 165–182.

Maurer, Trude. *Ostjuden in Deutschland, 1918–1933.* Hamburg: Hans Christians, 1986.

Mayer, Paul. *Ernst Rowohlt: In Selbstzeugnissen und Bilddokumenten.* Reinbek: Rowohlt, 1967.

Mehring, Walter. *Der Kaufmann von Berlin.* Düsseldorf: Claassen, 1979.

Meidner, Ludwig. *Gang in die Stille.* Berlin: Euphorion, 1929.

———. *Septemberschrei: Hymnen, Gebete, Lästerungen.* Berlin: Cassirer, 1920.

Meier-Cronemeyer, Hermann. "Jüdische Jugendbewegung." *Germania Judaica,* Neue Folge 27–30 (1969), pp. 1–122.

Meisel, Josef. "Hayei Shimon Dubnow." In *Sefer Shimon Dubnow,* ed. Shimon Rawidowicz, pp. 24–60. London: ORT, 1954.

Mendelsohn, Ezra. *The Jews of East Central Europe Between the Wars.* Bloomington: Indiana University Press, 1983.

Mendelssohn, Peter de. *S. Fischer und sein Verlag.* Frankfurt: S. Fischer, 1970.

Mendes-Flohr, Paul R. "Ambivalent Dialogue: Jewish Christian Theological Encounter in the Weimar Republic." In *Judaism and Christianity under the Impact of National Socialism,* ed. Otto Dov Kulka and Paul R. Mendes-Flohr, pp. 99–132. Jerusalem: Historical Society of Israel and Zalman Shazar Center for Jewish History, 1987.

———. "Fin-de-Siècle Orientalism, the Ostjuden and the Aesthetics of Jewish Self-Affirmation." *Studies in Contemporary Jewry* 1 (1984), pp. 96–139.

———. "Knowledge as Service: An Appreciation of Nahum N. Glatzer." *Jewish Studies* 31 (1991), pp. 25–44.

———. *The Philosophy of Franz Rosenzweig.* Hanover, N.H.: University Press of New England, 1988.

———. "Scholarship as a Craft: Reflections on the Legacy of Nahum Glatzer." *Modern Judaism* 13 (1993), pp. 269–276.

Meyer, Michael A. *Jewish Identity in the Modern World.* Seattle: University of Washington Press, 1990.

———. *The Origins of the Modern Jew: Jewish Identity and European Culture in Germany, 1749–1824.* Detroit: Wayne State University Press, 1967.

———. *Response to Modernity: A History of the Reform Movement in Judaism.* New York: Oxford University Press, 1988.

———. "Yahadut liberalit ve-tsionut be-germaniah." In *Tzionut ve-dat,* ed. Shmuel Almog, Jehuda Reinharz, and Anita Shapira, eds., pp. 111–126. Jerusalem: Zalman Shazar Center for Jewish History, 1994.

Mierau, Fritz, ed. *Russen in Berlin: Literatur—Malerei—Theater—Film: 1918–1933.* Leipzig: Philipp Reclam jun., 1987.

Milfull, John. "Juden, Christen und andere Menschen. Sabbatianismus, Assimilation und jüdische Identität in Lion Feuchtwangers Roman *Jud Süß.*" In *Im Zeichen Hiobs. Jüdische Schriftsteller und deutsche Literatur,* ed. Gunter E. Grimm and Hans-Peter Bayerdörfer, pp. 213–222. Frankfurt: Athenäum, 1986.

Miron, Dan. "Ashkenaz: Modern Hebrew Literature and the Pre-Modern German Jewish Experience." Leo Baeck Memorial Lecture 33. New York: Leo Baeck Institute, 1989.

———. "German Jews in Agnon's Work." *LBIYB* 23 (1978), pp. 265–280.

Mittleman, Alan L. *Between Kant and Kabbalah: An Introduction to Isaac Breuer's Philosophy of Judaism.* Albany: State University of New York Press, 1990.

Mitzman, Arthur. *The Iron Cage: An Historical Interpretation of Max Weber.* New Brunswick and Oxford: Transaction, 1987.

Moses, Stéphane. *L'ange de l'histoire: Rosenzweig, Benjamin, Scholem.* Paris: Edition du Seuil, 1992.

———. "Scholem and Rosenzweig: The Dialectics of History." *History and Memory* 2 (1990).

———. *System und Offenbarung: Die Philosophie Franz Rosenzweigs.* Munich: W. Fink, 1985.

Moses, Stéphane, and Albrecht Schöne. *Juden in der deutschen Literatur: Ein deutsch-israelisches Symposion.* Frankfurt: Suhrkamp, 1986.

Das Moskauer Jüdische Akademische Theater. Berlin: Die Schmiede, 1928.

Mosse, George L. *The Crisis of German Ideology: Intellectual Origins of the Third Reich.* New York: Grosset and Dunlap, 1964.

———. *The Culture of Western Europe: The Nineteenth and Twentieth Centuries.* 3rd ed. Boulder: Westview, 1988.

———. "German Jews and Liberalism in Retrospect." *LBIYB* 32 (1987), pp. xiii–xxv.

———. *German Jews Beyond Judaism.* Bloomington: Indiana University Press, 1985.

———. *Germans and Jews: The Right, the Left, and the Search for a 'Third Force' in Pre-Nazi Germany.* Reprint. Detroit: Wayne State University Press, 1987.

Mosse, Werner E., ed. *Entscheidungsjahr 1932: Zur Judenfrage in der Endphase der Weimarer Republik.* Tübingen, Germany: J. C. B. Mohr, 1965.

Murken, Barbara. "Tom Seidmann-Freud. Leben und Werk." *Die Schiefertafel: Zeitschrift für historische Kinderbuchforschung* 4, no. 3 (December 1981), pp. 163–201.

Myers, David N. "'Distant Relatives Happen onto the Same Inn': The Meeting of

East and West as Literary Theme and Cultural Ideal." *Jewish Social Studies* 1 (1995), pp. 75–100.

———. "The Fall and Rise of Jewish Historicism: The Evolution of the Akademie für die Wissenschaft des Judentums (1919–1934)." *Hebrew Union College Annual* 63 (1992), pp. 107–144.

———. *Reinventing the Jewish Past: European Jewish Intellectuals and the Zionist Return to History.* New York: Oxford University Press, 1995.

Nadel, Arno. *Jacob Steinhardt.* Berlin: Verlag Neue Kunsthandlung, 1920.

———. *Der Sündenfall: Sieben biblische Szenen.* Berlin: Felix Stössinger, 1926.

Nash, Stanley. *In Search of Hebraism: Shai Hurwitz and His Polemics in the Hebrew Press.* Leiden: E. J. Brill, 1980.

Niehoff, Maren Ruth. "The Buber-Rosenzweig Translation of the Bible Within German-Jewish Tradition." *Journal of Jewish Studies* 44 (1993), pp. 258–279.

Niewyk, Donald L. "The German Jews in Revolution and Revolt, 1918–19." *Studies in Contemporary Jewry* 4 (1988), pp. 41–66.

———. *The Jews in Weimar Germany.* Baton Rouge: Louisiana State University Press, 1980.

Nisbet, Robert A. *The Quest for Community.* New York: Oxford University Press, 1970.

Noam, Ernst. "Erinnerung und Dialog." LBI-AR, ME 477.

Nora, Pierre. *Les lieux de mémoire.* Vol. 1. Paris: Gallimard, 1984.

Nussbaum, Herbert. "Weg und Schicksal eines deutschen Juden." LBI-AR, ME 478.

Pappenheim, Bertha, ed. *Maasse-Buch. Buch der Sagen und Legenden aus Talmud und Midrasch nebst Volkserzählungen in jüdisch-deutscher Sprache. Nach der Ausgabe des Maasse-Buches Amsterdam 1723.* Frankfurt: Kaufmann, 1929.

———. *Die Memoiren der Glückel von Hameln.* Vienna: Stefan Meyer and Wilhelm Pappenheim (private printing), 1910.

———. *Zeenah u-Reenah Frauenbibel.* Vol. 1 (Bereshit). Frankfurt: J. Kauffmann, 1930.

Paucker, Pauline, and Justin Howes. "German Jews and the Graphic Arts." *LBIYB* 34 (1989), pp. 443–474.

Pfefferkorn, Rudolf. *Jakob Steinhardt.* Berlin: Stapp, 1967.

Philippson, Ludwig. *Saron.* 5 vols. 2nd ed. Leipzig: Oskar Leiner, 1863.

Pierson, Ruth. "German Jewish Identity in the Weimar Republic." Ph.D. dissertation, Yale University, 1970.

Plessner, Helmuth. *Die Grenzen der Gemeinschaft: Eine Kritik des sozialen Radikalismus.* Reprint. Bonn: Bouvier Verlag Herbert Grundmann, 1972.

Pöggeler, Franz. "Erwachsenenbildung in der Weimarer Republik. Persönlichkeiten und Institutionen." In *Sozialisation und Bildungswesen in der Weimarer Republik,* ed. Manfred Heinemann. Stuttgart: Ernst Klett.

Pöggeler, Franz, ed. *Geschichte der Erwachsenenbildung.* Vol. 4 of *Handbuch der Erwachsenenbildung.* Stuttgart: W. Kohlhammer, 1975.

Poljakoff, Solomon. *Sabbatai Zewi.* Berlin: Welt-Verlag, 1927.

Pommerin, Reiner. "Die Ausweisung von 'Ostjuden' aus Bayern 1923. Ein Beitrag zum Krisenjahr der Weimarer Republik." *Vierteljahrshefte für Zeitgeschichte* 34, no. 3 (1986), pp. 311–340.

Poppel, Stephen. *Zionism in Germany, 1897–1933.* Philadelphia: Jewish Publication Society, 1977.

Prestel, Claudia. "Bevölkerungspolitik in der jüdischen Gemeinschaft in der Weimarer Republik: Ausdruck jüdischer Identität?" *Zeitschrift für Geschichtswissenschaft* 41 (1993), pp. 685–715.

———. *Jüdisches Schul- und Erziehungswesen in Bayern, 1804–1933.* Göttingen: Vandenhoeck und Ruprecht, 1989.

Pulzer, Peter. *Jews and the German State: A Political History of a Minority, 1848–1933.* Oxford: Blackwell, 1992.

Rabinbach, Anson. "Between Enlightenment and Apocalypse: Benjamin, Bloch and Modern German Jewish Messianism." *New German Critique* 34 (1985), pp. 78–124.

Raeff, Marc. *Russia Abroad: A Cultural History of the Russian Emigration, 1919–1939.* New York: Oxford University Press, 1990.

Rathenau, Walther. *Briefe.* Vol. 1. Dresden: Carl Reissner, 1926.

———. *Impressionen.* Leipzig: S. Hirzel, 1902.

Ravid, Benjamin. "The Life and Writings of Simon Rawidowicz." In *Israel: The Ever-Dying People,* by Simon Rawidowicz. Rutherford, N.J.: Fairleigh Dickinson University Press, 1986, pp. 13–50.

———. "Le-hayav u-likhtav shel Shimon Rawidowicz." In *Iyunim be-mahshevet Yisrael,* ed. Shimon Rawidowicz, pp. 13–50. Jerusalem: Rubin Mass, 1969.

Rawidowicz, Shimon. *Sihotai im Bialik,* ed. Benjamin Ravid. Jerusalem and Tel Aviv: Devir, 1983.

Reichmann, Eva. "Der Bewußtseinswandel der deutschen Juden." In *Deutsches Judentum in Krieg und Revolution, 1916–1923,* ed. George L. Mosse, pp. 512–613. Tübingen, Germany: J. C. B. Mohr, 1966.

Reif, Wolfgang. *Zivilisationsflucht und literarische Wunschräume: Der exotistische Roman im ersten Viertel des 20. Jahrhunderts.* Stuttgart: Metzler, 1975.

Reinharz, Jehuda. "Achad Haam und der deutsche Zionismus." *LBIB* 61 (1982), pp. 3–27.

———. *Chaim Weizmann: The Making of a Zionist Leader.* New York: Oxford University Press, 1985.

———. *Fatherland or Promised Land: The Dilemma of the German Jew, 1893–1914.* Ann Arbor: University of Michigan Press, 1975.

———. "The Lehrhaus in Frankfurt am Main: A Renaissance in Jewish Adult Education." *Yavne Review* 7 (1969), pp. 7–29.

Reinharz, Jehuda, ed. *Dokumente zur Geschichte des deutschen Zionismus, 1882–1933.* Tübingen, Germany: J. C. B. Mohr, 1981.

Reinharz, Jehuda, and Walter Schatzberg, eds. *The Jewish Response to German Culture.* Hanover, N.H.: University Press of New England, 1985.

Rexroth, Dieter, ed. *Erprobungen und Erfahrungen. Zu Paul Hindemith's Schaffen in den Zwanziger Jahren.* Mainz: B. Schott's Söhne, 1978.

Richards, Donald Ray. *The German Bestseller in the 20th Century: A Complete Bibliography and Analysis.* Berne: Lang, 1968.

Ringer, Alexander. "Arnold Schoenberg and the Politics of Jewish Survival." *Journal of the Arnold Schoenberg Institute* 3 (1979), pp. 10–48.

———. *Arnold Schoenberg—The Composer as a Jew.* Oxford: Oxford University Press, 1990.

Ringer, Fritz K. *The Decline of the German Mandarins: The German Academic Community, 1890–1933.* Cambridge: Harvard University Press, 1969.

Rinott, Chanoch. "Major Trends in Jewish Youth Movements in Germany." *LBIYB* 19 (1974), pp. 77–95.

Rosenzweig, Franz. *Briefe und Tagebücher,* ed. Rachel Rosenzweig and Edith Rosenzweig-Scheinmann. Vol. 1 of *Franz Rosenzweig. Der Mensch und sein Werk.* The Hague: M. Nijhoff, 1979.

———. *On Jewish Learning,* ed. Nahum N. Glatzer. New York: Schocken, 1955.

———. *Sprachdenken im Übersetzen: Arbeitspapiere zur Verdeutschung der Schrift,* ed. Rachel Rosenzweig. Vol. 4, part 2, of *Franz Rosenzweig: Der Mensch und sein Werk.* The Hague: M. Nijhoff, 1984.

———. *Zweistromland: Kleinere Schriften zu Glauben und Denken,* ed. Reinhold Mayer and Annemarie Mayer. Vol. 3 of *Franz Rosenzweig. Der Mensch und sein Werk.* The Hague: M. Nijhoff, 1984.

Roth, Joseph. *Juden auf Wanderschaft.* Cologne: Kiepenheuer and Witsch, 1985.

———. *Werke.* Vol. 2. Cologne: Kiepenheuer and Witsch, 1990.

Rothschild, Lothar. "Die Geschichte des Seminars von 1904 bis 1938." In *Das Breslauer Seminar: Jüdisch-Theologisches Seminar (Fraenckelscher Stiftung) in Breslau 1854–1938,* ed. Guido Kisch, pp. 121–166. Tübingen, Germany: J. C. B. Mohr.

Said, Edward W. *Orientalism.* New York: Vintage, 1979.

Sakheim, Artur. *Der Zadik.* Frankfurt: J. Kauffmann, 1929.

Salzberger, Georg. "Zwischen zwei Weltkriegen: Die Gesellschaft für jüdische Volksbildung und das Jüdische Lehrhaus." In *Georg Salzberger: Leben und Lehre,* ed. Albert H. Friedlander. Frankfurt: Waldemar Kremer, 1982.

Sandrow, Nahma. *Vagabond Stars: A World History of Yiddish Theater.* New York: Harper and Row, 1977.

Sandt, Rita van de. *Martin Bubers bildnerische Tätigkeit zwischen den beiden Weltkriegen: Ein Beitrag zur Geschichte der Erwachsenenbildung.* Stuttgart: Ernst Klett, 1977.

Sartre, Jean Paul. *Anti-Semite and Jew,* trans. George J. Becker. New York: Schocken, 1948.

Schachnowitz, Selig. *Feuerzeichen.* Frankfurt: J. Kaufmann, 1928.

Schalit, Michael, ed. *Heinrich Schalit: The Man and His Music.* Livermore, Calif.: Private printing, 1979.

Schatzker, Chaim. *Jüdische Jugend im zweiten Kaiserreich.* Frankfurt: Peter Lang, 1988.

———. "Martin Buber's Influence on the Jewish Youth Movement in Germany." *LBIYB* 23 (1978), pp. 151–171.

Scheibe, Wolfgang. "Die Stellung der Erwachsenenbildung im Bildungssystem des Weimarer Staates." In *Sozialisation und Bildungswesen in der Weimarer Republik,* ed. Manfred Heinemann, pp. 325–338. Stuttgart: Ernst Klett, 1976.

Schine, Robert S. *Jewish Thought Adrift: Max Wiener (1882–1950).* Atlanta: Scholars Press, 1992.

Schiratzki, Selma. "The Rykestraße School in Berlin." *LBIYB* 5 (1960), pp. 299–307.

Schivelbusch, Wolfgang. "Auf der Suche nach dem verlorenen Judentum: Das Freie Jüdische Lehrhaus." In *Intellektuellendämmerung: Zur Lage der Frankfurter Intelligenz in den zwanziger Jahren,* pp. 35–51. Frankfurt: Suhrkamp, 1985.

Schlotzhauer, Inge. *Das Philanthropin, 1804–1942: Die Schule der Israelitischen Gemeinde in Frankfurt am Main.* Frankfurt: Waldemar Kramer, 1990.

Schneider, Lambert. "Beginnen. 1925–1932." In *Rechenschaft über vierzig Jahre Verlagsarbeit 1925–1965: Ein Almanach,* pp. 9–25. Heidelberg: Lambert Schneider, 1966.

Schocken, Gershom. "Gershom Scholem und die deutsch-jüdische Romantik." In *Philobiblion: Vierteljahrsschrift für Buch- und Graphiksammler* 27 (1983), pp. 111–120.

Schoenberg, Arnold, and Wassily Kandinsky. *Letters, Pictures, and Documents,* ed. Jelena Hahl-Koh. London and Boston: Faber and Faber, 1984.

Schoeps, Julius H., ed. *Juden als Träger bürgerlicher Kultur in Deutschland.* Stuttgart and Bonn: Burg, 1989.

Scholem, Gershom. *From Berlin to Jerusalem: Memories of My Youth.* New York: Schocken, 1980.

———. *The Messianic Idea in Judaism, and Other Essays on Jewish Spirituality.* New York: Schocken, 1971.

———. *On Jews and Judaism in Crisis: Selected Essays,* ed. Werner J. Dannhauser. New York: Schocken, 1976.

———. *Walter Benjamin: The Story of a Friendship,* trans. Harry Zohn. New York: Schocken, 1988.

Schönberger, Guido. "Das ehemalige Jüdische Museum in Frankfurt am Main." In *Synagoga: Jüdische Altertümer, Handschriften und Kultgeräte.* Frankfurt: Historisches Museum, 1961.

Schorsch, Emil. "Zwölf Jahre vor der Zerstörung der Synagoge in Hannover, Germany. Persönliche Erinnerungen." LBI-AR, ME 575.

Schorsch, Ismar. "Art as Social History: Oppenheim and the German Jewish Vision of Emancipation." In *Moritz Oppenheim: The First Jewish Painter,* ed. Elisheva Cohen, pp. 31–58. Jerusalem: Israel Museum, 1983.

———. "The Emergence of the Historical Consciousness in Modern Judaism." *LBIYB* 28 (1983), pp. 413–439.

———. "German Judaism: From Confession to Culture." In *Die Juden im Nationalsozialistischen Deutschland, 1933–1943,* ed. Arnold Paucker, pp. 67–73. Tübingen, Germany: J. C. B. Mohr, 1986.

———. *Jewish Reactions to German Anti-Semitism, 1870–1914.* New York: Columbia University Press, 1972.

———. "The Myth of Sephardic Supremacy." *LBIYB* 34 (1989), pp. 47–66.

Schütz, Christiane. "Kunst aus jüdischen Verlagen." In *Europäische Moderne: Buch und Graphik aus Berliner Kunstverlagen, 1890–1933,* pp. 141–162. Berlin: Dietrich Reimer, 1989.

Schwartz, Shuly Rubin. *The Emergence of Jewish Scholarship in America: The Publication of the Jewish Encyclopedia.* Cincinnati: Hebrew Union College Press, 1991.

Schwarz, Karl. "Berliner Jüdisches Museum (Aus den Memoiren von Karl Schwarz)." Robert Weltsch Collection, LBI-AR, 7185.

———. *Die Juden in der Kunst.* Berlin: Heine-Bund, 1928.

Seligmann, Caesar. *Erinnerungen,* ed. Erwin Seligmann. Frankfurt: Waldemar Kramer, 1975.

Shaked, Gershon. *The Shadows Within: Essays on Modern Jewish Writers.* Philadelphia: Jewish Publication Society, 1987.

———. *Ha-sifrut ha-ivrit, 1880–1980,* vol. 1. N.p.: Ha-kibutz ha-me'uhad, 1977.

Shapira, Avraham. "Buber's Attachment to Herder and German 'Volkism.'" *Studies in Zionism* 14 (1993), pp. 1–30.

Sharfman, Glenn Richard. "The Jewish Youth Movement in Weimar Germany, 1900–1936: A Study in Ideology and Organization." Ph.D. dissertation, University of North Carolina, 1989.

Shavit, Zohar. "On the Hebrew Cultural Center in Berlin in the Twenties: Hebrew Culture in Europe—the Last Attempt." *Gutenberg-Jahrbuch* 1993, pp. 371–380.

Shedletzky, Itta. "Belletristik und Literaturdiskussion in den jüdischen Zeitschriften in Deutschland, 1837–1918." Ph.D. dissertation, Hebrew University, Jerusalem, 1985.

Shoham, Chaim. "Jeremias—Prophet für jede Gelegenheit. Essay in Rezeptionsgeschichte." *LBIB* 63 (1982), pp. 51–57.

Siegele-Wenschkewitz, Leonore. "The Relationship Between Protestant Theology and Jewish Studies During the Weimar Republic." In *Judaism and Christianity under the Impact of National Socialism,* ed. Otto Dov Kulka and Paul R. Mendes-Flohr, pp. 133–150. Jerusalem: Historical Society of Israel and Zalman Shazar Center for Jewish History, 1987.

Simon, Ernst. *Aufbau im Untergang: Jüdische Erwachsenenbildung im national-sozialistischen Deutschland als geistiger Widerstand.* Tübingen, Germany: J. C. B. Mohr, 1959.

———. *Brücken: Gesammelte Aufsätze.* Heidelberg: Lambert Schneider, 1965.

———. *Entscheidung zum Judentum: Essays und Vorträge.* Frankfurt: Suhrkamp, 1980.

———. "Franz Rosenzweig und das jüdische Bildungsproblem." In *Brücken: Gesammelte Aufsätze,* pp. 393–406. Heidelberg: Lambert Schneider, 1965.

———. "Martin Buber and German Jewry." *LBIYB* 3 (1958), pp. 3–39.

Simon, Hermann. *Das Berliner Jüdische Museum in der Oranienburger Straße: Geschichte einer zerstörten Kultstätte.* Berlin: Union 1988.

———. "Jüdische Exlibris." *Marginalien: Zeitschrift für Buchkunst und Biblio-philie,* no. 101 (1986), pp. 60–67.

Simonsohn, Emil. *Die jüdische Volksgemeinde.* Berlin: Jüdischer Verlag, 1919.

Sinasohn, Max. *Adass Jisroel Berlin: Enstehung, Entfaltung, Entwurzelung, 1869–1939.* Jerusalem: Private printing, 1966.

Smith, Anthony D. *The Ethnic Origin of Nations.* New York: Oxford University Press, 1986.

Sommerfeld, Adolf. *Das Ghetto von Berlin. Aus dem Scheunenviertel. Kriminal-roman.* Reprint. Berlin: Verlag Neues Leben, 1992.

Sorkin, David. *The Transformation of German Jewry, 1780–1840.* New York: Oxford University Press, 1987.

Spael, Wilhelm. *Das katholische Deutschland im 20. Jahrhundert: Seine Pionier- und Krisenzeiten, 1890–1945.* Würzburg: Echter, 1964.

Spielmann, Diane R. "German-Jewish Writers on the Eve of the Holocaust." In *Reflections of the Holocaust in Art and Literature,* ed. Randolph L. Braham, pp. 55–77. New York: Columbia University Press, 1990.

Stachura, Peter D. *The German Youth Movement, 1900–1945: An Interpretative and Documentary History.* New York: St. Martin's Press, 1981.

Steiner, George. *After Babel: Aspects of Language and Translation.* Oxford: Oxford University Press, 1976.

Steinhardt, Jakob. *Haggada schel Pessach.* Berlin: Ferdinand Ostertag, 1923.

Stern, Fritz. *Dreams and Delusions.* New York: Vintage Books, 1989.

———. *The Politics of Cultural Despair.* Berkeley: University of California Press, 1961.

Stern, Heinemann. *Warum hassen sie uns eigentlich? Jüdisches Leben zwischen den Kriegen.* Düsseldorf: Droste, 1970.

Straus, Rahel. *Wir lebten in Deutschland: Erinnerungen einer deutschen Jüdin.* Stuttgart: Deutsche Verlags-Anstalt, 1961.

Strauss, Eduard. *Aufsätze und Anmerkungen, 1919–1945.* New York: Congregation Habonim, 1946.

———. "Der deutsche Jude Franz Rosenzweig." In *Franz Rosenzweig. Eine Gedenkschrift,* ed. Eugen Mayer, pp. 30–32. Frankfurt, 1930.

Strauss, Herbert A. "The Jewish Press in Germany, 1918–1939 (1943)." In *The Jewish Press That Was: Accounts, Evaluations and Memories of Jewish Papers in Pre-Holocaust Europe,* ed. Arie Bar, pp. 321–354. Tel Aviv: Jerusalem Post Press, 1980.

Strauss, Herbert A., and Christhard Hofmann, eds. *Juden und Judentum in der Literatur.* Munich: Deutscher Taschenbuch Verlag, 1985.

Strauss, Ludwig. *Der Reiter.* Frankfurt: Ruetten und Loening, 1930.

Stuckenschmidt, H. H. *Schönberg: Leben, Umwelt, Werk.* Zurich and Freiburg: Atlantis, 1974.

Tal, Uriel. *Christians and Jews in Germany: Religion, Politics, and Ideology in the Second Reich,* trans. Jonathan Jacobs. Ithaca: Cornell University Press, 1975.

Tau, Max. *Das Land, das ich verlassen mußte.* Hamburg: Hoffmann und Campe, 1961.

Theilhaber, Felix A. *Dein Reich komme! Ein chiliastischer Roman aus der Zeit Rembrandts und Spinozas.* Berlin: C. A. Schwetschke, 1924.

Tietgens, Hans, ed. *Erwachsenenbildung zwischen Romantik und Aufklärung.* Göttingen: Vandenhoeck und Ruprecht, 1969.

Tönnies, Ferdinand. *Gemeinschaft und Gesellschaft.* Leipzig, 1887.

Toury, Jacob. *Die politischen Orientierungen der Juden in Deutschland. Von Jena bis Weimar.* Tübingen, Germany: J. C. B. Mohr, 1966.

Tramer, Hans. "Eduard Strauss und seine Freundschaft mit Franz Rosenzweig und Martin Buber." *LBIB* 16–17 (1977–1978), pp. 147–158.

———. "Das Judenproblem im Leben und Werk Ludwig Meidners." *LBIB* 16–17 (1977–1978), pp. 75–132.

Trosman, Harry, and Roger Dennis Simmons. "The Freud Library." *Journal of the American Psychoanalytic Association* 21 (1973), pp. 646–687.

Tucholsky, Kurt. *Gesammelte Werke,* ed. Mary Gerold-Tucholsky and Fritz J. Raddatz. Paperback edition. 10 vols. Reinbek: Rowohlt, 1975.

———. *Politische Briefe,* ed. Fritz J. Raddatz, pp. 109–110. Reinbek: Rowohlt, 1969.

Tuguntke, Hansjörg. *Demokratie und Bildung: Erwachsenenbildung am Ausgang der Weimarer Republik.* Frankfurt: Haag und Herchen, 1988.

Verwaltungsbericht des Vorstandes der Jüdischen Gemeinde zu Berlin 1926–1930. Berlin, 1930.

Vital, David. *The Origins of Zionism.* Oxford: Oxford University Press, 1975.

———. *Zionism: The Crucial Phase.* Oxford: Oxford University Press, 1987.

———. *Zionism: The Formative Years.* Oxford: Oxford University Press, 1982.

Voigts, Manfred. *Oskar Goldberg. Der mythische Experimentalwissenschaftler: Ein verdrängtes Kapitel jüdischer Geschichte.* Berlin: Argon, 1992.

Volkov, Shulamit. "Die Erfindung einer Tradition: Zur Entstehung des modernen Judentums in Deutschland." *Historische Zeitschrift* 253, pp. 603–628.

———. *Jüdisches Leben und Antisemitismus im 19. und 20. Jahrhundert.* Munich: C. H. Beck, 1990.

Wassermann, Jakob. *Deutscher und Jude: Reden und Schriften, 1904–1933.* Edited by Dierk Rodewald. Heidelberg: Lambert Schneider, 1984.

———. *Der Fall Maurizius.* Munich: Langen-Müller, 1971.

———. *Fränkische Erzählungen: Sabbatai Zewi, ein Vorspiel.* Frankfurt: S. Fischer, 1925.

———. *My Life as German and Jew.* New York: Coward and McCann, 1933.

Weber, Max. "Science as a Vocation." In *From Max Weber: Essays in Sociology,* ed. H. H. Gerth and C. Wright Mills, pp. 129–156. New York: Oxford University Press, 1946.

Weintraub, Z. *Targumei ha-tora la-lashon ha-germanit.* Chicago: College of Jewish Studies, 1967.

Weiss, Avrom. "The Jewish Book-Plate," in *Katalog le-ta'arukhot tavei-sefer yehudi'im,* pp. vii–xi. Jerusalem: Hotsa'ot ha-arkhion ve-ha-museon ha-grafi, 1956.

Wendling, Willi. *Die Mannheimer Abendakademie und Volkshochschule: Ihre Geschichte im Rahmen der örtlichen Erwachsenenbildung von den Anfängen im 19.Jahrhundert bis 1953.* Heidelberg: Heidelberger Verlagsanstalt, 1983.

Wertheimer, Jack. "Between Tsar and Kaiser: The Radicalization of Russian-Jewish Students in Imperial Germany." *LBIYB* 25 (1982), pp. 187–215.

———. "The German-Jewish Experience: Toward a Useable Past." *American Jewish Archives* 40 (1988), pp. 417–423.

———. *Unwelcome Strangers: East European Jews in Imperial Germany.* New York: Oxford University Press, 1987.

Wertheimer, Jack, ed. *The Uses of Tradition: Jewish Continuity in the Modern Era.* Cambridge: Harvard University Press, 1992.

Whittick, Arnold. *Eric Mendelsohn.* London: Leonard Hill, 1964.

Wilhelm, Kurt. "The Jewish Community in the Post-Emancipation Period." *LBIYB* 2 (1957), pp. 47–75.

Williams, Robert C. *Culture in Exile: Russian Emigrés in Germany, 1881–1941.* Ithaca: Cornell University Press, 1972.

Wolf, Arie. "Lion Feuchtwanger und das Judentum." *LBIB* 61 (1982), pp. 57–78, and *LBIB* 62 (1982), pp. 55–94.

Wolf, Immanuel. "On the Concept of a Science of Judaism (1822)." *LBIYB* 2 (1957), pp. 194–204.

Wolff, Kurt. *Briefwechsel eines Verlegers,* ed. Bernhard Zeller and Ellen Otten. Frankfurt: Heinrich Scheffler, 1966.

————. *A Portrait in Essays and Letters,* ed. Michael Ermarth, trans. Deborah Lucas Schneider. Chicago: University of Chicago Press, 1991.

Wunsch, Albert. *Die Idee der "Arbeitsgemeinschaft": Eine Untersuchung zur Erwachsenenbildung in der Weimarer Zeit.* Frankfurt: Peter Lang, 1986.

Yerushalmi, Yosef Hayim. *Freud's Moses: Judaism Terminable and Interminable.* New Haven: Yale University Press, 1991.

————. *Haggadah and History: A Panorama in Facsimile of Five Centuries of the Printed Haggadah from the Collections of Harvard University and the Jewish Theological Seminary.* Philadelphia: Jewish Publication Society, 1975.

————. *Zakhor: Jewish History and Jewish Memory.* Seattle: University of Washington Press, 1983.

Yudkin, Leon. *Else Lasker-Schueler: A Study in German-Jewish Literature.* Northwood, England: Science Reviews, 1991.

Zelzer, Maria. *Weg und Schicksal der Stuttgarter Juden: Ein Gedenkbuch.* Stuttgart: Ernst Klett, 1964.

Zevi, Bruno. *Erich Mendelsohn: Opera Completa: Architetture e Immagini Architettoniche.* Milan: Etat Kompass, 1970.

Zunz, Leopold. *Zur Geschichte und Literatur.* Berlin: Veit, 1845.

Zweig, Arnold. *Die Juden auf der deutschen Bühne.* Berlin: Welt-Verlag, 1928.

Zweig, Arnold, and Hermann Struck. *Das ostjüdische Antlitz.* Reprint. Wiesbaden: Fourier, 1988.

Zweig, Stefan, ed. *E. M. Lilien: Sein Werk.* Berlin and Leipzig: Schuster und Löffler, 1903.

Index

Steiner, George, 105
Steinhardt, Jakob, 155, 166, 167, 168–170, *169*, 174, *175,* 179
Steinschneider, Moritz, 30, 102, 113, 125
Stern, Fritz, 1
Stern, Gerson, 218
Stern, Moritz, 177
Stern-Täubler, Selma, 110, 123
Strauss, Eduard, 77–78, 81, 82–84, 87–89, 215
Strauss, Leo, 86
Strauss, Ludwig, 151, 207
Strauss, Max, 206
Stravinsky, Igor, 157, 162
Struck, Hermann, 143, *144,* 166
Student fraternities, 20
Sturm, Der, 167
Stuttgart, 78, 91, 93–96, 98, 141, 215
Stybel publishing house, 200
Susman, Margarete, 107
Süßkind of Trimberg, 174
Switzerland, 22, 24, 25, 28, 151, 182
Synagogues: architecture, 2, 155, 181–184; burning of, 218; decoration, 25, 30, 171; decorum, 50, 53; libraries, 56–57

Talmud, 16, 63, 71, 72, 74, 79, 85, 146, 147, 170, 207; adult education courses in, 90–91, 92, 97; dramatization of Talmudic tales, 138–141; translations of, 110, 121, 138–140
Tarbut publishing company, 200
Täubler, Eugen, 101–102, 123
Taut, Bruno, 181
Tcherikower, Elias, 195, 196
Tchernikhowsky, Saul, 199
Tempeljuden, 145
Theater, 21, 30, 32, 138–141; Aryanization of, 213, 214, 216–219; Hebrew plays, 189–193; heretical Jews presented in, 150–151; Herrnfeld, 191–192; Jewish Theater Association, 192; and Lehrhaus, 97; modernism in, 153–154; Piscator, 153;

Russian avant-garde, 189–190; translations used in, 107. *See also* Yiddish theater
Theilhaber, Felix, 149–150
Theresienstadt, 164
Thesaurus of Hebrew Oriental Melodies (Idelsohn), 158, 159, 160
Threepenny Opera (Brecht and Weill), 153
Tillich, Paul, 95
Tilsit, 182
Toch, Ernst, 162, 163
Toller, Ernst, 32, 154
Tolstoy, Leo, 75
Torczyner (Tur-Sinai), Harry, 93, 109, 204
Translations, 4, 16, 17, 28, 58, 95, 101, 103–111, 202, 205, 207, 216, 220; of Agnon's work, 206; of art and art history articles, 195; of Beer-Hofmann's play, 191; Benjamin on, 105; by female scholars, 110–111; German, 104, 105–106, 108–109, 110; Goethe on, 104; Goldschmidt's Bible, 109–110, 176; Goldschmidt's Talmud, 121, 139–140; of Halevi's poetry, 105, 158, 163; and Jewish identity, 104, 105–106, 108–109; in journals, 33, 110; and Lehrhaus, 83; Liberal Jews and, 106–107, 109; Luther's Bible, 105, 108–109; Mendelssohn's German Pentateuch, 103; of mystical literature, 29; Orthodox Jews and, 108; Philippson translation, 104; rabbinate and, 106–107, 109; and religious observance, 108–109; of the Talmud, 110, 138–141; Torcyzner Bible, 109; by Wohlgemuth-Bleichrode, 104; women's Bible, 110–111; Zunz translation, 104
Trebitsch, Arthur, 133
Trilling, Lionel, 153
Trotsky, Leon, 117
Tse'enah u-re'enah, 110–111